WHEN THE SNOW MELTS

The Autobiography of Cubby Broccoli

WHEN
THE SNOW
MELTS

The Autobiography of
CUBBY BROCCOLI

With Donald Zec

B■XTREE

This edition published in 1998 by Boxtree

an imprint of Macmillan Publishers Ltd,
25 Eccleston Place, London SW1W 9NF and Basingstoke

Associated companies throughout the world

ISBN 0 7522 1162 5

9 8 7 6 5 4 3 2 1

A CIP catalogue record for this book is available from the British Library

For Dana, to whom I owe this book,
and so much more besides

AUTHOR'S NOTE

My friendship with Cubby Broccoli began in the early 1950s when he first arrived in Britain as an independent producer. From those days, then through the tumult of the Bond years, he had been approached by many biographers both here and in America, eager to write his life story. Cubby declined for one reason only, a desire to tell it all, candidly, but in his own words. He invited me in on these recollections which I began taping back in the late 1960s. Our sessions together at his home in Beverly Hills were inevitably interrupted by the seventeen James Bond films he steered into legend. There was a brief interruption while he underwent major surgery. Normal service was later resumed, albeit with the story-teller in a wheelchair and attended by nurses. He continued through into 1996. Having begun the task, Cubby Broccoli wanted to complete it. Regrettably he did not live to see his words in print. But they are his words; I'm happy to have been the messenger, and his friend.

Donald Zec

INTRODUCTION

On the morning of Sunday November 17, 1996, close to 2,500 invited guests, the famous and the less well known, crowded into the Odeon Cinema in London's Leicester Square to celebrate the life and work of Albert ('Cubby') Broccoli. He had died five months earlier at the age of eighty-seven, having fought a valiant and characteristically good-humoured battle until the end. Much of a man's worth in life can be measured by the reaction to his passing. The global tributes to Broccoli were unanimous in their recognition of his triumphs as a film-maker – not least for the James Bond adventures, the most successful series of movies in motion-picture history. On television, radio and in headlines around the world the eulogies confirmed the universal truth: if Bond had become a legend so too had Cubby Broccoli.

As *The Times* of London noted: 'The founder (with the late Harry Saltzman) of the James Bond films, Cubby Broccoli was one of the most successful producers in Hollywood. An American, it was his genius to perceive that the adventures of a British Secret Service Agent could make the stuff of international box-office.'

The comment is accurate, though it scarcely matches the mind-dazzling statistics of 007's thirty-six-year box-office success. We will come to these. Self-evidently the records, enhanced by the prestigious Irving Thalberg Award, place Broccoli among the 'greats'. Yet the 2,500 who filled the Odeon that November morning were less concerned with the producer, more with the man himself. Every word, every anecdote expressed in the semi-darkness pulsed with the resonance of genuine affection.

I have attended similar gatherings in Hollywood for departed film moguls and found them strong on acerbic one-liners, short on heartfelt reminiscences. But Cubby Broccoli had struck a different chord with all those in the theatre that day, and many more outside. Three successive James Bonds – Roger Moore, Timothy Dalton, and Pierce Brosnan – now richer beyond their wildest imaginings, spoke with palpable sadness of the man who had made it happen. There was a common thread to their tributes. They had been given an opportunity which even the best of actors can rarely aspire to. And with that opportunity came international recognition and the wealth and lifestyle that only superstardom can bring. But there was more: the unexpected bonus of a friendship that would be constant through good times and bad, whether they remained as James Bond or not. And this friendship, this sense of belonging to a family, not merely a film unit, was reflected in their speeches. There were real tears, not the glycerine substitute, in the eyes of this trio of 007s.

Conspicuously absent was Sean Connery. Great efforts were made to bring the first Bond to the gathering. We must accept that he was unable rather than unwilling to attend. But clearly, no man had a greater reason to be at the Broccoli memorial than Connery. It was here, at the Odeon, that James Bond first struck gold – with *Dr No* in 1962 – launching a raw and marginally unknown actor into orbit. Cubby Broccoli tells in this book of the genesis and exodus of Sean Connery in the Bond legend. It is way in the past and, in any event, overtaken by the success of later Bonds, the latest being Pierce Brosnan in the eighteenth film of the series. Nevertheless, Connery's non-appearance at the Broccoli Memorial inevitably caused speculation.

The records show that Sean's triumphant reign as 007 was tainted by bitter allegations, mostly about money. Serious allegations were made in print and subsequently withdrawn. (Cubby had persistently argued that it was the Bond distributors, United Artists, to whom Sean, rightly or wrongly, should have directed his complaints.) The actor's sense of grievance lingered on, though when Cubby died Sean was among the first to telephone Dana Broccoli offering his sympathies. That goodwill was not long-lasting. In an interview he gave to the *Sunday Telegraph Magazine*, returning to the theme of alleged 'short-changing' by the producers, he is quoted as saying: 'that's why I was always fighting with them [Broccoli and Saltzman]. Unfortunately they're both dead now, or fortunately, it depends on your point of view.' Crude perhaps, even by this actor's forthright standards. Perhaps it would have been difficult for Sean to face Cubby's widow after those words appeared in print; the more so since it was Dana Broccoli who, as we will see, was largely responsible for the decision to cast him as the first James Bond.

However, Dana had other thoughts that November morning in Leicester Square. 'Cubby loved everything about film-making,' she told the audience. 'But most of all he cared for each and every one of you. You were his extended family.' The eulogies that followed confirmed it. Actors, directors, and writers, on the rostrum or by video from Hollywood, echoed the theme. Prince Charles, in a personal letter to Dana, wrote:

> Cubby Broccoli held a special place in the hearts of very many people. He brought the character of James Bond to life and brought enormous pleasure to cinema audiences throughout the world. He was also extremely generous to my Trust and thanks to your dear husband it has benefited from the premières of many of the recent Bond films. Over the years these have raised nearly £650,000...I could not be more grateful for all he did over the years to help those less fortunate members of our society and I wanted you to know how much I appreciate his support.
>
> Yours most sincerely,
> Charles.

The last accolade of a whole string of glittering prizes.

On January 16, 1990 Cubby had his name embossed above a Gold Star on that famous Walk of Fame opposite Grauman's Chinese Theater. It was a wet and blustery morning, the rain falling impartially on his inscription, and those of Charlie Chaplin, Joseph Schenck, Eddie Cantor, Ingrid Bergman and Bing Crosby, and on the boarded-up windows of Smokin' Sam's Hollywood Bar BQ close by, which, like the Ming-style movie pagoda opposite, had seen more prosperous days.

A sizeable and noticeably happy crowd had gathered around that rostrum on Hollywood Boulevard to hear generous tributes to this veteran film-maker who astutely piloted James Bond, 007 into legend. The crowds applauded a municipal bonus. That day, by proclamation of the City of Los Angeles, would be 'Cubby Broccoli Day'. The tribute clearly pleased him. Glancing along the sidewalk at those other names – absent friends, many of them –

Cubby felt in good company. They represented his kind of Hollywood. The days when the creative process, not creative accountancy, motivated the industry; when making movies was a more enticing occupation than making deals.

After the ceremony Richard Berger, then chief executive of MGM/UA, the company distributing the Bond films – to its considerable advantage – declared that Cubby exemplified the best elements in film producing: good taste, style and commitment. The compliment was well intended. But only Cubby and selected insiders would know of the unseemly corporate turmoil within which he and his associates had to work. It is a long and disenchanting saga of billion-dollar manipulations; of buy-outs, buy-backs, wheeling and dealing, with ludicrously high-priced company chiefs arriving and departing at the speed of light.

The effect all these boardroom convulsions had on the not unimportant business of making movies is a significant part of the Broccoli experience. He tells it all in its appropriate time and place, and maybe more in sorrow than in anger. But on that euphoric January day he could forget studio politics awhile as he took handshakes around the gilt-edged metal star in the crushed-pink stonework. When he was photographed later with Dana and the children, Michael, Tina, Tony and Barbara, Cubby Broccoli's smile reflected a fair degree of contentment. The sidewalk recognition would take its place alongside the Order of the British Empire (OBE) presented by an aficionado of the 007 movies, Queen Elizabeth II.

But in career terms it is the judgement of the industry and its chroniclers that counts. On May 13, 1987 *Variety*, that respected oracle of the world's entertainment scene, published an almost unprecedented issue. Calling up a battalion of writers, it devoted thirty pages to a motion-picture landmark: twenty-five years of James Bond movies. It was a resounding tribute even by the standards of this Wurlitzer of showbiz organs. Initiates reading the blurb-speak headline '007 Sights $2-Bill in Ducats Overall' would have known in a flash what it meant. For the benefit of the others, this arcane intelligence informed readers that when the fifteenth Bond film, *The Living Daylights*, had run its course, 007's maximized earnings over twenty-five years were expected to exceed $2 billion. Further millions would be accrued with *Licence to Kill* and *Goldeneye*, the latter grossing a record $350 million in its first run. If these are formidable statistics, we can throw in the additional information that more than half the world's population has seen a James Bond film. Reason enough for *Variety*'s euphoric tribute in which assorted talents behind the phenomenon sought to explain how, in the words of an unusually agog *Newsweek*, it had become 'the most lucrative series in screen history'.

The significance of the anniversary – a quarter of a century of films based on the exploits of a single fictional character – was not restricted to the United States alone. On prime-time television in London; in special TV programmes across Europe; at film festivals as far apart as Deauville, France, and the Japanese capital, Tokyo; and in cover stories around the world, the name of the game was Bond, James Bond.

To comprehend the immensity of the event, we need to view the Bond phenomenon in its awe-inspiring totality. (His creator, Ian Fleming, would certainly have been awe-struck since, as he once confessed to this writer, he created Bond merely as a diversion during a period of intense boredom.) Unhappily, Fleming did not live to witness the prodigious global windfall in cash, television and merchandising that his brief moment of ennui would bring. 007 trench coats, vodka, cuff-links, toiletries, board games, T-shirts, attaché cases – the spin-offs from Bond's rakish persona were, still are, unlimited. Inevitably, after the spin-offs came the rip-offs. For just as the Beatles' explosion upon the 1960s induced a fallout of raucous and largely untalented imitators, Bond, too, spawned a worldwide stampede of assorted 007 look-alikes, more foot-in-mouth than tongue-in-cheek. The public's rejection of most of these recycled cheapies clinched an unavoidable truth: you can construct an exact replica of a Stradivarius fiddle which still manages to sound like a sawmill.

The records show that some of Hollywood's top operators tried to get 007 off the launching pad only to abort the projects with fingers burned, pride hurt. Others tried to make a fast buck by making spoof Bonds. They failed catastrophically, learning the hard way that audiences, especially Bond audiences, do not wish to see their hero smart-alecked off the screen. True, there have been some who, using Bond as their role model, have made their individual mark on the genre. Notable among these is Stephen Spielberg, who has paid generous tribute to Bond's huge contribution to this style of motion picture. Certainly the wit and derring-do of some of the later spy adventures were hooked to the generating current of 007.

Nothing confirms Bond's powerful entrenchment in the public's mind more than the way the film titles, familiar bits of dialogue, have been absorbed into everyday talk. When Gorbachov ushered in the hopeful vibes of *glasnost*, banner headlines in London newspapers announced, 'From Russia With Love'. Famous jewellers repeatedly introduce glittering window displays proclaiming, 'Diamonds Are Forever'. Critics searching for a phrase to describe their ambivalent reaction to a play admit to being 'shaken, not stirred'. And almost every tabloid newspaper labelled Britain's most daring bullion robber 'Goldfinger' – though, unlike the film, this character may not be released for some time. More grist to the mill. More power to a cult which had already received a famous endorsement by the White House when the late President Kennedy mentioned casually that the Fleming stories were among his favourite bedside reading.

Which brings us back to the man universally identified with the Bond legend, and the narrator of this life story: Albert Romolo Broccoli. It is a splendid name which reflects his Italian origins. This is the way he was formally addressed, notably in the citations for his Honorary OBE, France's Commander of Arts and Letters and, most important of all to a man who loved making films, the Irving Thalberg Award for a major contribution to motion pictures. (The prestige of this award, the highest that a film-maker can receive, is underscored by the fact that it is made at the Academy Awards ceremony. It is rarely given, and among the handful of recipients are Alfred Hitchcock, Cecil B. De Mille and Walt Disney.) But Broccoli was 'Cubby' to everyone else. To the industry on both sides of the Atlantic. To intimates and subordinates alike. Likewise to Ronald Reagan and Prince Charles, as he was to his friend Howard Hughes long ago.

It may be that another producer of talent, given the same circumstances, might have optioned the Fleming stories and hit the jackpot. Certainly Cubby Broccoli acknowledged that the Canadian producer Harry Saltzman partnered him in the creation of Bond, helping steer it through one box-office record after another.

But sustaining the series once Saltzman had departed; resuscitating the magic after the Fleming source material had dried up; above all, keeping Bond alive and menacing despite the formidable rivalry of Spielberg, Lucas and the reshuffled Rockys and Rambos, demanded more than the familiar producer's mix of shrewdness and power play. A strong nerve, for sure. Style, too. And an abundance of plain, audience-oriented savvy. Nor is an ability to lead from the front and engender commitment beyond the call of duty a disadvantage. Cubby Broccoli had all this under his capacious belt, added to the not insignificant bonus of the willingness to press hunches, take a gamble.

Any objective analysis of Bond's landmark success must take those assets as its starting point. Experts – and there has been no shortage of those – confess to being baffled by the difficulty of translating the Fleming adventures into vibrant screen material. On the face of it the tales appear to be a gift to a competent scriptwriter. In fact they have defeated some of the best operators in the trade. Any literary Don Quixote who believes he could write a Bond film with his free hand tied behind his back should study the contributions in later pages from two old campaigners in the field, writers Dick Maibaum and Tom Mankiewicz. They survived. But the clean-picked bones of many who failed testify to the exquisite agony of scripting a Bond movie. When the writers have finished scratching their collective temples to no avail, they inevitably came back to the producer, Cubby Broccoli, and latterly to his co-producers, his gifted stepson Michael Wilson and his daughter Barbara Broccoli.

This begs the question: how did Cubby Broccoli, the essentially modest son of an Italian immigrant, become one of the most respected and successful producers in film history? Broccoli, telling his own story for the first time, answered that by looking way beyond Hollywood's city limits to the back-breaking years long before, farming on Long Island. And even further back, in a touchingly delineated account of one immigrant family's shot at the American Dream. But others in Hollywood have emerged from a similar immigrant background, driven by the same stimulus, yet failed. What was it about Cubby Broccoli which led to such prodigious success and ultimately to the coveted Thalberg bust on the mantelshelf?

Maybe if Howard Hughes, that notoriously reclusive billionaire, were alive today he could offer us a clue. It was Hughes, on impulse, who sought to make acquaintance with the then unknown young Broccoli on his second night visiting Hollywood. The friendship which developed in all its quirky, round-the-clock intensity continued even after Hughes had virtually sealed himself off from the world. They kept in touch not by direct face-to-face contact but by remote control from that hermetically sealed penthouse atop a Las Vegas hotel. It is significant that when, after Hughes's death, the US Supreme Court was required to rule on crucially important domiciliary questions, Cubby Broccoli was called in as a leading witness. It offered the only light relief in an otherwise turgid drama on which barrel-loads of money were poised.

The posthumous media 'revelations' about Hughes have been heavy in weight but light on credibility. On this subject, Cubby Broccoli produced unimpeachable credentials. In this book, he gives us the reflections of a privileged insider. For these, incidentally, he required, among other virtues, a capacity for suspending disbelief and the ability to go without sleep for as long as it took. That friendship played no small part in getting Cubby Broccoli started on the roller-coaster of movie production.

There was another friendship that was equally fortuitous. Ian Fleming, the aloof, disdainful son of the English upper classes, approached Hollywood with a mixture of distaste and refined mistrust. But he accorded Cubby a kind of diplomatic immunity, in return for which, incidentally, Mr Broccoli was to make him far richer than his lightly pitched novels could ever have done on their own.

For the truth is that, in an industry not noted for its lack of malice, Cubby Broccoli had the cool cheek to be *liked*, if not loved, by most who work in it. Purveying Italianate affability, wrapped in Lacoste polo-necks and hairy tweed jackets, he ruled with a ladle of iron. By which is meant that he was as agreeable a character as ever cooked spaghetti for a crew on location when the standard rations failed to appear, or appeal.

Real achievers tend to reject the stereotypes of their trade, and Cubby Broccoli was no exception. As Hollywood's Hall of Infamy has frequently demonstrated, its most celebrated film-makers were scarcely nature's gentlemen. Indeed they were not required to be. As colourful as unhanged highwaymen, they were ruthless, controlled vast sums of money and could squeeze out a crocodile tear now and again to make their stars feel guilty and come into line. From the start, Cubby Broccoli distanced himself from that kind of role-playing. If he handled egocentrics, special pleaders and front-office megalomania better than most, it is because of his unwavering conviction that in the end these characters – I quote him – 'usually fall on their swords'.

Nevertheless it would be a mistake to read this civilized magnanimity as weakness. Uppity studio front men, actors stricken with their own awe, learned the hard way that Cubby Broccoli, to protect a production or a principle, fought like a lion. This suggests potent influences in the early Broccoli bloodline. Painstaking research by archivists confirms it. Yet this book would never have emerged but for the gentle determination of Dana Broccoli, Cubby's resourceful wife.

For Cubby initially had not wanted to write his life story. Too busy. Incredibly, at eighty plus, he was still very much the hands-on producer, hopping from London to New York, to Tokyo, location-hunting in China and doing a gruelling, life-threatening stint in Mexico. He was simply having too much fun living his life to find the time to talk about it. But Dana believed that her husband's contribution to motion pictures, and the fateful events counterpoised with it, added up to a story worth the telling. More specifically, both had come through two major crises late in Cubby's film career, revealing as much about their resistance under fire as about the testing realities of the film business.

The most traumatic of these was a protracted legal battle on which rested the fate of their whole multimillion-dollar empire. Yet despite the enormity of the stakes involved, the episode finally became more like black comedy than mere bloody jousting between expensive lawyers. The Kennedy clan's fashionable legal heavyweight Sargent Shriver was one of the many on the opposing side who, hoping to confront the usually affable Cubby, collided head-on instead with the Albert Romolo version. The whole bitter skirmish, fought out in a five-star lakeside hotel in Switzerland, was, in the words of Norman R. Tyre, Broccoli's leading attorney, 'a great battle to fight, and win'. Its ramifications, the serene Alpine backdrop giving way to a piece of pure farce in Paris, led to another revelation.

Cubby's legal opposites discovered early on in the fray that they also had to take on Dana Broccoli. In the event they misread her soft, disarming smile – to their considerable detriment. Not surprising then, that her husband frequently warned the uninitiated, 'Dana takes no prisoners!' (She would be just as formidable an ADC to Cubby, when decades later, Bond and its future became trapped in the crossfire between a leading world bank and a flamboyant financier of breathtaking chutzpah named Giancarlo Parretti. And there would come a time when Cubby, precariously poised between life and death, would say quite simply: 'I just wouldn't be here but for Dana.')

Thus while Cubby carried on making movies, Dana instructed the Istituto Genealogico Italiano in Florence to scour the centuries for hard evidence of earlier Broccolis. Roots, Italian style. The two calf-bound tomes which eventually arrived at the Broccoli home in Beverly Hills revealed an embarrassment of noble, Papal, aristocratic Broccolis linked directly to the child born Albert Romolo Broccoli, on Long Island, on April 5, 1909. Well, Cubby owned to being mildly embarrassed. When you have held Licence Number 5743 of the City of Los Angeles, permitting you to sell Christmas trees on a Beverly Hills street corner, it may unnerve you to know that equally humble characters once kissed the Papal ring of a former Broccoli. But there it is in black and white. On the finest vellum. Under the heading 'Genealogical Documents of the House of Broccoli', we learn:

> The earliest traces of the family Broccoli, nobles of Naples, can be found in Lucca, where records of the noble family date back to 1194. Their ancestors were the powerful Paganelli...known to have given the church a Pope, Pope Eugenio III, in 1149.

From then on, over the years, the line split five ways, one of these settling in Carolei, four miles from Cosenza in southern Italy. Here the archivists close in on Cubby's direct antecedents:

> Carolei, Parish of Santa Maria Assunta, Cosenza. The Brocculo, Broccolo, and later Broccoli. The documented genealogy leads to Guiseppe, born about 1690, father of Michele Angelo and Pietro. Among their descendants was one Francesco Maria, born March 29, 1771, married to Rosaria Sammarco.

'It is interesting to note,' the researcher declares, 'that in the Parochial Deeds concerning the birth of his children, the above-named Francesco Maria Broccoli is referred to as "Magnifico", a title which at that time was attributed to persons of a higher rank which equalled that of "Noble". Such distinction attributed to Francesco Maria Broccoli is proof not only of the man's high ranking, but also of the family being one of the most conspicuous of Carolei.'

And so on, from Francesco the Magnifico to Natale Broccoli and his wife Saveria. One of their descendants, Pietro, married Caterina of the House of Ruffolo, 'one of the oldest and noblest in Naples'. Pietro was awarded the title of Count. Born of that blue-chip union were Giuseppina Maria, on April 30, 1826, and Antonio Maria Broccoli, on November 9, 1828. Antonio married Rachele Lento at Carolei on February 8, 1863. Home at last. The first-born of their six children was a son, Giovanni. Cubby's father.

I knew Cubby Broccoli for almost forty-five years. I was writing a newspaper column when he arrived in England in 1952 as an independent producer. Journalists are warned against forming too close a friendship with those they write about. This applies particularly to leading figures in the film industry, where the blandishments are notably princely. The notion is that such intimacy might compromise a writer's independence, put a gloss on his critical judgement.

But then along came Cubby Broccoli and out went the rules of the game. He presented us with an immediate dilemma: how could we avoid being his friend, shrug aside the essential good nature of the man? We could not and we did not try. Columnists might have preferred him to project, say, the ruthlessness of a Harry Cohn or the heel-clicking theatrics of an Otto Preminger. There are more headlines in hell-raisers than in the gentler samples of the breed. But Cubby was a good guy, and gritting our teeth, we had to learn to live with it. Cubby's arrival in Britain was pivotal for him and, as it turned out, for the British film industry and the famous Pinewood Studios. He would later build there the largest film stage in the world, dubbed appropriately the '007 Stage'. Britain's most powerful film union would place him among a rare elite of honorary members. Moreover, the Queen, Prince Charles and the late Diana, Princess of Wales, seeking films to launch their favourite charities, would ring once and ask for Cubby.

If my admiration – all right, affection – for the man is showing, I can name the place and the year when the symptoms first developed. Nairobi, 1955. Cubby and his then partner Irving Allen were filming *Safari*, starring Victor Mature. Cubby, myself and a couple of the film crew climbed aboard a small aircraft hired to take us north to the location. The pilot's handlebar moustache and gung-ho humour suggested a former Battle of Britain pilot yearning for the old days. The heavy equipment was loaded on to the tiny charter plane, then the passengers climbed in. I silently estimated that the freight plus the humans put us uncomfortably close to an overload. But why worry with Captain Marvel at the controls?

We roared down the runway in the direction of Mount Kenya. About two feet off the ground the plane shudders, revealing no further interest in the flight plan. I can see the white on the pilot's clenched knuckles. The plane falters and thumps back on to the runway. Engine at full revs, the barbed-wire perimeter fence appears to be coming as fast towards us as we are to it. The pilot – I distinctly hear him sigh, 'Oh dear!' – guns the brakes and cuts down the engine. We slew round and are now approaching the fence. Sideways on. One wing is dipped and we are on grass where tarmac was the preferred surface. Nobody speaks. All of us are thinking hard. Action from pilot. He restarts the engine. A propeller turns. The intention is clear. 'Where're you going, friend?' Cubby asks, courteous as ever.

'Ah,' responds our hero, twirling the left segment of his moustache, 'I think we'll have another go.'

'You *think* we'll have another go!' Cubby echoes. 'Listen, my friend, we're not on this plane just to prove what a good pilot you are. I tell you what we'll do,' he continued in a more conciliatory tone. 'We'll take more than one plane. Two planes, maybe. Or if necessary,' he adds expansively, 'we'll all have a plane each! You,' he throws in with a burst of generosity, 'can have this one!'

The pilot seems pained: 'No need for...' His protest is stifled by a Broccoli command straight out of a John Wayne movie: 'This flight is cancelled as of NOW!'

A minor example of Cubby Broccoli getting his priorities right. One ought not to die for a movie. Not one starring Victor Mature, the White Hunter, for sure.

Indeed, Cubby Broccoli's perception of civilized priorities was intrinsic to the way he lived and worked, and to his deeply affectionate relationship with his family. He had his heroes, made no claims as to his own achievements, leaving that for others to judge. He went on making pictures for the love of it. Only a critical illness abruptly cut short his activities. By January 1995 the seventeenth James Bond film, *Goldeneye*, was in production in England, with Pierce Brosnan as the new Bond. In 1998, *Tomorrow Never Dies* became one of the top box-office successes of the year. Michael Wilson and Barbara Broccoli were again the joint producers. But the unseen hand on the tiller was Cubby's, steering, encouraging, leading from the front. The fact that he was still doing so in his eighty-sixth year is remarkable in itself. But more compelling was the short but not inconsiderable drama which had preceded it. In brief, the gamble of life-or-death surgery of the most critical kind. We will come to that.

The many accolades Cubby Broccoli has accrued over the years define his professional dimension. This candid recounting of his life enables us to measure the man.

Donald Zec, London, August 1998

PROLOGUE

Rendezvous on Long Island

There is a picture I hold in my mind which is as vivid now as it was on that overcast day nearly seventy years ago: May 20, 1927. I was a teenager cranking the Fordson tractor ready for ploughing our few Long Island acres before going to school. My thoughts at the time were the thoughts of almost everyone in America; of a young man about to embark on what most people regarded as a suicide mission.

The whole countryside on that misty morning was as quiet as a graveyard. Then suddenly I heard the faint sound of an engine overhead. I searched the dawn sky as the sound became louder. Then I saw it: an odd-looking aircraft dipping awkwardly beneath the rain clouds. The plane was so low I felt I could almost reach up and touch it. It was no more than five hundred feet above me and coming in straight overhead. I scarcely believed it as I read the logo on the fuselage: *The Spirit of St. Louis*.

My heart began to thump with excitement…Charles Lindbergh! He was flying with his cockpit window open and looking down. I ran toward the plane and began to wave. He spotted me and waved back with a big sweep of his arm. I was thrilled beyond belief. There was something so personal about it. Just the two of us in a fleeting, shared moment on Long Island as he rattled north-eastward on his journey. I recall now a whole turmoil of emotions and actually having tears in my eyes. Subconsciously I thought the unthinkable: maybe I might just be the last person to see him alive. I remember quite clearly whispering, 'God help him make it', and continued waving as the plane faded to a speck on the horizon.

I wasn't the only one to have these fears. Almost everybody in America was talking about this crazy character from Minnesota named Charles A. Lindbergh who was aiming to become the first man to fly solo across the Atlantic. The newspapers had made it headline news in the run-up to the fateful mission. The New York tabloids rated the flyer's chances as a wild longshot. They called him 'the Flying Fool' and wrote off his flight as a 'suicide mission'. One reporter, who could hardly be accused of being overly sensitive, asked Lindbergh's mother, a proud and patient lady: 'How do you feel about the fact that your son might be dead in twenty-four hours?' Another such character enquired: 'Have you come to New York to bid him a last goodbye?' It was sick and I remember how angry it made me at the time.

That anger was not shared by my father. He believed life was hard enough without gambling it on some damn young fool's escapade. 'You watch,' he said. 'He'll finish up with the fish in the sea!' He said this partly to rile me, sensing my almost hero-worship of a young pilot not much older than myself. His cynicism reflected the mood of the times. This was the jazz age. The basic human virtues of achievement and pride in one's country had somehow got lost in the stampede from one new craze to another. Prohibition had opened doors to organized crime. America badly needed a hero. Charles Lindbergh had loaded up his small, 220-horsepower Ryan monoplane with 5,000 pounds of extra gasoline. To compensate for the critical overload he cut down his emergency equipment, knowing that if he had to ditch he stood to lose more than his plane. I kept vigil by the wireless all through the night, as did a vast audience of Americans.

Then it happened! The headlines screamed out from the front pages. Lindbergh had made it. He did it. Thirty-three hours after that unforgettable hand-wave over Long Island, he bounced down in darkness on Le Bourget airfield. We had our hero.

That incident had a profound impact on me. Cynicism for some can be inspiration for others. It was for me. Charles Lindbergh had been written off, bad-mouthed, put down by those not fit to share his company. If he had listened to them he would never have taken off. But he had this belief in himself and wasn't afraid to fail. Believe in yourself, ignore the gypsy warnings, aim at the big horizon – that, to me, was the message of the Lindbergh flight. Almost anything is possible for those who dare to try. It is a message that has stayed with me all my life.

ONE

The earlier characters in the Broccoli bloodline included a fine assortment of noblemen, magnificoes, Papal dignitaries and others. But by the time the dynasty filtered down to the Calabrian branch of my family, there couldn't have been much collateral to go with the coat of arms. The Broccolis of Cosenza must have been seen as poor relatives to their northern kinfolk in the castles of Tuscany.

Carolei, in the parish of Santa Maria Assunta, was where my paternal grandfather, Antonio Maria Broccoli, was born and where, in 1863, he married Rachele Lento. It lies four miles outside Cosenza, the main town in the region of Calabria. At that time it was a forgotten village in an unforgiving landscape. Apart from a flint quarry and a couple of ancient churches, it had nothing to offer and less to hope for. The same could be said for the rest of the region. Most of the inhabitants in the small towns and isolated mountain villages had just the one ambition: to get the hell out. And most of those had their sights, and their dreams, set on one place only: the United States of America.

Who could blame them? The pattern of their lives was dictated by nature. And nature had seen to it that Calabria drew the short straw. Droughts in summer. Devastating floods in winter, turning rivers into torrents which churned up the soil and wiped out livelihoods overnight. Hunger was a fact of life. So was poverty. There were epidemics, too, particularly of malaria, until the American army was able to eradicate it after World War II.

It was into that kind of existence that my maternal grandmother, Marietta Arnone, was born, married and raised a family. She was a strong woman and typically Calabrian. The environment created the breed. You had to be especially tough to survive. I remember my grandmother as a tall, almost stately-looking woman. Her features seemed somehow more German than Italian. She had a beautiful, oval-shaped face, with high cheekbones and pink and white skin. She pinned her long, dark hair up in a bun and could look quite severe, which was misleading. In fact, she was an exceedingly generous soul with the strength of a man and the instincts of an angel.

She married a young cavalryman stationed in Cosenza. Giovanni Vence was everything village girls dreamed of in a uniformed horseman. He was a good-looking, zesty extrovert who lived life the way he rode: at never less than a gallop. He had obviously been a brave character, and I have inherited a collection of his campaign medals to prove it.

Giovanni Vence had his card marked by Garibaldi. He had served under the famed patriot and guerrilla leader, and clearly some of the old warrior's impetuosity had rubbed off on him. He was the sort of character who'd rush into a burning house and haul out the family without worrying whether his moustache might be singed. In the 1880s in Calabria, wenching and wining were the only diversions on offer to the military. According to the stories handed down, Giovanni was terrific at both. And marriage was not going to cramp his style. Released from duties, he and other soldiers would ride out on a galloping binge around selected hostelries. Stewed as all Hades, he'd then clatter back to married quarters, where my grandmother was waiting to pull off his boots and read him the riot act.

Marietta was always uneasy, for the roads were treacherous all year through neglect and frequent rock slides. She feared the worst, and the worst happened. Returning from one rollicking late-night session, Giovanni and a couple of comrades decided to race one another back to the barracks. Giovanni's horse slipped and crashed into a wall. My grandfather was killed instantly. Cosenza had another widow on its hands. No major tragedy in those days to people who never put the odds on a full life expectancy at more than evens. But to my grandmother, who had loved this dashing Garibaldian, it was catastrophic.

Marietta now had three young children: Cristina, who would one day marry and bring me onto the scene; Giuseppe, who Stateside would be called 'Uncle Joe'; and Aunt Minnie. The pension for a soldier's widow, even one with three small children, couldn't have been more than a pittance. But my grandmother was never a complainer. She didn't envy a soul. Not even Luigina, her sister, who had married well.

Luigina's husband, Pasquale de Cicco, was a tough, rough young farmer who was fazed by nothing, afraid of nobody. He was shrewd, ambitious, and from the outset aimed at grabbing a better life for himself and his family in the USA. He worked a small parcel of land with a frenzy. Considering the prosperity that this would one day bring him, he might just as well have been panning for gold.

Broccoli had been growing in Italy for centuries. But Calabria produced the best; the finest in the world, according to the experts. One variety, the Calabrese, is especially succulent and tender. A spin-off, the Bouquet or Nine Star variety, is way up in the gourmet class. Personally, I'm not besotted by it. It's just another type of cauliflower I guess. But nobody would have dared say that to my ancestors. After all, it was this vegetable that carried their name, and the fact that they gave the plant a dominant spot in the family coat of arms shows the respect they had for it. The insignia of most noble families usually feature crimson lions with their tongues sticking out. My ancestors weighed the animal against the vegetable and figured the plant had more going for it. They have the thing sprouting proudly beneath the crown and visor. The official legend reads: 'a bend, azure, charged in the base of a "broccoli" in bloom gules, stemmed or accompanied in the chief by three etoiles of six points or, set per fess.'

I'm proud of the fact that a vegetable that bears my name should have turned out to be that important. And I suppose if you're going to be named for a vegetable, it might just as well be the best. Pasquale de Cicco felt that way about his broccoli. He knew the quirks and characteristics of every variety. Always with an eye on Calabria's unpredictable weather, he carefully calculated sowing times and soil preparation. Everybody in Cosenza knew the way Pasquale felt about his broccoli. It was a passion which came close to an obsession. But one day the pay-off would be enormous, not only for Pasquale, but also for the younger de Cicco, who would marry a Vanderbilt (and not necessarily to his advantage).

Although that day was still some way off, already events were conspiring to bring it closer. By the early 1880s emigration fever was sweeping through Italy, particularly in the south, where life was hardest. Italians were emigrating to America in their thousands, Calabria sending out the largest contingent of all. Except for a lucky few, it was a region of negatives: no industry, no jobs, no hope and no future. The pressure was on for anybody who could raise the then fortune of forty to fifty dollars to buy a steerage ticket and make it to the New World. The Italian writer Corrado Alvaro summed it up in one sentence: 'Flight is the theme of Calabrian life'.

It was certainly the one thought buzzing through my grandmother's mind day and night. But how do you make this kind of leap – hauling yourself and your family on a strange ship three thousand miles to an even stranger country? Not much money. Not a word of the language. Dragging bewildered, frightened kids along with you. There were thousands, millions like my grandmother, of course. And not only Italians. Russians, Poles, Germans, Irish, crowded the cargo boats hoping to find refuge, if not gold, on the streets of New York. I have a great deal of respect for that class of immigrant. Gratitude is part of it. By the time we were born they'd fought the battle and won it. There will never be another generation like it.

Marietta, the soldier's widow, couldn't have had any illusions about travelling steerage to the United States with her three children. She'd heard all the stories: of immigrants cramped in holds that had been used for cattle on the outward journey; bad food, disease; double-bunked on filthy straw mattresses. There was big money in this wretched human cargo. And even when the transatlantic liners got into the act, travelling steerage was only marginally better than it was for the cattle. It was a simple numbers game. You could stack around a thousand passengers into steerage, which was more than the combined total of First and Second Class passengers. Two toilets per hundred passengers was primitive, but in 1897 nobody was too concerned. Steerage carried a stigma. The perceived impression was that most of these unfortunates had dubious habits and suspect morals.

Luckily for Marietta, fate had organized a subplot in her favour. Germany's leading shipping company at the time, Norddeutscher Lloyd, had been through a crisis. Losing money, it badly needed a winner. It set out to build the fastest, most luxurious liner in the world, and came up with a four-funnelled floating palace called the *Kaiser Wilhelm der Grosse*. This achieved two important objectives: one for the Norddeutscher Lloyd shipping line: winning the

Blue Riband for the fastest transatlantic crossing; the other for the Broccoli line: bringing my grandmother and her children to America. I have no problem figuring out which was the greater achievement. So, sometime in early October 1897, Marietta Vence, Cristina (aged thirteen) and the younger Joe and Minnie, carried their bundles up the gangplank.

Years later, eager to know, I asked them: 'What was it like?' I persisted because I felt I owed them so much. They gave me life, and a bonus: they gave me America. I was interested to discover at what cost. I know all about the 'immigrant experience'. Everybody in the United States knows that. But what was it like for *them*? It was not an experience they were eager to relive. But finally they started to remember.

It is a cold day and the children are shivering inside their topcoats. Marietta, tall, strong, the traditional shawl over her pinned-up hair, pulls them closer to her. They're tired and bleary-eyed from the tedious overland journey from Cosenza to the embarkation port of Bremen, north Germany. They are three of 1074 passengers jam-packed in steerage. Italians, Poles, Ukrainians; the usual goulash of emigrating humanity. (Also on board, so the story goes, is a young Italian inventor named Guglielmo Marconi. He is thirty-three years old and has been hired to test some wild idea about sending radio messages from ship to shore.)

An announcement over the loudspeaker tells the steerage passengers that if they want more air, they can get it forward of the spar-deck. Well, air is cheap. And there are freebies. Marietta and her three children stand in line to be issued with a knife, a fork, a spoon, a plate, a metal cup and a single blanket. 'We want all our passengers to be comfortable,' the deck officer says. And somehow my grandmother and the kids manage to find space, some straw mattresses and some double bunks. It may be rough, but the ship is moving westward. Out come the mandolins, the concertinas, the cold sausage and the vino. The kids are dancing, Orthodox Jews praying. There's a celebration. An Italian woman has just given birth to a baby in the ship's infirmary. Shrewdly, she had timed her departure date so that the delivery would be in five-star luxury.

Compared to the cargo boats which transported the earlier emigrants, Marietta's contingent are not complaining. There are wooden tables, benches to sit on and odd corners of privacy among the stacked freight. They can't get anywhere near the First Class area, but the word soon gets around. In the ornate dining-room, with its cathedral-like windows, the orchestra is playing 'Dixie'. On the menu for the first day of sailing: Fillet of new herrings; Blini au caviar; Potage tortue claire; English sole meunière; Boiled salmon with lobster sauce; Prime ribs; Châteaubriand; Vienna fried chicken; Carré of lamb; Asparagus; and Soufflé Kaiser Wilhelm.

Marietta slices a salami and doesn't envy those characters up there in the slightest. The next sausage she buys will be in the United States of America. Maybe she jibs a bit when the First Class passengers are given their mid-voyage treat, a conducted tour of steerage to 'see the immigrants'. Transatlantic slumming to enliven the cocktail hour.

Five days and nights, and the journey's almost over. Nothing between Marietta and a new life in America, except Ellis Island. Not that she and the children will go straight there. The ship first docks at Manhattan Pier to disembark the First and Second Class passengers. The steerage passengers are put on 'hold' for hours. Finally they're transported to the immigration landmark of Ellis Island, the ugliest twenty-seven acres of landfill on the whole New York coastline. Before the days of Ellis Island, immigrants were unloaded at Castle Gardens, which was no holiday camp either. But at least the place left the wretched, frightened newcomers with some dignity. But once the immigrants – there were Poles, Irish and Germans too – began flooding in, the authorities became more selective. Ellis Island was created with two objectives, to screen the mass arrivals more carefully and to keep out undesirables. In fact something like a quarter of a million people were refused entry for a variety of reasons which gave the island its sinister reputation. My grandmother had heard all about it and recounted to my mother the terrible fears she had that she and the family might be turned away.

So Marietta, Cristina, Joe, and Minnie are checked, labelled, examined, questioned, penned behind wire among batches of thirty. I have this vision of them in my mind. Frightened faces caged behind wire netting. Marietta, a proud woman, was scared, for sure. If she or any of the kids was rejected it would mean steerage back to Calabria. But she was also resentful. There was a stigma attached to the immigrants from steerage. Italians travelling

First and Second Class were waved through without a second glance. Being poor, Marietta and her fellow-travellers in steerage were also considered suspect. They were put through the wringer, struggling to make themselves understood, humiliated by the intimate physical examinations. (It would take a little time before the immigration authorities exploded the myth that only the poor are ill or acquire social diseases.)

As Marietta obediently stood in line so that she and the kids could have their teeth and lungs checked, she remembered seeing a food stall with the names of the snacks written in Italian. Pane di Segala 4 cents, Piccoli pasticci 6 cents, Prosciutto 18 cents, Formaggio 12 cents, Limonata 4 cents. That echo from the old country must have touched a nerve as she stood there alone and vulnerable in the vast concrete reception hall.

Then finally they heard the thump of the rubber stamp and they were through. There is a unique picture at the Library of Congress in Washington, taken at Ellis Island at the time, which perfectly captures that moment. It shows an Italian woman, another Marietta, leading the rest of the family out of the immigration compound. She carries a heavy sack in one hand, a bulging straw carrier in the other. Between her teeth, the vital papers and the railroad tickets. I look at it now and think of my grandmother. I imagine what must have been going through her mind. She won't understand a word of the language. She's going to have to doss down in a cold-water tenement in the extremes of the New York climate. She is going to have to work harder than she ever did before. She will have to sleep at night in a room probably shared by the whole family, as fatigued as an overstretched galley slave.

And yet if her daughter, my mother, was anything to go by, Marietta would have had her chin up as she passed through that barrier with the landing permit between her teeth. The immigrant barge would soon set them down on New York's waterfront. From then on it was the survival of the fittest, and the bravest. Part of the crowd. Into the melting pot.

TWO

My grandmother must have known what kind of life lay ahead of her as she and the children spilled off the train at Astoria, Long Island. Work didn't frighten Marietta Vence any more than it bothered the hundreds of other Italians in her particular shipload. Everybody was into the same stampede.

Mass immigration hit New York in the 1870s. In 1897, when Marietta arrived, almost two million Italians had flooded into New York, the largest number of them from southern Italy, where they had the worst unemployment. Many were unskilled, some illiterate. But they were a special class of humans. They worked with a passion, kept the family together and lit a candle regularly on the basis that somebody up there must love them. They were grateful for what they had. Which wasn't much. But they were here, in America. They had a stake in it. They were going to make it. Not exactly in style, but that didn't matter. The sky was the limit.

Some of them ended up in and around Mulberry Street, in an area which became known as Little Italy. Everything about those packed streets – the sounds, the smells, the colour and especially the food – made those early characters feel like they were at home. They set up stalls selling secondhand clothes or pots and pans, worked in sweatshops darning silk, altering clothes, or slaved in shoe factories or the woollen mills.

Those who had come over with some real money – and hadn't been separated from it by waterfront crooks – went to the end of the subway lines and beyond. There they could pick up land cheap, raise vegetables, keep a couple of goats and some pigs, and they were in business. (Many before had been taken by slick operators. It produced a hit song called 'Only An Immigrant', a real tearjerker about innocents who had been fleeced on arrival.) But these cheats would have had to be pretty smart to take my grandmother for a single lira. She was street-wise a century before that word slid into the language. Anyway, she had three mouths to feed in addition to her own. What little cash she had was eating money, not risk capital. She would have to get acquainted with tenement life, and quickly.

The building she finally holed up in was on Hoyt Avenue, Astoria. It was a typical New York tenement: four storeys, brick-built, depressing to look at and not much better to live in. There were two communal toilets in the hallway. You could identify the ethnic origins of the families who lived there by the cooking smells. You didn't need to enquire where the Germans lived. You just pointed your nose in the direction of the sauerkraut. The aroma of gefilte fish, Friday mornings, told you that the Jewish family above them was preparing for Sabbath. You identified the polacks by eliminating the other two.

Marietta secured a couple of small rooms on the top floor. Her garlic would soon upstage all the others. Her personality would do likewise. I have more than a special admiration for this lady. She was a terrific human being. She was the power base with a strong influence on all of us – my mother, father, uncles, everyone. People often ask why I work so hard. I guess the simple answer to that is, that's the way it was. My grandmother's credo was, you worked not only because you had to. The alternative was idleness; and that, in her book, was unthinkable. You made sacrifices. Cristina, her eldest child, was thirteen. She ought to have gone to school. She didn't. What English she learned was self-taught.

While her younger brother, Joe, and her sister, Minnie, would get some kind of education, Cristina, tough luck, would have to help Marietta out with the rent and the food. Even as a child she'd been wonderful with her hands. Embroidery, delicate needlework – she could do exquisite work. At thirteen she landed a job making artificial flowers. She earned maybe thirty-five cents a day turning them out. The factory was in the big city. It meant taking the elevated railroad, the 'El', from Long Island early in the morning and coming back late in the evening. I guess half of what she earned went this way. But she kept working.

My grandmother had also brought a special talent with her from Italy. She had learned to be a midwife. In a remote spot like

Trenta, outside Cosenza (where my mother was born), doctors were scarce and midwives delivered most of the babies. By all accounts, my grandmother was the best; a no-nonsense angel with rolled-up sleeves who loved the kids, especially those she brought into the world. She set herself up as a midwife on Hoyt Avenue. The word soon got around, and in a couple of years she had established a big reputation among the tenement blocks all along the street. Doctors who called her in to help liked her style. Busy, persuasive and strong, she was great in a crisis. She didn't just survive. She wasn't just going to be a struggling immigrant. She was going to be a useful citizen.

There were a lot of problems among the tenement families of the day which had nothing to do with pregnancies. Some had difficulty with the authorities and couldn't fight their corner in a language anybody could understand. Some families were hard up because the father was out of work. Gradually, Marietta found herself playing the female equivalent of the 'Godfather'. Not in the Mafia sense, but in the way people came to her with all kinds of problems. If someone badly needed some money, she'd loan it to them. If they couldn't repay her in cash, they'd bring her some fruit or something they'd cooked. If someone had got into trouble and had to go to court, Marietta would go in and plead with the right official. She could do this because she had put herself through a crash course in English. At night, when the kids were sleeping, she would sit in the kitchen learning basic English from the headlines in newspapers. She would get booster shots from Cristina, Minnie and Joe, who were learning fast.

As Cristina grew into a mature, seventeen-year-old beauty, Marietta was worried. Not so much because of the journeys she made alone to the big city on the El. What concerned Marietta, like any other mother, was that her daughter should meet a good man, make the right marriage. And 'right', in the Calabrian sense, was probably the guy around the corner. The concept of 'like with like' isn't peculiar to Italians. Minorities pitched into strange environments tend to close ranks. It's safer, more secure that way. Anyway, they prefer the food. Calabrians, buried in the mountains miles from the big towns, were perhaps the most closed-in community in Italy. The challenge of New York drew them even more tightly together. So I guess Marietta had more than a passing interest in the news that Cristina had met this character, Giovanni Broccoli.

'Where does he come from?' she asked her daughter, secretly relieved that the chap had to be Italian.

'Calabria.'

'Ah, Calabria!' Her daughter had struck a chord. 'And where in Calabria?' (My grandmother was pressing her bet.)

'Carolei, I think, Mamma.'

'Carolei!' It was so close, Giovanni Broccoli was virtually the boy next door.

'Why don't you bring him home to meet Mamma?'

The man who would be my father had passed his first hurdle. But he was twice as old as Cristina. Like other Italian immigrants, he had to grab whatever work he could get. With New York bursting at the seams, construction and excavation offered the best chances to the huge pool of labour. The Italians were way back at the end of the line. If my father had any bitterness in him it was because of the insulting injustices of that period. He remembered there were three wage rates operating at the time: one for the locals; a second, lower one for the blacks; and a third, even lower, for the Italians. Their biggest enemies were among the Irish who were stirred on by the Ku Klux Klan, who viewed immigrants with contempt and whipped up anti-Jewish and anti-Catholic prejudices.

But Giovanni Broccoli was strong. He could carry bricks or lift rocks like anybody else. At least as well as the Irish, who fought to keep out 'dago' competition with their fists and shillelaghs. He started off as a hod carrier. No great shakes, maybe, for the privilege of marrying Marietta Vence's shapely daughter Cristina. He came to their home, and my grandmother liked what she saw. Giovanni was powerfully built, short on charm, but he tried no fancy stuff and looked my grandmother straight in the eye. Anyway, the Broccolis of Carolei were a family Cosenzans knew about. And, luckily for the boyfriend, respected.

Cristina Vence and Giovanni Broccoli were married in the spring of 1902. A son, John, was born a year later. I was born six years after that, on April 5, 1909, in that tenement on Hoyt Avenue, my parents having moved in with my grandmother. Mine was not exactly a dignified entry into the world, either. Years later I was given the following version of the event.

My grandmother, being a midwife, was obviously going to

handle the delivery. When my mother's time came and I was due for general release, my grandmother was already on hand. But there was an emergency. I was a breech birth, and it seemed I was having trouble breathing. There was some doubt as to whether I would survive: no paramedics then, of course. Not necessary, as it turned out. My grandmother, so they tell me, resorted to an old Calabrian custom. Somebody ran out and caught a chicken. It had to be a black chicken, apparently. They shoved the chicken's head into my mouth, and pretty soon I appeared to be making the same squawking noise as the bird. The strategy worked. I began breathing properly. Panic over. Afterwards my brother John used to tease me about it. He claimed they didn't stick the bird's head in my mouth but in the other orifice. Personally, that distinction never bothered me, though I can't speak for the chicken.

Anyway, I survived. Which meant another hungry mouth joined the top-floor occupants of the Astoria tenement. Grandmother's sister, Luigina, wasn't having it all that easier just a mile away. Her husband, Pasquale, was an overbearing Calabrese. I used to visit him when I was a child. My father and mother would take me there, and I could see that the two men didn't exactly love each other. I remember old man de Cicco as a tough character. Prussian-like almost, with mutton chop whiskers and a habit of talking down to my father, which drove Giovanni mad. Most times he told my mother he didn't want to visit the de Ciccos. My father was, with all his gruffness, a proud man. He wasn't going to be put down by this domineering roughneck.

Old man de Cicco could be disgusting, too. I remember a night when we all went over for supper. Something had happened previously and the two men were obviously spoiling for a dogfight. But my mother, always the peacemaker, warned my father: 'Don't make trouble. Let's have a nice family evening together.' Giovanni shrugged his shoulders and nodded. But these coarse-grained Calabrians had their own way of settling arguments. My father was prepared, for Cristina's sake, to make peace. He was demonstrating, by offering his hand, that the rift between them was over. But when de Cicco returned the handshake, he soundtracked the gesture with a thunderous fart. It was disgusting, of course, and in any other circumstances involving different characters, it would have been intolerable.

However, these men were cut out of rough soil. They had their own basics of communication, their own rituals. De Cicco explained afterwards that he was only trying to ease the tension between them. At the time my father went white with fury, but, out of respect for Cristina, kept his cool. He stared at de Cicco and uttered, in Italian, an ancient insult whose crudity matched the level of de Cicco's humour. The two sisters looked scared. Then suddenly old man de Cicco laughed. Giovanni had given as good as he got. 'Let's eat,' he said.

For all their arguments, de Cicco and my father had much in common. Both were proud Italians taking up the challenge of making good in America. They shared a common enemy, too: the Irish labourers who resented these 'dagos' coming in and stealing the best jobs. It was a lie, of course, for the Italians took their chances like all the other immigrants. But that didn't stop the Irish contingent – Tammany Hall types – laying into the Italian 'competition' whenever they could. (Both envied the Jewish immigrants, geniuses with the scissors and the needle and thread, who were dragooned into the sweatshops of New York's garment district. They would one day have sons named Milton Berle, Jack Benny, Danny Kaye and Kirk Douglas.)

It couldn't have been easy for Pasquale de Cicco any more than it was for my father; both from farming backgrounds, they'd been thrown into hauling bricks, clearing sites, digging sewage trenches – the brutal side of the construction business. They both belonged to the Hod Carriers' Union, which gave the card carriers more problems than protection. Even within the Italian section, cliques formed. Most often these were from the same Italian village. Their leaders, called the *padroni*, supplied the squads of labourers – hand-picked by them – took all the pay from the bosses and divided it up among the workers. The wage packets were a shade lighter by the time the *padroni* had taken their cut. They claimed it had to be done this way because they could speak the language whereas most of the labourers could not. In 1897 two-thirds of the Italian labour in New York was controlled by the *padroni*. By 1900 they represented almost the entire workforce building the New York subways.

Yet even the *padroni* had it rough. They had their counterparts among the Irish, and there was always an unofficial war between the 'micks' and the 'dagos'. When a building project was announced, they'd all stream along to the site to make an early pitch for a job. When the Irish saw the Italian labourers coming, they threw rocks at them to keep them away. My father and de Cicco were blood brothers in these situations. They punched their way into getting a piece of the action. At night, during the worst periods, Marietta and her sister, Luigina de Cicco, waited for the battling 'dagos' to come home with bloody noses and maybe a couple of teeth missing. It wasn't a lifestyle either of them was going to put up with for long. They hadn't come to America to mix concrete and fight the Irish.

Giovanni Broccoli had a sharp mind behind his abrasive image. And though he wasn't the demonstrative type, he loved his children in his own brusque manner. And he loved Cristina, my mother, even more. Damned if he was going to be beaten by the 'system' or the *padroni* who controlled it. Even while he was climbing ladders with a hod of bricks over his shoulder, he was planning to get into something better. He bought books and went to night classes, learning engineering and contracting. He brought all his pay home, which my mother would salt away. I used to hear them talking and planning late into the night. They had only one aim, obsession really: to save enough to buy a farm. That was their dream, and they were going to realize it no matter what that meant in sweat and humiliation.

So my father had to go where the jobs took him. After a while we'd only see him weekends. Later on he'd go away for as long as six months. My mother had to cope alone, raising the family on the money Giovanni sent her. But it was my grandmother Marietta who held us all together. I never went hungry. At five years old I was turned out as smartly as any of the other kids at the local school. I hadn't yet learned the tricks the gangs in the tenements used for survival.

The whole area was in a kind of ethnic upheaval, the kids inheriting the street generosity and the prejudices of their elders. At five, coming from a home where Italian was mostly spoken, my card was clearly marked. Dago. In those days, if you were called that, it was a put-down. An insult. But if we called each other that, then it was said affectionately. Nowadays my friends in the motion-picture business often ask: 'Hey, dago, how're you doing?' with the same friendliness. Sammy Davis Jr's close pals would call him 'Smokey'. It was the subtle inflection given the words which mattered. (I seem to remember Frank Sinatra once had a plane he called *The Flying Dago*. I think he painted over the name whenever he flew across Italy.)

Influential Italian groups in the United States have objected to the use of the word in films or television even in fun. I can understand that, though it doesn't bother me that much. Usually the portrayals on television are pretty bad. But on Hoyt Avenue, when the kids called me 'dago', affection had nothing to do with it. I was one of the wops and they let me know it. But I never had a chip on my shoulder about it. Queensberry Rules didn't operate in those days. You lived, survived, by the rules of the streets.

I remember the day they were going to show a film at the school. I was as mad with excitement as any other half-pint going to see a picture for the first time in his life. The film was *Little Lord Fauntleroy*, starring Mary Pickford. My mother bought a ticket – a big deal for her. I remember that day clearly. Walking through the schoolyard with all the other kids of the elementary school. A couple of them came up to me and said, 'You going to see *Little Lord Fauntleroy*?'

'Yes,' I replied, feeling pretty proud.

'We don't believe you. You really got a ticket?'

'Yes, I've got a ticket.' And like a prize patsy I showed it to them.

One of the ruffians just whipped the ticket out of my hand and ran like hell. I stood there too dumb to know what to do about it. I started to cry and do what all kids do in these situations: I ran home to my mother. I told her what had happened. 'Don't worry Cubby,' she said. 'The film will be on for a few more days. I'll get you another ticket. This time somebody will go with you.' I guess that was my first encounter with rogues in the film world. (There would be similar confrontations years later, on which more than the price of one ticket would be poised.)

So eventually I got to see *Little Lord Fauntleroy* and it was absolute magic. I've never lost that feeling of wonder that motion pictures had on me right from the start. From then on I went to films whenever I could: sometimes with my brother John or with my cousin Pat, Pasquale de Cicco's son. The equipment would be primitive, the seats hard, the theatres no better than your average flea-pit. But it was an enormous thrill for me.

There wasn't much fun around the rest of the family. My father was away most of the time. My brother John had gone to New

Jersey to work with my uncle, Joe Broccoli. New Jersey was opening up fast. They were building the roads that would one day take cars and freight right across America. John had learned to drive a truck. He worked with contractors, laying the concrete for the roads and bridges of the new scheme. I learned to drive when I was twelve. I could barely reach the pedals, and felt twenty feet above the ground, but my father said, 'You've got to know how to drive. One day it won't be a truck, it'll be a tractor.' He was still dreaming about that farm.

His big break came when they urgently needed skilled construction workers for the Croton Dam. This was a vast enterprise built on the Croton River, a tributary of the Hudson. Thirty-five miles outside New York, it was built in 1842, but there was still plenty of reconstruction going on fifty or sixty years later. Important work, too, since it provided almost all of New York City with its water supplies. My father landed some work out there, and was grateful for it, even though it was tough, especially in the hot summers and freezing winters.

I could see how lonely my mother was. Not much of a life for her. Now and again she must have wondered whether it was any better than life in Cosenza. Marietta consoled her. One day it will be better, you'll see. It certainly was for Luigina. Her husband Pasquale had taken everything the mobs could throw at him. He was going to have his farm. He hadn't travelled steerage across the Atlantic for nothing. He had brought something with him to America none of these hooligans could match. A packet of broccoli seed; his own precious crop from Calabria. When the New York customs asked Oscar Wilde whether he had anything to declare, he boomed back: 'I have nothing to declare but my genius.' Pasquale de Cicco had nothing to declare except a packet of seed. (In the event, he had more luck with the vegetable than Wilde had with his genius.)

Broccoli was the first thing de Cicco planted when he'd scraped enough cash together to rent a farm at Astoria. It covered about twenty acres. We were going to wait for our spread, putting the dollars and cents away each evening. But my father and mother were glad at least one branch of the family had got a stake in American soil. From now on it was a matter between Pasquale de Cicco, the weather and the Almighty.

He was tough. And in any event, farming could never be as

rough or demeaning as fighting the jeering hooligans on the construction sites. My father was going through all that working on the Croton Dam. The workers slept in makeshift dormitories, ate their meals at long wooden tables, shaking out into their own ethnic groups, with the Italians well distanced from the Irish. There were accidents, fist fights, particularly on the Catskill Aqueduct, where major construction had to be undertaken to bring New York its water.

But Giovanni was earning money. Every wage packet brought him and Cristina closer to achieving what they wanted most: their own farm, like the de Ciccos. They got even closer when my mother was offered a job as cook-housekeeper to H.N. Marvin, the inventor and radio pioneer. She was second cook, in fact, but she could prepare anything, not just typically Italian food (though after a while her pasta figured high on the menus when Marvin did formal entertaining).

The Marvins lived in a huge mansion in maybe thirty acres on Boston Post Road, Rye, New York State. It was a lovely old establishment with tall windows, root cellars, caves, built among tall trees, back from the road. After the tenement on Hoyt Avenue, the sauerkraut and the blocked toilets, this was five-star living for us. I remember sensing how vulnerable my mother felt as she said goodbye to Marietta and her friends on the street, moving into a strange house, among strange people, her husband away most of the time. But there was a lot of Marietta's stoicism in Cristina. She always did what was asked of her, never complained, took what was coming.

Harry Norton Marvin turned out to be a gem of an employer. He was a brilliant inventor and innovator, without being your conventional eccentric retreating behind dials and flashing lights. He liked my mother and took an interest in me, too. I was now going to Rye Free State Elementary School. When I'd come home in the evenings, if he wasn't working on an experiment, he'd tell me about some of his inventions. He had first been an associate of Thomas Edison. Together they installed the first electric light plant in New York. One night in 1888, in Edison's office at 65 Fifth Avenue, Marvin and Edison together threw the switch that brought the first electric light to New York City.

But that was only openers for Marvin. He went on to invent the Marvin Electric Rock Drill, which developed into the pneumatic road drill used everywhere today. A couple of years after that, he and a character named Herman Casler invented the Mutoscope. This was the forerunner of the motion-picture machine. Originally in penny arcades, they're collector's items today. Marvin's pioneering work in the making of motion-picture cameras was crucial. He demonstrated some of the earliest contraptions to me; they were fantastic. With Casler and an English inventor, W.K. Dickson, he invented the biograph, the first true movie machine. He filmed moving pictures of the famous train called the Empire State Express. The effect on the first-night audiences in New York was stunning. One woman became so excited she fainted and had to be carried out.

Marvin and a couple of associates formed the Biograph Company at 11 East 14th Street, to make motion-picture shorts. The first two unknowns they hired to act in them were a young beauty called Mary Pickford and a serious-looking performer named D.W. Griffith. Marvin was the first man in the world to take motion pictures of royalty. He was brought to England by royal command to film King Edward VII.

His son Robert and daughter Marguerite adored him, proud of the man who had worked with Edison. He retired once, then got restless and invented the automatic palm-reading device you see in all the fairgrounds. I remember seeing him fiddling with something when, after school one day, he'd let me look over his shoulder in the laboratory. Small copper wheels, turned by cords, moving a needle across a dial. It developed into the first automatic tuning device, now used universally on radio sets. He sold the idea to the Zenith Radio Company. The whole field of films and radio owes plenty to this friendly genius. What I admired most about the man was the fact that he found time to talk to me, and to listen. He demonstrated a lot of his film equipment, how the cameras worked and so forth, and in a way became quite an influence on my life. He used to tell me how he thought film photography would develop in the future. I couldn't have had a better introduction to motion pictures. Marvin never treated me as though I were the son of the hired help.

Many of Marvin's patents had paid off and he was very wealthy. He was also a man of great taste, who owned fine pictures and sculpture, displayed in a gallery at the house. One day he noticed me looking at his paintings, running my hand over some of the sculpted pieces he kept in this gallery.

'You like them?' he asked.

'I think they're terrific!'

'You'll find brushes, paints, clay in there. Why don't you see what you can do?'

I spent hours in the gallery painting and making odd figures with the modelling clay. It was obviously going to be the only gallery that would ever exhibit the stuff. But apparently old man Marvin was impressed. 'The boy is good. He has a talent,' he told my mother. 'You ought to try and get him to study painting and art.' A nice thought, but I saw a couple of immediate objections. One, I didn't see myself getting anywhere in the future with the paintbrush or chisel. Two, though my parents wouldn't have stood in my way, I knew they could never work a farm without their two sons.

Still, Marvin's encouragement wasn't wasted on me. Motion pictures are just a series of images in fixed frames. It involves composition, visual balance, style and the ability to catch and hold the eye. I learned a lot about those values studying Marvin's works of art. He would explain certain qualities to me which applied as much to film-making as they did to painting. I was hooked on what he said, and remembered it.

Whenever his children were having fun, holiday time, he saw to it that I somehow got involved with them. There was a period when the young Marvin grandchildren and their friends would go off skiing in the Adirondack Mountains. Skiing is not the kind of sport hod carriers' sons automatically drift into. I had no skis. The trick, in those days, was to use split barrel staves and lash them onto the feet. Your feet smelt like a brewery, but you could get down the smaller hills without breaking your neck.

Pasquale de Cicco and his family – Angelina, Pat, Louise, Joseph, Cristina and Anthony – were now living on the farm land he'd rented outside Astoria. He had made money. If he'd been a shade smarter, he'd have bought the place and become richer even quicker. When he took it over, it was mostly barren land. He raised spinach, turnips, carrots and beets, which he used to truck to the Harlem Market on 116th Street and First Avenue.

But Pasquale's prize crop was broccoli. When he first brought his broccoli seeds to America, he discovered other farmers had tried to grow the vegetable in New York State, Texas, virtually everywhere. But they failed. The plant bore flowers and came out all wrong. They blamed it on the soil, the weather, even the bees, which they accused of pollinating the plant and screwing it up in the process. All of which was joy to Pasquale. His broccoli was the de Cicco strain, a very fine seed which sold for something like sixteen dollars just for one ounce. Gold dust. The de Ciccos sang all the way to the bank. Luigina could see the contrast in lifestyles between herself and her niece Cristina. She understood my mother's loneliness, with her husband miles away on a construction site while she was living in an upstairs room in the Marvin mansion.

Pasquale could occasionally be condescending to my father. He ignored the fact that Giovanni had been promoted to site superintendent, earning status and a bigger pay packet. And it was all to a purpose: his own farm. So when Luigina begged the Broccolis to live with them in Astoria, Giovanni backed off. It was a matter of pride with him. He didn't need anything from the old rascal. As long as he could work, then the family could eat. But, gently as ever, Cristina eventually persuaded him that the move made sense. Moreover, after two years' cooking for H.N. Marvin, she was ready for something better. It would be good for her sons too, she insisted.

The move would mean further spats between my father and Pasquale de Cicco, who I expect enjoyed some malicious pleasure at the thought of having his old rival under the same roof, working for his keep. But he was denied that satisfaction. My father gave in sufficiently to allow my mother and the two sons to move into the de Cicco farm. But not him. Giovanni preferred to spit on his hands and make his own way someplace else.

The de Cicco farmstead at Astoria was small for a business which was expanding all the time. De Cicco had fixed a deal with one of the main seed companies in New York, to whom he sold the valuable broccoli seed he imported from Calabria. He was quietly building a fortune, which years later would enable my cousin, Pat de Cicco, to enjoy the lifestyle he reckoned he was cut out for: fun and beautiful women.

It was Pat, incidentally, who was responsible for the name 'Cubby', which early on replaced my given names of Albert Romolo. There was, at the time, a cartoon character who for some reason reminded Pat de Cicco of me. I never saw the resemblance. But Pat figured I was the dead ringer for Abie Kabibble, as famous as Peanuts today. And that's what he called me. Over the years Kabibble was shortened to 'Kubbie' and finally 'Cubby'.

Pat and I became very close on the Astoria farm. Our friendship lasted right until the end of his life. I miss him now. He had style and was closer to me and the family than almost anyone else. But there was always this closeness between the Broccolis and the de Ciccos, with the exception of the two at the top, Giovanni and Pasquale. The more Pasquale prospered, the more Giovanni was aware of the disparity between them. It made my father work all the harder, even more determined to buy a farm and go it alone.

Soon de Cicco saw no sense in continuing to pay rent to a landowner. He had enough cash now to buy his own holding: a big spread further out in Smithtown. Luigina insisted we all moved there with them. My mother worked hard on that farm, and helped out with the cooking. She was never the type of woman who looked for a free ride in life. She came from the old school. Duty was everything. She obeyed the rules as a wife, and as a mother. There were rules, too, if you were living under somebody else's roof. Even the old tyrant Pasquale conceded that Cristina Broccoli pitched in as hard as anybody else on the farm. She continued to be like that when, later on, there were plenty of other hands to do the work. These days they call that attitude the 'work ethic'. With my mother it was simply the sort of effort you made if you were a human being. She never thought of herself as being deprived, unlucky. She just accepted that she was born into a way of life in which expectations were limited. You just rolled with the punches.

My father, in spite of his abrasive manner, wasn't any different. And one day it all paid off. He had raised just enough money, together with what my mother had saved, to buy his own farm. First step towards the American Dream, Broccoli version. He could, at last, bring the family back together again under one roof. His own. I remember there was a lot of joy around my family at that time. My father was more pleased than all of us. Pasquale de Cicco couldn't patronize him any longer, though I suspect he was secretly pleased Giovanni Broccoli had got his stake at last.

The farm my father bought was a modest spread of twenty-five acres at Lake Grove, close to Lake Ronkonkoma, Long Island. It was right at the end of the motor parkway from Mineola. Twenty-five acres of rough land which I guess at the time nobody else wanted. But it looked good to the Broccolis.

Giovanni had thrown his hat into the ring, and hoped that Pasquale de Cicco was watching.

THREE

It was not much of a farm to begin with. A couple of Fordson tractors to turn the soil over. Storage sheds for the machinery and seed. But there was a fine old farmhouse, which had what we called a summer kitchen. It was in the basement, a large, clean area where we could seat a dozen or more at a long, scrubbed table. It had a stone floor, which kept the place cool in the summer. No matter how early I got up, my father was always in there ahead of me, cooking his own breakfast. It was usually the Giovanni Broccoli 'special'. He would empty what was left of the previous night's spaghetti or macaroni into a pan and fry it in olive oil, like a pancake.

'Have some,' he said to me once.

'What, in the morning?!'

'Sure, in the morning. It's all right in the morning.'

Then an afterthought: 'It's also all right in the evening.'

So I had some and it was delicious.

The game plan was to plant radishes, spinach, lettuce and, of course, broccoli: anything we knew could sell in the market. We couldn't afford to take on permanent labour. This would be hired when the land needed to be developed or when it was time to harvest the crops. So in the early days we relied almost entirely on family labour: my father, mother, my brother John and myself. I did my stint every morning before I went to school. I'd either help with the ploughing, repair some of the machinery or crawl along the furrows weeding out the crops. I'd then get cleaned up and walk the couple of miles to school.

John had already finished his education after only one year at high school. He could see he was needed on the farm, and that was the end of it. It seemed tough on him, so I asked my parents: 'How about my quitting school so that I can work full time with all of you?' My mother wouldn't hear of it. 'Never. We have enough farmers in the family. You've got to finish your schooling.' Not that she and my father had any great ambitions for me. Some parents, immigrant parents especially, want their sons to be lawyers, accountants, doctors – never actors, and least of all, producers – but they were happy to leave the choice of a career to me. 'Get the education first, then you can do what you want.' I understood their feelings. The one obsession of all immigrants was to get a stake in America by seeing that their kids would have it different, build a better life.

Harry Cohn, that old buccaneer of Hollywood movies, was the son of Russian immigrants. Their life in a crowded tenement on New York's Lower East Side, was as wretched as it was for all the other immigrants, class of 1900. It had a lasting effect on Cohn. He was asked once why he worked so hard as a studio boss. 'So *my* sons won't have to sleep with *their* grandmother!' he snapped back. My father was just as determined. He was going to work his tail off to make sure he was the last hod carrier in the Broccoli line.

I'd been thinking about what I would do when I left school. At one time I decided I'd study to become a civil engineer, maybe get into building railroads, bridges: the sort of things you help create, that you can stand back from with some sense of fulfilment.

I'd always been interested in drawing and design, but I gave up that idea, and also the notion of studying law. But I did go some way toward becoming a journalist, doing a night course at New York City College. But that idea, and others, had to be put on the back burner. The Broccoli farm needed every pair of hands it could get. We worked from daybreak to nightfall – ploughing, sowing, planting, fixing the machinery – after which my mother and father would flake out, exhausted. Even now it hurts when I think about it.

My brother John and I never minded the work. We both had the muscle for it and in any event it was our farm, our family. It was watching our mother, Cristina, out there in the fields that was painful. I remember this bent little figure with greying hair tied back, on her hands and knees in the worst of the summer heat. She'd be pulling out the weeds and spiky grass with her bare hands, crawling along furrows that seemed to go on for ever. She'd stop awhile, sit up and wipe the sweat from her forehead; then on with the back-breaking routine.

And that wasn't the beginning or the end of it. Her work began, as it did for everyone else, at daybreak. When we started hiring hands, she had to rise early to cook breakfast for the lot of us (apart from my father, who was satisfied with his fry-up of the left-over pasta). No ordinary breakfast, either. These guys we hired – a dozen or more at harvest time – would put away huge steaks, sausages, eggs, fried potatoes and gallons of coffee. After they'd stuffed themselves with that lot and gone back to the land, my mother would clean up, wash the dishes and then go out and join them. Rain or shine. Good days or bad days. If she felt ill or tired we never knew. I couldn't bear to see it. I used to say, 'I should be doing that, Mom, not you.'

'You do your share,' was her answer. 'Anyway, don't worry. I enjoy doing it.' Long after, when she really didn't have to go out there, she'd disappear occasionally from the kitchen. We'd start hunting and find her in the fields.

'I can always do *something*,' she used to say. They were unique, that generation of immigrants. They took on burdens that today people half their age would run away from.

As the produce began to sell, my mother and father hired seasonal labour. They'd thin out the newly sprouting carrots, build hothouses to cultivate plants for the early spring. These were migrant workers, and you were lucky if they stayed. There were some Italians, Hungarians and other immigrants who were glad to get the work. They were marvellous workers, most of the time. But they had their weaknesses like everybody else. Farm work is a seven-days-a-week chore. Some of these characters would work up quite a thirst, go out on Saturday nights and get roaring drunk. They'd come back either hung-over and legless, or they wouldn't come back at all. We had one such Hungarian named Jake, who was typical. He was a key man, and he worked with a passion. Then he'd go on a bender, spend all his money and maybe come back three days later, sheepish but ready for work.

But the character who was really the linchpin of the whole set-up was a wonderful old Italian named Biaggio Cavalere. He was a weather-beaten sonofabitch (I use the term affectionately) with gigantic hands and a face like a hawk. He was an independent southern Italian, as perverse as an overworked ox. He had once worked for Pasquale de Cicco. Maybe they were too much alike. Whatever the reason, my father managed to head-hunt him off the de Cicco farm. Behind the impatient, grizzled front he put up was a good and kindly soul. Like many Italians, he sent all the money he earned back home to his family in Italy. The cash he sent was invested in property over there. The relatives were poor. His hand-outs, as regular as the seasons, fed, clothed and housed them.

Biaggio did every job that was going on our farm. He took care of the animals, planted the seeds, drove the tractors, loaded up the trucks. He was the first one up in the fields as dawn broke; the last one in at night. He behaved as though it was his farm. If we had a good season he was happy. If bad weather had wiped out a whole field of crops, he was as moody as if it had been his money that had gone down the tubes. The pendulum swung between making a small profit or the disaster of a price drop, when it was cheaper to throw the stuff into the river. The whole business was a gamble, the farmers being the least able to carry the loss.

I remember vividly what it was like. The truck is finally loaded up, so heavy the springs are almost flat on the axles. In that load is everything you've grown with your bent back and your bare hands. You've got radishes, spinach, tomatoes, cucumbers, all washed, bundled and crated. It looks beautiful up there, and you're proud of it. The truck is only a four-tonner, but it seems like there's ten times that weight aboard. You've got stuff for the general market. You've grown special ethnic items like the horse-radish Jewish housewives grate up as 'bitter herb' for the Passover service. Also the *heimischer* cucumbers, the small ones they'd pickle, and the root vegetable kohlrabi. So here's your truck all ready to go, and it's your effort, your money, your future up there. You climb up front and your mother and father wave you off to the Harlem Market. Your mother wipes her hands on her apron and says, '*Buona fortuna.*' Your father is more practical. 'Don't crash the truck,' he says. You drive along the dirt road off the farm, and the truck is so heavy it's rolling like a ship in a storm. You slow down, thinking of all that lovely stuff on board and the money you hope to get for it.

Now you're in the Harlem Market and they assign you a stand where you spread out what you've brought. And you make it look like a work of art. But you know inside you that this isn't going to impress all these hustlers, who don't give a damn about art. They're there to squeeze you till it hurts. You know there's no point in telling them that your mother had to go down on her hands and knees to produce this stuff. They'd just tell you you're breaking their hearts. They look down at everything you've washed and buffed to perfection, then sniff at you and start turning the screw.

'How much are the tomatoes?'

'Five dollars a case.'

'Give you three dollars.'

'No, we can't do that.'

'Three dollars, that's it.'

'Impossible. The crate alone cost two dollars.'

'You can have the crate back.'

You're arguing with these bastards now, and you know you're going to lose. You don't want to drive home to Lake Ronkonkoma with all the produce back on the truck. So you either let them take you apart, or you say 'The hell with it' and cart the stuff away with you. You've done it before. Many times you'd hoped to come back from Harlem having sold your vegetables at market value, managed to squeeze out, say, fifteen hundred dollars for the entire truckload, or even two thousand on a good day.

Sometimes, though, you run into a special brand of hustlers. You tell them it's the best produce for miles around. They tell you that the prices have hit rock bottom that week and maybe they won't buy anything at all. You've driven miles and these bums in Harlem are ready to cut your heart out. You tell them that you're small farmers who can't afford to hire mechanics when the equipment breaks down; that you've had to repair the harvesters, the tractors, and all the other machinery yourselves and probably won't cover your expenses even if they did meet your price. 'That's your problem,' they say. By now you're desperate and ask their final bid.

'One hundred and fifty bucks for the lot.'

'You're kidding...!'

'A hundred and fifty and that's coming down any minute...'

A hundred and fifty? At that price it's no deal. But you dare not take the stuff back to the farm. So you load up the truck and drive along to the banks of the Harlem River. And you take this beautiful fresh broccoli, the green spinach, the cucumbers and the Passover radish, and you heave it all into the water. And then, sick at heart, you drive the empty truck back along the Jericho

Turnpike and your father and mother are standing by the gates. They see the truck is empty, and get the wrong idea.

'You sold everything? Get a good price?'

'No.'

'How much then...?'

'Nothing. We threw the stuff into the Harlem River.'

Your mother bites on her lip. Giovanni Broccoli goes red from the neck up. He is angry but understands.

'You did right, boys,' he growls. 'Screw them!'

I had finally quit school. I didn't figure it was such a big sacrifice, either. John had cut out of high school after only one year. I could no longer take the situation where my mother is on her knees in the fields and I'm comfortably on my backside in the classroom. My father's health wasn't holding up too well. He'd developed some ominous heart symptoms, though he made no fuss about it. But I knew my mother worried. For all his occasional surliness, my father was a good man, and generous, too. He often gave fruit and vegetables away if he thought some of the neighbours needed stuff but couldn't afford it. He couldn't afford it himself, but he couldn't bear to see their kids go hungry. They'd come to the farm with their pinched faces and scrawny infants, look at the fruit and vegetables and ask: 'How much?' My father would name a price which would be half of what he might ask in the market. He'd look at the expression on their faces. If it was obvious they couldn't afford it, then he'd give it to them.

Of course, once the news got around, the traffic increased. But Giovanni was foxy enough to sort out the needy from the freeloaders. Sometimes my mother might complain that he was giving away all the profits. But inwardly she approved. She was a born giver, too, and raised her family that way. She knew herself what it was like to be hungry. Both she and my father were liked in the neighbourhood.

Everybody took my father for what he was, a difficult, forthright pain in the ass, but an honest and decent man. He hated any kind of pretence. But he never made a big thing about it. I only once remember him giving me advice. And I've never forgotten what he said. Somebody had been bragging about something, or maybe he'd read an item in the newspapers. Anyway, what he wanted to get over to me was the difference between big talk and the reality; the bogus and the real McCoy. But he didn't use any of those words. What he said was:

'Remember always, Alberto, when the snow melts you see the dog shit!'

Philosophers may have expressed the point more elegantly. But I prefer the Giovanni Broccoli version. You don't forget advice like that in a hurry.

I was now a full-time worker on the farm. We'd extended our crops, and we'd added Polish labourers to the workforce. You could hear all kinds of languages out there in the fields. But the workers all had one shared ambition: to get their 'papers', to become American citizens. They had jobs and a roof over their heads. But they were transients, 'foreign labour', and there's no pride where there's no status.

Biaggio Cavalere wanted to be an American citizen more passionately than all of them. He knew he had to work for it. He was weak on the English language: bad at reading, worse at writing. I'd catch him muttering to himself, a pencil stuck awkwardly in a calloused fist, and I could see he was getting nowhere. I felt sorry for him. 'Biaggio, there are certain things you have to do,' I told him. He eyed me suspiciously.

'Like-a what?'

'You have to learn about America, our laws, our customs, our history and so forth...'

Biaggio got a copy of the questions he was likely to be asked and I trained him to write his name and other details legibly. Then I gave him a run-down on our distinguished line of American Presidents. I had a problem here. I could never get him to pronounce 'Lincoln' correctly. He would smile, imitate my lip movements, then say, 'Klincoln.'

'It's *Lincoln* with an "L",' I stressed.

'And that's-a what I'm saying: "Klincoln",' he shouted.

I arranged to take Biaggio to a court on Long Island for the hearing. He put on his best suit, got a shine on his boots and told me: 'Do'n-a worry. I'm ready.'

'I'm not worried, Biaggio,' I said, which was the only time I ever lied to him. I was very worried, remembering he had the shortest fuse on the farm.

'Just remember to face the judge and answer truthfully.'

'Course I'm-a gonna face-a de jorge...'

'Judge.'

'I said-a "jorge". What-a you think – I'm-a dumb?'

I grilled him all the way to the court. 'Who was George Washington?'

'It's-a easy one,' he laughed. 'George-a Washington was-a da first President-a United States...'

'And who was Abraham Lincoln...?'

'Do'n-a worry,' he winked, then raised his voice. 'Abraham Klincoln was also President...'

'Do you remember what he was famous for?'

'Of course I remember everything like-a my own name!'

We go into court. And immediately we're off to a bad start. Biaggio is murdering the English language and drawing laughs around the court. He doesn't like this at all, and looks venomously at me. I had coached him, and not too brilliantly, he must have decided, considering the laughs he is getting. But the judge is friendly and patient.

'What is your name?'

'My name is Biaggio Cavalere.'

'Where do you live?'

'I-a live...Ronkonka.'

More laughter. Except from Biaggio. I sense he's going to blow it. The judge nods encouragingly.

'You mean, Ronkonkoma?'

'Dat's-a what I said,' beams Biaggio.

'Thank you.'

'Ronkonka!' Biaggio says again to prove his point.

The judge passes on that one.

'Are you married?'

'Yes-a, I'm-a married.'

'How many children do you have?'

'I got-a two children.'

'But Mr Cavalere, here on the paper it says you have three.'

'Oh yes-a, Mr Jorge. I got-a two *now*, but I got-a one started which is-a no-finished yet.'

Now everybody is laughing, including the judge. Biaggio can't see what's so funny. The judge decides to throw him an easy one.

'All right now, Mr Cavalere, what did Abraham Lincoln do that made him so famous?'

Biaggio was waiting for it. The big one.

'Well-a, Mr Jorge, I tell you. Abraham Klincoln became-a famous because he was-a-frigga da sclaves!'

'He what...?'

'He frigga da sclaves!'

Biaggio brings the house down, and I am not looking forward to taking him back to the farm. It is becoming a terrible ordeal for this simple farm worker, though the judge is clearly on his side and puts the question asked of all would-be citizens of the United States.

'Biaggio, tell the court why you wish to become a citizen of the United States?'

Biaggio decides the question is superfluous. What more did they want? He gripped the rail in front of him and addressed the court.

'Look-a, Mr Jorge, if you-a wanna give me the papers, hat's hokay. If you no wanna give me the papers, hat's hokay too.'

The judge looked at him and smiled.

'Biaggio Cavalere, you are a citizen of the United States of America. Good luck!'

We had at last persuaded my mother that her farming days were over. But she still insisted on doing the cooking, and there might be sixteen at one sitting, with another mob to feed later in the day. At a certain time of the year the farmers would kill the pigs to be made into sausages and *sanguinacio*, a special delicacy made from their blood. This was party time for everyone. If you were invited to a pig party, that showed you had status. It was a great Italian cookout with home-made wine, singing, the children dancing. My mother stood over the open fires turning the sausages, my father walked around filling the glasses. It was good to see them happy like this. But now and again my father would go pale and stand quite still. He could no longer work the way he used to, though that didn't stop him going out into the fields. 'Take it easy, Poppa,' we told him, and he said, 'Sure, when I've finished.'

He loved his farm, especially in the summers. He would stand in the sunlight and look at the land. His land. He looked at the long lines of ripening vegetables, tomato plants, dwarf cucumbers and especially the broccoli. We had told him that it was on the menus in the finest restaurants in New York. That pleased him. I believe he felt that he had made something of this life. He had never wanted much for himself. Everything he did was for us. But he was running out of steam.

It was on one of those very hot New York days when it happened. I had just turned my back. I remember he had a hoe in his hand and was cracking jokes with six or seven others working in the fields. I was looking the other way, when John shouted to me, 'Cubby, come over here...Pop's on the ground!' I rushed over. My father was still sort of smiling from the jokes he'd been putting around. I thought he'd just passed out. But that was the moment when he had died. We lifted him up and put him in the truck. John and I drove him up to the house.

Our mother was terribly distressed. She kept repeating his name. He hadn't suffered. It was all over in an instant. He deserved that. He would have hated to have been alive but unable to function with all his old vigour. The Croton Dam, the farm, these were a couple of roots he put down and could be proud of. It was a big blow to John and me. There was never great intimacy between us and our father, but he knew we loved and respected him. It was when he was gone and we started to think about it that we began to measure the kind of man he was.

It was a sad day, the day of the funeral. All the neighbours turned out to salute him. And all the workers on the farm. He was buried at Sayville, with John and I standing at the graveside, Cristina between us. We knew she was grieving deeply, but as always, she kept her emotions to herself. I was going to miss the old villain. We'd had a good relationship which required no words to express it. We had both understood that. Best of all we understood each other. I guess he was as good a Broccoli as any of the others who came before him. Maybe even better.

FOUR

John and I realized we had got about as much as we could out of the Long Island farm. If we were to expand, we'd have to take on more acreage. What looked like a great opportunity came up in Florida. The Seaboard Airline Railroad, extending its lines along the Florida coast, was looking for ways to build up its rail revenues. The company offered farmers franchises to develop thousands of acres of rough land which would eventually bring trade and people to the railroad. The deal was that the farmers put up the money for the actual farming and the company would stake them for a certain amount of the development.

On offer were five or six hundred acres of virgin land in the Okeechobee area on Florida's east coast. It would take more money than the family could raise, so a partnership was formed. Joining John and me was another Italian, Joe Savino, who was a cousin on the de Cicco side, and a couple of friends, Herman Sharfe and Nick Barbado. My mother decided she couldn't go with us. The spirit was willing but she recognized that physically the whole adventure would be beyond her.

We worked that land for two years, and I don't think chain gangs had it any rougher. It was sour land, full of snakes, tough meadow roots and submerged saw-grass, which was murder to shift. But if we could get the soil right, we could grow almost anything: cereals, peanuts, potatoes, tomatoes, and close to Lake Okeechobee itself, sugar cane. Before you could plant a single crop or put seeds down, the land had to be drained. First we hired railroad workers to come in and build dikes and ditches every twenty acres. We had to create canals and sluices to drain the poisons away. That done, we had to plant cow-beans just to build up the soil. Once these had come up, you had to plough the stuff under again. All this took two years, but it seemed at last that we were going to make it.

Then we had our first disaster. John and Joe Savino had gone down in the roadster patrolling the cultivated areas, including the dikes and ditches. These were routine checks to make sure the drainage was clear. The car had stopped and Joe got out. John wanted to park the car in a better spot, and started backing up, half standing. He had this Remington rifle wedged between his leg and the steering column, the muzzle facing upward. We always carried it to kill the snakes. There were plenty of these around: water moccasins mainly, which are deadly killers. Suddenly the car began to slide down the slope of the ditch. John dropped back into the driving seat to jam his foot on the brake. As he did so his foot caught the hammer of the gun. It fired and shot him in the rump, the bullet glancing off his hip-bone.

John was bleeding badly, and Joe rushed him to a drugstore at Okeechobee, to get something to staunch the flow. The drugstore was closed, but Joe hammered on the door.

'What d'you want?' a voice called out.

'I've got a man here who's been shot. He's bleeding and I want you to help me. He needs some bandages, some emergency attention.'

'Sorry, we're closed.'

Grabbing hold of the Remington, Joe said, 'Listen, you'd better open this goddamn door or I'll break the glass and blow your head off!'

The drugstore owner opened the door; his face was white. He saw that John was bleeding badly, and he applied tourniquets and sutures while Joe watched, still holding the rifle.

'Where's your hospital?'

'It's at Fort Lauderdale.'

'Too far. You got a doctor here?'

'Yes, there's a doctor. He happens to be at the back.'

'Get him out.'

The doctor appeared and it was clear he'd been drinking. But Joe decided this was no time to quibble.

'Can you stop the bleeding ?' he asked, showing the part of John the bullet had hit.

'No problem,' the doctor said. His speech was slurred and Joe could tell he was from the north. He wondered whether he could see John's ass, let alone the needle. But he did a terrific job, and I'm sure he saved my brother's life.

The accident put John out of action for a couple of weeks. We got back on course, though, and produced a great crop of vegetables. There they were: carrots, onions, tomatoes, lettuce, acres of broccoli – all ready to be harvested. Then blight swept through and wiped everything out. The four of us stood there and stared. All those months of work, in that Florida heat, shrivelled into ruin. There are no easy options when that happens. You just have to start the whole cycle all over. We did that, and again the soil repaid us for all the sweat we'd put into preparing it. Acres of produce, beautiful to look at, ready to be picked.

We'd had the blight. What the hell else could happen? The answer was a hurricane. A real Florida special which tore up the dikes and sluices, scything through our crops like a gigantic meat grinder. It flattened sheds, made a shambles out of our precious acres and cleaned us out. There was nothing left for us to do but hand back everything to the Seaboard Airline Railroad. The fact that the company went bankrupt didn't help us one little bit. I said there was nothing left, but I forget the one exception. The broccoli. It is a hardy vegetable and its roots were strong enough to hold firm in the hurricane. I can understand now why my ancestors were so keen to have it in the family coat of arms. That vegetable kept the partnership afloat for a while.

Pat de Cicco had this beautiful La Salle roadster with the familiar folding windshield. We packed the broccoli into crates, stacked these in the back of his car and hauled them around the big hotels on the Florida waterfront. We were in luck. Running the restaurant of a five-star hotel was a man named Joe Panney, who had been a leading restaurateur in New York before being enticed down to Florida. Panney happened to love broccoli. He introduced Hollandaise sauce, making it a favourite delicacy in New York's classier restaurants. We sold the crop to him at twenty dollars a crate. We'd bring the stuff round to the kitchen entrance, pick up the cash, then go round the front, order dinner for four and enjoy the show. This featured some of the top entertainers of the day. The biggest was Morton Downey, the Frank Sinatra of his day. Al Jolson was the other main draw.

Back in New York, Pasquale de Cicco had died, making Pat a

wealthy man. But even before then, Pat had decided that farming was strictly not for him. He was a tall, good-looking guy with impeccable taste, who dressed with style and had the wealth to indulge his reputation as the most sought-after playboy in town. All the most eligible heiresses in New York were drawn to Pat, and not merely because of his money. When he went out on the town in his elegant grey-flannel suit, the custom-made brogues and the hand-blocked trilby hat from London's St James's, he was every inch the English gentleman. When I got back to Long Island, Pat was back on the playboy circuit mixing with the smart set in the finest places. One day he phoned me. 'Why don't you come to New York for a weekend and have some fun?' I went over in my one good suit, which might have passed for a Saturday night out in Mineola but was the wrong gear for de Cicco territory. He complained I looked like Li'l Abner.

'You can't go to the 21 looking like that,' he said. 'I've got a reputation to keep up. Here, borrow one of my suits.' My first encounter with New York's chic society was at the 21 Club. In those days it was a very exclusive establishment where even the most eminent clientele had to go through the ritual of knocking on the door, whereupon a small panel would open and they'd be scrutinized carefully to make sure they had the right credentials. Pat slid into all this as though he'd been born to it. He was now a favourite 'item' in the society columns, which gave him points with the captains in the best restaurants.

Pat introduced me to Prince Michael Romanoff, a suave and delightful character who claimed kinship with the aristocratic Romanovs of Tsarist Russia. The fact that most people knew this was bogus didn't detract from the respect we paid to 'His Imperial Highness'. Now and again a serf among us might cast doubt on Mike Romanoff's alleged blue-blooded connections, and Mike would get so angry he'd throw a punch at the guy. But this would be a rare reaction, for mostly he was a man of great dignity. He had a photograph on his dressing table which most people took to be a magnificent fake. It showed Tsar Nicholas II and his family. At one end of the group, with what looked like an arm around Prince Alexis, was none other than 'Prince' Michael Romanoff. Mike was a bit hazy about when it was taken. Maybe some astute artwork had been added. Either way it didn't bother his friends, who could never fault him for trying.

One time Mike was called in to advise on a movie. The director, Lewis Milestone, was born in Russia. Ben Warner, at that time boss of Warner Brothers, had been born in Poland. Both men spoke Russian. Ben Warner's son Jack confronted Romanoff.

'OK, you say you're a Russian prince. Now Ben and Lewis are going to speak to you in Russian. We'll soon see what kind of a Russian prince you are!'

Mike stiffened up.

'You should know by now, my ignorant friend, that I never use my native tongue unless I am in my native land.'

Though Mike may not have been royalty, he had all the dignity associated with it. He cornered the best tables in the best restaurants, usually with some beautiful woman or society hostess in tow. He would order the finest champagne and caviare. Later he would run his own restaurant in Hollywood, where he would frequently hole up at a corner table playing some fierce chess with Humphrey Bogart. He became the most lovable phoney on the coast. We had a close friendship which lasted right up to his death.

New York in the mid-thirties and forties was probably the most exciting city in the world. Broadway exploded with talent which dazzled this one-time farmer's boy in his Li'l Abner suit. Earl Carroll, one of the greatest-ever impresarios, put on reviews that were a byword in the world of entertainment. N.T.G. – Nils T. Grantlund – virtually ran New York's night-life. With the fun came those celebrated scandals like the character who was arrested for dunking glamorous ladies in bathtubs filled with champagne. All this was nectar to my cousin Pat, whose style had put him well up in the social calendar.

I now had my own problems. The Okeechobee débâcle had left me in limbo and short of cash. My brother John had left Long Island to get married in Florida. He'd taken his savings and bought a restaurant in St Petersburg. Some of the top baseball players used to eat there, but they didn't just come for the pasta, though it was great. Everybody down there loved John. He was a sweet man, good-natured and a devoted brother. My mother and I used to visit him down there, and it was really good to see the pleasure he had in running the place. He loved sitting around with these marvellous old baseball players like Enos Slaughter and Yogi Berra, and all the famous Yankee ballplayers. They'd sit with their beers, reminiscing about their finest games. It was great to see the way John had landed on his feet.

Farming was over as far as I was concerned, too. I needed a job. Ironically, I landed one which wasn't all that far away from the soil. It was with the Long Island Casket Company, owned by Agostino d'Orta, who was way out on the fringes of the family. Remember Marietta, my maternal grandmother, and her sister Luigina, Pasquale de Cicco's wife? Well, there was a third sister, Maria Grazia, who virtually came to America so that she could die alongside the others. She married Francisco Faraco, and they had a daughter, Rosie, who married Agostino d'Orta. This made Agostino a relative, which was why he approached me on hearing that I was looking for a job. The work itself didn't attract me that much; it was never going to be a barrel of fun.

I liked Agostino, as most people did. Originally he had been an expert wood craftsman, specializing in making miniature furniture. Carved perfectly to scale, these pieces were beautiful to look at. Going from miniature furniture to making children's caskets may not have been a logical development, but Agostino was immediately successful. This reflected the times, I guess. Infant mortality must have been high then, certainly in the poorer tenement areas.

Agostino's workmanship was so good, he expanded into making caskets for adults. When that part of the business began to flourish, he decided he needed someone to help organize the business. Somebody who could talk to New York's major undertakers – there were about thirty of them, companies like Thomas and Quinn. I got to know all the leading funeral directors. One I particularly remember was a fellow named Hazzi Crook, which for an undertaker might be a pretty hard name to live down. He acquainted me with some of the rules of the game, particularly in regard to persuading the bereaved to pay upfront. 'Get 'em while a tear is in the eye!' was his maxim. As he explained it: 'Once the loved ones are buried and the tears are dry on the faces, you'll find it much harder to collect.' Fortunately I wasn't in that end of the business.

Although I worked hard and became Agostino's top man, I could never shake off the morbid aspects of the trade. Seeing those consignments of baby caskets going out every day was depressing. I couldn't help thinking of the grieving families. After a while, though, I was able to keep my emotions out of it. There came a time when I could walk into morticians' parlours and not worry too much that the deceased might be lying there along with the company's caskets. Yet much as I liked and respected Agostino, I wasn't going to spend my future there. When you came down to it, there wasn't much to choose between casket manufacturers and undertakers.

After some months without a break, I decided to take a holiday. Pat de Cicco had been pressing me to join him for a couple of weeks' vacation in California. He had become a Hollywood agent, and a very successful one, representing film cameramen. But while this gave him a lot of clout among producers and the big stars of the day, his charm and sociability counted even more.

'Grab a plane and fly down, we'll have some fun,' he said. 'You need a break from the factory.'

I had never been in a plane before. In 1934 flying was still considered an adventure and a bit of a risk. But I was going to *Hollywood*, which, to the family back east, was just as much of an adventure and an even bigger risk. Stories of lurid scandals made Cristina Broccoli a shade apprehensive about what might happen to her son. So my mother didn't care too much for the whole idea. The rest of the family, though, were ecstatic. Here was the Italian boy going to Hollywood! This was the biggest thing to happen to the Broccolis in years.

The relatives streamed out to the airport at Newark to give me the big send-off, Italian style. They brought gallons of wine and beer. There's a lot of hugging and kissing: maybe twenty-five to thirty Italians getting into the act to say goodbye. Everybody is laughing and crying, warning me against this and that, and uncorking more bottles of vino and slapping me on the back.

At last I get on the plane, a Lockheed Lodestar. The weather is so cold my goodbye smile seems to have frozen solid on my face. It is midwinter, very cold and overcast. I look around and see that I'm one of four passengers. The only other people on the plane are stewardesses and airline personnel. A storm is now blowing up outside, but since I hadn't flown before, it doesn't bother me that much. Soon the plane is bouncing around, and at one point I look out at the wings and see chunks of ice falling off. Knowing nothing about ceilings, weather patterns and so forth, I fall asleep in the midst of all this. Of course, being half-stewed helps. The plane is making a hell of a racket, but as I'm mostly semi-conscious, it doesn't bother me.

Finally we land. The stewardess shakes me. I look out of the window and assume we've made one of the scheduled stops on the way to the coast. Maybe Buffalo, or someplace similar. But the more I look out the window, the more familiar everything appears to be. I know I've seen this place before. I step down and realize I'm back in Newark Airport. The weather had been too bad for the plane to continue, so it had turned back. The airline puts me up in a hotel. I consider informing the family, but decide this would only bring them all out again.

The following morning we take off and after about eight stops wind up in Reno, Nevada. I step off the plane and this really is the Western scene. Everybody's wearing these big stetsons, belts with silver buckles, cowboy boots, and I feel I'm a long way away from the Long Island Casket Company. In the airport you can buy guns, pistols in ornate holsters, and outside the sun is beating down on the desert. The characters around me are either talking about guns, cattle or gambling. In those days they had these punch-boards where you push tiny tubes through holes and there are prizes if your number comes up. I have nothing else to do, so I go to work on that. The Italian boy has only been away for twenty-four hours and he's already gambling in Nevada! As I recall, I won a six-shooter but was too scared to take it with me.

At this point I had to switch to another airplane, belonging to the Trans-Continental Western Airline. I believe it was an old three-engine Fokker or Ford, a low-altitude type with no heating. It was one of the original planes in Howard Hughes's aviation empire. The pilot is Jack Frye, who also happened to be president of the airline. It's very cold, and we have no blankets. The guy seated next to me introduces himself.

'My name is Jake Factor.'

'Any relation to...?'

'Max Factor? Yeah, he's my brother.'

By coincidence, I had only just read an item about him in a New York newspaper. Known to the FBI and the underworld as Jake 'The Barber' Factor, he was at the time said to be a friend of Al Capone.

I settle back and try to sleep. This is difficult because the flight is getting even rougher than the one I took the night before. In those days you had to get enough altitude to fly over certain mountains. The pilot had to circle in the valley, between the peaks, until he'd achieved sufficient height to clear them. If the weather is bad, the wind throws the plane – and you – about. This can be a very unnerving experience.

Finally we sort of crawl over a mountain and drop into Burbank Airport. Beautiful California! There are palm trees. The air is warm and scented with the flowers growing all around. Pat is there to meet me. He says hello to 'The Barber', whom he already knows. We get into this sports car: the suave, wealthy man about town and his hick cousin who is seeing Hollywood for the first time. We're riding past those famous street signs: Hollywood Boulevard, Vine Street, The Brown Derby, Sunset Boulevard, Schwab's Drugstore, Grauman's Chinese Theater...They're all there and I can't believe it! Pat knows what I'm thinking, and is grinning all the time. Divorced from Thelma Todd, he's now living alone in a beautiful cottage apartment on a street with enormous palms stretching on either side. We're hardly there more than a few minutes when there's a ring at the door.

'See who it is, Cubby, will you?'

I open the door. It's Cary Grant. *The* Cary Grant, dropping by to borrow something from Pat. On the doorstep, smiling that famous matinée idol's smile. I call Pat, and it's obvious he and Cary Grant are buddies. I'm knocked out at meeting this famous movie star. Then Randolph Scott shows up. There in the doorway is the famous Western star, pumping my hand and saying any friend of Pat's is a friend of his. I haven't been in Hollywood a day and legends are dropping by every hour on the hour.

'You're going to see more tomorrow night,' Pat says. 'We're going to the Colony Club.' This was one of Hollywood's most fashionable clubs, strictly reserved for members and their guests.

When we arrived, Pat left me to have a drink at the bar while he went to make a phone call. I had a handful of silver dollars with me that I'd picked up in Reno. The bar is long, and I'm seated on one of the stools, idly spinning one of the silver coins. A tall, lean character is seated four bar stools along the counter. He's watching me and the spinning dollar.

'Heads or tails?' he asks.

'Heads.'

I lost, and he took the dollar.

'Spin another one.'

I spun another dollar.

'Head or tails?'

'Heads.'

I lost again.

'Heads or tails?'

And I lost that one, too.

'Well, I guess we'll call it a day,' he said. 'I'm three dollars ahead. Can I buy you a drink?'

'Well, thank you, but I have one right here.'

Then Pat came up and said, 'Hiya, Sam' – I found out later that was what the guy's closest friends called him – 'meet my cousin, Cubby Broccoli.'

'Hello,' the man said to me, shaking my hand. 'My name is Howard Hughes.'

FIVE

I'd been in Hollywood only a week, but I was getting more and more interested in the way the studios were run and who controlled them. The place had an enormous undercurrent of excitement. Going round these huge studio complexes with Pat de Cicco was an education. The men who held absolute power in those days had been mostly immigrants. They were of the same generation as my father, Giovanni, and Pat's father, Pasquale. They had been just as tough, and were probably targets for the same kind of prejudices. But their achievements were colossal. They created more than a major American industry. They taught the world how to make motion pictures. Their genius – ninety per cent gut feeling and ten per cent knowledge – was evident in the stars they created, and the marvellous film classics which stand for all time.

I remember looking at Goldwyn Studios and thinking that the guy born Shmuel Gelbrisz, who once sold gloves in Lodz, Poland, had done pretty well in California. Likewise, Louis B. Mayer, the rag picker from Minsk; Ben Warner, the cobbler who, even when he was President of Warner Brothers, couldn't throw the habit of picking up small nails and putting them between his lips. And, of course, Harry Cohn, son of a German tailor, who built the powerful Columbia Studios. Maybe you couldn't love them all, but you had to respect them. True, they could make their stars nervous and their subordinates sweat. But the bottom line was, they made motion pictures and made Hollywood a legend.

Take just one of these buccaneers: Louis B. Mayer. At one time he had under contract Greta Garbo, Clark Gable, Wallace Beery, Lionel Barrymore, Joan Crawford, Robert Taylor, Jean Harlow, Spencer Tracy, Nelson Eddy, Jeanette MacDonald, Laurel and

Hardy, the Marx Brothers, Judy Garland, Gene Kelly, and Frank and Esther Williams. They were all great professionals. Authentic superstars. Nowadays that word is applied to almost anybody who gets a record into the charts or who appears in the soaps. The star system died a long time ago. But it had much going for it while it lasted. The stars had a kind of stature and magic you don't see much of these days. When any one of them entered a room, the effect was electrifying. Who today has the same kind of impact? Of today's so-called superstars, how many will be remembered twenty years from now?

I went to my first Hollywood film première in a rented tuxedo. No other city in the world could match the glamour, the excitement and the spectacular celebrity turnout. The huge crowds, the searchlights sweeping the sky – and maybe Lana Turner or Joan Crawford, swathed in white mink and loaded with jewellery, stepping out of a big limousine like a queen. It was all part of the business, and I was beginning to get hooked on it. Pat was certainly keen for me to get work in Los Angeles. He had the notion that meeting more people might steer me into something. I suppose that's what they mean by serendipity. Not long afterwards I landed a job with the Paris Beauty Parlour Supply Company. They were based in San Francisco, selling hairnets, shampoos, conditioners and small hair-driers to the trade. San Francisco is a wonderful city, but it doesn't go overboard to salesmen peddling hair products. Any career which is predicated on dandruff has to be speculative.

My deal with the company was this: they would stake me in cash to the value of their products. I would then go out and sell enough items to cover the advance. I checked into a cheap downtown hotel, which didn't smell as fragrant as the potions I had in my samples case. The room was small and decrepit, with a window that wouldn't shut. This was convenient for a rat which used to skitter up onto the window-sill and wait to be fed. I knew it was waiting to be fed, because when I complained to the management, they said, 'Oh yeah, there was a guy before you who used to feed a rat. Must be the same rat.'

They didn't like it when I insisted they shut the window. I suppose the rat had a complaint, too, having his room service shut off without warning. One day I caught him brushing his whiskers up against the window-pane and I felt guilty, so I let him in and gave him some of my breakfast, which in any case was more to his taste than mine. As a matter of fact, I got to like him. Looking back, he was probably the only friend I had there at the time.

I worked hard at trying to shift my wares. Unfortunately, sales were thin. There was an adverse imbalance between the advance I was given and the money I got back to cover it. The significance of arithmetic was not lost on the company, either. The fact was, my sales were insufficient to feed me and the house rat. I remember my total bankroll was exactly eighty-five bucks and no cents. I considered my options. I could either hang in there and hope; turn it all in and try for another job in the town; or take a long walk on the streets of San Francisco and think things out. I took the third option, which turned out to be a smart decision. I walked three blocks and recognized an old friend, Bob Howard, walking toward me. He wanted to know what I was doing in San Francisco. I told him and he laughed.

'You're selling hairnets? What do you want to do that for?'

'That's all I could find.'

'What are you doing today?'

'The same as yesterday. I've still got a case of stuff to get rid of.'

'Fancy going to the races?'

'When?'

'Today. What can you lose?'

The answer was eighty-five dollars. On the other hand, what could I do with it? Well, I'd need some of it for the bus fare back to Los Angeles. The rest wouldn't keep me going for long anyway. So we went to the Golden Gate Racetrack. Minutes before the start, I walked down the stairs toward the clubhouse. An official stopped me.

'Here, you'll need this return check to get you back into the Turf Club. You can't be readmitted without it.'

I bought a programme and there's a horse running named 'Return Check'. I couldn't ignore the signs. So I bet five dollars across the board on him. He wins at thirty-five to one. It was a long time since I'd seen that kind of money. In the second race I back another long shot, which comes in first at twenty to one. Before I know it, I'm leaving the track with eight hundred and fifty dollars. I resigned from Paris Beauty Parlour Supply Company without breaking any hearts there. Then I took the Greyhound bus back to Los Angeles.

Pat was there to meet me – he was that kind of guy. He was eager to know how his cousin had fared in San Francisco. No great shakes, he conceded, but I'd come back with more money than I'd taken out with me. That had to be seen as a plus. We moved to a house near the Chateau Marmont Hotel, off Sunset Strip. Our house belonged to William de Mille, brother of Cecil B. de Mille. Pat and I would give these great Sunday brunches, attended by the playboy bachelors. They made up a colourful group: Bruce Cabot, Errol Flynn, Greg Bautzer and other characters, including an ex-disc jockey named Buddy Ernst.

The last-named had been a radio announcer who'd done well. Well enough now to be flying his own plane. At one time he was sharing quarters with Pat and myself at the de Mille house. He was a crazy Dutchman and we were never sure what he was going to do. One day he said he had to fly up to some place in northern California and asked me to go with him. In a loose moment I said yes.

Buddy was flying this high-wing plane with a single engine. Ten minutes out above the clouds I could see he was somewhat morose. Really despairing. He began telling me his problems. Apparently he'd just broken up with a lady friend, a German–Polish beauty named Lyda Roberti. It had hit him hard and before he got on the plane he'd belted quite a few drinks. This only made him more miserable. He stared out toward the horizon. 'You know, Cubby,' he said bitterly, 'I really feel like packing it all in.'

'What are you talking about, Bud?'

He started swinging the plane around in the sky.

'I just think I'd like to end it all. What have I got to live for?' Then he puts the nose down and I'm getting very nervous indeed.

'Yeah, Bud…well, that's great, you know, but what about old Dad here? He's in the plane too…' I'm hoping he's kidding. But clearly he isn't. He's sobbing now and losing all interest in the controls. Finally I convinced him he had plenty to live for, friends he could count on, one of whom was sitting there right beside him. He appreciated my logic and pulled the nose of the aircraft up. I've never been so quick to get off a plane in my life.

Naturally everybody laughed when I told them of my experience with this unpredictable flying Dutchman. But they were the sort of guys who would think it funny; Flynn for sure, and Oscar Levant, who was as sharp with his wit as he was brilliant with his piano playing. George Murphy, who was a great Irish-American, a polished actor and dancer, was also in the group. He eventually gave up movies to become senator for California. And then there was Busby Berkeley, whose spectacular dance settings and unique choreography were part of the genius that created Hollywood.

These were the types who'd come to our Sunday brunches. First, we'd all go to Mass at the beautiful Church of the Good Shepherd in Beverly Hills. This was a social as well as a religious occasion, and you didn't have to be strictly Catholic to attend. In fact, some of our group were strictly Jewish, but they would reverently light a candle with the rest of us. There would also be a handful of hungover penitents staggering in for the eleven o'clock service, which eventually became known as the Alka Seltzer Mass. Aside from this, the Sunday Mass in that lovely church in Beverly Hills was a serious moment away from the hard bargaining and the hustling of movie-making. Almost every Sunday a sober young attorney named Greg Bautzer would be in a pew there with a partner, Bentley Ryan. It will be some time before Greg becomes Howard Hughes's personal friend and attorney, and one of the most articulate but volatile personalities in town.

We were all of us fledgelings then; in career terms, barely flexing our muscles. In fact, I had nothing to flex, being still out of work. We were very, very broke. I mean, seriously short of eating money. We had rented a bungalow out in Tarzana, which in Hollywood terms was strictly on the wrong side of the tracks. There were three of us: Pat, me and the third member of the family, a Dobermann pinscher which was Pat's pride and joy. He was a beautiful animal named Hans, and Pat insisted that, whatever the situation, the dog would eat before we did. I was very anxious about this because the bills were piling up and we were running out of excuses.

However, there was hope on the horizon. Pat announced he was going to Florida with the influential Joe Schenck on some deal to shift oranges from California to Florida, which is like taking coal to Newcastle. Pat left me in charge with a warning that Hans meant more than life to him and that I would neglect him at my peril. He didn't care too much about what I ate but wrote out in detail the menu for the dog.

But the Florida deal was slow to materialize, and the petty cash in the bungalow was fast disappearing. One day a couple of characters arrived and repossessed the car, explaining that Mr de Cicco had forgotten to keep up the payments. Twenty-four hours later the telephone was cut off for the same reason. The dog didn't care – he was eating twice a day.

Next day the gas cylinders ran out and a red notice was dropped in threatening to cut off the electricity. Every time there was a ring at the door I dived under the table and kept my hands clamped around Hans's jaws in case it was someone coming to remove the furniture.

I was finally down to my last fifty cents. All I could think of was my cousin Pat sunning himself on some millionaire's yacht in Florida and eating. The dog didn't seem to like the way I was eyeing his dinner. But I had sworn an oath that the mutt would get his full rations. With that last fifty cents I walked ten blocks in the afternoon heat to a post office and sent Pat a telegram:

'HOW DO YOU COOK A DOBERMANN?'

An hour later Pat wired a money order for $100. you could never fault the priorities of a de Cicco.

Good fun, but I was twenty-three years old and still unemployed. I hadn't come to Hollywood just to drift around. I managed to find a job with an exclusive Beverly Hills jeweller, John Gershgorn, who had many well-known clients among the stars and in the top echelons of the major studios. I opened the establishment each morning and helped clean the jewellery. I also had to deliver merchandise to selected customers. I was bonded for $15 million, which was more of an indication of the value of the consignments than of the messenger.

One day I had to deliver a tray of jewels to a man called Irving Thalberg at MGM Studios. I wasn't told, but I imagined that the expensive trinkets were almost certainly for his wife, Norma Shearer, a classic beauty who was a legend even then. What I did know was that Thalberg was as fastidious in his relationships as he was about the films he made. A courteous and highly sophisticated gentleman, he, along with Howard Hughes, the fabled John Gilbert and Howard Hawks, had been one of the most eligible bachelors in town. Peggy Hopkins Joyce, a stunning showgirl with a string of millionaire industrialists among her famous divorces; Bessie Love, a bright young star; and particularly the formidable Constance Talmadge, were once his special companions.

With that track record, I was a shade apprehensive at the thought of meeting this famous producer. He was Hollywood's *wunderkind*, a man much respected, admired and feared. He had masterminded classics like *Mutiny on the Bounty*, *The Barretts of Wimpole Street* and *Romeo and Juliet*; and had also put the Marx Brothers on the map. Unlike some of the other studio chiefs, he was a refined and polite individual, and unquestionably one of the great creative forces in our industry. (Forty or so years on I will be proud to have an office in the building that bears his name, and the Irving Thalberg Award on my mantelshelf.)

On that day, however, in MGM's lobby, I was nervous, wondering how the great man might receive me. I need not have worried.

A slim, serious-looking figure in spectacles came out to greet me.

'Mr Broccoli?'

I nodded.

'I'm Irving Thalberg. You have some things to show me.'

I produced the tray of jewellery, and he selected a sapphire bracelet and a clip, together worth perhaps $20,000.

'Can you leave them with me?' he asked.

'Sure I can leave these with you,' I said. 'I was told that would be perfectly in order.' (I wasn't going to be the one to question Irving Thalberg's bona fides.)

He smiled. 'On the other hand,' he said, 'take them with you back to John, have him clean them up and gift-wrap them for me.'

I walked out of MGM feeling a shade taller than when I'd walked in. I'd been scarcely more than a messenger, but I'd made a sale. I'd also met Irving Thalberg. I didn't know then that he had barely a couple of years left to live. He died at the appallingly early age of thirty-seven. Hollywood could ill afford to lose him. I remember the funeral. I stood on Wilshire Boulevard and had my first glimpse of how Hollywood saluted its fallen heroes. Around 10,000 people lined the route to the Temple on Wilshire to watch the 1,500 mourners file in. The operatic beauty Grace Moore sung the 'Psalm of David' and sobbed to a halt halfway through. The Reverend Edgar Magnin, the man they called 'The Rabbi to the Stars', read a message of condolence from President Roosevelt. Later, when the casket was being carried into the sanctuary at Forest Lawn, Wallace Beery, one of the 'greats', flying his own plane, dropped flowers from the sky. That was Thalberg. He was the kind of producer one rarely encounters these days: sensitive to the fragile talents crucial to the making of a successful motion picture. He was as good a role model for an aspiring producer as one could find.

Jewellery was OK, but it was never going to be a career. I wanted to get into the film business. It was Joseph Schenck, head of Twentieth Century Fox, who finally got me through the door. It was not exactly a case of making friends and influencing people, because the job I landed probably paid less than what was received by the guy who swept the floors. I did all the menial tasks which come under the heading of third or fourth assistant director. If the director wanted a cup of coffee, or needed an actor to be called onto the set, I arranged it.

The studios didn't like intrusions of people who'd been nominated by the top brass, which was odd, because most of them had got there like that anyway. But they made sure I wasn't much more than a gofer, which was all right with me because I had a foothold there and I learned fast. I began climbing the ladder pretty quickly. Everything about the business fascinated me: the cameras, the editing, the complex logistics of putting a movie together. I was fascinated by the characters who appeared in front of the cameras. And dating quite a few of them now.

Pat de Cicco had come to Hollywood for another reason beside the attraction of the sunshine and *la dolce vita*. In New York he had met, and been dazzled by, Claudette Colbert, a beautiful and cultivated lady; and when she moved to Hollywood, Pat rapidly followed after her. She was then the highest-paid actress in Hollywood, earning more than $400,000 a year. A delight to be with, she mixed with an élite group of stars who had learned their craft on Broadway and weren't slow in letting Hollywood know it. William Gargan was one of these. His name may ring no bells today, but he was one of the most prolific performers of the 1930s and early 1940s. He played 'good guy' roles in dozens of very profitable movies.

Gargan had been brought from New York after scoring a major success in a play called *The Animal Kingdom*. MGM were looking for actors to play opposite Joan Crawford, who was starring as Sadie Thompson in *Rain*. She was then the queen of Hollywood, and her leading men were expected to show proper deference to her. Unfortunately, my friend was not easily impressed. At a welcoming dinner party given by the director Lewis Milestone on Catalina Island, Gargan was seated next to Joan. Giving him full eye contact, she began listing some of her greatest screen performances and wondering which of these he most admired. He cut her short.

'Miss Crawford,' he said, 'I have never seen you on the screen in my life!'

Crawford went into shock. Milestone wished he was back shooting *All Quiet on the Western Front*. News of my friend's gaff was soon favourite 'happy hour' conversation. Bill Gargan had charm, wit and style. Everybody wanted him over to dinner. Late on in his career, he had a critical throat operation which left him without a voice. Bad enough for anyone, but a disaster for an actor. He and his wife Mary were close friends of the Leslie Howards. We used to visit them in their enormous house with its traditional English décor. Leslie used to greet us at the door in that impeccable manner which hostesses found so devastating. They liked this touch of the slightly rakish intellectual. Actually, from my personal knowledge, he was a lustful old ram who used to chase chambermaids all over the house, in the best traditions of the English country squire. These peccadilloes weren't unusual in Hollywood, which seemed to hold a monopoly of beautiful, unattached girls. And all was forgiven if you had talent, or more importantly, sold tickets.

It's a long time since I was an energetic bachelor in his late twenties, escorting such beauties as Joan Marsh and Rochelle Hudson. We would go to various nightclubs and restaurants, the big event being Sunday night at the Trocadero. This was owned by Billy Wilkerson, then publisher of the *Hollywood Reporter*, the best-read trade paper on the coast. Everybody came to these shows, which were intended as shop-windows for supposedly amateur performers. So many young artists got their big break there: Judy Garland, Red Skelton, Deanna Durbin, Bob Hope; the 'Troc' launched many of the big names of today. All the studio chieftains would be there, hoping to filch a potential superstar from under the nose of a rival. Louis B. Mayer would sit at one table, Joe Schenck at another. If the buzz had got around that a really exciting 'find' was coming on, then every leading producer would show up. The place would be packed and you'd be lucky to get in.

On lesser nights, when some of the acts would be truly terrible, Billy Wilkerson would bring his famous 'hook' into play. This was the old burlesque hook with which acts dying the death would be yanked offstage in the middle of a gag, a song or even a balancing act. Billy kept one at the Trocadero. I remember this guy who used to play the mandolin. He was once the number-one mandolin player in New York – and he couldn't forget it. Once he'd got started at the Trocadero, they couldn't get him off, and the audience became restless. Billy Wilkerson shouted over to Tommy Seward, his brother-in-law, who worked for him: 'Get the hook and pull that sonofabitch off the stage!'

I owe a great deal to Joe Schenck. The break he gave me at Fox may have been low down on the totem pole, but it got me started. Many other people had reason to be grateful to him, too. He was a fine man and a good friend to Pat and me. We used to go over to his house at weekends for a barbecue, or he would come over to us. Danny Kaye became known as the best man in town for preparing Chinese food. I became the pasta genius, with no rival apparently, in the spaghetti and meatball category. Joe was very partial to this dish, so it was only a question of deciding whether it was his place or Pat's.

Everybody looked up to Joe. He was one of the most honest and respected men in the industry. I recall that whenever there was a major crisis it was Joe everybody looked to, to come in and pull the fat out of the fire. It was because of this willingness to take the flak that he became caught up in a movie-industry scandal. The case involved the notorious union boss Willie Bioff and the payment of so-called protection money. Almost all the studio heads were enmeshed in the affair. But the authorities decided they would settle for one head to roll. That martyrdom fell to Joe Schenck: the sacrificial lamb.

The episode has to be seen in the context of Hollywood around 1940–41. At that time there were more cinemas in America than there were banks. Fifty million people went to the movies every week. The money was pouring in, and so were the hoodlums, greedy for what they could hustle or steal. Bioff, a fat-jowled Chicagoan, ran the stagehands' union. And he wasn't too particular how he did it. He had worked as a newsboy in Chicago, then in an ice-house. He had been employed by mobsters to run special errands for them. He gravitated to Hollywood, where he

operated the union with the double barrel of blackmail and
extortion. He would simply demand a fat cash pay-off from the
studio bosses. If he didn't get it, he'd pull the plug and close them
down. When he saw how easy it was, he demanded a two-million-
dollar 'sweetener' from the entire movie industry. He told Joe's
brother, Nicholas Schenck, President of Loew's, Inc.: 'If you don't
get the others together and come up with the money, I will close
every theatre in the country.'

It was a question of either submit or see the industry on its
knees. The studio heads met and decided they had to concede the
game to Bioff. Each came in turn with a bundle of money. Joe
Schenck identified himself as the donor and went to prison. After
a few months he was given a Presidential pardon. Yet Joe, through
all the years I knew him, was never bitter. He survived and carried
on enjoying a life in which, as we'll see, Marilyn Monroe played
a sweet supporting role. (Bioff, on the other hand, didn't have it
so good. He went to prison, came out and changed his name. He
hung around the fringes of Las Vegas for a while. Then, one
November day in 1955, he got into his Ford pickup and switched
on the engine. The explosion threw him twenty-five feet from the
wreckage. His widow said he didn't have an enemy in the world.)

Joe Schenck was a leading force in Hollywood. Great achievers
like him rarely get through their lives unscathed. More often than
not, their true worth goes unrecognized, the media getting a lot
more mileage out of gossip. As Joe's friend, I knew the extent to
which he'd been misjudged by the newspapers. He had sacrificed
– temporarily at least – his freedom and his reputation to save the
necks of many other people.

I had an even closer friend, Howard Hughes, whose
contribution to world aviation – and incidentally to the United
States – received far less recognition than it deserved. Instead, his
ever-publicized eccentricities, and the wretched manner of his
dying, dominated the obituaries, overlooking what really
mattered: his courage, his patriotism and his vision.

[Howard Robard Hughes was born in Houston, Texas, on
Christmas Eve 1905. He was fortunate. He was born into wealth
derived from a drilling bit invented by his father, 'Big' Howard.
The bit's incredible 166 cutting edges could gouge through rock
more efficiently than any other oil-drilling tool. Oil companies

were permitted only to lease the Hughes bit, which was patented throughout the world, paying $30,000 a time. When oil chiefs complained that this gave Big Howard a monopoly in the oil-drilling business, he disagreed. They could always use a pick and shovel.

Money from the patent bankrolled a lifestyle unequalled even in the richest echelons of Houston society. Big Howard liked beautiful women, and had married a lively, strikingly attractive creature, the granddaughter of a Confederate general. Extravagant, extrovert as they were, it was almost inevitable that their son would be the complete reverse. The boy spent most of his time alone, his almost painful shyness made worse by a stammer and slight deafness. His joy was to be left in his father's workshop, where he could tinker around with the collection of tools on the bench. At thirteen he built his own radio set. He'd inherited that skill, the inventive touch, from Big Howard. He also inherited a more intriguing preoccupation of his father's: an intense interest in beautiful, famous women – Hollywood stars for preference. (In this area, Howard junior was destined to have the edge on his father.)

At eighteen, with both his parents dead, Howard Hughes was a multimillionaire, owning seventy-five per cent of the Hughes Tool Company. Without his father looking over his shoulder, the gaunt, six-foot four-inch Howard Hughes could launch into the three passions of his life: flying, motion pictures and women. His first film, *Swell Hogan*, was a disaster. It was never released. His relatives came to Hollywood hoping that the flop would have 'got movies out of his system'. They misread Big Howard's son. He dispatched them back to Houston and sailed into several small-budget productions, all of which made money. A mere detail to Howard Hughes.

What mattered was that he was learning the movie business in a style that stupefied his associates. He pitched into every aspect of it with a ferocity and single-mindedness that later would be focused on his famous flying exploits. He set out to make *Hell's Angels*, which still stands as a classic, both for its spectacular aerial-combat sequences and its landmark achievements at the world's box offices. When *Hell's Angels* was almost complete, Al Jolson's voice was heard in *The Jazz Singer*, making silent films as obsolete as yesterday's news. Talkies were in. *Hell's Angels* seemed ready to be scrapped. Instead of dumping the picture, he added a soundtrack to it which cost an additional $2 million. The original female star, a Norwegian actress, was replaced, because in her role as an English socialite her accent on the soundtrack would get her, and the picture, laughed off the screen. In that case, his associates pleaded, at least replace her with a known actress. Hughes, as politely as ever, disregarded their advice. He was not to be criticized for it, either, since the unknown he chose was named Jean Harlow. The film made her and history.

Success being contagious, Hughes continued in the early thirties with two further classics, *The Front Page* and *Scarface*. In between movies this tall, dashing pilot in a leather jacket and tilted fedora enjoyed those other ecstasies, females and flying. In the air he was as daring as any of the stunt flyers he used for *Hell's Angels*. On the ground, in the company of women, however, he was awkward, diffident, as hesitant in starting relationships as he was in terminating them. This perturbed him, since even as an escort-turned-lover, Howard Hughes had to be the best, if not a record-breaker. His occasional stammer and imperfect hearing added further inhibitions. So there were many evenings when he would be alone: needing company, but not seeking it. As on the night at the Colony Club in Hollywood. Seated further along the bar, also on his own, is Cubby Broccoli, idly spinning that silver dollar. Even then, in his early thirties, Hughes made friends warily. But there was something easy and disarming about this pleasant-faced character at the bar that made Hughes challenge: 'Heads or tails?' He won three dollars and a good friend for life.]

I was extremely close to Howard Hughes. I admired him not just as a friend, but for being a wholly decent man. Books have been written about him by so-called experts claiming to reveal the secrets of this admittedly complex and reclusive individual. Well, I've read most of this stuff and the image that emerges doesn't match the man I knew and liked immensely. There was, it's true, an abrupt and disturbing change in his personality after a devastating flying accident in 1946. We will come to that incident and its aftermath. Yet even years later, when he'd virtually cut himself off from the world, he kept in touch by a kind of remote control. He knew what I was doing, wherever I was living in the world, and was uncannily aware of any problems I or my family might be facing.

There was Hughes the studio boss; Hughes the aviation innovator; Hughes the powerful company magnate; and Hughes the polite but persistent wooer of beautiful women. Any character achieving success in all those fields had to be a versatile and fascinating man. He was reserved and spoke very little, yet dominated every situation. Socially, he was always at the controls. Yes, he had his eccentricities. I should know, since many of these involved my very urgent and personal attention. Sometimes the demands he made on his friends tested your patience to the limits. But he did it with such charm, you bit the bullet because of the man he was. In any event, if you were Hughes's friend, you accepted his often bizarre behaviour as a small price to pay for knowing one of the most intriguing and important men of the century.

Nothing Howard Hughes did was ever on the small scale. When he became interested in something, or someone, his approach was like a field commander planning his campaign strategy. No goddess wooed by Hughes, to be courteously discarded later, could ever complain that he hadn't taken care of every essential detail of their brief relationship. Perfectionism as a lover was as crucial to him as it was in his flying, or the running of his business. One day, early in our association, he disappeared abruptly from the Hollywood scene. I checked with others in the Hughes 'circle' – Walter Kane (a devoted employee and friend), Cary Grant, Greg Bautzer, Bill Hearst (the son of William Randolph Hearst), Charlie Farrell and Pat de Cicco – to see if they knew where he had gone. He hadn't informed them, either. When he wanted to cover his tracks, no private eye or investigating agency could ever get near him. The loyalty of his friends helped to plug every loophole.

Where was Howard Hughes? He was at Caltech, studying one aspect of aeronautical engineering he had not yet mastered. It was a crash course, with the tutor concerned sworn to secrecy. He'd done the same sort of thing a couple of years before. He went missing for two months, and his studio colleagues went frantic. Passionate about flying, he had changed his name to Charles Howard and landed a job as a co-pilot with American Airlines. If he was going to own an airline (TWA), he wanted to get an insider's view, from the cockpit.

Most of us enjoyed playing golf in a laid-back, non-competitive way. This didn't suit my highly motivated friend. Anybody could play ordinary golf. Howard Hughes had to be the best. He studied the manuals, watched the champions on film, had private sessions with a golfing friend, Bill Guest. He worked and worked at his swing, meticulously measuring the length of club in relation to the angle of approach – and became a scratch golfer. Once he could beat the hell out of us, he lost interest and quit the game.

He wasn't concerned with winning trophies, though one day he would halve Lindbergh's flying time, setting up a new trans-atlantic record. That, like his other feats, demanded tremendous determination. And a lot of guts. He was afraid of nothing, and about as easy to intimidate as a cobra. His one, almost pathological, obsession was his need for privacy. It forced him and his friends into a cloak-and-dagger relationship involving clandestine meetings, mostly at night, and sudden flights to secret destinations. If you didn't know the man, you'd say this behaviour was eccentric, if not paranoid. Then you'd remember his frustration over his increasing deafness and realize that he could hear better in the quiet of the night.

He also happened to believe in what he called 'natural sleep'. You stayed awake until you felt tired. Then you went to sleep for as long as it took: an hour, or a day and a half. And you didn't necessarily have to sleep in your own bed. Hughes could sleep just as easily on the floor of his office. Or in the back of an old Chevrolet. At three o'clock in the morning he would be wide awake. He would often call me around that time, always with the polite preamble: 'Hi, Cubby, I hope I'm not disturbing you.' (I don't know what else he was doing, at that time of the morning.) Nobody had their sleep shattered more frequently than the friends of Howard Hughes. Yet it is the measure of the man, I suppose, that none of these sleepwalkers ever seriously complained.

Although Hughes demanded your time, he could be caring, in a very generous and spontaneous way. For instance, if you phoned and he detected you had a cold, before you knew it his personal physician, Verne R. Mason, would be knocking on your door to see if you were all right or needed anything. There were many occasions when he put his private planes and the resources of his massive organization at your disposal, to help cope with a sudden crisis. This ability to recognize a problem, then press a button or invent a scheme to solve it, was basic to Howard Hughes.

The stories about his romances with the famous sex symbols of the day have been told, recycled in acres of print from the scandal sheets to the *New York Times*. Since his death, all these ladies have been coming out of their boudoirs with kiss-and-tell revelations of how he allegedly pursued them, how they had to fight off his almost embarrassing attentions. I find this very amusing indeed, as from my own personal knowledge, many of these shrinking violets made all the play. They were about as resistant as a revolving door.

The fact is, no matter how important an actress you were, an affair with Howard Hughes, or even just a dinner date, gave you status. You might not have wished it known that, say, Harry Cohn had grabbed you in his inner office, or that Darryl Zanuck had inveigled you into a weekend at the George V in Paris. But if it were known that Howard Hughes had flown you in his private plane to Vegas, or to some secret assignation elsewhere, you had your head above the rest. The reason for it was partly the aphrodisiac of power, partly because of his attentive, well-mannered style. But mainly because, for many years in Hollywood, he was the man to know. He was the most talked-about personality in the papers. He was a daring aviator, an industrial buccaneer and (after divorcing Ella Rice in 1929) a millionaire bachelor. He was not all that articulate with women. He had this boyish hesitancy reminiscent of James Stewart in his early romantic roles. They all found him 'charming' – Katharine Hepburn, Madeleine Carroll, Hedy Lamarr, Jane Greer, Jane Russell, Janet Leigh, Ruth Warwick, Lana Turner, and Gene Tierney – though Ava Gardner is said to have slugged him with a brass bell in one of her more impetuous outbursts.

(The reason for my late friend Ava's boisterousness revealed another aspect of the Hughes persona: a reluctance to be upstaged by a possible rival. Ava, being a very independent lady, naturally resented Howard's highly efficient network which kept tabs on her movements. Hearing that she had been seen dancing at the Mocambo club well into the early hours, he ordered her over to his house for a reprimand. Ava apparently swore at him. According to her, he slapped her. The nearest object within reach was a brass bell. As I heard it later, she knocked him cold.)

It was easy to see why these actresses found Hughes irresistible. He had a habit – or strategy – of inviting the girl's mother along on some of the dinner dates. This could be very disarming, and also very pleasing to these Moms, who picked up a little oblique rejuvenation in the process. Finding no instant rapport with Lana Turner, Howard spent the rest of the evening in earnest conversation with her mother. Another time he flew Gene Tierney and her mother in his private plane to a lunch in Tijuana. He didn't just reserve a table: he booked the entire restaurant and had a Mexican band serenade them over their chilli. His generosity to some of these creatures was legendary. He bought some of them houses, setting them up for life. Now and again there would be a lady who figured that the largesse fell short of what she was entitled to. A European actress to whom Hughes had given a lovely home considered he ought to buy one for her mother, too. She complained to me about it. I told her: 'But my dear, you already have a home that Howard bought you.'

'Yes, I know,' she pouted, 'but that was for me. It was not for my mother. When Mr Hughes comes to me in the middle of the night I do not want my mother in the house. She should have her own house.'

Hughes found it difficult to handle situations like these. Those aspects of a relationship – the details – made him uncomfortable. He always seemed baffled by the reluctance of these women to accept that the relationship was over. The flowers concluded the affairs for him – but not for them. When we were alone on our various flying trips, he would express his bewilderment about women. But around this time I was beginning to have a little bewilderment of my own.

SIX

I can't recall where Gloria Blondell and I met. She was the sister of Joan, the zesty blonde who made some of the great comedies and musicals of the thirties. We liked each other from the start. She strongly resembled her famous sister, although her hair was more sandy-coloured than blonde. She was a fun lady and we hit it off well together. I brought my mother down to meet Gloria, and my brother John came over from Florida. They both took a shine to her, and were delighted when I told them that we were planning to marry.

My cousin, Pat de Cicco, didn't share in the family euphoria. He figured that as bachelors we had a great thing going for us. Why spoil it? In fact, minutes before the ceremony – at a pleasant little chapel in Las Vegas – he took me to one side. 'Now look, Cubby, you see that door over there? That's the way out. If you have any doubts at all, want to change your mind and want to retreat through that door, don't worry. I'll cover for you. I'll handle everything. You can grab a plane and leave everything to me.'

What amused me about this offer was that it was almost a replay of that great wedding scene in *It Happened One Night* where the bride's father offers the same escape route to his daughter, a runaway heiress played by Claudette Colbert. Pat had good reason to recall it since he and Claudette were at one time pretty much taken with each other. But he was quite disappointed when I declined his generous offer.

Being married made me take a closer look at my career prospects at Fox. I was improving my status there, but I was keen to get closer to production. Howard Hughes was now making *The Outlaw*, originally titled *Billy the Kid*. It was an important production for several reasons, the main one being the launching of Jane Russell. Howard Hawks was hired to direct it. He had impressed Hughes with a couple of his earlier pictures, *Scarface* (which Hughes produced) and *The Dawn Patrol*. Both were typical of Hawks's style as a director: no frills, no nonsense, letting the action tell the story in a direct and uncluttered manner. The aerial footage on *The Dawn Patrol* was brilliantly handled, understandably, since Hawks was, like Hughes, passionately interested in flying. I could have asked Hughes for a job on the picture, but didn't. There was a tacit understanding between us that our friendship must not spill over into professional considerations, and anyway I wasn't going to put Hughes in that position.

But I had met Hawks before, and we had an easygoing relationship, friendly enough for me to approach him about getting a job on the picture. He needed an assistant, and he hired me. When Hughes found out, I think he was glad I'd observed the rules of the game. *The Outlaw* was interesting in the way it revealed Hughes's infuriating (to a director) obsession over detail. I watched the two men together, and it was never going to be a tranquil partnership. Hawks was a tough, forthright film-maker with a low tolerance threshold when it came to producers running interference on a movie. He was an expert game fisherman and hunter who enjoyed wandering around in wild country with a gun in his hand. He could drive supercharged racing cars around the circuits and was still riding a motorbike when he was well past seventy. As you would guess, he was not the type who would easily roll over in the face of one of Howard Hughes's idiosyncrasies. And my late friend Howard had plenty of these. When I came on the scene they had already hired the male lead, Jack Buetel, to play Billy the Kid, and two other actors, Walter Huston and Thomas Mitchell.

The search was now on for the heroine. Hughes already had under contract a sexy fifteen-year-old named Faith Domergue. But he was looking for something with more meat on the bone for *The Outlaw*. It was the general consensus at the time that Hughes was a 'bosom man'. He confided that much to his friends, who mostly demonstrated the same partiality. He had obviously made up his mind that this would be the dominating feature in the candidates short-listed for the role, and sent out for photographs of possible performers. The one he and Hawks looked longest at was a statuesque creature, tall, beautiful, and with thirty-eight vital inches toward Hughes's blueprint. Her name was Jane Russell, a thirty-dollar-a-week receptionist to a foot doctor. Hawks showed me the photo and asked me what I thought.

'I think she's terrific,' I said.

'Howard thinks the same.'

Howard must have been thinking a lot of other things, too. I was due to go with the unit up to the location in Arizona. The night before, he telephoned.

'I understand you're going up to Flagstaff with the crew,' he said, but mentioned nothing about the fact that Hawks had hired me. 'I'd like you to do me a favour. It's a long ride up there in the train. Jane Russell will be on it. Have you met her?'

'Yes, of course.'

'Well, I'd appreciate it if you'd see to it that she gets everything she needs on the journey.'

'Sure, Howard.'

'Oh...and Cubby...'

'Yes?'

'Keep all the characters away from her!'

This inevitably begs the question which Jane Russell answers in her autobiography. She claims she never slept with Howard Hughes. I believe her. Not all of his 'protégées' were totally obliging. Charming and generous though he was, even Howard Hughes had his rejections. Ingrid Bergman was one, despite Hughes telling her that he'd bought RKO Studios just for her. (Elizabeth Taylor would one day join that rare handful, to the considerable frustration of my persistent friend.) There were two reasons, I suppose, why Hughes asked me to keep an eye on Jane Russell on the Flagstaff location. One, I was married. Two, he trusted me. He could have hired bodyguards, but that would have fuelled rumours about him and Jane. Anyway, it was no hardship keeping an eye on Jane Russell, who was very attractive indeed.

Hawks pitched into the movie with his usual energies, but began to have doubts when Hughes started taking a hand in day-to-day production. When Hughes saw the first rushes in his Romaine Street office, he complained to an associate that there were no clouds in the scenic shots. He phoned Hawks and conceded that the director was doing a great job, but asked for some clouds in the next scene. Hawks, who had a commitment to direct *Sergeant York* with Gary Cooper, saw a way out. He told Howard: 'You evidently don't like what I'm doing. Why don't you take over the picture?'

The same situation had occurred on *Hell's Angels*. Hughes never needed a second invitation to take over at the controls. He brought us all back from Flagstaff, and rescheduled the whole production at the studio. There was a lot of writing going on and also a lot of no-writing. Sometimes he would shoot more than twenty-five takes of one scene. But his big preoccupation – it became a famous obsession – was how to get the maximum impact of Jane Russell's breasts. The scene called for Jane's wrists to be tied by leather thongs between two trees. As she writhed sensuously in her attempt to break free, he studied her cleavage through the viewfinder and frowned with dissatisfaction. He wasn't hitting the jackpot. The bra, he decided, gave the Russell bosom an artificial look. Here was a flying ace and aeronautical genius engrossed with the business of getting a pair of boobs to bounce out of the screen. I laughed at it, but Hughes was serious.

'It really is just a simple engineering problem,' he said. So he designed his own cantilevered bra, which he believed would have the desired effect. It was bizarre, to say the least. Back at Hughes Aircraft, Air Force chiefs were waiting to see Howard's latest design, a highly secret revolutionary medium-range bomber capable of flying at the then record speed of 450mph. 'Where's Mr Hughes?' they enquired.

I could have told them. Mr Hughes was busy over a drawing-board demonstrating to me just how Miss Russell's bosom could achieve immortality by the simple application of cantilever dynamics. In the event, he was to have far more success with the boobs than with the bomber.

Jane, who was smart, obediently accepted the redesigned brassière. But she didn't wear it for the vital scene. 'When I tried it on,' she would say later, 'it was uncomfortable, ridiculous. Obviously, what he wanted was today's seamless bra, which didn't exist then. I just put on my own bra, covered the seams with tissues, pulled the straps over to the side, then put on my own blouse.'

Hughes was satisfied and the scene was shot. Maybe he was entitled to include the seamless bra among his many innovations. This perfectionism, eccentricity – call it what you will – was tolerated by most of us because there was never any unpleasantness involved. For all the demands he made, Hughes was always courteous, apologetic even. Though he was often angry, I never saw him lose his temper. Like all men exerting his kind of power, he hated to be rebuffed, professionally or personally.

He did some crazy things at times, but if you judge a man by his motives, then Hughes comes out pretty well. I don't believe anything he did was motivated by personal ambition. He rarely discussed politics with me, but it was obvious he was a strong Republican with a strong desire to see the United States at the top of the league. He had his enemies. His interests covered vast territories from oil drilling to space-age exploration. He trusted fewer and fewer people. Whenever he made arrangements for us to meet, it was always cloak-and-dagger stuff, straight out of a spy movie. If I was going to meet him at some studio, he worked out to the last yard the distance I'd have to travel so that he could calculate how long it would take me to get there. On arrival at the studio gates I'd maybe blink my headlights and the gateman would wave me through. Then there'd be another car ahead of me which I would have to follow in the darkness, until finally I'd find Hughes in some small, nondescript office.

Though he owned RKO at one time, he never once visited the place. He preferred to operate out of his headquarters at 7000 Romaine Street, Hollywood, or from a small office at Goldwyn Studios. (It was there, incidentally, where Hughes learned how to cut and edit a film. He had to know all about that, too.) An average rendezvous with Howard Hughes would begin with a phone call, often in the middle of the night.

'Did I disturb you?'

'It's three a.m.!'

'Well, could I come over?'

'Sure, come over when you like. Why, what's the matter?'

'Nothing, it's just that I don't want to make any phone calls from where I am.'

So he would drive over, make his phone calls and leave. On another occasion he phoned to ask if I could spare the time to fly to San Francisco. I was free at the time, so I agreed.

'Listen, a suite has been booked for you at the Fairmont. When you get there, someone will call you. [He'd give me the name.] This person will talk to you about...[he outlined the confidential project]. When that has been completed, stay in your suite. I will fly up to meet you there.'

I followed the plan. I got the call from the stranger. I then waited in my suite, but nothing further happened. Hughes didn't show up. I couldn't get him on the phone. His underlings had no idea where he was. He'd just flown off in secrecy, telling no one. I flew back to Los Angeles. A couple of days later he was on the phone, full of apologies. The more angry I became, the more contrite he was. An explanation followed which made sense, and I forgot and forgave – the standard response of the friends of Howard Hughes. Why? Because with it all he was great company. Every episode was an experience. Part of the excitement was never knowing what was going to happen, or where.

A rendezvous point would always be established with Howard's customary precision. He would meet me in a rented car. He had a fleet of Cadillacs at his disposal, but preferred the anonymity of an old Chevrolet from a rental company; this way he could be sure that no insider could have bugged the car. It wasn't paranoia. There was enough evidence before, and a lot more since, to justify his suspicions. I got into his car one night and we drove up to the gates of the vast Hughes Aircraft Company. The moment the guard recognized him, he snapped to attention. Hughes didn't care for that sort of thing, but the guards always jumped when they spotted him. We drove out to the airstrip, where, isolated in the darkness, was one of his personal planes, a converted bomber. He reached over to the back seat and picked up what looked like an old shoe box.

'What have you got there?' I asked.

He looked inside. 'Peanut butter and jelly sandwiches and a couple of cartons of milk. Want some?'

'Sure, I'm starved.'

Hughes wore an open-necked shirt over his pants, and the famous brown hat on his head. Ordinary shoes, not the tennis trainers everybody said he wore. When he did wear them, they accused him of being an oddball. Now every half-baked producer or director wears them and nobody calls them eccentric. The plane took off with Hughes piloting it with one hand, a peanut-butter sandwich in the other. I would have preferred him to have both hands on the controls, particularly on take-off, but no one, not even a friend, told Howard Hughes how to fly a plane. As we lifted up from the strip, the full measure of the Hughes empire was spread out below, a brilliantly lit complex still humming with activity far into the night. Massive undertakings in aircraft development, satellite systems and defence contracts. And here was the man at the pinnacle of it all with a sandwich between his teeth and other thoughts on his mind.

'It would be nice to know where we're going,' I said. 'I've got to be at the studio tomorrow morning.'

'Yeah, sure, OK.'

This was typical Hughes double-talk. I'd find out soon enough.

We landed at Las Vegas. Another inconspicuous car took us to the Flamingo Hotel, where two or three suites were permanently reserved for Hughes. He washed up and went down to a long table right alongside the stage. Mr Hughes was expected. You could feel the excitement and the tension when this tall figure with the moustache and well-brushed hair weaved his way to the table.

From then on, Hughes concentrated on the two attractions that had lured him to Las Vegas: girls and gambling. To be strictly accurate, Howard was no big expert in either field. For all his track record with Hollywood goddesses, he was often uncomfortable at first meetings. He could be as awkward as a turf-kicking cowboy. Part of this had to be due to his increasing deafness. Also, having been raised by a domineering father and a socialite mother, he was alone much of the time and hadn't learned how to feel easy with strangers. He was a near-genius at almost everything he undertook, but he struck out on his social relationships. He and I got along, I suppose, because I understood and respected his craving for privacy. Also, we agreed on most things, and I liked him.

I don't think he had much happiness out of life, except the fun he could command at Las Vegas. It was a great place to visit in the 1940s. You didn't go there merely to gamble. It was a really lush playground attracting gorgeous women, colourful high-rollers and the greatest entertainers in the business. Hughes loved to be there. Going there at any time was an event; going there with Howard Hughes was an experience: everything arranged on impulse, journeys to a secret rendezvous in unidentified cars, late-night flights with Hughes at the controls, every detail taken care of by discreet subordinates.

The chance to see Hughes arrive in this kind of style brought hordes of excited revellers crowding around him at the casinos. They expected to see this multimillionaire toss fortunes onto the crap tables. He quickly disillusioned them. In fact, when the two of us gambled together it was a joke. I remember one evening – at that time I was earning around $200, at the most $250, at the studio. We decided to shoot craps. I went in with ten or fifteen dollars on the line. Hughes, standing alongside me, took out a roll of hundred-dollar bills, peeled one off and threw it on the table.

'Let me have some chips.'

The guy counted out twenty five-dollar chips.

'Oh, I don't want them all in chips. Just give me fifty dollars' worth, the rest in cash.'

'We can't do that, sir. We don't have cash to use.'

I felt embarrassed. Onlookers were pressing round us to see The Man going in with some heavy action. Instead, my wealthy friend was behaving as though his eating money was on the line. I was in for fifteen dollars – big stuff. Howard put down a five-dollar chip. There was a lot of murmuring going on, so I said quietly, 'Howard, why do you only put down five dollars?'

'Out of line. You make your bets, I'll make mine.'

Of course, at the end I lost all my chips and Hughes came away with a bundle of winnings from his five-dollar bets. The outcome he looked for in any challenge: he'd beaten *them*.

Vegas was his kind of excitement. He began to relax the moment we took off from Los Angeles. Seated beside him in the plane, I could sense the tension easing in him as he swung the aircraft north-eastward over the High Sierra. You would see nothing but blackness below, and then suddenly this oasis of twinkling lights framing the glittering ribbon of Vegas's 'Miracle Mile'.

'There she is, Cubby,' Hughes would say with a grin. 'Let's go down and have some fun.'

And it was all fun in those days. Firstly, because Hughes felt free to move around – though a tragic event would soon change that – and secondly, it was the time before the Mob arrived on the scene.

Any business handling the vast amounts of hard cash from Vegas's slot machines and casino tables was bound to entice the wrong kind of characters. It was easy money, it was legitimate, and infiltrating the 'action' was no problem to the Chicago professionals. They began taking over by stealth. They assumed control of the best hotels, installed plausible front men to run them. They skimmed fortunes off the nightly 'takes' and pretty soon Vegas acquired unpleasant overtones. (One day Hughes would change all that, though he would be too frail and too ill to reap the benefits.) The dubious influences calling the shots there became so diffused, you could never identify them. Frank Sinatra claimed that any entertainer appearing at the most fashionable hotels in Vegas must, at some time or other, have worked for a member of the 'syndicate'.

These characters were nothing like the stereotyped mobsters with the busted noses and ears, guys whose English included a lot of 'dem', 'dese' and 'dose'. These boss men knew how to fit in. Once they had become rich and bought their homes in Beverly Hills, they were eager to be accepted in Hollywood society. They spent a lot of money and effort on it, too. They wore English-cut suits, employed impeccable butlers, and being natural extroverts, were very popular indeed.

I played squash with one of them at the Beverly Hills Club. He was handsome, polite and immensely charming. Sometimes I would run into him at big fights or at the Mocambo in Hollywood. He lived in a mansion in Holmby Hills, and being very much the ladies' man, was always with a pretty girl, or girls. Jean Harlow let it be known that she found him irresistible. His name was Benjamin Siegel, 'Bugsy' to his intimates, on account of his protruding eyes, though few dared call him that to his face. Few need to be reminded of this character's notoriety and his pre-eminence in the crime world. But there was nothing on the surface to indicate the fact. He wore hand-blocked, snap-brimmed hats, soberly cut pinstripe suits, English custom-made shoes and well-tailored overcoats with fur collars. His shirts and shorts were elaborately monogrammed. To those who knew his record and didn't care, he had the gangster chic which brought a tremor of excitement to their parties. I had no idea who he was. To me, Benjamin Siegel was just a friendly, casual squash partner who never said or did anything out of line.

(This view, however, was not shared by everyone. On June 20, 1947, while Siegel was seated on a chintz love-seat at his lady friend's home on North Linden Drive, Beverly Hills, a sharpshooter beyond the window loosed several steel-tipped bullets into him. He was dead before he hit the floor.)

Working for Howard Hawks on *The Outlaw* taught me a lot about film-making on both sides of the camera. I now had the problem of finding a job that would take me further along that road. Hollywood at that time was running at peak production. The theatres were doing sell-out business. My prospects looked pretty good. Pearl Harbor, December 7, 1941, changed all that – as it changed everyone, everything else, in America. Suddenly, film grosses, Vegas, the celebrity game, didn't seem to be that important any more. Hollywood found its wartime role, and I no longer needed to look for a job. Anybody connected with film or entertainment generally was urgently hauled in as a massive back-up to the armed services. When I think back, the way Hollywood pitched in with its energies and its talent in World War II was magnificent. Propaganda, morale-boosters, warnings against careless talk, how to black out windows, dig shelters, identify enemy planes – Hollywood was thrown into a crash programme of official film-making. Given that kind of challenge, the motion-picture business really goes into overdrive.

My role was decided for me. I received a call from a retired naval officer, Captain Jack Bolton. He had connections in both Hollywood and Washington. He was put in charge of Entertainments for the Eleventh Naval District, and also for the Hollywood Victory Committee, which selected all the stars who would tour camps, hospitals and various service installations. Captain Bolton wanted me as part of the set-up. I was glad to get into the Navy, and joined on November 23, 1942. I've always loved boats. One of the last trips I'd made was crewing in a yacht race from Los Angeles to Honolulu and back. It was on the *Paisano*, a sixty-foot Staysil schooner owned by a scriptwriter friend of mine, Tom Reed, who was racing for the Pacific Writers Yacht Club.

We sailed out on July 4, 1936 from Santa Monica to celebrate the opening of the newly completed Santa Monica breakwater. Tom Reed was the skipper, Harold A. Corbin and Don Luckham took over as navigators, while Murray Ward, Dick Jordan, Ronnie Burla, John Swope and myself were the rest of the crew. It was a tough race won eventually by the *Dorade*, a fifty-two-foot yawl which in 1931 had won the Transatlantic Race to Plymouth,

England, beating the rest of the fleet by two days. In the same year she won the Fastnet Race in foul weather, so we knew we were up against the favourite. Anybody who could beat the field in the Atlantic was in good shape to take on the Pacific.

While we took the conventional route out past the west coast of Catalina Island, the *Dorade* did the wide sweep between Santa Cruz island and Santa Barbara island. We made a pretty unforgettable arrival. With thousands of Hawaiians watching in moonlight on the shore, we crossed the line at 12.36 a.m. Sunday morning, July 19, fifteen days from the start. We finished sixth. Not bad as it turned out. The *Dorade* made yachting history, recording triple trans-Pacific triumphs: first to finish, first overall and first in her class. The whole jaunt took thirty-two days.

But life wasn't going to be quite so jaunty for Yeoman First Class Albert Broccoli of the Eleventh Naval District. We had an office in downtown Los Angeles. Ray Stark joined up around the same time. Our outfit had representatives from the Marines, the Coast Guard and the Navy. Stark – a major force in Hollywood today – was then an agent with a considerable number of clients. Even though we were all in uniform, Ray could never quite forget that he was a Hollywood agent. It was amusing to hear him say to a client over the phone: 'Look, I think I can get you three thousand dollars a week', when we were all on service pay and Navy rations.

Most of the time we were in transit, putting various shows together. I had a free hand to order aircraft to fly our shows out to naval stations at San Francisco or way out in the Middle West. At various times I'd be shipping out Bing Crosby, Dinah Shore, Dick Powell, Bob Hope, Milton Berle, Dorothy Lamour and Danny Kaye. One day Ray Stark and I tried to work out what it would cost if he had to pay all these people. We'd be talking in scores of millions today. These stars we sent out everywhere were great; they worked round the clock, going from one station to another. We flew them to places where thousands of young servicemen were waiting to be shipped out, or to hospitals where some of them were brought back, many of them amputees. There was no let-up: requests for personal appearances by particular favourites flooded in from all over the place.

Now and again there would be a minor disaster. Nobody had the time to vet every lyric or piece of material in the script. I recall one night when I had fixed for some good singers to perform at a naval hospital in San Francisco. We had one marvellous young girl who sang a string of great numbers. She was in the middle of one of them, 'I Don't Wanna Walk Without You, Baby', when she looked down and saw men with their legs amputated. She realized, in horror, that she was singing the wrong song for that audience. She just choked on her words, burst into tears and flew off the stage. But the touching thing about it was the way in which those same guys yelled for her to come back. They hadn't related the words to themselves, and even if they had, it wouldn't have fazed them. I think the reason for this was because all these top entertainers genuinely felt a warmth and a rapport with the millions of servicemen they entertained.

The classic example of this was Bob Hope, who has probably 'played' more military establishments in more war zones over more years than any other entertainer in the world. Only Bob could breeze into a ward full of amputees and men with their plastered legs raised high and quip: 'Don't get up, fellers!' The guys in uniform appreciated Hollywood's high profile in the general war effort.

We fixed weekend parties in stars' homes where servicemen were served drinks by the pool, mingling with the big names. There was the legendary Hollywood Canteen, an idea of the late John Garfield, where, if you were in uniform, you could dance cheek to cheek with Marlene Dietrich or waltz with some other slinky goddess. I remember Hedy Lamarr trading kisses – right on the lips – for $25,000 worth of War Bonds. Lana Turner, the lady I would bring into the Charlie Feldman stable, 'kissed' $50,000 worth of bonds in one day. The list of Hollywood – and Broadway – stars whose talents were demanded, and given, in the war would fill the casting directories. Walt Disney's genius at animation was, according to the experts, worth every award that was going. Even Veronica Lake, the girl with the peek-a-boo hairstyle, did her stuff. She scissored hanks of it as part of a documentary on industrial accidents, then auctioned them for War Bonds.

I used to love watching from the wings as, say, Bing Crosby sang in front of a couple of thousand enraptured faces. Bing and Bob Hope were the two great draws for the boys in uniform. I took Crosby with me to an air station up at Santa Ana. I was an unenlisted man, so I couldn't go into the Officers' Clubs. (I had two other top-class entertainers with me at the time.) The Commodore of the station was impressed that I'd brought talent of this class, with Crosby top-lining the show. He was so appreciative, he said to me, 'Come along, let's go have a drink at the Officers' Club.'

'I'm sorry,' I told him, 'I can't go into your club. But thanks just the same.'

'You are my guest. Come in.'

So the three of us – Crosby, the Commodore and I – went in and wandered over to the bar. I didn't drink. I just stood there.

A young ensign marched over and said to me, 'Yeoman, you're out of order here. You don't belong in the Club. You'll have to leave.'

'All right, sir,' I replied, and started to leave.

Crosby had a drink in his hand. 'Hey, where're you going?' he asked.

'I've just been ordered out of the Club.'

'By whom?'

'This ensign,' I told him, nodding towards the fresh-faced youngster, all shiny and officious in his brand-new uniform. Crosby put down his drink.

'Mr Broccoli is with the show, and is a guest of the Commodore.'

'I'm sorry, Mr Crosby, sir,' gurgled this gung-ho character, 'but unenlisted men are not allowed in the Officers' Club.'

'Don't worry, Bing,' I said. 'I'll go into the NCOs' Club.'

'Fine,' Crosby said. 'I'll go with you.' We left to have a drink with the lesser ranks. The Commodore, red-faced and embarrassed, came chasing after us. He'd dealt with the ensign, he said, and would we please come back in?

Crosby laughed. 'If it's all the same to you, Commodore, this place suits us fine. These guys are talking to me, and I guess I hate to leave in the middle of a conversation.'

There was no repeat of this situation, because by the time I was discharged from the Navy, on November 20, 1945, I was an ensign myself. It had been a lively and eventful three years. A privilege in many ways. I'd met some fine and brave characters, and seen an aspect of Hollywood that outsiders tend to forget. I was now out of uniform and out of work. My personal life had struck a reef, too. It hadn't taken long for Gloria and me to realize that the marriage had been a big mistake. There was no particular catalyst in the breakdown. I liked her and she liked me, but we weren't suited for permanent life together. The divorce, when it came, was by Hollywood standards a friendly severance of the partnership. 'We remain good friends' is a worn-out cliché, but in fact Gloria and I were exactly that. There were no children by the marriage. No recriminations after it was over. She married again: a very pleasant chap in the television business. Then unfortunately he died, but she never remarried.

Howard Hughes's uncanny ability to find me, no matter where I happened to be in the world, always impressed me. He had a ferociously loyal band of unseen, unnamed characters who could locate anyone or anything instantly, all around the globe. One day he phoned me and asked what I was doing at the weekend.

'Oh, not much, Howard – just going to take it easy.'

'Maybe we could fly somewhere interesting together.'

'Thanks, but I'm tired. I just feel like a quiet couple of days.'

'OK,' he said.

David May and I had planned a boat trip together, and we wanted to stock up with provisions before we sailed. It was early, just daybreak, when we left for the seventy-minute drive down to Balboa. We drove right down to the pier, which is a long one with telephones for the boat owners. Anybody nearby hearing the ring would shout out the name of the boat for someone on it to take the call. We got all our gear loaded onto the boat. Then David said, 'Cubby, where are the watermelons?'

'Just a minute, I'll go and get them,' I said. 'I think we left them on the pier.'

I went back, picked up the watermelons and was just about to return to the boat when the phone rang. It was seven-thirty a.m. in Balboa. Howard Hughes was on the line. We had told no one where we were going, not even the staff at David's house. But Hughes knew. His long arm had reached out and grabbed me in a distant phone booth.

'Is that you, Cubby?'

'Yes.'

David laughed when I told him Howard had been on the phone. He couldn't figure out, either, how Hughes had managed to keep

tabs on us. We got to Catalina Island and were relaxing on board
the boat when out of the sky came this seaplane, doing a wide
sweep overhead.

'That's your friend Howard,' May said. 'You'd better wave to
him.' It was not going to be an easy, relaxed weekend. But the
episode demonstrated that, for all his power and battalions of
people ready to jump on his command, Hughes was a lonely man.

The more solitary he became, the more persistent people were in
trying to get close to him. As far as I was aware, he never had any
bodyguards. He relied entirely on his arm's-length lifestyle and the
discretion of his intimate friends. Everything to him was a matter
of trust. He trusted me and I recall him asking me on one occasion
to make some payments on his behalf. He asked me to take two
sums of money to a certain television station: two lots of $20,000,
as I remember it. I gave these identical sums to two political
figures, one a Republican, the other a Democrat. I don't remember
what the money was in aid of, but I do know Hughes was making
sure that neither recipient had an edge over the other.

All kinds of characters were constantly trying to move into his
orbit. One of these was Johnny Meyer, who later became a close
confidant of Howard's, and a very loyal friend. The way it
happened shows that in making friends, Hughes trusted his
instincts; the same way he piloted planes: flying by the seat of his
pants. Meyer had been a friend of Errol Flynn, but that ceased
because of objections by Flynn's then wife, Lily Damita. She didn't
like Johnny, accusing him of being a disruptive influence between
her and Flynn. Johnny pressed me several times to introduce him
to Howard Hughes. I found that difficult, because Hughes had
made it clear he didn't want to meet anybody new. Part of the
reason was his almost pathological shyness. It was also a matter of
whom he could trust. He was becoming more the mystery man
every day. Moreover, Johnny was a very forceful and aggressive
guy, and I wasn't sure how Hughes would take him.

One day Howard, Pat de Cicco and I were about to fly from
Santa Monica Airport over to Catalina Island on Howard's flying
boat. He was at the controls, Pat was seated behind him, and I still
had to get on board. Then a car pulled up, and out stepped Johnny
Meyer. He had learned that we were leaving – I don't know how.
He stopped to talk to me. Howard had started the engines and
waved for me to get into the plane. I pointed to Johnny Meyer. I

didn't know what the hell to say. He nodded his head towards the open door. I climbed in and went forward to the cockpit.

'What seems to be the problem?' asked Hughes.

'Well, this chap Johnny Meyer has been dying to meet you, and he's come by somehow...'

'Did you invite him?'

'No, I didn't invite him. He just found out in some way what we were doing.'

Hughes took a second to decide.

'All right. Look, let's not hold up any longer. I'm flying to a flight plan. Tell him to come in and sit down. We'll take him with us.'

So I called to Johnny to board the plane, and we flew to Catalina. The part of the plan I hadn't mentioned to him was that we were joining Errol Flynn there, which was bad news for Johnny, who had been put off-limits by the fiery Lily Damita. Also on Flynn's boat, the *Sirocco*, was an experienced archer named Howard Hill, who had worked with Flynn on films like *Robin Hood*. Hughes put the flying boat down on the water with his usual expertise. But once there, the engines stopped, and it was hard to control. It had a sea anchor – just a big old bunch of rope coiled up into one big knot – which we threw out, and it held the flying boat steady. We went to get out through the front of the plane to climb down forward, by means of a lazaret standing on the bow of the boat, waiting for someone to pick us up.

'Go out and see if you can hold the boat steady,' Hughes said to me.

I got out, Pat got out. Hughes was standing by the bow. It looked as though we were in very shallow water, maybe a foot or less. Pat said to me, 'Why don't you get down and see if you can hold the boat?'

'I don't fancy that, Pat.'

'For Chrissakes...I'll do it myself!'

He got out of the plane, in his English blazer and soft grey flannels, and found himself up to his neck in water. He started cussing and spluttering. Howard creased up laughing. Flynn, Lily Damita and the expert archer were doubled up also. Then out came Johnny, who saw what was happening, and he started to laugh, too.

Suddenly Lily Damita looked over and shouted, 'Who's that? Is it that goddamn Johnny Meyer?'

Johnny darted below decks, and Howard wanted to know what all the excitement was about.

'That was Lily Damita saying don't bring Johnny Meyer over to their boat,' I told him.

In fact, as I was explaining this, Lily fired another warning shot across our bow.

'Cubby, come on over here, but don't bring that goddamn Johnny Meyer with you!'

'What the hell's she got against him?' Hughes asked.

I told him I didn't know, though of course I knew well enough.

'Look, why don't you and Pat go over,' Hughes said. 'I'll stay here with Johnny.'

Pat and I went over to the *Sirocco*, while Hughes stayed aboard his flying boat out of courtesy, loyalty, to the rejected Johnny Meyer, whom he had only just met. Lily Damita was furious. Hughes was the principal guest. But Flynn understood, and so did I. When you invite a guest under your roof – even in a flying boat – the rules say you stick by him. Howard's rules, for sure. It was the beginning of the strong bond that grew up between them. One thing I know: that boat trip established Johnny Meyer's future. This was one pointer to the kind of man Hughes was.

Another was the way he reacted if anyone he knew was in trouble. I don't recall an occasion when, if tragedy hit any of his friends, he, or one of his men, wasn't on the phone enquiring how the situation could be helped. And we didn't need to inform him of the problem, either. The Hughes grapevine worked infallibly through the world.

I had little contact with Howard Hughes during the war. Pearl Harbor challenged all of his ingenuity and inventiveness. Given the chance and an A-1 rating, he'd have been a fighter pilot from day one. But his imperfect hearing ruled that out. In any event, he and the Hughes Aircraft Company had a lot more to offer over the drawing-board. On the Saturday night preceding the dawn attack on Pearl Harbor, he was in his office grappling with design problems on the new medium bomber, the D2. He worked almost through the night; as usual, adjusting his sleep patterns to suit his schedule. He heard the news about the Japanese attack just as he was about to turn in.

Howard's reaction was predictable. He went hell out on his

military projects: a pressurized airliner that could fly into the stratosphere; a revolutionary strut for aircraft landing-gear; a reshaped wing for a fighter; a new brand of artillery shell; an ammunition holder for bombers that trebled the rate of fire; and a fuselage that could withstand greater stress. So much for the screwball eccentric!

But the secret project which had kept him away from his friends at the time was a new kind of photo-reconnaissance aircraft, code-named XF-11. He had invested $6 million of his own money into it. One of the test pilots volunteered to give it the first trial. Howard wasn't having that: he had laboured hard over the prototype, and he was eager to see what it would do. Just a few seconds after take-off, the plane went wildly out of control. It crashed in Beverly Hills, scything through two houses on North Linden Drive, then bulldozing between two more on North Whittier.

It was not just luck, but a miracle for Howard that Sergeant William Lloyd Durkin was on leave and having dinner with friends a few houses along the street. He heard the death rattle of the plane's engine and correctly diagnosed impending disaster. Seconds later he heard the crash. He ran out and saw what was left of the XF-11 smouldering between the houses. As he ran towards it there was an explosion, with flames flaring out of the fuselage. It didn't stop him. By the time he reached the plane, Howard had crawled out and collapsed onto the wing, which was also ablaze.

The sergeant pulled him away, managed to smother his clothes, which were alight, then called for help. It wasn't until late evening that he discovered he'd saved the life of Howard Hughes. It was a brave thing to have done and Hughes rewarded him with a handsome income.

However, the injuries Hughes had suffered were devastating. Doctors rated his chances of survival at a thousand to one against. They scarcely expected him to last the day out. He had a fractured skull, a collapsed lung, nine broken ribs, second-degree burns on parts of his body, lacerations everywhere, and his heart had been pushed out of alignment. All this in addition to severe shock. It was a great blow to those of us who were close to him.

When the dust began to settle it dawned on the media and their millions of readers that Hughes was no playboy aviator. He had guts. He wasn't going to risk somebody else crashing in this untried prototype. Less than a week after the crash he instructed his doctor, Verne R. Mason, to deliver a message to the Air Force. It read: 'Look in the wreckage, find the rear half of the propeller, and find out what went wrong with it. I don't want this to happen to somebody else.'

Only a few of us were allowed past the armed guards outside Hughes's room at the Good Samaritan Hospital. These included Cary Grant, Lana Turner, Greg Bautzer, Jean Peters and Errol Flynn. It required quite a performance to smile at this bandaged hero who grinned weakly back at us from his bed. In the critical days when his life hung in the balance, some of the stars he romanced began to re-evaluate their opinion of him. They realized that behind all the awkwardness and shy detachment was a serious character with not an ounce of fear in him.

Hughes survived that crash, but the total effect it had on him was catastrophic. Firstly, the medics had pumped him full of morphine after dragging him from the wreckage. They did this because they were pretty sure he was going to die, and the morphine could at least remove the agony of it. After this, they gave him big doses of codeine. In addition he'd be swallowing tranquillizers – anything to relieve the constant pain. It's important to say this in answer to the lurid picture the media painted of Howard as a chronic drug addict. In all the years I knew him he was totally against drugs. Moreover, he took a pretty poor view of characters who dabbled in them. He didn't need them and I think the records show that he could take pain more stoically than most.

But whether out of panic or incompetence, they shot the stuff into him on a scale that inevitably risked addiction. Maybe they had no alternative, but the amount of painkillers he received was bound to have long-term effects. He was just too ill to resist. Before the crash, the Howard I knew had been a good-looking, boyish character, full of energy and high spirits. When I saw him a year later, some of the spark had gone out of him. I wonder to this day which was worse for my late friend: the effects of that terrible crash or his increasing dependence on the massive doses of drugs he was given afterwards.

I knew that the first thing Howard would do when he came out of hospital in August 1946 was to get back into the cockpit. There was no point my telling him that one major crash was enough in a man's life. It was his problem and his alone. But when he made his formal application to the Air Force at Wright Field for permission to test-fly the XF-11, he was turned down. He was furious. It had been a mechanical fault – a suspected oil leak had thrown the right propeller into reverse pitch – and Howard was damned if he was going to be knocked out of the box because of it. As usual, he didn't waste any time talking to intermediaries.

'I'm not going to let those bums do this to me,' he said as he flew out of Los Angeles heading for a showdown with the top brass of the USAF. From what he said afterwards I gather he laid it on the line; he'd put a lot of thought and time into that plane; he knew it right down to the last nut and bolt; it was his baby. And incidentally, it was also his life. Then he pitched in with some novel collateral: $5 million if the plane crashed with him at the controls. It was an offer they couldn't refuse. They had no cause to do so, either. He had proved himself to be one of the greatest aviators of his day. He had collected every land speed record that was going; broken the transcontinental record; and somewhere along the line found time to conceive the Constellation and hit on the time-saving idea of the Polar route across the Atlantic, taking advantage of favourable wind currents and the earth's rotation. How the hell could they turn down his request to fly the XF-11? They didn't.

But then something else happened which I could see really infuriated him. Side by side with his film interest, Howard was trying to build TWA into a major airline to rival Pan American Airways, which at the time virtually monopolized the lucrative transatlantic route. He secured similar rights, which riled a certain senator from Maine, Ralph Owen Brewster, Pan Am's influential lobbyist in Washington. Brewster wanted to introduce a bill that would in effect knock TWA out of the race. Hughes decided to take him on, arguing that in his book the skies were free. As chairman of the Special Senate Investigating Committee, Brewster announced he would hold an inquiry into Hughes's multimillion-dollar contract to build the world's largest plane, a flying boat they called 'The Spruce Goose'. We all knew what was behind the move: an attempt to discredit Howard and thereby push TWA out of the reckoning. As I remember it, there was a lot of talk about money being spent entertaining service chiefs who might be in-fluenced to edge contracts towards the Hughes Aircraft Company.

(It was here that Howard's flair for picking the right people as his associates was amusingly demonstrated. Called as a witness to explain the way entertainment expenses were incurred, Johnny Meyer demolished his inquisitors. He had the spectators laughing on every line and the senators looking decidedly uncomfortable.)

Howard, who was not due to appear in Washington until the last week of the hearing, was socializing in his usual style with Cary Grant, Pat de Cicco and me. He'd taken to wearing a moustache now to hide a scar, and looked in pretty good shape. Just to prove it, on April 5, 1947 he test-flew the XF-11 for an hour and a half. When he stepped down from the plane, all his associates and the workforce at Hughes Aircraft lined up to applaud him.

On August 6 he flew to Washington to fight his corner against Brewster – 'a little unfinished business' was how he described it to me. It was the media bonanza of the year. Fifteen hundred spectators, a crowd of photographers, film crews and reporters saw my friend arrive in a smart double-breasted suit, white shirt and tie. He was a hero before he'd even opened his mouth. I watched him on TV – we all did – and he was self-assured, confident and surprisingly outgoing for a man of his reserve. They couldn't get him on the 'money for favours' charge. In fact, Howard hit back, taunting Senator Brewster: 'Why not tell about the two airplane trips you bummed off me?' It went down pretty well with everyone, except the senator. They tried to make out he'd profited by war contracts. He proved the reverse. He showed he'd thrown in millions of his own money developing aircraft, and lost over seven million on the Spruce Goose alone.

Anyone watching could see that the inquiry was tilting in Hughes's favour. The records show that when he walked into the Senate Caucus Room with his attorneys and other associates the whole audience applauded. For the first couple of days on the stand Hughes and Brewster hammered at each other, with Hughes, much to Brewster's irritation, homing in on Pan Am. Bringing that issue into the proceedings focused on the senator's personal interest in the airline and the shift in favour of Hughes became evident. The more these interchanges went on, with Brewster wriggling on the hook, the more the audience applauded and cheered. In their eyes this was a famous, record-breaking pilot taking on a man who patently had an axe to grind.

At one point Howard was asked about the absence from the

hearing of his associate Johnny Meyer.

'Do you know where he is?'

'No. No, I don't.'

'Well, he was instructed to be here,' said Homer Ferguson, the chairman. 'And I am just advised by the counsel that he is not here and they are unable to locate him.'

There was some laughter at the back of the court and Ferguson's irritation showed.

'He works for you, does he not, Mr Hughes ?' he said sharply.

'He works for my company,' said my friend, smiling.

'It may be funny to you that he is not here.'

'I didn't laugh, Senator,' Hughes replied, still grinning. 'Somebody laughed back there.'

'You also laughed, did you not?'

'Laughing is contagious, Senator.'

It was showtime and the audience were relishing Howard's performance. A smarter chairman might have left it at that. Instead, Ferguson drilled on and on about Meyer's absence. At one point the senator challenged: 'I will ask you again.'

'What?'

'Will you bring Mr Meyer in at two o'clock session?'

'No, I don't think I will,' Howard said.

'Will you try to bring him in?' Ferguson repeated, pleading now.

'No, I don't think I will try.'

On August 11 the committee abruptly adjourned the hearing for three months. (It was rumoured that Ferguson was under heavy pressure from Republicans warning him the whole business was becoming a fiasco. Howard had gone to Washington and demolished his accusers. Outside the court he told reporters that he was pleased to have vindicated his position, noting that his opponent Brewster was 'too cowardly to stay here and face the music'.)

The hearing was scheduled to reassemble on November 5. The hiatus gave Howard the opportunity to nail one particular gibe which had infuriated him at the hearing. The senators had made great play about the Spruce Goose never actually having flown. Howard was determined to get the monster airborne if only to take the smile off their faces. A couple of weeks or so before the renewed hearing, he told me he was going down to Long Beach. Apparently he was going to put the flying boat – pretty much a mystery plane to the world at that point – through some simple taxiing trials. He was casual about it. In fact he'd secretly gone through intensive flying practice, landing and taking off on water. Not even his closest friends knew that he had secretly put the rebuilt Sikorsky S-43, which had crashed back in 1943, in a whole series of test runs on the Colorado River near Parker Dam. On November 1, at Terminal Island, Long Beach, Hughes unveiled his creation.

When the crowd of press men had their first look at the 'Goose', tall as an eight-storey building and with a wingspan longer than a football field, they were speechless. As the packed spectators watched on the shoreline, Howard piloted the plane smoothly along the surface of the water. The wind blew up and the trials ended. The crowds and reporters drifted away. The following day he repeated the trial. The speed got up to ninety miles per hour. It was too tempting for my adventurous friend. As the enormous craft sheared through the water, he gently eased it upwards, and a cheer went up from the thousands lining the harbour. Yachts and pleasure boats sailing around to watch the tests, sounded their klaxons. The plane flew for a mile before landing perfectly back on the water. It was a beautiful sight.

Afterwards Hughes, usually nonchalant, grinned like a schoolboy. He had done more than write another footnote to aviation history. He'd sent a conclusive piece of evidence to Washington. When the headlines hit there three days before the resumed hearing, his adversaries privately conceded that the flight was too big an act to follow. That one-mile test-run over Long Beach offered testimony no smart-ass attorney could match. My friend rested his case. He saw no need to return to the witness stand. The hearings closed on November 22. A report followed which failed to give any substance to the charges. The thrust of Brewster's accusations had been lost in the slipstream of the Spruce Goose's historic but one and only flight.

Long after the hearings, Hughes discovered that throughout the whole proceedings a Washington police lieutenant had tapped his phone and bugged his suite at the Carlton Hotel, apparently on Brewster's orders. That information shook Howard. It went a long way towards fuelling the obsessive secrecy that later cloaked his whereabouts and his movements. Always shy of the limelight, he was outraged by the news that he had been eavesdropped, his suite bugged. From that time on he pulled the shutters down, incommunicado except to the few friends and associates he trusted.

Christmas 1947 was approaching and I was still trying to become an agent. To put it accurately, I needed a job – by which I mean I needed the money. A friend of mine, Bert Friedlob, married at that time to the actress Eleanor Parker, had a wild scheme and was looking for partners. It involved selling Christmas trees. There was some crazy character who had cornered this market and offered franchises to various groups to sell them on street corners all over Los Angeles. This was a big operation: there were probably eighty franchises spread over the city. Friedlob saw a chance of making some real money in this field. He asked me and our mutual friend David May, of the May Company, to participate. I was staying with David then. He was reluctant to be an active partner in the deal in case he got landed with a lot of unsold trees and was sued as a result. But he put up the money, making it possible for Bert Friedlob and I to get into the Christmas tree business. There was another partner, Norman Hanak, who also got into the deal. As a matter of fact, one franchise owner was Charlie Evans, brother of Robert, who was to become head of Paramount, which shows that nobody in those days was too proud to earn a buck this way.

I wouldn't like it to be thought that selling Christmas trees on a street corner in Los Angeles was easy money. You slept in a trailer all night long, with fires lit all around to keep yourself warm. The trees were stacked outside, and you had to keep half awake to make sure nobody would walk off with one (this being the season of goodwill to all men). So you don't sleep much, you can't get a shave, and you hang in all day hoping you'll make a sale. First I had to get a business licence from the city authorities. I got Licence Number 5743, which authorized one Albert Broccoli to sell Christmas trees on the north-west corner of Wilshire Boulevard and Doheny Drive, in the City of Beverly Hills, from December 5 to December 25, 1947. It had to be paid for in advance, and set the partnership back one hundred dollars, with a further fifty as a cash bond. It was an exhausting business. Now and again I began thinking, I've got a partner, David May, who owns a chunk of real estate apart from the May Company; I have a multimillion-dollar friend, Howard Hughes; I'm the former naval ensign who took

Lana Turner out to dinner; and now I'm hustling trees on a street corner. Yet as I remember it, my particular pitch did well, though there was a problem with some other gentlemen who had run off with the money, not having paid for their trees.

All in all, I look back on this stint as a minor event – except for one incredible, memorable coincidence. Early one evening, just before Christmas, a stunning-looking lady stopped at my lot to buy a tree. She had her small son with her. She had raven-black hair, large eyes and pale, delicate features. Having chosen a tree, she wondered where she could get a stand for it. I offered to make one for her, nailing a couple of crossed boards together and pinning the tree to it. We wished each other 'Happy Christmas' and she walked away into the night. No reason for me to believe I'd ever see her again. To chic beauties of that class, when you've seen one Christmas tree salesman you've seen them all. But not in this particular scenario.

For that lady, my lovely Dana, and I were destined to meet twelve years later. She remembers my selling her that tree on the corner of Wilshire and Doheny. I recall it even more vividly. There are some customers you just cannot forget.

SEVEN

My licence to sell Christmas trees in Beverly Hills ended on December 25, 1947. I had no intention of applying for a renewal in 1948. Though I had made some money, it was never going to be the kind of enterprise that could support the lifestyle I was now enjoying in Hollywood.

Joe Schenck's Mediterranean-style house on Sunset Boulevard had become the centre for some of the best – and most influential – parties in Beverly Hills. Joe and I had become very good friends. He also liked the way I cooked spaghetti. So did a particular house guest of his at the time, Marilyn Monroe. She had moved in with the now seventy-year-old boss of Fox when she was still not much more than a starlet. You hear a lot about the bunch of smart characters who claimed they discovered Marilyn. Those who had the chance but let it slip from their fingers are a shade less boastful. Certainly Harry Cohn saw no particular star magic in her – though, according to Marilyn, that didn't inhibit him from making a play for her right there in his office. There were some other producers, too – one of them became my partner – who demonstrated the same unerring judgement, turning their back on one of the greatest legends of our business. But Joe Schenck wasn't interested in Marilyn the Star. He just loved having this sweet and giving creature as a friend. Many times I'd see his face light up when she walked into the room.

At that time Marilyn's friend Johnny Hyde, an agent, was wildly in love with her. He had serious heart trouble. He had been married twenty years, but he had this one obsession: Marilyn Monroe. Unfortunately for him, it was a one-way passion, for Marilyn insisted on staying with Schenck. The sexual attraction between my elderly friend and this voluptuous house mate had to be very one-sided. But Marilyn had her problems, too. She'd had some bad affairs, which had left her uneasy and vulnerable. Few men chased her for the benefit of her conversation. But here was Joe, kindly, considerate – and, according to the best intelligence, a sporadic and undemanding lover – offering her aid, comfort and tender, loving care. There's no doubt Marilyn enlivened the last years of Joe's life. We'd all sit together by the pool, and just to hear her laughter was a tonic to him.

The partnership of Friedlob and Broccoli (Christmas Trees, Inc.) having been dissolved, I was back to square one. I was still on the fringe of the agency business, and it was going to take time to improve the situation. Bert Friedlob and another friend, Bob Topping, who was married to Lana Turner, were looking to improve their situation, too. They had organized a deal promoting midget racing cars. They had about thirty of these machines, which were beautifully engineered, and a team of expert drivers. There was a big public for this kind of sport in those days, and football grounds and similar stadiums were hired and converted into racing circuits. I was fascinated by the sport, which had taken hold in America. I came into the deal, all of us believing that the success could be repeated in Europe. We contracted to race the cars first in London. This meant transporting the valuable cargo of cars and drivers by boat. I went with them first to New York, then over to Ireland, then finally on to London docks.

We went all out converting the soccer pitches into racing circuits, but immediately there was a hullabaloo from the football-going public, who complained we were destroying what to them was sacred territory. I could understand their concern. Anybody trying to convert Yankee Stadium into a dog-racing circuit might find the New York fans just as friendly. With the newspapers cool on the project and soccer fans staging angry protests, I got that sinking feeling that another dream was going down the tubes. But we were in so deep we just had to carry on.

Neither Friedlob nor Topping wanted to come out onto our first brand-new circuit in full view of the crowd, so I became an official starter. The result was a minor fiasco, if not exactly a major disaster. It had been necessary to resurface the former football pitch to take the heavy-duty racing tyres, but something had gone wrong in the process. There was more dirt than speed, and the cockney I overheard sneer, 'It's a load o' bleedin' rubbish!' wasn't that far out. At the end of it all the crowds drifted away and so did our money. Topping had put in the most and lost it all. He had hoped to prove to his brother, who owned the New York Yankees, that he, too, was a great entrepreneur. Instead, it had been a disaster which soured him and the whole trip. I just wanted to forget it and get back to America.

Mrs Topping, however, wanted to go to Paris. In truth, we all wanted to go to Paris as a break after the London failure. I was hoping we'd have a ball. Unfortunately, Topping liked to drink. This fuelled an additional problem: he and Lana were constantly fighting. I had been looking forward to some great French cooking, good wine and relaxation, but instead I was caught between these two close friends whose marriage was falling apart, and not too pleasantly, according to the dialogue. They split up when we got back to the States.

I was glad to get home. I guess I realized finally that I wasn't cut out to be an entrepreneur. For better or worse, I was going to battle it out in motion pictures. My experience at Fox hadn't been wasted. I knew what cameras could do; I'd sat in on production meetings; I stood alongside some of the best directors, listening, watching and learning. I observed how the real producers – not the hustlers – operated. I recognized how all the creative elements had to be orchestrated to bring ninety minutes of magic to the screen. It was all going to be a valuable apprenticeship for the time when I would put myself on the bed of nails as a producer.

I came back to Los Angeles to work for Charlie Feldman full time. I had brought Lana Turner into his agency, which was a big plus for him and a boost for me. Charles K. Feldman was one of the most important and respected agents in Hollywood. A striking figure with a California tan, he dressed with style and had the shrewd mind of a born dealmaker. Having been a lawyer, he could construct contracts which even the producers he squeezed had to admit were masterpieces. There was hardly a major production that didn't have a Feldman player either in it or short-listed for the lead.

I liked Charlie because he was a straight shooter and was afraid of no one. This was crucial to an agent who had to take on some of the very sharp practitioners operating in our business. If you worked for Charlie Feldman in those days, you had status. Watching him with some of his stars was highly instructive. If you're a good agent, or for that matter a good producer, it is not just a question of manoeuvring an actor into a role, agreeing terms, writing the contract and calling it a day. You have to nurse fragile egos which, at their worst, can cost a production a lot of money in time-wasting or unacceptable extravagances. It would not be long before I'd have to cope with some choice examples myself.

I have said that Charlie Feldman had status, which meant, of course, that all studio doors were open to him and his associates, including me. There was one embarrassing exception: MGM Studios, then dominated by the all-powerful Louis B. Mayer. On the day I arrived, I had four clients with me. One was Robert Wagner, but I can't recall the other three, though I know they were in the same big league. I was there to see Pandro Berman, who was one of Metro's most prolific and gifted producers. As we entered the lobby the receptionist said, 'Yes, can I help you?'

'My name is Broccoli, of Famous Artists. I have four clients with me and I have an appointment to see Mr Pandro Berman.'

He recognized the actors I had with me, and told them they could all go up. I started to go with them, but he stopped me.

'I'm sorry, Mr Broccoli, but that doesn't include you.'

'I beg your pardon?'

'My instructions are you are to be barred from the lot.'

'On whose orders?'

'I'm afraid I'm not at liberty to tell you.'

There were two policemen behind the reception desk to clinch the point.

Wagner and the others went up to the executive offices, leaving me completely shattered in the lobby. This was MGM in its greatest years, with stars like Gable, Garbo, Robert Taylor, Greer Garson, Spencer Tracy – the sublime talents of our business – and I had been barred when I had barely got my foot in the door. It must have shown on my face. Eddie Mannix, a key figure in the Metro hierarchy, spotted me as he walked past.

'Hey, dago, what's the matter? You look miserable.'

'I don't know what the hell is going on,' I said. 'I was just going up to Pandro Berman's office with four of my clients when I was told I'm barred from the lot.'

'Who told you this?'

'The reception desk.'

'Come with me.'

As we walked through the entrance some flunkey shouted: 'Mr Mannix, Mr Broccoli has been barred from the lot.'

I'm not sure what Eddie's response was, except that it was two words and the guy got the message. We went up to Eddie's office, and he brought out a bottle of Jack Daniels.

'OK, dago, have a drink.'

I felt better.

'OK, now tell me,' he said. 'What have you done to be barred?'

'I have no idea. I've just come along with some clients.'

'Well, what could you have done?'

'I can't imagine.'

'There must be a reason.'

'Maybe, but I don't know what it is.'

'Excuse me a moment,' he said, and disappeared into another office. He came back looking angry.

'Yes, Cubby, that's the way it is. You've been barred. Don't worry about it. I'll see what it's all about and I'll call you back at your office.'

I went back and told Charlie Feldman that I had been shut out. He said nothing. Nor did Eddie Mannix call me back. Nobody would talk about it. I discovered later that the order had come directly from Louis B. Mayer. Charlie's sin had been simple and unforgivable: he was having a secret affair with Mayer's girlfriend. And the fact that later Charlie married her altered nothing. Anybody moving in on Mayer's personal territory was automatically excommunicated. And that went for Charlie's chosen representative, too. Hell hath no greater fury than a duped mogul.

[Jean Howard, a slim beauty from Texas, was twenty-four years old when she met Mayer. She had been a dancer with the Ziegfeld Follies before being brought to Metro for a screen test. She made an impression, and the test was shown to several producers at MGM. The timing was fortunate. Mayer's wife had become increasingly ill following a hysterectomy. She went into acute depression and was finally admitted to a mental clinic. Mayer, Hollywood's most powerful tsar, looked for consolation elsewhere. It was not easily forthcoming. In his fifties, stocky, bespectacled and elderly-looking, Mayer could scarcely expect any beauty, with or without talent, to fall in love with him. But he fell in love with Jean Howard. He pursued her with the same single-mindedness with which he ran his studios. He pestered her, hoping one day to marry her. He also called in private detectives to monitor her movements and the company she kept. They gave him a full account of her clandestine meetings with Charlie Feldman. According to eyewitnesses, 'L.B.' went berserk, emptied a tumbler of Scotch down his throat, roared like a bull, then stumbled across the room, threatening to throw himself out of the window. He didn't. He had a big schedule that year. Not long after, Jean Howard and Charles Feldman were married.]

Working for Charlie Feldman was a challenge and an education. Famous Artists was a prestigious agency, and Charlie dominated it. Once he opened the store he went out for results and, though we were good friends, expected the same from me. I was given two specific areas to cover: RKO and the Motion Picture Center. The second was an independent operation run by a man who had made his money selling vegetables wholesale. He bought and refurbished the studios, leasing them out to independents. Burt Lancaster, Harold Hecht and Carl Foreman once had offices there. Another film-maker working at the Motion Picture Center then was the likeable and very audible Irving Allen. One day we would form a highly successful partnership, but on the occasion I called at the studio I was simply there to sell him an actor. Correction: I was there to hustle him into hiring an actor. A few days earlier Charlie Feldman had said to me: 'Look, you've got to do me a favour. There's a guy by the name of Len Kutnick with whom I've done some real-estate business, and he wants to get into pictures. Will you try and see what you can do?'

Since Charlie paid my salary, I regarded getting Kutnick a job as being crucial to my prospects. I met him and was glad to see he was a tall, strong, good-looking guy. What he wanted more than anything else was to get a part in a Western. Leaving aside the question of whether a chap named Kutnick who's in real estate is ideal cowboy material, there was also the question: could he ride a horse? Mr Kutnick beamed when I queried him on it. Not only could he ride a horse, but he owned two beautiful steeds, silver saddles, six-shooters and a Western outfit that wouldn't have disgraced Gucci.

This eagerness gave Kutnick points as far as I was concerned. It occurred to me that Irving Allen would appreciate his dedication and give him a job. But I had qualms when I dropped by the Motion Picture Center to see Irving. This was because an average response from Allen to any proposition was a sour grin and a suspicious glance through his bifocals. This was a kind of holding-pattern reaction whereby producers appear to be disinterested while keeping their options open. Irving, who had many good points, had an additional reason not to turn down offers out of hand. I had once suggested Marilyn Monroe to him, but he brushed her aside, saying he much preferred another Marilyn, whose second name was Maxwell. So when I asked him whether he needed any actors, he immediately said no, but added: 'Why, what have you got in mind?'

'I've got this guy who has these two beautiful palomino horses, silver saddles, the lot. Pay him what you think and you can have him.'

Irving made a rapid calculation and reasoned that with horse, saddle and gear thrown in, he had a bargain cowboy.

'OK, tell him to be here at eight o'clock tomorrow morning.'

Len Kutnick was there at seven, dressed like Roy Rogers, and leading this beautiful palomino. Irving was impressed. The face under the brand-new stetson may not have been in the Gary Cooper mould, but it was close. He had one line of dialogue, which was something as original as: 'They went that-a-way!' Kutnick was thrilled. He hadn't figured on getting lines, too. Everything was set for the scene. Irving called, 'Action!' Kutnick the Cowboy delivered his words, and everybody fell about. Maybe it was because he was nervous or slightly depleted in an essential area, but Kutnick's voice came out like a choirboy's. He squeaked in a strangled falsetto which caused the sound man to punch his equipment and ask everybody: 'Did I hear right?' Irving Allen's moon-shaped face went puce.

'Listen, Mr Kutnick, is there any way you could pitch your voice a little lower?'

'Sure,' said Kutnick obligingly. But the second attempt wasn't any better. He still squeaked where he should have roared.

'Cut!'

Kutnick tipped his stetson back on his head and looked enquiringly at the director.

'I tell you what,' said Irving, with great restraint. 'Don't bother to speak, just point.'

'No problem,' said Kutnick, and dead on cue pointed toward the canyon. Now all he had to do was ride the horse. Allen drew him aside to explain the scene.

'This is the situation,' he said, Kutnick listening intently. 'There are three outlaws in the story having a shoot-out. After the gunfight, they have to jump on their horses and gallop over the white rail. You're the third outlaw. I want you to leap onto your steed and head out after the other two guys.'

Kutnick's jaw clenched as he slowly pulled on his black kid gloves.

'Action!'

Two cowboys on two horses are up and away. The third, Kutnick, falls off the horse and is flat on the ground. He tries to pull himself up, but Allen is on a tight budget. He can't waste any more time.

'*Stay there*!' he shouts. 'Props, put an arrow in his back. The Indians got him!'

But the hustle had paid off. I had steered Charlie's friend into a movie, which, considering all the circumstances, had been quite an achievement. This raised my stock with Charlie, who figured that anybody who could get Kutnick hired had to be a good agent. I was now handling important talent and earning money. Which was just as well. I was planning to marry again.

I had met Nedra Clark in Palm Springs. She was a tall, beautiful lady and pretty fantastic, considering the nightmare experience she suffered in her first marriage when very young.

[Nedra's marriage was a disaster, and eventually she moved in with her mother, taking the couple's little boy with her. One night her estranged husband came in, and in a moment of insane rage, killed the boy, Nedra's mother and all but murdered Nedra, too. She was wounded badly but recovered. Later she married a well-known singer, Buddy Clark. They were happy together, but then, unbelievably, a second tragedy shattered her life. Her husband was flying back from a ballgame in San Francisco. The plane developed engine trouble – some said it ran out of fuel – and the pilot had to come down on a roadway. It was a messy landing, but miraculously the plane stayed in one piece. Buddy Clark was the only passenger who had not fastened his seat-belt. He was thrown from the plane and died instantly: the single casualty of the disaster.]

Nedra was a resourceful lady, however, and in spite of all the hell she'd been through, she kept her grief to herself. Early on in life she had been a model, so she knew many people on the fringes of show business. She was good company, and very popular at the Springs. There was some kind of conspiracy between her friends and my friends to get us together. Frank Sinatra, who had known her and Buddy Clark, was very keen for us to meet. So we had several dates together, and the first hint that we might marry came from the Hollywood papers. But we weren't rushing our fences. She had been shattered by two appalling events in her life. I had been divorced, though thankfully it had been a friendly parting from Gloria. Nedra had a pretty house on Saltaire Terrace at San Vicente, a street which ran straight down to the beach. She lived there with Penny, her daughter from her marriage to Buddy Clark. She was a beautiful child about seven years old, and Nedra adored her; in fact, worshipped her. I could understand that, considering how much she had already lost in life. I remember people saying, after Buddy's death in that plane crash, 'How much more can a person have to take?' It wasn't long before that question was answered. I was in my office at Famous Artists when a friend of Nedra's called me.

'Cubby, I have some terrible news. Penny's been killed in an accident.'

'Where is Nedra now?'

'She's having lunch at Lucy's [a favourite meeting place near Paramount] with her friend Jean Long. We feel you're the only person who can break the news to her.'

I got into my car with this dreadful feeling. How do I tell this woman, who has already been hammered over the years, that the daughter she cherishes is dead? I walked into the restaurant, which, as usual, was filled with agents, producers and artistes from Paramount, RKO and Fox. I looked around the room and saw Nedra and her friend Jean sitting at a table laughing, enjoying each other's company. I walked over to them and said, 'Nedra, you have to get in the car and go with me. We have to go to the hospital. Penny's been injured.'

'Don't tell me she's dead!'

'Come with me.'

I grabbed a quick drink, dreading every second ahead of us. We set out fast for the hospital at Santa Monica. As we got nearer, Nedra turned to me and said slowly, 'You're going to tell me she's dead, aren't you, Cubby?'

I made some kind of answer, but eventually, when we reached the hospital lobby, I just had to tell her the truth. She would know soon enough. I had to prepare her. She took it bravely. They wouldn't let her see the child. There was no screaming. She just sat there quietly, with tears in her eyes, and we talked for a while. Then she asked me to drive her home.

Nedra and I were married in December 1951.

EIGHT

Now that I was married, I decided to leave the agency and try to get into production. I liked Charlie Feldman, and had enjoyed working with Famous Artists. But it was the time to make a move. I had gained a lot of experience on the creative side of motion pictures, as well as in the logistics of putting a production together. Pat de Cicco had financed a film called *Avalanche*, which Irving Allen was producing and directing. I joined them, though as a début for an aspiring producer it didn't add up to a row of beans. The budget was around $87,000 and the actors, as I recall, were Roscoe Kearns and Bruce Cabot. A strictly routine kind of picture. As a matter of fact, it was the first motion picture made for theatre exhibition that went out on network television. It seemed to be on all the time in the really black-and-white days of TV. Eagle Lion, who made a smart deal with us, came out well. Pat got his money back, and I was in production.

I had become interested in a book called *The Red Beret*. It was a 1940 story about British paratroopers that offered scope for some action sequences. I was convinced it was a good subject for a commercial picture, but the problem was raising the money to buy an option on it. I had practically no spare cash. Irving Allen wasn't that solvent, either. But we agreed to go into partnership on the deal, putting a couple of hundred dollars down to hold the book for a week or two while I went shopping for finance. (I'd been fairly successful as an agent, but not to the extent of having salted away spare cash.) I managed to get RKO interested, Howard Hughes putting up some money to get commission work on the script.

Howard, meanwhile, was having his usual fun pursuing film stars. He was besotted by Janet Leigh, one of the bright young actresses of the day. He thought she was fantastic and made a deal with her to make a picture for RKO. But personally he couldn't get close to her. One obstacle was the presence of Arthur Loew Jr, the grandson of Marcus Loew of Loew's Inc. Arthur was a rich young man in his own right but was determined to succeed without pulling family strings. He had notions of being an actor. Hughes, typically, didn't like the idea of being edged out of the running by a younger rival.

Around this time Irving Allen was having problems completing a picture. He needed someone to release the picture and put up some completion money. He asked me if I would try to interest Hughes in taking over the picture. Irving required a release deal and $175,000. I had no problem persuading Hughes, because Irving always did a good professional job producing saleable films. Howard, of course, wanted to know who was in the picture.

'Didn't I read somewhere about Arthur Loew being in the picture?'

'No, Howard,' I said. 'What you read about was that Irving was *talking* about putting Arthur Loew in the picture.'

'Look, where is the picture being made?'

'I don't know. In New Mexico, I believe. Somewhere like that.'

Hughes said, 'Well, I'd be interested in giving him a release and complete financing if he would put Arthur Loew in it and keep him out on location for some time.'

I was puzzled by this. You can't be vague when it comes to production costs.

'What do you mean, "some time"? If you keep him out there too long, it'll increase the budget...'

'I don't give a damn about that,' he replied.

I couldn't help seeing the irony of it. Here's a man who wouldn't give me a job because he didn't want the stockholders to think he was favouring his friends. And now he's saying a picture can go over budget so long as the boyfriend of a girl he wants can be hired and then kept on location.

I had no personal interest in the intrigue. I just wanted to help Irving get his picture completed. I got hold of him, though I didn't dare tell him about Hughes's bizarre request.

'Look, I think I can swing this deal for you if you can put Arthur Loew into the picture,' I told him.

'I was figuring I might do that anyway,' Irving said.

'Good. Now how long do you think the location schedule will be?'

'Well, if I don't want to go over budget I'll be out on location for another four or five weeks.'

'Do you think you might go another six or seven weeks?'

Irving frowned. 'No, I don't think so. Why?'

'Well, it doesn't matter, Irving, if you do.'

Irving shrugged. He'd never had a deal before where the backer was practically inviting him to go over budget. The contract was signed. Irving got his release, and his completion money. And Hughes had succeeded in exiling a serious but unsuspecting rival.

As was once said of Thalberg, wherever Hughes sat was the head of the table. So it was no surprise that stars, even married ones, were drawn towards this polite but unpredictable Casanova. The star who intrigued him most of all was Elizabeth Taylor. She was then very much in love with Michael Wilding, and Hughes, who knew everything that was going on around him, must have been aware of the fact. But Howard wasn't inhibited by that detail. To him, Elizabeth Taylor was a terrific woman with all the attributes he admired – full-bosomed, beautiful, and fun to be with. He called me one day to enquire what Nedra and I were doing for the weekend. I told him we were going to Palm Springs, and that Elizabeth Taylor was coming down to visit us.

'Where are you staying?'

'Probably the Racquet Club, or somewhere like that.'

'To hell with that,' he said. 'I have a house down there. Use it. You'll enjoy it more than a hotel.'

This farming-out of houses among friends was standard practice at the Springs. So Nedra and I moved into the place. It was a large house, comfortable, but not pretentiously laid out. I had all the usual crowd come over: Pat de Cicco, Walter Kane, Johnny Meyer and others. Elizabeth had arrived, and I arranged a special dinner party. I told her Howard Hughes was in town and that he might drop by.

'Oh,' she said, 'it'll be nice to see him.'

They had, in fact, met a couple of times before. Elizabeth knew how to talk to people like Howard. He liked her sassy spirit and directness. Hughes had an Irish chef who was very good in the classical style. The man was marvellous at constructing impeccable dinners, though his IQ wasn't as impressive as his cuisine. He had helpers in the house but insisted on coming out of the kitchen and serving too. Of course, he knew Howard intimately, having been his chef for some time. He had been ordered to be discreet at all times and never let on publicly that he knew who Howard Hughes was, let alone recognize him.

The dinner proceeded well. Everybody's having fun with a lot of laughing around the table, when there's a knock at the door and Howard comes in. We all greet him, glad to see him, and Elizabeth kisses him on the cheek. We'd left a vacant chair beside her. They chatted for a while, and it was obvious, to me at least, that he was trying to impress her. Not all that successfully, as far as I could judge it. The party was going fine, everybody drinking freely, laughing and talking, when suddenly this genius of a chef asks, *sotto voce*, but loud enough for everyone to hear: 'Could I ask who the gentleman is who just came in?'

Now of course we all knew he'd worked for Hughes for years. He was trying to show how discreet he was.

'You silly ass,' Johnny Meyer hissed. 'That's Howard Hughes!'

'Not the round-the-world flyer!' gasped the chef. We all broke up, including Hughes.

'That's fine,' Hughes laughed. 'Just bring some more coffee.'

Having prepared the ground with Elizabeth, Howard called her up a couple of days later. But she declined his offer for a dinner date, saying she was busy. On the third or fourth day, he called in again at the house. He was carrying a black box, maybe twenty-four inches long by six inches in width. He took her to one side, and after chatting to her for a minute or two, opened it up. It was full of jewels, worth probably a million or more. He pressed her to select one of the pieces. But she shook her head. She wanted no part of it. She announced that night at dinner that she was leaving. She couldn't get a plane out of Palm Springs. The word was that Hughes had somehow managed to get her flight cancelled. He did everything to keep her there. But Elizabeth had a mind of her own. She started phoning around to see if she could charter a plane. Finally Hughes saw he wasn't going to win. Part of him admired the way Elizabeth dug her heels in. Other stars might have been cautious in offending a man of his power in Hollywood. So he did the gracious thing.

'Look, Liz,' he said, 'if you're that eager to get back to LA, I'll fly you there myself.'

Elizabeth paused a second or two, then nodded. 'OK, Howard, that'll be fine.'

He flew her back, and had a car take her home.

But he still didn't capitulate totally. He had Wilding checked out, and was told that rumour had it that the actor suffered from epilepsy. He reported this to Elizabeth, resorting to anything to prevent her marrying Wilding. It was, of course, the worst thing he could have done. Elizabeth cold-shouldered him and married Wilding, with whom she happened to be deeply in love. I was sorry for Howard. He was smart about almost everything, but as awkward as an adolescent in forming meaningful relationships with women. Yet I loved him, and the few others who were close to him felt the same way. Friendship with Howard had its annoying moments, but you took the rough with the smooth. There was a lot more good in the man than his biographers give him credit for.

Irving Allen and I had agreed on a deal to make *The Red Beret*. Terence Young came over to work on the script. Though he owned the studio, Hughes never set foot in RKO. The man who ran the place was a fellow named C.J. Tevlin, who somehow resented the fact that a modest independent producer like myself should have an office at the studio; worse, be a personal friend of the man who owned it. I don't know how Irving and I managed to get the project going. It was cliff-hanging all the way. We had to pay Terence Young, who would direct the picture as well as write the script. He started writing, commuting between Pat de Cicco's house on Benedict Canyon and the studio.

However, there were difficult problems to overcome – most crucially, finding the right actor for the role of the paratroop officer. You start, in these situations, by asking: who's the biggest box-office draw of the day in the handsome-hero category? The answer, at that time, was unquestionably Alan Ladd. By a coincidence useful to us, he had just quit Paramount because they wouldn't pay him enough money. I believe he was getting $100,000 under contract. He demanded $150,000 or $200,000, but the studio refused. We thought he'd be great in our picture and wanted to talk to him. Irving decided to leave it to me to approach him, which I thought odd at the time.

As I drove out to his house I started thinking, here am I, going out to try and hire the biggest box-office star of the day, and I can just about pay my rent! I had met him a few times, but couldn't claim to know him very well. But as often happens, especially in Hollywood, near strangers discover they have mutual friends. Billy Wilkerson, then publisher of the *Hollywood Reporter*, was a close friend to us both. I knew this and phoned him.

I told him about our project, and he also thought the part would be good for Ladd. Billy fixed for us to meet Ladd at his ranch house, way out in Hidden Valley. When we drove in, he was on the roof, doing some shingling. He shouted a warm greeting to me, then asked, 'Who's that down there?' Recognizing Irving Allen, he laughed. 'For Chrissakes, Apples, where've you been? I haven't seen you in a long time.'

He hadn't seen Irving, in fact, since he'd worked for him at Universal, where they were doing a serial called *Tailspin Tommy*, which Irving was directing. Although Ladd was just one of the grips, he had this burning ambition to become an actor. But every time he raised the subject, Irving brushed him off with: 'What d'you wanna be an actor for? That way you wouldn't work for months. This way you get a pretty good cheque each week. I know, because I sign it. Forget it. Stay as a grip. You'll make more money in the long run.'

So obviously Irving had been reluctant to contact Ladd about our movie, in case the actor remembered what a brilliant talent-spotter he'd been at Universal. Now there was this other reminder of those days: the nickname 'Apples', which he acquired because of his original name, Applebaum. Everybody at the studio found 'Apples' much more friendly. (Later, when we got to England, Irving finally jettisoned the name 'Applebaum'.)

Ladd climbed down from the roof and we talked about *The Red Beret* over a Jack Daniels.

'OK, it sounds good,' he said. 'I don't know about going over to England, but we'll talk about it. You'll have to talk to my agent, Lew Wasserman.'

Wasserman was a top agent, tough but highly respected. We sensed it wasn't going to be an easy ride for us. We drove back to the studio to continue work on the script. Though the deal had to be fixed with Lew Wasserman, we well understood that it was Ladd's wife, Sue, who ultimately had to be convinced. Her influence on Ladd was total. She masterminded his career, watched over him, protected him, supervised his every move. And most times she was right. While Wasserman would have to approve the contract, it was Sue Ladd's hand on the master switch. We decided to talk directly to her. Her initial reaction was: 'Well, you know, the deal you guys want to make, $150,000 and a piece of the picture, isn't really so good for Alan. He can get more.'

This was arguable. We were pretty sure, though, that he couldn't get what we were prepared to offer, $200,000 plus ten per cent of the profits – not the gross, but the profits. We went to see Lew Wasserman and put that offer to him.

'No way,' he told us. 'You guys, you're just starting out. This is an amateur operation and Ladd is number one at the box office!' (Today, for a star in, say, the Stallone category, it wouldn't be $200,000. Twelve million might open the discussions.) Time was running short, and so was our development money. Finally, in desperation, I called Sue Ladd. I knew she was hot on the idea of going to Europe and taking the whole family with her. I told her Wasserman had turned down our deal, and explained we had moved up from $150,000 to $200,000.

'What!'

'And ten per cent of the profits.'

'Stay by the phone,' she said briskly. 'I'll call you back.'

A few minutes later she phoned and said, 'Will you guys meet me at the house at five o'clock?'

We drove over to the house on Mapleton Drive to find Lew Wasserman sitting in the corner, ashen-faced. He was a big man, a big agent, but Sue was unmistakably in the driving seat. She spoke first.

'Lew, Alan and I want to make this deal. You work out the details with the boys.'

'Well, Sue,' Wasserman said slowly, 'I think it's crazy. These boys are talking about the Eady Plan and stuff like that, which doesn't mean anything.'

(The Eady Plan was a levy put on cinema takings which gave a percentage back to producers of wholly British films.) Sue Ladd had her answer ready.

'I know what you're saying,' she said, 'but you haven't been able to get Alan any more than the boys are offering you right now, so I want to do this deal. I'd like to make it a three-picture deal [as we had suggested], and an all-expense-paid for the kids and everybody going over, and a nice house in the country...'

'Sure, sure,' I said in a daze. 'Why not.'

I'm promising all this and I haven't got five cents. Wasserman nodded reluctant agreement. And when I think back on it, he hadn't been all that out of line. I drove away from the Ladds' house with all these thoughts flying around in my brain. We had half a script and a qualified yes from Alan Ladd, but it was still a long way to the top of the mountain. The film had to be made in colour, but at the time, with the studios working to capacity, it was almost impossible to get a firm commitment from Technicolor. Sue, rightly, had insisted the films be made in colour and with a distribution guarantee from a major studio. The majors had already taken up all of Technicolor's available commitments. Without them, we'd have had no picture.

Again it was Billy Wilkerson who came to the rescue. He went straight to the man who owned the process, Dr Herbert Kalmus. Like practically everyone else in Hollywood, Dr Kalmus respected Wilkerson, whose influence in the industry extended far beyond his power as the publisher of the *Hollywood Reporter*. He was a major figure during the industry's most productive years. He was a giant, a friend, and I miss him. He spoke to Kalmus, who gave us the valuable commitment we needed.

We had Technicolor now, but there was still the question of a signed distribution deal with RKO; in other words, the guarantee of financing. Without it the whole house of cards would collapse. Those who think this aspect of motion-picture production is easy should think again. The territory between getting an idea for a movie, then getting it off the ground and rolling, is littered with the bodies of those who've tried it and failed. It was always a struggle in those days. A matter of horse-trading and hope. Getting a distribution deal whereby a major company guarantees finance against a not exactly immodest return is always a tough exercise. It isn't made any easier when the character who has to sign the papers is an enervating recluse who never even visits the studio he owns.

I had the necessary papers drawn up. All Howard Hughes had to do was sign the commitment for RKO to distribute the picture. But for some reason or other, he was ducking it. I chased around and finally cornered him at Walter Kane's house. Not unexpectedly, our hero was in the toilet, and, as usual, on the phone. (He resorted to this kind of privacy when he didn't want anyone to overhear the conversation.) I tapped on the door, but Howard was too engrossed in the call to answer me. I waited a little while, then knocked again.

'Who's that?'

'It's Cubby.'

'What the hell do you want?'

'I've got a commitment here which you promised to sign, for RKO to distribute the film *The Red Beret*. Every time I try to get you, you're either on the john or someplace I can't reach you. You've been promising to sign it, and you haven't done so. I'm not letting you out until you sign it.'

I heard him chuckling, then he said, 'Pass it under the door.'

I slid the document to him, and he signed the damned thing and pushed it back under the door. As I drove away I wondered how many other major film deals had slid into production from under a lavatory door.

But the sequel was even more bizarre. RKO did not distribute the picture after all. C.J. Tevlin, Hughes's man at the studio, had always objected to our presence there. Furthermore, he was cool on the project itself, and had stated his objections to his employer. Howard had given him the job of running the studio, and he was going to run it his way. He leaned on Howard, who finally conceded: 'OK, let Cubby take the picture someplace else.' This made me nervous. We'd promised a fortune to Alan Ladd, and his wife was already glancing through England's glossy *Country Life* magazine to see which lordly manor might suit her and the family.

Fortunately, *The Red Beret* was beginning to pick up some momentum of its own. Paul Lazarus of Columbia heard that RKO had backed out. He mentioned it to his chief, Leo Jaffe, who had been trying to get Alan Ladd for a picture. Columbia called me and wanted to talk.

I said to Howard, 'Look, there's a possibility we can take this to Columbia. Is that all right? We owe you a lot of money.'

'That's OK. You'll pay me when you've made the deal.' It was all as simple – and as crazy – as that. We had agreed the property, Alan Ladd; the director and writer, Terence Young; and a good commercial subject, and were all ready to go. There had been that bizarre sequence with a film contract – and my future – passing to and fro under a toilet door. All settled. But then, because one character at the studio gripes, Hughes hands the project over to Columbia. Such is the nature of the business. It would also turn out to be the least of my problems.

Nedra and I had moved into the Warwick Hotel in New York while the final negotiations were taking place. It was that location which gave us the name 'Warwick Films' – '*War-wick*' to us – for our company. I remember what great hopes we all had when the four of us – Nedra and I, Irving and his wife Nita – arrived in London. It was cold, though, and to convince us we were in London, foggy, too. I'd taken an apartment in Portland Place, not far from the BBC. It was an ancient building which reflected the lifestyles of its former aristocratic owners – like being freezing and impossible to heat. Nedra quickly settled in, making it a home. And getting to know London.

She had met Irving Allen before, and knew how to handle this gruff, unpredictable character. When we first arrived in England, fighting to establish ourselves as independent producers, he could be a cantankerous associate, though with a bark much worse than his bite. You wouldn't have accused him of being strong on all the social graces. Sometimes, if, as husbands do, he raised hell with Nita, then Nedra stepped in and raised hell with him. But the partnership began well. We did our daily journey to the studios where *The Red Beret* was being shot.

Alan Ladd played it smart with the British press when he gave his first London interview. I'd briefed him well on British sensitivities regarding Americans playing heroes in wars involving British troops. The furore over Errol Flynn's *Objective Burma* (a campaign in which no American troops were involved at all), produced violent protests. So when the press heard that Ladd, an American (playing a Canadian in the story), was making a film about Britain's famous airborne army, a few eyebrows were raised. But Ladd was charming. Seated on the edge of an armchair next to Sue, who was shrewdly drinking afternoon tea, Ladd explained: 'The story is of a Canadian who joins the British Paratroopers in order to *learn*, not *teach* the job. All the big decisions in the film are made by the British.'

It was disarming, and it also happened to be true. Terence Young clinched the point by assuring the reporters: 'I can promise

Le più remote origini dei Broccoli, nobili del Napole-
tano, vanno ricercate a Lucca, dove risultano in alto stato fin dal 1194.
I loro progenitori erano i potenti Paganelli, che furono signori di Mon-
temagno, castello presso Pisa, noti per aver dato alla Chiesa un Pon-
tefice in Eugenio III nel 1145. I Broccoli vantano, pertanto, appar-
tenenza alla nobiltà antica di Lucca, che discendeva dai feudatari di
contado di origine Carlovingia o Longobarda.
Il ramo fiorito nel Napoletano fu decorato del patri-
ziato ereditario di San Marino nel 1869. I Broccoli si sono
stanziati anche a Carolei (Cosenza).

The Broccoli family coat of arms.

Above: Italian immigrants step ashore on Manhattan with their bundles and their hopes c. 1897.

Left: Cubby's grandparents, Giovanni Vence and Marietta Arnone Vence with children, *left to right*, Cristina, Joe and Minnie in southern Italy, c. 1888.

Cubby's maternal grandmother, Marietta, beloved matriarch and midwife, in Astoria, New York.

Cubby as a child with cousin, Pat DiCicco, in the saddle.

Charles Lindbergh and *The Spirit of St Louis* in 1927 – Cubby's inspiration.

Left: John Broccoli (Cubby's older brother) and Cristina Broccoli (Cubby's mother) in Florida in the 1950s.

Below: Cubby at sea, *third from right*…The crew of the *Paisano* yacht race, July 1936.

Left: Cubby Broccoli, hands on the tiller, in California, c. 1936.

Below: Howard Hughes: aviator, film-maker and friend, in 1947.

Right: Gloria Vanderbilt and Pat DiCicco at their wedding in Beverly Hills, 1941.

Below: Cubby with Gloria, his first wife, *left*, and her sister, actress Joan Blondell, *right*, c. 1942.

Cubby in naval
uniform with his
mother, Cristina,
c. 1945.

Albert R. Broccoli's licence to sell Christmas trees on a corner in Beverly Hills (1947). One particular customer lingered in Cubby's thoughts...

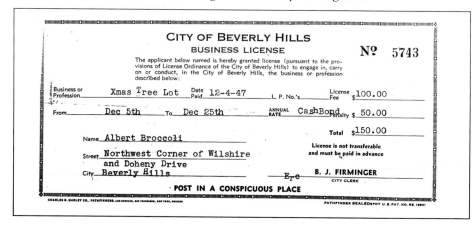

CITY OF BEVERLY HILLS

BUSINESS LICENSE

Nº 5743

The applicant below named is hereby granted license (pursuant to the pro-visions of License Ordinance of the City of Beverly Hills) to engage in, carry on or conduct, in the City of Beverly Hills, the business or profession described below:

Business or Profession __Xmas Tree Lot__ Date Paid __12-4-47__ L. P. No.'s _____ License Fee $ __100.00__

From ___Dec 5th___ To ___Dec 25th___ ANNUAL RATE Cash Bond Penalty $ __50.00__

Name __Albert Broccoli__

Street __Northwest Corner of Wilshire and Doheny Drive__

City __Beverly Hills__

Total $ __150.00__

License is not transferable
and must be paid in advance

By __B. J. FIRMINGER__
CITY CLERK

· POST IN A CONSPICUOUS PLACE ·

CHARLES R. HADLEY CO., PATHFINDERS, LOS ANGELES, SAN FRANCISCO, NEW YORK, CHICAGO

PATHFINDER SEALEDSPOT U.S. PAT. NO. RE. 18931

Dana, the young actress and Cubby's future wife.

Nedra (Cubby's second wife), Cubby, Nita and Irving Allen at the races in
England c. 1952.

Facing page: Paratrooper, released in the UK as *Red Beret*.

ALAN LADD
AT HIS GREATEST
IN THIS RIPCORD THRILLER THAT RIPS AT YOUR EMOTIONS!
PARATROOPER
The skies
go black
with thousands
of fighting men
hurtling
into battle!
also starring
LEO GENN
introducing
SUSAN
STEPHEN
Screenplay by RICHARD MAIBAUM and FRANK NUGENT
Story by Hilary St. George Saunders, adapted from his book, "The Red Beret"
Produced by IRVING ALLEN and ALBERT R. BROCCOLI Directed by TERENCE YOUNG
A WARWICK PRODUCTION • A COLUMBIA PICTURE Reprint

Cubby on the *Kista Dan*, 1954.

The film crew of *Hell Below Zero* in 1954 at the South Pole monument to Ernest Henry Shackleton, Explorer. Stanley Baker is standing to the right of the stone with Cubby standing next to him.

Fire Down Below crew on location (Cubby on the left in white suit and hat) in 1957. Columbia Pictures/Warwick Production.

Fire Down Below film poster.

Right: Cubby and Dana Broccoli with best man Cary Grant on their wedding day in June 1959, Las Vegas, Nevada.

Below: Peter Finch as Oscar Wilde, 1961.

```
                                              8/23/61
        L/T

        Harry Saltzman - Warwicfilm - London


        Blumofe reports New York did not care
        for Connery  feels we can do better

                        CUBBY
```

New York says 'No' to Connery.
However, Broccoli stood firm.

Five shots of Sean Connery during his early days. Even here, the charisma which
was to make him the first in the Bond dynasty is evident. Cubby's resolution to cast
him paid off.

you, Alan Ladd doesn't win the war.'

The press were satisfied, and the picture started. I felt proud making a subject of this importance with a top American star. It was the beginning of a relationship with British technicians, stunt men, musicians and others that I would cherish for close to forty years. Several of those people I started out with in the early 1950s are still my working associates and friends. We were coming in at a time when independent production dominated the scene. John Wolf and Sam Spiegel, for instance, teamed up to make *The African Queen* with Humphrey Bogart and Katharine Hepburn. American producers and finance were welcomed in Britain, because it kept the studios humming and technicians in work, and brought dollars into the country. Moreover, there was then, as there has always been, a tremendous reservoir of talent there. Maybe Britain hasn't produced the greatest number of international stars – though Olivier, Guinness, Finney, Gielgud, Dudley Moore, the Beatles etc., are formidable candidates – but the supporting players have always been first-class.

It is normal to feel a bit apprehensive when starting out on a picture. But we had no qualms. We had a top box-office star and a good script which one of my oldest friends, Dick Maibaum, wrote from Terence Young's first draft. Maibaum was to bring his writing to many of my pictures after that, including some of the most successful Bonds. (His death, years later, was a great personal loss.) He had a fine track record as a screenwriter. He was also a genial character, easy to get on with, which is no small bonus in the nervous atmosphere of motion-picture making. His greatest plus as a scriptwriter was on construction. He was good on ideas, too, but his strength lay in constructing a viable framework on which we could build. No scriptwriter, at least not on the kind of pictures we make, can operate in isolation. We know what we want and make our own creative input, then writers take these ideas and run with them.

As far as the script was concerned, *The Red Beret* presented no particular problems. Terence Young, a wartime British officer, directed action stuff with style, and he and Alan Ladd got on well. But there were peripheral difficulties, inevitable in an overseas production where the reputation of a box-office idol is very much on the line. Sue Ladd knew her way around the motion-picture business. She understood how to talk to producers and, in a sense, was acting as co-agent to Lew Wasserman. Alan Ladd was completely dependent on his wife. He had faith in no one else, and was right to feel that way: she protected him the way a tigress protects her cubs. Alan was a sweet man. If he didn't like something, he didn't gripe about it on the set. He'd quietly make his complaint to Sue. She would raise hell with everybody, and Alan would sort of disappear until the smoke cleared.

But there were some embarrassing incidents with Alan. These arose out of the complex he had about his height. He had this fixation about being shorter than the average screen hero. I don't know why it bothered him. He did pretty well, despite being short of a couple of inches. But he was concerned, and when an actor is worried it shows. The first incident occurred when we moved to Shepperton Studios, on the Thames just outside London, to shoot the interiors. We introduced one of the co-stars on the film to the Ladds, the distinguished British actor Harry Andrews, whose death in the late 1980s robbed me of a good friend and the acting profession of an outstanding talent. He was a powerful, exceedingly tall man who, in the film, looked absolutely terrific in military gear. He towered over all of us, but, more embarrassingly, he towered over Alan Ladd.

Sue called me and Irving into our office and asked, 'Who is that guy you introduced?'

'He's Harry Andrews. The best there is. He's going to play the Sergeant-major in the story.'

'No he's not.'

'What d'you mean, he's not? He's perfect for it.'

'I don't give a damn how fine an actor he is,' Sue insisted. 'He is not playing the Sergeant-major.'

When this happens on a production it's a challenge a producer can't duck. Alan Ladd began to get nervous and it showed.

So I said, 'Sue, look. Andrews has already been advertised as playing the part. It's been in all the papers. It will be very difficult to change things now. So what if he does tower over most of the men? Sergeant-majors are supposed to be big and tough. He's perfect casting.'

Alan Ladd was shrewd as well as talented. 'Now wait a minute, Sue,' he said. 'You have to recognize there'll be repercussions...' He feared, correctly, what the gossip writers might make of the item. Finally, I reasoned Sue into accepting the situation. But it took me until three o'clock in the morning. And as it turned out, Ladd loved working with Andrews and wanted to make further pictures with him. It wasn't a question of having Ladd stand on a box. There are ways of building a set with changing levels so that you can make the height adjustments between stars without being obvious. There are more superstars than the public are aware of who suffer from this kind of dilemma: too tall or too short. But, like Jane Russell's cantilevered brassière, it's amazing what can be achieved with a little smart engineering.

However, Ladd's height problem still nagged at Irving, who was a decent character but short on tact. Everything seemed to be going well on the picture until he had to shoot some second-unit shots on one of the other stages. He had it all set up for Ladd to go in and shoot. He hadn't put a box there, which would have been bad enough. Instead, he had erected a pile of six or seven books, and looking across to the number-one box-office star of the day, he called out: 'OK, Alan, stand up on there.'

Ladd froze. 'What do you mean, "stand up on there"?'

'Well, we've got to shoot this scene and...'

Ladd didn't wait to hear the rest of it. He looked at me for a moment and then, without a word, walked off the set.

'Alan, where're you going?' asked Irving, now red in the face. Ladd didn't answer, but when I joined him outside he was furious.

'You see that dumb sonofabitch, he embarrasses me, Cubby. I'm not going back in there.'

Later my apologetic partner phoned Ladd and soothed him back onto the set. There was no intentional slight on Irving's part. On the contrary, he was a good-hearted guy, but finesse was not his strongest point – not when it came to making motion pictures anyway. Much later, our disagreements long forgotten, we met occasionally to talk over old times. He had mellowed and was a much frailer man – he was to die in 1988. We had our differences, but also our successes. I miss not seeing him around.

Thinking back, I had a lot of sympathy for Alan Ladd. An actor's ego is crucial to his performance. Everything is wrapped up in it: his self-esteem, his confidence, his creative energy. When that ego is affronted or damaged, everything falls apart. An actress's self-image can be even more fragile. I learned a lot about these hang-ups as an agent. Once you're a producer you have to know how to handle it. But, compared with some of the ego problems I was scheduled to face years later, *The Red Beret* was a breeze. Alan didn't have any illusions of grandeur. He was a professional, and did what was asked of him. Sue, on the other hand, scrutinized everything, particularly the script. No leading actor is ever in every scene in a movie. There have to be gaps where other actors or action shots don't require the star. But Sue Ladd was determined that her famous husband should be in as many scenes as possible. Once she went through the script and counted maybe ten or fifteen different pages where Alan wasn't involved.

'Where's Alan? He's not in the script here!'

'Sue,' I said patiently, 'Alan is not there because he's not supposed to be in those scenes.'

'Well, why do we have those scenes?'

'Just read the script. You will find those scenes are necessary to the story.'

And so it went on. It's a familiar ritual for producers. And in any event, I can't fault a wife who battles in the best interests of her husband. I'm blessed with that kind of good fortune myself.

As it turned out, the picture emerged as one of the biggest box-office successes in England in that year, 1953, despite a cool reception from the critics. As the saying goes, nobody liked it but the public. I like good notices and I'm grateful when I get them. But I don't make pictures for critics. You can't fill a theatre with them. Several times I slipped into London's Empire Theatre to feel out the audience response. I do this with every picture I make. I like to sense what keeps them on the edge of their seats. I want to see if they laugh in the right places. Frankly, with all due respect to my friends in the Fourth Estate, this is more instructive to me than any review, no matter how flattering it is. *The Red Beret* was a big hit.

Warwick Films was away and running. Our début in Britain had clicked. I was now an independent producer.

NINE

All motion pictures have their problems. *Hell Below Zero*, the second of our three-picture deal with Alan Ladd, presented massive physical as well as logistical difficulties. Based on a book by Hammond Innes, *The White South*, the whole action is played out on whaling ships in the Antarctic. These days, computers, model-designers and scientists can create anything you want in a laboratory, from a landing on Mars to World War III. Back in 1953 there seemed only one way to make this picture: get out there among the whalers, and shoot.

Taking a whole film unit to the frozen waters near the South Pole, with the special film stock, camera equipment, clothing and medical supplies, was like planning a Polar expedition. A lot hangs on second-unit production. This gives you the visual realism you need. Irving Allen had a lot of experience at this, but somehow decided that he could confidently leave the frozen Antarctic to me. Apart from Alan Ladd, we had Stanley Baker, Jill Bennett and other British talent in the picture. Ladd didn't come out on the location. In the first place, we could manage without him, using a double in the long shots. But whether we needed him or not, there was no way his devoted Sue was going to expose him to the sub-zero hardship on a whaler.

Mark Robson, the director, was involved in the studio, which left me to lead the entire Antarctic expedition. I put together a film unit of thirty-five, the kind of characters who understood what they'd be up against. We now needed a ship to take us there. We chartered one from a great Scottish seafarer named Harper Gow. He had the icebreaker *Kista Dan* berthed at Cape Town, and ordered the captain to stand by, ready to take us to the whaling area.

The plan was for the *Kista Dan* to rendezvous in the Weddell Sea with the factory ship *Southern Harvester*. Sailing from Cape Town to the Antarctic isn't exactly a cruise. The further south you get, the bigger the scattered ice floes get, until finally you run into solid ice. The frightening stuff is the submerged ice, which is as hard as steel, and can slash the bottom out of a ship. Most of the ice isn't visible, and the only way you can detect it is to have a lookout high above the ship. At deck level, you don't see ice which is submerged, or rising dangerously to the surface, until it hits you. But we were lucky. We had a good skipper, who 'read' the ice with an experienced eye. And although the *Kista Dan* was not a big vessel, it had a bellyful of power and sliced through ice like a knife through cheesecake.

What with the submerged ice and storms – at night, when these threw us around like dice in a cup, we gave up any notion of sleep and played poker through to the dawn – it was hard going. But I was lucky in having great guys to work with. Sir Stanley Baker, the fine British actor, was marvellous to have around. Born and raised in the coalmining area of Wales, he remained good-humoured in the worst of the Antarctic conditions. He became a good friend. His death, far too early, was a great loss to us all. As the second-unit director we had Tony Bushell: a tall, gutsy character, upbeat, with a lot of charm. Ted Moore, the cameraman, was another true professional who could operate at temperatures twenty below zero as though he were at Pinewood. John Wilcox, the lighting cameraman, was the same, and we also had some fine stunt men with us.

At last we saw a huge ship loom out of the mists. It was the *Southern Harvester*, where the real action would take place. A handful of us were invited aboard to meet the captain. We had to be hoisted up in large baskets on a derrick, like freight, then lowered onto the deck.

I expected to see the sort of skipper you find in the movies: braided cap, smart uniform, a couple of service ribbons and a courteous salute. Instead, there was this mean-looking Norwegian with a pock-marked face, dressed in a brown pinstripe suit and matching cap, looking about as friendly as Captain Bligh. I got the instant impression that he was taking us aboard under protest, and he confirmed this when we talked in his cabin. He threw his cap down on a table and, speaking with a heavy accent, told us: 'Look,

I don't like strangers on my ship. I've been asked by Harper Gow to take you aboard because you want to film. We are highly superstitious with strangers, especially when we are fishing for whales. Strangers have been known to keep whales away. However, I have given my word to Mr Gow, and I will accept fifteen of you on board my ship. No more than that.'

'We need more than fifteen...' I said.

'Never mind that!' he interrupted. 'Take it or leave it.'

The man was putting out very unpleasant vibes. I told him I didn't like ultimatums. He told me *he* was the skipper, then added a final warning: 'If, when you are aboard and we do not begin to catch whales, then I will put you off the ship.'

I said nothing, weighing my options. The *Kista Dan* was still standing by. If I let it go, I was stuck with this joker for better or for worse, and the situation appeared to be deteriorating by the minute. On the other hand, if I refused his conditions and left, the whole enterprise could be scuttled. He read my mind, and was smart. He'd have some explaining to do to Harper Gow if we refused to come aboard his ship.

'Bring your gear aboard and let the *Kista Dan* go,' he said. 'You will be confined to the lower deck, fore and aft. You will be able to move around the ship only on my orders. Meanwhile, would you like a drink?'

'Captain,' I said, 'I would like a drink, I would like to get my crew and equipment aboard, I would like to shoot my picture, please...in that order.'

The gear was transferred to the *Southern Harvester*, and we let the *Kista Dan* leave. Fortunately, egocentrics were no new breed to me. That bit of Norwegian bravado was just a signal to remind me who was running the ship. But I was prepared to let things simmer for a while.

The night before heading to the whaling areas is the one occasion the skipper unlocks the hard liquor. It was New Year's Eve, and the captain let his crew of more than thirty men, mainly Scots, Norwegians and Danes, get royally drunk. He had to do this because he was already well stewed himself. I stood watching these roughnecks from the upper deck. They wielded these long cleaving knives, used to slice the whales, and I noticed that, in the general conviviality, these were flashing around as in a Japanese ritual, with all the participants seeing how close they could get without losing an ear or a nose. Now and again they drew blood; at this, everybody laughed and poured the victim another drink.

'Looks dangerous to me...' I said to a ship's officer.

He laughed. 'They love it. It relieves the boredom. Tomorrow, with the whales, they work very hard.'

That night we received a radio message from London. Stanley Baker had become the father of twins, a boy and a girl. What the wire did not tell him was that his new-born daughter was giving the doctors cause for concern. There was nothing Stanley could have done about it. There was no point in wiring that additional fact. The agony of knowing the truth, stuck out in the Antarctic, would have been harder to bear.

The dawn came, though in fact there is very little darkness in that part of the world: it is almost perpetual daylight. It was a spectacular sight when the *Southern Harvester* slid slowly among the whaling fleets. We could now identify them all – Russians, Japanese, Norwegians and other Europeans, some close enough to hear – as they prepared for what must be the bloodiest competition on the high seas.

As the whaling began the ship came alive. The experience was both exciting and sickening: carnage outside the ship, a commotion inside, especially on the deck of the factory ship. I hated seeing the beautiful beasts harpooned, mechanically lifted, then sliced in these floating abattoirs. But that's what we were there to film, and realism isn't always easy on the stomach.

Some of the whales they took were highly prized: every inch could be used, to provide a whole range of products. Others were considered largely expendable. In this case the head was removed and the ambergris was taken out of the body, which was then dumped back into the sea. The head was kept, however, to be processed into whale oil.

These whales had their own special stench; they produce a hideous grey liquid which, ironically, is the fixative of some of the world's most expensive perfumes. But even in one piece, dead whales didn't smell that good. It is when they've been toppled onto the deck and the carvers get at them, that the smell really hits you. It is no place for weak stomachs, especially on a rolling ship. After about six weeks of this, *Hell Below Zero* seemed a pretty accurate title.

On the other hand, by now everybody was friendly. At night, when we were all pretty exhausted, we played dominoes with the crew. Different as our work and lifestyles were, eventually we got along fine. We had to. There was no place else to go. When the time came, they really didn't want us to leave. But we had our footage, and everyone was ready for home.

At last the *Southern Opal* arrived to take us out of the whaling area. This large tanker collected all the whale oil, simultaneously transferring the bunker fuel to the *Southern Harvester*. Now all of the crew began shaking our hands and embracing us, while the captain, pleased with the catch, said how much he enjoyed having us aboard. A couple of the scientists in the ship's laboratory had a special gift for me as a memento of the long location: two whales' penises. They explained why the penis was the most valuable part of the creature. It is a huge thing, even in repose, used apparently for making many fancy items, including high-quality ladies' gloves. They could see my gratitude was a little transparent. I was figuring what I would say to the British Customs. But then they asked me if I knew Bing Crosby and Bob Hope.

I was mystified. 'Yes, as a matter of fact they're friends of mine,' I said.

'Well, we'd like to make them a couple of golf bags out of these, and one for you. They're waterproof.'

Which, apart from anything else, must be convenient for the whale. Months later, when I was in California, I told Bing and Bob to expect these golf bags. Bob was particularly enthusiastic, as he saw some great gags in there somewhere. Unfortunately, something went wrong in the ship's laboratory and the bags never materialized. But it was a nice gesture. At least two whales might have been able to claim they were in show business.

We travelled on the *Southern Opal* for some time before we rejoined the rest of the crew on the *Kista Dan*. When eventually I disembarked at Montevideo, all the footage we'd shot was unloaded, and I flew with it to Los Angeles, where it had to be processed – a long and detailed business.

I had learned a great deal making this film: how to keep the cameras operating in freezing conditions, how to keep the lenses from steaming up in the heated areas of the ship, how to solve technical problems concerning the raw film in extreme temperatures. There were other bonuses. I had seen things I'd never encounter normally. Apart from whales, there was a terrific abundance of seabirds, penguins and seals. Miles and miles of seals. They were friendly, too: I'd walk up to the young ones and they'd turn over just like puppies, wanting to be scratched on their tummies or necks. How anybody could club them to death amazes me. There were two other wonderful things I'll never forget about the South Pole: the brilliance of the light and the absolute purity of the air.

I had not been home for long before I was back on location, a situation which would soon develop into a habit. It was the mixture as before: second unit, stunt men, doubles and so forth. The film was *The Black Knight*, Alan Ladd's third picture for us. It was a period piece, set in King Arthur's time, and I wouldn't claim it was the most important subject filmed under the Warwick banner. But with Alan Ladd in the starring role, its saleable value was guaranteed. Once again, with Ladd absent, finishing another film, we had to use a double for long shots. This was easy, because most of the time the Black Knight was helmeted and in full armour. On location in Spain, we used the double with his visor down. Back in the studio, when we needed a close-up of Alan's face, we had the visor up. We temporarily renamed the picture *Visor Up–Visor Down*. Maybe it should have stayed that way. The girl in the picture was played by Patricia Medina. When Irving and I planned the film, for some obscure reason we decided that the female role should be played by a blonde, and styled the costumes and hair accordingly. We forgot this, and cast Pat Medina, who was a striking brunette. I made the deal which brought her from the States to London. When she arrived, Irving and I saw at once we had a problem. As I've indicated, Irving was never going to get any medals for diplomacy.

'Now look, Pat,' he said, 'we shot the double as a blonde and you're a brunette. Either you dye your hair or you're going to have to wear a wig.'

Pat Medina was a very forthright lady, and came from good solid British stock.

'I'm not going to do either,' she said.

'What do you mean?' Irving shouted. 'We're paying you a hell of a lot of money, and you've got to do one or the other.' She frowned back at him. 'What is this nonsense anyway?'

'Well, you see,' said Irving, 'the story is a about a vestal virgin...'

Pat interrupted with a shriek of laughter. 'Who, me? A vestal virgin! You have to be out of your mind, Irving!'

My diplomatic partner, figuring that he'd obviously insulted Pat, leapt in quickly. 'Look, it's only in the story! They're going to lay you on this stone and sacrifice you.'

Finally I placated the 'vestal virgin', who agreed to wear a blonde wig in the sacrificial scene, and we got on with the movie. I have this to say for Irving: he was a good second-unit director. In his own no-nonsense, sometimes abrasive way, he got things done. Most people could tell the difference between his bark and his bite. But not one particular Spaniard. This was a guy who had to lead a cavalry charge down a hill. He led a couple of charges at full gallop. But Irving, through a megaphone, is shouting, 'It's too slow... Faster!'

This guy comes belting down, the rest of the cavalry galloping behind. Hooves are flying, cameramen are scattering, but again Irving shouts, 'Cut! I want it faster...faster!'

This guy is looking at Irving. He's riding like hell and he can't figure out how much faster he can possibly go. In mid-gallop he gets his testicles caught between his armour and the saddle, and he's in agony by the time he reins in his sweating horse. He gets off, walks painfully up to my partner, and in the only English he is certain of, snarls: '*Fucky fucky Irving Allen*!' before remounting his steed and departing. Irving thought it was very funny, but then none of *his* equipment had been caught in the saddle.

The episode was a prelude to a recurrence of a familiar problem. Once we moved into the studio, Sue Ladd was there, intently scrutinizing Alan's dialogue, fiercely guarding her hero's unblemished image. It was obvious she considered he needed more scenes in the picture. The writer, Alex Coppel, had given us a workable story, but we decided we needed another writer to build on it. And fast. It demanded a frenzied weekend of writing to produce sufficient pages to start shooting on the Monday morning. (Nothing unusual: many a great movie has been born out of panic.) There were plenty of good writers around, but few with the skill to operate at that lightning speed, and under pressure. I mentioned our dilemma to the director Raoul Walsh, who happened to be in England at the time.

He said to me, 'Why don't you use this guy Bryan Forbes? He's a hell of a good writer.'

'I know Bryan, he's a friend of mine,' I replied. 'But he's not a writer, he's an actor.'

'Well, he's a better writer,' Raoul said. 'My advice is you get him.'

I managed to reach Bryan at a friend's house in Kent. Irving and I explained the spot we were in, and Bryan grabbed the first train to London. From what he told me later, our call had apparently come at a crucial moment in his life. His career was in limbo. He was eager to get started and earn some money. I warned him he didn't just have to satisfy us and Alan Ladd: contractually, Sue Ladd had script approval on Alan's behalf. By the Monday morning, Bryan had produced exactly what was needed. At least Irving and I were totally satisfied. We all drove happily down to Pinewood Studios, pleased that we had pages which the director, Tay Garnett, could shoot. End of euphoria. We ran into the same kind of flak we'd had on *The Red Beret*. It was almost a repeat of the confrontation over Harry Andrews. Sue Ladd had read the pages and got in early, ready to take on the Marines. I was not immediately involved in the explosion.

[But Bryan Forbes, who was, recalls the impasse with the alert ear of the born writer:

'I was summoned to Ladd's caravan on the set, where I met him and his wife for the first time. Alan was polite, but distant. Mrs Ladd, on the other hand, got straight down to business.

'"Alan Ladd," she said, "does not steal a horse, period." I looked round for an interpreter.

'"I'm sorry, Mrs Ladd, I don't quite follow."

'"Get Irving down here," she said, firing her voice at some acolyte standing behind me. Irving duly put in an appearance with Tay Garnett.

'"What's the problem, Sue?"

'"I'm telling you, Irving Allen, Alan Ladd does not steal a horse."

'"What horse, Sue? What're you talking about?"

'"This Limey writer you got here, he's got Alan Ladd stealing a horse. He steals a horse, we lose the Boy Scouts Association of America, we lose the fan clubs, we lose the Daughters of the American Revolution. So unless you change it, we're catching the next plane out of here."

'"Let me see the pages again," Irving Allen said, playing for time. Then: "It's a good ballsy scene, Sue. What more do you want?"

'"I don't want him to steal a horse."

'"He's got to get out of the place, hasn't he?"

'"Not on a stolen horse."

'"You want him to take a taxi?"

'"That's your problem. You keep the stolen horse in, you'd better look for another star. We're on the next plane."

'Everybody turned to me. I said, "Look, Mrs Ladd, how would it be if Alan Ladd jumps off the battlements behind the hay wagon? This Saracen comes up and says, 'Sire, this is the horse you ordered!'"

'Mrs Ladd pondered the brilliant compromise, weighing it against the possible loss of the Alan Ladd Fan Club, the Boy Scouts Association and the Daughters of the American Revolution.

'"Yeah, I'll buy that," she nodded. "It's good."

'The cameras rolled again. Cubby laughed his way back to his office. And my career as a screenwriter had begun.']

Warwick Films was now a flourishing partnership. Irving and I had established ourselves as independent producers, and were developing several new subjects. Africa had always attracted film companies, from the days of Tarzan onwards. The intrepid white hunter coolly taking on a charging rhino, stalking a wounded lion, rescuing the girl from the treacherous rapids, may be a cliché, but it has always been great entertainment. Hemingway produced the definitive white hunter in *The Snows of Kilimanjaro*. We had Victor Mature starring in *Safari*. Now, Victor is a very nice chap, easy to work with, fun to have around, and (as De Mille discovered in *Samson and Delilah*) a pretty good-looking hunk of male. But nobody expected him to be a hero offscreen – any more than I expected Alan Ladd to gallop across the Spanish plains, visor up. Victor laid it out for us before we started.

'Look, you guys, I'll do whatever you want, as long as you remember I'm a devout coward – even in San Diego! I'm gonna be worse in Africa.'

I understood how he felt. At the time we flew out to Nairobi, in the fall of 1955, Mau-Mau terrorism was officially over, but there was a certain amount of residual tension and isolated raids on villages. A state of emergency remained in force. Though Jomo

Kenyatta had troops out protecting them, many of the whites in threatened areas carried guns.

There are also other, more subtle problems a producer has to face in bringing actors and technicians on location in the tribal areas in Africa. It is essential to respect the local customs and taboos. The Kikuyu, the main tribe of the area, were a disciplined back-up to the government forces. The Masai tribe had seen enough second-unit crews before, and were not too fazed by the cameras. But they are an intelligent, intensely proud and beautiful tribe, so respecting their sensitivities was crucial. Respecting Mature's sensitivities was just as vital. Not too difficult, either, once we understood that he was scared of anything that crawled, flew, brayed, roared, buzzed or went bump in the night. Though I'd told him that we would guard him – correction, *I* would guard him – night and day, he insisted in his contract that two armed white hunters be assigned to him twenty-four hours of the day.

Our first base out of Nairobi was at the Mawingo Hotel, Nanyuki, at the foot of Mount Kenya. This was a marvellous place, which later became the Safari Club, created by the late William Holden, a fine gentleman and a great actor, and Ray Ryan, who had gone to Kenya and fallen passionately in love with the place. It was a two-hour drive from there to the location at Isiola, where we built an airstrip. British settlers had created a beautiful spring, which gave us our drinking water, ice-cool and pure. It was half enclosed by a forest of tall trees. Beyond that was scrub land, dotted with mud huts, fever trees, grazing elephants and giraffes – everything we needed for our picture. Returning there each evening after shooting was a wonderful experience.

The camp we'd set up at Isiola included the usual assortment of tents to take wardrobe, camera equipment, make-up and showers, and had a central marquee for the kitchen and mess area. Compared to other Hollywood-in-Africa productions, with white-coated 'boys' pouring champagne, ours was strictly a three-star location. Mature insisted on sharing a tent with me. He reasoned that if anybody was going to be safe, it would be the producer. We had a large tub in the tent, with hot water provided by one of the native boys. He also kept a fire burning through the night, to deter animals from straying too close. We had a refrigerator, which functioned on wood alcohol. The alcohol was intended for this purpose only, but the tent boy used to drain it off and drink it. He would then pass out cold, the fire would die and strange animals would appear in our tent.

One night I woke up and heard Mature stirring in his bed. It was a king-sized bunk, because Mature is a very big guy. Mine was the same, because I'm no lightweight either. Victor, in response to a call of nature, had wandered out into the African night. Our tent boy was snoring on the fridge alcohol. I thought it was brave for Mature to take his chances outside the tent, even though one of the two white hunters was probably standing by. When Victor returned to the tent, I saw a big black thing follow him through the cheese-cloth curtains. It was enormous, and seemed to hover high above his head. It was a giant bat. It landed on the metal crossbar which supported the tent roof, and hung from it, head down, immediately above Victor's bed.

I yelled out, 'Victor, as you came in, you let in a big bat, and it's hanging right over your bed!'

'Yeah, yeah,' he grunted. 'You're very funny, dago, but stop with the jokes. I gotta get some sleep, otherwise I won't be able to work in the morning.'

'I also want you to work in the morning, but I'm telling you, there's a bat right over your head!'

'For Chrissakes, Cubby...' Victor reached for a torch, shone it up to the crossbar, screamed and slotted himself under his bed. The bat, attracted by the noise, followed him under there. There was a terrific commotion, which woke our hungover tent boy and brought a gun-bearer rushing into the tent. The bat and Mr Mature flew out in opposite directions.

Naturally, after that incident, the 'devout coward' was even more apprehensive. We had a scene where Mature, the white hunter, goes into the water to rescue the girl (Janet Leigh), whose canoe had been swept over a waterfall and into the river. All he had to do was go in, pick her up and carry her to shore. There were some whispers that crocodiles had been seen in the water. They would come in, swim upstream and lie sunning themselves on the beach there.

'I ain't going into that water!' Mature said.

'Victor, what do you mean?' I asked. 'We've got to shoot the scene, and we can only shoot it with you in the water.'

He thought about it. 'All right, I tell you what I'll do. I'll go in if you'll go in.'

'OK,' I said, 'but I promise you you've got nothing to worry about.'

We drove up to the area, and the camera crew prepared for the scene. Our advance hunter had gone forward with the bearers to make sure the water was clear. Which was just as well. By the time we arrived, he had shot five crocodiles – not all that big, but big enough. If the shooting party had been smart, they would have removed the kill before we got there. Instead, Victor saw these five crocodiles on the beach and flipped.

'That's settled it! I'm not going in there!'

Now, one of my pressure points in persuading Mature to go into the water was that journalists had been invited on the location.

'Do you want them to record how the brave Victor Mature was scared to go into the water?' I said.

'You bet your ass they can!' he scowled. He pointed to the bank. 'I thought you said there weren't any crocs in the water.'

'Look, come on, Victor. I'll go in first, then you follow me.'

The cameraman already had his tripod set up. Janet Leigh was floundering around in the water ahead of us, supposedly having just been swept over the waterfall, waiting to be rescued. We walked together, the white hunter and the producer, the producer a yard ahead of the white hunter. It occurred to me that my associate ought to have been in there, too. Irving and I were supposed to have a fifty-fifty partnership. Suddenly I felt things bumping against my legs.

The cameraman saw us flinch, and called out: 'It's all right, they're only catfish. Don't worry.'

But Mature was still scared. He hesitated.

'For Chrissakes, Vic,' I hissed, 'go out there, pick up Janet in your arms and put her on the beach!'

In a kind of daze, Mature lifted his co-star out of the water, and walked with her towards the bank. Then something really large hit his leg. It was too much.

'Screw this...I'm not gonna do it!' he shouted, dumped Janet Leigh into the river, then scrambled up onto the shore. I should have known. Something like this had happened to Victor before. He didn't mind talking about it, either. Filming *Samson and Delilah* for De Mille, Mature had to wrestle with a lion. The original idea was to put a young lion in the scene, secretly tethered by the paws or immobilized in some other way. But Mature wasn't having that. He said he would only shoot the scene if they would change the lion. De Mille agreed, and convinced him that the young lion had been replaced by the old MGM lion, who'd had all its teeth removed. There was also a sharpshooter standing by, just in case the animal got too frisky. Hedy Lamarr, playing Delilah, stood waiting.

'Action!'

Victor moved towards the lion, but the closer he got, the more scared he became. De Mille, always stern, was now fuming.

'It's not the young lion, it's the old one! He's toothless, for heaven's sake!'

'Look, you bald-headed sonofabitch, I don't want to be gummed to death either!'

I have a lingering memory of our African location. Just before we wrapped, Victor had taken a bunch of natives aside – actors, extras and a couple of stand-in grips – and taught them a short chorus of what he said was an ancient battle song. When he'd gotten them all into a platoon order, drums and all, he marched ahead of them in full white hunter's gear, the whole bunch of them chanting, '*Mendl, Mendl, kack 'n fendl...Mendl, Mendl, kack 'n fendl...*'

Victor said it was Yiddish. It sure wasn't Swahili. But the grinning marchers behind him loved it. And they loved Mature. At night, when the camp-fires were lit, voices could still be heard in the darkness crooning, '*Mendl, Mendl, kack 'n fendl...*', which could pass for a lullaby at night, unless you happen to know that it translates as 'Mendl, Mendl, shit in the pan...'

It was to that happy refrain that we folded our tents and left Africa.

TEN

One of the best stories to come out of World War II was of Colonel H.G. ('Blondie') Hasler RM, who led ten Marines into Bordeaux Harbour, where they planted limpet mines on German warships. The tiny boats they used were shaped like cockleshells, giving us the title of our next picture, *Cockleshell Heroes*.

We assembled some great British talent in the film, led by the late Trevor Howard, whom I always admired. He was an actor of great range, brilliant in almost everything he did. José Ferrer directed as well as playing a leading role in the picture. It was a major project which needed talent of that class to match it. Dick Maibaum did his customary expert job giving us a first-draft screenplay. I've made many films over the years, but I know few writers with Maibaum's skill at getting an idea down on paper with a construction that holds up. You can't start without that any more than a ship can move without a compass.

The film, which we shot in Portugal, centred on an entirely British operation. To get the authentic servicemen's dialogue, the cockney humour and the flavour of that period of the war, we needed an English writer who himself had been involved. I thought immediately of Bryan Forbes again. First, because of the good work he'd done for us on *The Black Knight*. Second, because this was his kind of story. When you get top professionals together on a production, things tend to go well. This movie was no exception, though there was one minor incident which emphasizes that producers must pick their jokes as carefully as they cast their actors.

Once again my late lamented partner Irving Allen proved how trigger-happy he was from the lip. We ran the rushes each evening at one of the Rank cinemas in Lisbon. José Ferrer had several good close-ups of himself in his acting role, paddling his boat first on the one side, then on the other. This made Irving restless. He didn't like it at all, and I guess he was right. There were just too many rowing shots, particularly of Ferrer, his face right in camera, paddling interminably through one shot after the other. Irving sat there fidgeting and picking his teeth, becoming increasingly exasperated. Suddenly, out of the darkness of the cinema, rasped that unmistakable voice of his.

'Jesus Christ! If there are any more of these shots, we'll have to change the title from *Cockleshell Heroes* to *Rowing up the River*!' I saw a figure leap over the rail and run out of the cinema. It was Ferrer, who'd heard the remark and was obviously upset. Irving, of course, was being funny, and as usual I had to pick up the pieces. I couldn't find Ferrer for hours that night. When finally I caught up with him, he didn't want to come in to work the following day.

'You've got to keep that so-and-so off the set!' he said angrily (an ultimatum that would recur uncomfortably in future confrontations on my pictures). Apart from that odd lapse, the production went smoothly. The picture was a big hit, especially with British audiences. They felt we had dealt accurately with this limited but immensely brave operation by their Marines.

After *The Red Beret* and *Cockleshell Heroes*, Warwick Films was now established internationally, and attracting major stars. *Fire Down Below* was an indication of this success. The cast was Rita Hayworth, Robert Mitchum, Jack Lemmon and Herbert Lom; director, Robert Parrish; writer, Irwin Shaw. We went out to Trinidad to make this picture. Parrish is a good director, who learned his craft working as a film editor for John Ford, George Cukor, Max Ophuls and other film-makers of that stature. Jack Lemmon was not as big a star then as he was to become. But any producer would have been proud to have him in a picture. He is dedicated and a hard worker. And a fine actor. Luckily for us, Rita Hayworth, though always unpredictable, produced none of the traumas that were soon to blight her, physically and emotionally. Even Mitchum, an old friend and a great performer, did nothing to confirm his reputation as a hell-raiser and formidable drinker.

But things happen on location, especially in the Caribbean, where the sheer languid beauty of the place isn't exactly conducive to the tight schedules of movie making. Well, put it this way: it wasn't exactly conducive to Mitchum. The story of the film was straightforward enough: two partners in a fishing and smuggling enterprise fall out over a woman. But with talents as fragile as Rita's and as volatile as Mitchum's, I could never be sure how the chips would fall. There were many delays and a variety of production problems, and the technicians became restless and started slowing down. That made me restless, too. You don't make movies on a blank cheque.

We did much of the shooting on a boat. One morning I arrived and saw that nothing at all was happening. The sun was shining, the conditions were perfect and everybody was sitting around listening to the waves lapping the side of the boat. What they were not doing was shooting a picture. I looked at Bob Parrish. 'What the hell is going on?'

Parrish points to Mitchum, who is prostrate on the deck, blissfully stoned out of his mind with booze.

'Well, wake him up, for Chrissakes!'

The director, who knew Mitchum as well as I did, shook his head.

'Not me! You wake him up.'

I got a bucket of water out of the sea, stood over Mitchum and sloshed it over his face. Jolted out of his stupor, he wiped the sea water out of his eyes.

'Who did that?'

'I did.'

'What did you do that for, Cubby?'

'Hell, Bob, you were asleep. You're supposed to be working. Now come on, let's get going.'

Mitchum drowsily replied, 'OK...wardrobe!'

It wasn't that he didn't want to work. Like many of the great actors of his era – Bogart, Cooper, Wayne – Mitchum delivered. He was just bored: the occupational hazard of filming in an exotic location. There is a lot of hanging about between set-ups. Lying around in the sun doing nothing can be very addictive. And expensive. Throwing a bucket of water in Mitchum's face doesn't appear in the *Producers' Manual*. But it's as good a trick as any to get a hungover actor on his feet.

The film had a moderate reception, and won no medals. I remember it mostly for the fact that it was on this picture I met England's Bernard Lee. He was a fine actor and a fine man.

Bernard would not only become one of the bedrock performers of the Bond films, but a very good friend, too.

We made a string of pictures in those days, many of them not very memorable. Commercial products like *Odongo*, *Pickup Alley*, *April In Portugal* (made by a separate unit during the filming of *Cockleshell Heroes*), and *How to Murder a Rich Uncle*, written by John Paxton and directed by actor Nigel Patrick. We cast it, shot it, then long after, in London, I ran into Michael Caine, who said to me, 'Cubby, you probably wouldn't remember it, but did you know I once worked in a picture for you?'

He was right: I didn't remember it.

'When was that?' I asked.

'It was back in 1956, on *How to Murder a Rich Uncle*. You short-listed two of us for a small part on the picture, though you needed only one. You looked at us both, but finally chose me. It wasn't much of a part. I had a scene where I was punting up the Thames with a pretty girl, in a sort of background shot. Do you remember the other actor with me, the one you rejected?'

'No, I don't remember...Who was it?'

'It was Sean Connery.'

Both actors were virtual rookies in the business then. Neither of them, the then Maurice Micklewhite and the former Tommy Connery, could have had the faintest notion of the success that would one day hit them. And with singularly contrasting reactions.

If 1956 was not a memorable year for Warwick Films, it certainly was as far as my personal life was concerned. Nedra gave birth to a baby girl, whom we named Tina, after my mother, Cristina. It was a great joy for us. Having lost two children in appalling tragedies, and been brutally treated by one husband, widowed by another, that Nedra could have put together a normal life was a marvel to me. But she did, though I don't think she ever fully recovered from those terrible blows early on in her life. Now she had Tina, and with Tony a flourishing two-year-old, at last there was some equilibrium in her life. She liked London, knew her way around the restaurants and was very popular with the film crowd.

The 'marriage' between Irving and me, on the other hand, was beginning to run out of steam. We had made a lot of pictures together – some good, some I'm not too eager to remember – and had quite a stake in independent production in Britain. We were beginning to disagree about stories, and we made mistakes. The worst of these was forming our own distribution company, Eros. Irving Allen was convinced that it would be advantageous for us to finance and distribute our own pictures. I went along with the scheme, but I had some misgivings, mainly because I hated moving into uncharted waters. I knew next to nothing about distribution, and I wasn't sure that Irving knew much more. In any event, he sold me the idea and I went along with it. So I have no complaints on that score.

But it was a total disaster. We lost almost everything we had. We both went into a kind of limbo to lick our wounds and figure out how we were going to get back into action. A successful film might just pull us out of trouble. The problem was, how to find the right property. There's no particular genius required here. You have to look, listen and read. And even then, when you think you've found the right story, there is an enormous gulf between its acquisition and getting a distributor interested and a deal struck. But Irving and I had been pretty successful at it. We'd crashed with our distribution company, but we were still in business, albeit with not much spare cash lying around.

In the hiatus following the failure of Eros, Irving spent much of his time at Newmarket, where we kept a string of racehorses. He loved the sport, which his success as a partner in Warwick Films enabled him to pursue. I enjoyed it too, still do. But at the time, the débâcle over the distribution company was one gamble too far. What we both badly needed as film producers was a safe bet. In the back of my mind was an idea I'd had for a long time: filming one of the books of Ian Fleming. James Bond appealed to me on several levels. Fleming's fictional character offered exciting scope for all the basics in screen entertainment: a virile and resourceful hero, exotic locations, the ingenious apparatus of espionage, and sex on a fairly sophisticated level.

From the very beginning I believed that 007 had enormous screen potential, though I was not the only one. Other characters had gone along that route before me, only to stumble over the specifics or fall at the first hurdle. We'll come to that. But, for the record, since many have claimed to have had a hand in the 'discovery' of Bond, I think it relevant to point out my early appearance in the field. The more I thought about the project the more convinced I was that this was the subject I had long been building toward. I had arranged to meet with Ian Fleming and his associates in London. I told Irving how enthusiastic I was for Bond and sent copies of the Fleming books to him at our stud farm at Newmarket so that he'd know what to talk about at the meeting. I wasn't sure he would read them. I was a shade nervous at his apparent lack of interest over the phone. Nevertheless it was important that he knew enough about 007 to face Ian Fleming and his two associates at the meeting. But just before that day I received a phone call at the office. It was from Dr Saxe, our GP in London.

'Cubby, I'd like you to come over,' he said. 'I have to talk with you.'

I was confused. I couldn't think why he'd contacted me. I was OK as far as I knew; so was Nedra. But apparently she hadn't been feeling well, and had gone to see him a few days earlier. She didn't think it was important enough to tell me. But Dr Saxe didn't waste any time.

'I'm sorry, Cubby. We have to put Nedra in hospital. She has cancer.'

It was brutal news. On top of everything that Nedra had endured, she now had to face this illness. The consultant had diagnosed cancer of the bladder. I discussed it with Dr Saxe, who was convinced that the only hope lay in immediate surgery. There was no way I could hide the truth from Nedra: she needed a major operation. She would want to have a say in where it should take place. I persuaded her that the best idea would be to be treated in New York. We both knew excellent specialists there, and she'd have the surgeon of her choosing. It was remarkable the way she took it all. Whatever she felt – and it must have been plenty – she managed to keep her composure in front of Tony and Tina. But they were obviously bewildered by the sudden flight from London, moving into the Savoy Plaza in New York, the urgent consultations between us and the doctors.

I took Nedra to the Doctors' Hospital, and we had several eminent doctors brought in. They carried out an exploratory operation, then quickly patched her up. The disease had spread too far, and extensive surgery was out of the question. I had to face the fact that this poor lady, who had endured so much, wasn't going to make it. The grief caught up with me. The two children wanted to see their mother. But Nedra told me not to bring them up to her room. She didn't want them to have that memory for the rest of their lives. The nursing care was magnificent. The doctors did everything they could to ensure Nedra suffered no unnecessary pain. Slowly, and peacefully, she passed out of our lives. We took her home to California, and she was buried in Inglewood.

The show goes on...and I had left it in my partner's hands. While I was in New York, Irving had to negotiate for the Bond options, alone. I had misgivings, not because I doubted his ability to talk to Fleming and the writer's associates. What bothered me was that he was obviously lukewarm on the whole project. To be fair, he didn't make any secret of it. I said to him before I left London, 'I think we have a great property here, Irving.'

He rubbed his chin. 'Well, I don't know, Cubby. I'm not sure it's such a good idea.'

I had already talked to Columbia about optioning the Bond books, but they were more interested in what Irving and I were currently involved in. My partner had assured me he'd read the books but, rightly or wrongly, I didn't get the feeling that he'd really gone through them. The feedback I got from his meeting with the Fleming people at Les Ambassadeurs in London was not just negative: it was terminal. Irving had been his usual candid, forthright self. And candidly and forthrightly, he blew it. He told them that he didn't share my views about the feasibility of making films of the Bond books. He went further. In a judgement as unequivocal as if it had been delivered on the Mount, he declared to Ian Fleming and his literary agent, Robert Fenn, and my dear friend Ned McLean: 'In my opinion these books are not even good enough for television.' (Twenty-five years and two billion admissions later, he had slightly adjusted that opinion.)

He then excused himself to return to Newmarket and the horses. The Fleming contingent were justifiably put out, wondering why they'd bothered to attend the meeting in the first place. So the tenuous link I had with the James Bond books in 1958 was broken. Fortunately, not for ever.

But I wasn't too concerned about making movies at that time. I had to put my life together again, and help Tony and Tina cope with what, even to their very young minds, must have been a shock. This was going to be a slow and delicate process. Friends are great in this sort of situation. My cousin Pat de Cicco, one of the biggest-hearted guys I ever knew, helped me over the first hurdles. Pat hid a lot of wisdom and compassion behind that playboy image of his. He didn't offer a lot of verbal bromides; he was just there when I needed him. Slowly, I got back into some kind of momentum. One weekend we found ourselves in New York together. We had a date at Bill Hearst's house, where we were going to cook an Italian dinner. We decided to go to this place on 116th Street to buy the groceries.

I said to Pat, 'You know who I'd like to see? – Andrea Cirolli.'

Cirolli had been an old friend to both Pat's father and mine. He had been like a little 'Godfather' of that neighbourhood. My father, when he used to go to the market, would stop by and play cards with Cirolli and his friends. Giovanni Broccoli, the plain old simple farmer, knew these people from way back. In the summer they'd come out and visit us on Long Island. In the winter they'd all go out hunting rabbits. When Cirolli used to call on us, he'd give us kids five-dollar gold pieces, or maybe the two-and-a-half-dollar gold pieces which were around at the time. I knew he had to be a very old man by now, but I felt this urge to go and see him. Pat and I stopped at this 116th Street tavern. It was about eleven or twelve o'clock, and they were sweeping the place out, getting ready for business. It was chilly, and we had on trench coats.

I asked the barman, 'Is Mr Cirolli here?'

'Who wants to know?'

'I'm an old friend of his – my father was an old friend of his...'

There was a little kid there helping to sweep the place, about ten years old. The guy made a gesture, and the kid ran out into the street. We didn't know where he'd gone. It should have almost gone unnoticed, except that later on we remembered: we just saw this gesture which sent the kid running out.

So the guy said to us, 'Well, I don't know. Could you wait a minute?'

As we're sitting there, the door opens and in come three men. One of them is a rather handsome-looking chap with a very fine Borsalino hat, cashmere suit; well-groomed, shoes polished, clean. A couple of other fellows are with him.

'Which one of youse guys is asking to see Mr Cirolli?' he asks in an accent straight out of Damon Runyon.

'My name is Pat de Cicco,' my cousin says. 'This is Mr Broccoli. Mr Cirolli was a friend of my father's, and of Mr Broccoli's father.'

'Well, I'm over here asking the questions because Mr Cirolli is a very dear, dear friend of mine, and so we'd like to know who wants to see him.'

I knew by the way this guy was talking that this was not a frivolous enquiry. Pat got the message at the same time. He sort of smiled and said, 'Well, we don't exactly *have* to see Mr Cirolli. It's just that he used to come out and visit us on the farm years ago, with Mr Caruso and Mr Broccoli's father, and we're just curious...not having seen him for years, to see if he's all right and so forth...'

'Yeah, he's OK. Do you really *need* to see him?'

'Oh no...' we said together, Pat making a move to get out of the place. But I pressed on. 'We don't have to see him, of course, but is he in good health? And if he is...'

'Well, maybe I can talk him into coming out to see you.' The guy then went out and came back with this frail old man who used to be the power in the district. He spoke to me in Italian.

'Who is this who wants to see me?'

I said, 'Mr Cirolli, I am the son of Giovanni Broccoli. Mr de Cicco is the son of Pasquale de Cicco.'

'Oh...Pasquale de Cicco...Giovanni Broccoli...' he said, shaking his head. '*Non mi ricordo...*'

Now I started to get a little worried, because these gentlemen were looking at me and obviously didn't like the way the conversation was going.

'Do you remember my mother, Cristina?' I said. 'We used to make the sausages at pig time. You used to come out when they killed the pigs. And you would bring us the gold coins, and we'd have a big pig-roast party – and a lot of fun.'

The old man said, 'Well...I don't know about parties and...', his voice trailing away.

'My father used to come in here from the farm, in the market...' Now I'm almost pleading with the old tyrant. 'He used to play Abriscolo with you...' (Abriscolo is an Italian card game, like Gin.)

'*Aaah...Abriscolo...aaah, sí!...Abriscolo! Giovanni tu padre... sí, your father...*'

And it all comes back to him. And he's smiling.

'Ah yes...how's your mother? How's your father?'

'My father's passed away. Mother's fine.'

'I'm sorry about Giovanni. But it's good to see you. Have a drink. Give Mr Broccoli anything he wants.' The guy turns to me and says, 'My name is Frank Uale.'

Now I knew why I was nervous. Frankie Yale – formerly Frank Uale of Brooklyn – was a notorious character regarded by most at the time as Public Enemy Number One. He was a top-class racketeer who specialized in contract murders. Al Capone was one of his hired bouncers and bartenders. He stared at me and said, 'What did you come down here for?'

'We're going to cook a little dinner tonight at Bill Hearst's place. He's the son of William Randolph Hearst...'

'I know who he is...'

'...and we want to buy some Italian olive oil, some garlic and tomatoes.'

'Come with me.'

We go to these stores which had obvious syndicate connections. You could tell that by the way the guys behind the counter react at the sight of Mr Yale.

'Mr Broccoli wants some of these tomatoes to make spaghetti sauce, eh! That means you give him the best tomatoes, you hear me good?'

I said, 'You don't have to go to all this trouble, Mr Uale. I just want a few...'

'Shaddup!' He's watching the shopkeeper. 'Nah, not that! Give him the other, the imported ones, you stupid sonofabitch!' Now he smiles at me and asks, 'How many you want?'

'Oh, maybe four cans.'

'Give him a dozen!'

'That really will be too much...'

'A *dozen*! Put them in the car.'

'OK, what else you want?'

'Well, some grated cheese, a pound perhaps.'

'What's-a-marrer with you? A pound! Give him three pound! Oil?' (This guy knew his spaghetti.)

'Just a little, Mr Uale.'

'Give him a gallon!'

'It's only a small dinner party, Mr Uale. We've got enough tomatoes, cheese and...'

'Put all the stuff in the car. Now, what else you need?'

'Well, we were going to get some *cannoli*.'

'Come with me.'

We walk across the street to this pastry shop. He probably owned it. In the back of the shop they've got a betting syndicate going. You could hear them punting away. We sit down and he says, 'Have some *cannoli*.'

We have one of the cream horns. The rich, sweet pastry is delicious.

'Have another one,' he says.

'Oh gee, that's too much, we just want to...'

'*Have another one!*'

So we have another one.

'How much *cannoli* you need?'

'Oh, say about ten.'

'Pack two dozen of the *cannoli*.'

And the man goes into the back of the shop, where they keep the packets of *cannoli*, and picks up a box, but before he can move, Uale jumps up, runs around to him and Bang! slaps him around the face.

'These are my friends,' he shouts. 'Mr Broccoli and Mr de Cicco – friends, you hear me? When I say I got friends, you pick them the fresh *cannoli*, not the *cannoli* from last night, you know what I mean? You know what I'm talking about!'

'Oh yes, sir, yes, sir...'

Then, as we're walking across the street, Pat and I look at each other. We look like a couple of cops with our trench coats on. Now there are four of us – another character has attached himself to Uale – and as we're walking I feel as though it's a scene straight out of *The Untouchables*. Except it's not booze in the car but enough oil, tomatoes and *cannoli* to run an Italian restaurant.

As Uale sees us into our car, he asks, 'When you coming to New York again?'

'Well, we're going over to London to make some films.'

'Well, when you come through, I don't wanna hear you came into town without coming to see me, you hear? I'll hear about it. I'll know you're in town.'

'Oh yes, we'll definitely do that, Mr Uale,' I said.

'Not Mr Uale. You call me Frankie.'

(One sunny July afternoon Frankie Uale was nailed to the seat of his car by bullets fired from revolvers, sawn-off shotguns and a tommy-gun. This was the first time a tommy-gun was used to kill a New York gangster.)

The year 1958 proved to be eventful. Warwick Films had only

been in existence since 1952, yet Irving and I had made close to twenty pictures. Three of these were released within a year: *No Time to Die*, *The Man Inside* and *Killers of Kilimanjaro*. We had another film planned, which would turn out to be the last one we would make together. Meanwhile, I was back in California, having flown directly there in spite of Mr Yale's insistence that I stop over in New York. I arrived in Los Angeles to find Cary Grant had called. Despite his easygoing manner, Cary was an introverted character who kept out of the mainstream of Hollywood social life. He had his own problems, but he knew I was in town, and alone. Howard Hughes had called, too. He was aware I was back on the West Coast almost before the wheels of my plane had hit the tarmac. His personal information service operated as efficiently as ever. We were seeing much less of each other. The change in my friend after that catastrophic plane crash was startling. It was clear to me that his so-called eccentricities, his obsession over hygiene, his fear of human contact even with close friends, were all the aftermath of that disaster.

But the one part of him that was never diminished was his genuine concern and loyalty for his friends. He knew that Cary and I were flying to Las Vegas. Howard was there, too, and there was some talk that he might join us. He loved that whole scene: the glamour, the big shows, the beautiful women and the crowds around the gambling tables. But he was always the perfectionist. He could only be there on his own terms. He could only have enjoyed that scene as the good-looking, dynamic man of the moment. The playboy instincts had long since died in him. He didn't show up. But I can never be in Vegas without remembering Hughes in his better and happier days there. The centre of attraction. Calling the shots. Focal point of the action.

Cary and I were staying at the El Rancho Hotel, owned then by a good friend of ours, Beldon Katleman. It was New Year's Eve, and I had a dinner date at the Flamingo Hotel with a girlfriend named Dorothy. There had been some gossip about us in the Hollywood papers. She was becoming increasingly interested in marriage, and I was just as eager to disillusion her. In this kind of unsatisfactory situation, conversation becomes a bit stilted, and I was relieved when she left me for a moment to talk to a friend. The lady in question was an exquisite beauty with thick, raven hair falling around a lovely face with a pale, delicate, camellia-like skin.

She was graceful, perceptive, and I adored the way she laughed. A thought flashed across my mind that I had seen her somewhere before. She was with a group of people she didn't appear to be at ease with, and spoke of wanting to get back to Los Angeles. Her name was Dana Wilson. She had a lovely open manner. I had her telephone number. Her friend Dorothy, having read the signs, scribbled it for me as a parting gesture.

I had to get back to England, and it was some months before I returned to the States. But I'd thought a great deal about this lady I'd met at the Flamingo. I planned to call her, but by coincidence ran into her again at the 21 Club in New York. I asked her if she remembered meeting me in Las Vegas.

'Yes,' she smiled, 'I remember the occasion very well.'

'I'd like to see you again.'

'Oh?' She hesitated. There were loyalties involved here. 'Aren't you and Dorothy...?'

'No. I'm not going with Dorothy. That was just Hollywood talk,' I said with a sinking feeling that I wasn't getting the better of these exchanges. 'When can I see you? Can I call you?'

Pause. 'Yes,' she said, and I left. I walked back, somewhat confused, to my hotel. It was obvious to me that getting to know Dana Wilson – like walking on eggshells – involved treading with extreme care. Understandably too, the more I learned about her.

[The reserve displayed by Cubby's new-found friend Dana stemmed from a scrupulous upbringing in a well-connected New York family. Her main interests were music and drama. After graduation, she went to Cecil Clovelly's Academy of Dramatic Arts at Carnegie Hall in New York, where she met Lewis Wilson, an actor from a New England family, who was attending the American Academy of Dramatic Arts, also at Carnegie Hall. His father had been a Unitarian minister in Massachusetts; his mother was the daughter of Senator Gregg of New Hampshire. The Wilson background was strongly intellectual and political, with a Senator, a Governor and a Congressman among its offshoots. Lewis Wilson, the second son of four children, had always wanted to be an actor, which cut against the grain of the family tradition. He was the only one who did not go to college, which was bad enough. By deciding to become an actor, he compounded the felony.

So this 'black sheep' went to drama school in New York and met Dana, and they were married. Dana became a leading lady in the Boston Stock Company. A son, Michael, was born after America entered World War II.

Lewis Wilson brought his talents to Hollywood, where he was under contract to Columbia. Tall, with a strong build, he became the first-ever Batman. Dana had no particular interest in becoming part of the movie scene. She was more interested in writing and continued with it when Lewis was drafted into the Army, to serve in Europe until the end of the war. During that time she wrote a novel. When Lewis was discharged, she helped him try to re-establish himself in movies, with mixed results.

Meanwhile, Dana wrote for films and the couple moved to Pomona, California, where they joined the Pasadena Playhouse. Lewis had a few TV jobs, but ultimately they split up. Dana and her son Michael moved first to Hollywood, then to Beverly Hills. What attracted her about the place was its serenity, not its celebrity connotations. Whatever the future held for her, she was never going to be a 'Hollywood wife' – that unreal creation of Jackie Collins's novels. Her plans were clearly defined: Michael would go to military school, college, then probably into law. She would continue to write, while displaying the cool diffidence essential to a beautiful divorcee in the Hollywood jungle. It was this reticence that Cubby Broccoli was determined to overcome.]

I called the following night in New York, but the hotel said Dana was out. I had a date with an attractive Eurasian lady at the El Morocco, then probably the most exclusive place in town. Fate had obviously taken an interest in my relationships. As we walked to our table, I saw Dana dining with a man of unmistakable European appearance, but apparently without the cultivated manners normally associated with it. There is a class of individual who believes he scores points – especially with a woman – by being obnoxious to waiters, making a flourish of sending the wine back, snapping his fingers to get attention; and this character was playing a full hand. If he thought he was impressing Dana, he was a mile adrift. I could see she was becoming increasingly annoyed. They left early.

I called Dana the next day, which led to several dates and an awareness – from where I sat at least – that we liked each other.

We both had plans to fly to California. We said goodbye, and I promised I would call her in Los Angeles. 'I'd like that,' she said, so I felt pretty elated when I took the early flight to LA.

ELEVEN

As the films I had produced with Irving Allen began to be released across America, some of their success rubbed off on my family, especially my mother. Her thrill was to walk past a cinema with a friend or neighbour and point at the name 'Broccoli' in the producer credits on the marquee. She didn't know very much about the business, and wasn't that interested in it, either. But she guessed it was probably OK if millions stood in line to buy the tickets.

Years after my father, Giovanni, died, she married again. My stepfather, William Labbate, was a good man of Italian descent, and Cristina and he lived contentedly together out on 43rd Avenue, Corona, Queens. He died years later. By June 1944, when Cristina became an American citizen, she was sixty and a widow. The naturalization certificate described her as having a fair complexion, brown eyes and grey hair, and being five feet two inches tall. This was all the Department of Justice needed to know on the Petition, Number 336112. I could have added: soft, gentle features, the dark-ringed eyes which always carried a hint of her childhood in Calabria, and that human quality she managed to convey without uttering a word.

She was a wise mamma, made, like most Italian mothers, for motherhood, love and emergencies – like a crisis calls for spaghetti. Her chosen territory was the kitchen, centre stage for all the pleasures and the sorrows of our early family years. Even when she lived comfortably, luxuries (or what she thought were luxuries) made her feel uneasy, slightly guilty. She was enjoying possessions that others didn't have. There was a dignity about her, even in a print apron stirring a saucepan of soup. Both my brother John and I were devoted to her. I finally persuaded her to come and live in

California. She would have been really happy to have John there too. But he had married and moved to Florida, the distance between us growing even wider when I started my film operations in England.

John and I kept track of each other by phone wherever I was in the world. He was very proud, telling all his chums about his kid brother, the 'film producer'. He would tell them what a good guy I was, which was embarrassing because I wasn't all that good. He would tell all these veteran ballplayers who sat around his restaurant in St Petersburg to go and see my films; he'd name-drop all the famous film stars I mixed with. I was touched by it, not because the celebrity side of it added up to a row of beans, but because of the genuine affection behind it all. We did love each other. It was just bad luck that a geographical separation prevented us from being together. What made it worse for me and Cristina was that John had developed heart trouble. We'd both go down to Florida now and again, though the last time I saw him I went alone. It was a sad experience. He was trying to be cheerful, brotherly, but I could see he was suffering. He had a successful business, but he was ill and having serious problems over his marriage. I tried to persuade him to leave St Petersburg and come to California, where I could spend more time with him. But he felt it was too late for him to make that kind of move. He really looked sad when I left him. Four months later his heart caught up with him and he died.

It hit me hard. My mother, of course, was heartbroken. We brought him back to New York and buried him on Long Island.

When I think back, my pursuit of Dana Wilson wasn't exactly textbook wooing. My two closest confidants at the time were my cousin Pat and Cary Grant. Both were acknowledged experts in the game. Pat – tall, suave and a sharp dresser – attracted women with a mixture of charm and good-natured needling. Cary got his mileage out of a boyish exuberance and looking as tanned and healthy as a Malibu lifeguard. I have a feeling I tried to project the lot. I had called Dana several times in California, but apparently she hadn't yet left New York. This didn't look like a good sign to me. I persisted with calls to both coasts.

Cary, who was now divorced, was dating a strapping Yugoslav basketball player named Luba, who had been in their Olympic team but defected to the West. It created quite a sensation in Hollywood at the time. Defecting Slav basketball players do not generally fall into the arms of the likes of Cary Grant. Cary had phoned to say that he was taking her to Las Vegas, and invited me to join them there. I went, but despite the action on hand, I was thinking too much about Dana. I continued to phone her, and finally managed to reach her mother in Los Angeles. She was a sweet lady, but for some reason the call made her nervous. Suddenly getting a call from Las Vegas from a guy by the name of Broccoli took this refined and virtuous soul by surprise. When I asked if Dana was there, her response was a firm 'No, she's not here!'

'When is...can you tell me when she's arriving?'

'I'm sorry, I don't know when she's coming.'

'Do you think...?'

'No.'

I was beginning to wonder how Pat or Cary would have handled the situation. (I would have felt much easier had I known at the time that Dana was really wanting me to call, and was looking forward to our getting together. But I guess protocol demanded that I suffer a little along the way.) At last she touched base in Los Angeles. I called, and there was all sweetness at the other end of the line.

'I'm in Las Vegas and I'm coming home to LA tomorrow,' I said. 'I'd like to see you. Let's go out to dinner one evening.'

'Certainly, I'd love to. When are you getting in?'

I told her the flight number, and took a gamble.

'It would be nice if you met me.' You've blown it, Broccoli! I told myself. But I'd made the offer, and I had to run with it. 'I can get a car. I just thought it would be nice if you met me. I'd like to see you.'

There was a pause. Had I got the right balance between persistence and eagerness?

Apparently, yes.

'All right, I'll arrange to meet you,' Dana said.

I am not suggesting I prepared for our rendezvous as meticulously as a matador gets into his 'Suit of Lights', but it was close. I was in pretty good shape at the time: I weighed one hundred and seventy-five pounds, was tanned, and though I didn't have Cary's flat steel midriff, it didn't show under my English

blazer and charcoal-grey pants. And to add the final touch of
casual sophistication, I wore a cravat. A touch of Noël Coward in
Nevada. The fact that I remember the whole sartorial effort more
than thirty-seven years later shows the importance I attached to
the occasion. I stepped down, me and the cravat, from the plane,
and spotted Dana, who looked delicious. Maybe it was the cravat
or my St James's Street brogues, but I decided that the situation
called for some clever remark with just a hint of a barb to it – a
kind of de Cicco special. Dana pulled up in a beautiful, brand-new
Chevrolet convertible, and before I realized it, I said, 'Where did
you get this bucket of bolts? Wouldn't you like a Cadillac?'

The offer was bogus as hell. I just thought it sounded good.

'Mr Broccoli, if I wanted a Cadillac, I would have bought a
Cadillac!'

Freeze. In two seconds flat I'd gone from one hundred and
seventy-five pounds of sun-tanned sophistication to Mr Broccoli
the smart-ass. Now I'm burbling something about Chevrolet
making great convertibles. Suddenly she turns and smiles at me
and normal relations have been restored. Dana has that civilized
dimension that judges people more by what they mean than by
what they actually say.

It must be obvious from what I've written that I was clearly in
love. It was my good fortune then, as it is now, that Dana felt the
same way about me. We'd both had misfortunes in marriage. We
now had a chance of happiness, and felt sure and secure in our
relationship. I gave her a ring, and we became engaged. Six weeks
later we were married. The wedding was held in Las Vegas in the
garden of our late friend Beldon Katleman and his then wife
Mildred. Cary Grant was best man. Dana's son, Michael, about
sixteen at the time, came down from school. And he knew the
rituals. The night before the wedding, he said to his mother, 'Mom,
how about Cubby having the traditional stag night out on the
town tonight? Cary and I will go with him.'

Dana thought it was a great idea, but Cary backed off.

'I've got to get up early tomorrow, so I'm going to hit the sack
early,' he said. 'And you'd better do the same.'

But Michael was in Vegas, and I saw this as a great opportunity
to get to know him better. I learned in a flash what an alert and
mature mind there was in that young head of his. Halfway through
the evening, he looked at me and said, 'You sure you want to go

through with this marriage?' He's sixteen, he's not yet at law school, and he's interrogating me!

'What do you mean, am I sure? Of course I'm sure. Why do you ask?'

'Well, you know, she hasn't been married for some time. She's a very independently minded lady. I'm saying this just so that you should know what you're getting into!'

I was taken aback, but there was an honesty about it which I liked.

'Yeah, I know what I'm getting into, Michael,' I said. 'And I think you and I are going to get along fine, too.'

My stag night then went into overdrive. It was now close to eight o'clock, I'd had no sleep, was hungover, and I was getting married at eleven. I called Cary Grant, who had been up for an hour gulping in the desert air and doing maybe a hundred push-ups.

'Sleep well?' he asked.

'Not a wink.'

He prescribed an instant steam bath. Beldon Katleman, my host, said this couldn't be arranged, because the attendants didn't arrive until noon. All three of us were wondering how the bride would react to Dr Jekyll appearing at the ceremony as Mr Hyde.

A jug of coffee, a hunk of pumpernickel and a cold shower later, I arrive, spruced up for the wedding. I feel a wreck, and look it. Dana looks fresh, stunning and ice-cool in the desert heat. The sun is hammering down on my head, my knees are folding, I don't know where I'm at, and Dana is looking at me. Cary is highly amused. Michael is begging for an aspirin. I glance round a haze of faces and spot Mike Romanoff, Tex Feldman, David May, Billy Wilkerson, Beldon and a lot of other friends. I have this sheepish grin of the remorseful sinner. The preacher is wilting in the heat. Finally the ceremony is over. It is June 21, 1959: the beginning of the happiest, most fulfilling period of my life.

TWELVE

Dana and I flew to London, and soon the warm thoughts of that wonderful wedding in Las Vegas faded into the hassle of making another motion picture. It was *The Trials of Oscar Wilde*, the last under the Warwick banner with Irving Allen. The success or failure of a film often hangs on a question of timing. Make the right subject at the wrong time, and though you might have Oscar-winning performances and material, you can die at the box office. Though we didn't exactly start from strength – we'd lost our shirts with the failed distribution company and had to finance this picture with our own money – we still thought we'd got it right.

We had barely announced the film when another company, headed by Gregory Ratoff, hustled an outfit together and also commenced a picture about Oscar Wilde. This led to a spirited skirmish between opposing lawyers, but with neither side backing down it became a race to see who would be first in the cinemas. Though being second could be damaging – even a bad film on the same subject could act as a spoiler – it didn't worry me unduly. In the end the better picture would be the winner. What mattered was getting a good script, a sensitive director and an actor who could bring out the complex dimensions of the central character. This is decision time for a producer. Wrong choices in those three key elements can be fatal.

In the event, we had an embarrassment of riches. We engaged Britain's Ken Hughes to both direct the film and write the screenplay. A shortish, physical lightweight, with the pallor of the dedicated indoor man, Hughes was imaginative and exactly right. He had flair and above all, judgement. The script he produced against the clock, under extreme pressure, was brilliant. It demanded an actor of the same calibre to match it. We chose the late Peter Finch, and I am not the only one who believes that as Oscar Wilde he gave the performance of his life. Hughes based his script on John Fernald's play *The Stringed Lute*, and on *The Trials of Oscar Wilde* by Montgomery Hyde.

We set Ken a shooting schedule of just six weeks. It was asking for the moon, but he came through. First, there was a complete fusion between his ideas as the writer and his vision as the director. Second, he had a supremely professional cast. Alongside Peter Finch were James Mason as the shrewd prosecuting attorney, Carson; John Fraser as 'Bosie' (Lord Alfred Douglas), who viciously destroys Wilde; and Lionel Jeffries as Bosie's father, the Marquis of Queensberry. They were all excellent.

But the revelation was Peter Finch, who mastered one of the most subtle and demanding roles an actor ever faced. He got Wilde absolutely right: the degeneracy, the flamboyance and the tragedy. I have never known an actor prepare himself for a part as thoroughly as Finch did. He had to transform his slim, rugged, Australian looks into the paunchy effeminacy of the self-indulgent aesthete. He put on fourteen pounds, eating a lot of bread and potatoes and drinking maybe a half bottle of whisky a day. The liquid intake gave him no problem whatsoever. He read everything about Oscar Wilde, and everything Wilde had written. At one time, when he was reading some of Wilde's poems, he actually broke into violent sobbing. Somehow Wilde's personal agony, the scandalous self-destruction of a genius, had got to him. And it was all there, beautifully portrayed, in his performance.

I knew instinctively, after the final scene, that we'd made a damn good movie. Just how good, was yet to emerge. Disaster comes in various guises. It was the sort of picture which demanded a special kind of promotion; a fashionable audience, with maybe a late supper at the Café Royal, where Wilde, the brilliant wit, once held forth. But we had to be content with a midnight showing for a single charity performance. Even the circuits were grudging in their bookings, despite the critical praise coming from all sides. Margaret Hinxman, one of Britain's most respected critics, wrote: 'The battle of the Wilde Ones is over, with a clear-cut victory for *The Trials of Oscar Wilde*. It is one of the finest film biographies I've ever seen. Its merit rests on the monumental performance of Peter Finch as Wilde...'

Paul Dehn wrote in the *News Chronicle*: 'How knowingly we all scoffed at the casting of Peter Finch as Wilde! And how formidably Peter Finch wiped the grin off our faces in the picture's first minute, reducing us thereafter to that happy state of credulity where a performance ceases to be an impersonation and the actor becomes the man.' While Derek Monsey, in the *Daily Express*, referred to Finch's '...magnificent acting right up in the Olivier class', and added: 'Directed with a startling and almost insolently brilliant bravado by Ken Hughes who also wrote the script; photographed in colour at times of a breathtaking beauty; redolent of the vulgarity, the artificiality, the nostalgia and also the decadence of the nineties, this is a tremendous film. One of which the British film industry can...and should...be proud.'

I, for one, was proud. This picture deserved to do well. It had earned, through Peter Finch's performance alone, a worldwide audience and total exhibitor support in the United States. Which brings us back to the question of timing. Would the susceptibilities of the American public – as perceived by the chicken-hearted distributors – stand up to the homosexual revelations which were central to Wilde's downfall? Today critics would probably say our film wasn't explicit enough. In the spring of 1960 all kinds of moral pressure groups closed ranks against us. At the head of this self-righteous battalion were the Legion of Decency. An anachronism today, but twenty-five or thirty years ago, if a movie didn't have the Legion's seal of approval, distributors treated it like a leper.

Loew's were delighted with the picture, but feared a damaging backlash from the Mothers of America, Alan Ladd's Boy Scout lobby and all the other organizations who failed to recognize the integrity of the picture. They insisted we remove the scene in the courtroom where Carson challenges Wilde:

'Mr Wilde...did you know this valet?'

'Yes, I knew him.'

'Did you give him a cigarette case?'

'Yes, I gave him a cigarette case.'

'Did you kiss him, Mr Wilde?'

'Good heavens, no! He was too ugly!'

I refused to remove that scene from the picture. Without it, the whole prosecution case made no sense. The result was, the Protestant, the Catholic and the Jewish organizations all came out publicly against the film. The best we could hope for was isolated bookings in art houses – this despite the fact that Wilde was required reading in almost every American school. We finally managed to get several bookings in New York, and then the Paramount Theater in Hollywood. The night the booking geniuses selected for the West Coast opening was the eve of the Day of Atonement, the most sacred day of the year in the Jewish calendar. Not the day when thoughts of worshippers dwell on the likes of Oscar Wilde.

Ken Hughes, Dana and I drove up to the cinema, which is opposite Grauman's Chinese Theater. The big arc lights they reserve for the big openings swept the night sky. But there wasn't a soul in town, and scarcely anyone in the theatre. We had made a picture that would win awards throughout the world. But when we sat down, we counted fifteen people in this huge cinema. We sat there, Dana and I, holding hands, and I don't mind confessing, we wept. I don't remember whether we sat through the picture or not. What I do remember is that my practical and devoted Dana pulled me away from the scene of the disaster, into a pub next door. As I recall, the establishment specialized in semi-lethal Hawaiian mixes. I also remember we had lots of them. I suppose we were more angry than anything else.

We weren't alone in this. Ken Hughes had been brilliant. To have directed and scripted a film of this calibre, then see it die in a virtually empty theatre in Los Angeles, must have sickened him. The actors, too – Finch, especially – had to feel that they'd been robbed. Dana and I flew back to London for the real clincher: the film had won three major British awards, and seven awards in Moscow. But I was up against the wall. My partnership with Irving Allen was over. We had disagreed professionally, though personally it was a good, indeed very warm, relationship. We were able to shake hands and go our separate ways without hard feelings. Now we had to find our own way out of the debris. The total impact of the several reverses I'd suffered raised a serious question: is this the end of Cubby Broccoli in the film business? Justified or not, that is the thought that went through my mind. The film company we had created had gone, taking most of my money with it. I had several ideas floating around, but no resources to develop them. If nothing materialized, I would have to wrap up and take the family back to America. And Dana was expecting a baby.

I don't panic in these situations. But all these nagging thoughts resolved into one question: where the hell do I go from here? It was then I saw in full perspective the many qualities of Dana Broccoli. I could see then, as I have appreciated ever since, that whatever happened in my life and career, I would never have to go it alone. Dana would always be in there, as resourceful an aide as any husband could hope to have in his corner.

After the disastrous opening in Hollywood we flew back to London depressed and apprehensive. In that year, 1960, I was a producer with nothing to produce. Short on funds, prospects nil and with a pregnant wife. I remember pacing the floor in our apartment at Fountain House, London, in the middle of the night. The crisis was not just a question of money or lack of creative ideas: my confidence had taken a beating. Any producer would have felt the same, seeing a picture hailed as a masterpiece die the death through bad timing and mischievous, uninformed campaigning. Dana heard me wandering around the apartment; she had her sleepless nights too. She got up and we sat together in the kitchen.

'Look Cubby,' she said. 'Something's bound to turn in your favour. You've proved yourself as a film-maker. You're a hard worker. You may have lost your money, but not your energies and talent. If it comes to it I can rent my house in California, sell my jewellery. You're not alone. I have the strongest feeling that this is just the beginning for you. Something will happen.' Dana's words were not just a booster shot of some magnitude from a very devoted wife: she turned out to be a prophet, too. Something did happen – and beyond anything I could have imagined.

It is the nature of our business that whenever it spawns a really sensational success, all kinds of characters come out of corners to claim credit for it. The emergence of James Bond, first as a movie, then as a landmark and finally as legend, is a prime example of that syndrome. Accounts of the Bond phenomenon have filled acres of newsprint, produced several coffee-table books, been the subject of TV specials and fuelled a media bonanza for more than thirty-five years. What has never been told with any accuracy is how it all really happened. It began, as I recall, with a conversation. Wolf Mankowitz, a gifted British novelist and scriptwriter, met with me to discuss a script we'd been working on together called *Arabian*

Nights Adventure, an idea I had suggested to him.

I felt pretty exhilarated that week. Dana had given birth to a lovely baby girl, Barbara, who had her mother's large eyes and beautiful skin. And now our family was complete. After we were married Dana came to London. She was thrilled at the thought that Tina and Tony were there, part of the good-sized family she always wanted. I remember her telling me, long before, that after her first marriage ended she hoped that if she married again it would be to a man who already had children. She and her son Michael had always been close and affectionate. Dana opened her arms to Tina and Tony so that they would feel part of the family from the very beginning. That is why she insisted on officially adopting them. This was partly because of her natural maternal feelings towards them; but, more importantly, she wanted it made clear that if anything happened to me she would be completely responsible for them as if they were her own children. She feels no differently today. Dana is a very sensitive person and could see the situation from Tina and Tony's perspective. No matter how much joy we wanted to create for them and around them, there was bound to be a sense of loss and a feeling of hurt. Dana was sensitive to those feelings, just as she hoped, when they grew up, they would be to hers. But it was going to require a lot of love and understanding.

I now had a look at Wolf Mankowitz's script – with no great enthusiasm, as I recall. No reflection on the writer, but it's a long and difficult haul from an idea to an acceptable shooting script. Wolf felt he could tailor *Arabian Nights Adventure* into a commercial proposition given some humour and hokum. But the more I turned the pages, the less I liked the idea. I didn't see it as the sort of subject that could turn the corner for me.

'I'm sorry, Wolf,' I said finally, 'but I really can't finish this script. It's OK, but it's not something I think I can make into a picture. I think we'd better drop it.'

Wolf nodded.

'That's all right, Cubby. Have you got anything else in mind?'

'Yes. I've always had this urge to film Ian Fleming's James Bond books.'

'Why don't you? Nobody else seems to want to make them.'

I recounted the events of a year earlier, when I'd tried to secure the option: how I'd been forced to leave the negotiations to my partner, and how these had proved to be abortive.

'I tried to get the properties, but someone else has the options on them now,' I explained.

'I know who that is,' Wolf said, 'but I don't believe he can make it. He hasn't been able to put a deal together, and I think he only has about thirty days of the option left. You must know Harry Saltzman?'

'I've never met Harry Saltzman.'

'Well, I know Harry. Why don't I arrange for you to meet him?'

'OK, you do that. Whenever you can arrange it, I'll meet him.'

I got back to my apartment and Wolf telephoned me to say, 'Harry is coming in tomorrow morning to see you in your office.'

[Harry Saltzman, a Canadian by birth, with a background in the legitimate theatre, was an exponent of what was called the 'kitchen-sink' movies, because of their stark and basic realism. He was behind such films as *Look Back in Anger*, *Saturday Night and Sunday Morning*, and the Olivier classic *The Entertainer*. Shaped like a well-fed mandarin, watchful eyes set in a roundish face, Saltzman was a very colourful character indeed. In his progress towards becoming a successful independent producer, he appeared to have picked up the abrasiveness and verbal blitzing associated with the 'Big Producer' stereotype.

Harry could, however, also be as benign as a favourite uncle, though this fell short of actually twinkling. He considered himself to be a gourmet of class, occasionally infuriating friends he entertained by sending back their meals as they were poised to take the first bite. It would be said of him later that, had he been at the Last Supper, he would have sent the food back. So, cherub he most assuredly was not. And at the time he was scheduled to meet Cubby Broccoli, Harry had problems.

First, the option he had secured on the Bond properties was fast running out. Second, the era of the kitchen-sink drama was fast going down the drain. Incontestably, they were well made, and produced talent on the scale of Richard Burton and Albert Finney. But the public was weary of the turgid bellyaching Britain's *cinéma vérité* appeared to focus on. So in his own way, Saltzman, too, was at the crossroads. Yet there could not have been two more contrasting individuals meeting for the first time in a Mayfair office.]

Harry Saltzman turned up, but surprisingly, he didn't want to talk about James Bond. He said to me, 'Look, I've got a terrific story. I wrote a synopsis. It's a great idea, and we can do it together. I'd like to go into business with you.'

'Mr Saltzman, thanks and all that, but I really don't want to go into business with anybody. I've just come out of a partnership, and I'm not eager to go back into one.'

Harry Saltzman wasn't easily dissuaded.

'Well, when you and I get going, we'll be great. I know you're a nice, easygoing guy and I'm an easygoing guy, so we'll get along fine.'

'I'm only interested, Mr Saltzman, in the Fleming options you have. If you haven't been able to put it together...'

'Nah! The Fleming books are a bit of nonsense!'

I remember that phrase, 'a bit of nonsense'. Nor could I forget the alternative scenario he was suggesting.

'I've got another story I've been working on. It's called *Rapture in My Rags*. It's about a scarecrow.'

'A what ?'

'A scarecrow.'

'Look, Mr Saltzman, Wolf Mankowitz told me that you might be interested in selling me your option on the Fleming books.' (This meant all the titles with the exception of *Casino Royale*, which had been sold earlier.)

Harry hedged around, then finally said, 'Listen, I don't need money. I'm in good shape: I've just finished *Look Back in Anger* and...'

I let all that pass. What mattered to me was following my hunch that Fleming's books, James Bond, had great film potential. I could see that the only way I could proceed with the project was by going into partnership with Harry. For better or for worse I was reluctant, and it showed. But the danger was, if he dropped the option someone else might immediately pick it up. I was convinced that sooner or later others would catch on to 007. Rather than take that chance – Harry might even have considered renewing the option – I agreed to go into business with him.

'We'll make a deal,' he said. 'We'll draw up a piece of paper now.'

Mark Elms, who had been managing director of Warwick Films, was still working in that office. Harry talked to him and brought out this piece of paper.

He said cheerfully, 'You'll have forty-nine per cent, I'll have fifty-one per cent.'

I said less cheerfully, 'No, Mr Saltzman. If you want to make the deal with you having fifty-one per cent, forget it.'

Saltzman half smiled. 'What's the difference? It's only a couple of per cent.'

'Look, Harry, forget it!'

'All right, we'll have it drawn up. Fifty-fifty.'

'Fine.'

We shook hands. I left with the distinct feeling that this was going to be an interesting partnership. It was agreed between us that I would leave for New York in two days to discuss a possible deal with Arthur Krim of United Artists. I had, in fact, made a prior arrangement with Mike Frankovich of Columbia Pictures to discuss Bond with them. But I suspected this would be no more than a formality, since their interest in the books was zero. I wasn't sure how much Krim knew about the Bond books, either. His nephew, David Picker, however, a young and eager man, had read all Fleming's works, so I knew I had someone in there who would be primed on the discussions.

'Don't you think I should be there?' Harry asked me.

'Of course, if you wish,' I said. 'We'll go together.'

Arthur Krim, the civilized, powerful chief executive of United Artists, had made encouraging noises over the phone about the Bond idea. He said he looked forward to making a picture with me. I told him I'd be bringing my partner, Harry Saltzman. The name rang no bells, but that was OK with him. We should both come in and make a deal.

We flew to New York, me with Dana, Harry with his wife Jacqui. At the appointed hour, Harry and I entered Arthur Krim's office. I wasn't prepared for the battalion of executives he'd assembled for the discussions. With Krim were his partner Bob Benjamin, David Picker and all the publicity chiefs: clearly they felt they were on to something big. They spoke in awesome terms about sums approaching $1 million. (Twenty years later they'll be casually mentioning billions.) With all that top brass on show, I felt excited. Churning away in my mind was the absolute conviction that James Bond was going to be a revelation in motion pictures. We had some argument about the music rights: no small item in the logistics of film-making, for many a movie has produced gold discs from its soundtrack. They insisted on owning all the music rights, since they were putting up all the money. We countered by saying we had our own music company. 'In that case,' they declared, 'you may as well leave now. We're prepared to talk about everything else, but not about the music rights.'

The budget was agreed at $1 million. Our share of the profits – after they had recovered their investment – would be sixty per cent for us, forty per cent for them. We all shook hands. We had a deal. It had taken no more than thirty-five or forty minutes. I was thrilled. This was going to be a major production, backed by a famous company, aimed at world audiences. I couldn't wait to break the news to Dana. But as we walked out, I observed that my new-found partner appeared disgruntled.

'Harry, we did it!' I said. 'That's the fastest goddamn deal I ever made in my life!'

'We haven't got a deal,' he replied.

'What do you mean, we haven't got a deal?'

'We'd better go over to see Frankovich and Leo Jaffe at Columbia.'

Although this would be only a formality, Columbia having expressed no enthusiasm for the idea, Krim and I agreed that I should go to them to get their blessing for the UA deal. I would have done so anyway out of loyalty to a studio with whom I'd had a long and successful relationship. Krim respected that obligation. I would go there for that reason, but also to appease my highly apprehensive partner. We walked over to the Columbia offices on Fifth Avenue. There were some lively exchanges between Columbia executives and Saltzman which made me wonder a bit about the future of my partnership with him. But as I forecast, Columbia had no interest in Bond, releasing me from any obligation to them. I felt relieved. Krim had given his word. I was back in business.

My partner still seemed unconvinced, however. I said, 'Look, Harry, we shook hands with Arthur Krim. I've known him for many years. He's an honourable man. What he says, he means.' But I couldn't persuade him. He demanded something more tangible than Krim's word. 'OK, Harry, wait right here,' I said, and went back in alone to see Arthur Krim.

Krim, who was on the phone, looked up. 'What is it, Cubby?'

'I know this may sound odd,' I said, 'but could you do me a favour? Can you draw up a letter of agreement, a letter of intent, just setting out the terms of the agreement?'

'Yes, of course I can. When are you getting back to London?'

'I'll be back in London in about a week, but I don't want it in London. I'd like you to draw it up so that I can have it tonight.'

He leaned back, staring at me. 'What do you mean, tonight?'

I felt uncomfortable. 'Just a letter, Arthur, broadly stating what we have done, outlining the agreement.'

'But Cubby, you have my word.'

'Of course, Arthur, I know I have. But don't ask me to explain anything. I just would like to have that letter, if you could draw it up by tonight or tomorrow morning.'

He paused thoughtfully, and then smiled. 'Oh yes, Cubby, I understand,' he said. 'You'll have that piece of paper in your hotel tonight.'

That hazard out of the way, I raced back to the Hampshire House to share the good news with Dana.

'Let's celebrate, on the town,' I said. We had a drink at the Sherry Netherland, and then went on to the El Morocco. Dana was smiling curiously at me, though I was too pleased at the turn of events to question why.

'Let's have some champagne,' I said.

'Yes...let's!' Her tone was decidedly meaningful. The champagne arrived.

'What'll we drink a toast to?' she said.

'Let's drink to Barbara, the baby.'

We did, and then we drank to the success of the negotiations. I thought that about wrapped things up. Then Dana asked me, 'Do you know what today is?'

'Yes,' this genius responded. 'It's the first day of summer, June 21.' We raised our glasses.

'Now I'll make a toast,' Dana said. 'Happy wedding anniversary!' It was our second, and I had forgotten it. Every husband will know the semi-paralysis that sets in on being confronted by his wife with this information. The temptation to bluster it out is irresistible.

'Oh yes, I know,' I burbled. 'Happy anniversary!' (It was just as well they didn't have lie detectors at the El Morocco.) Dana kissed me and laughingly exited to powder her nose. I called Joe, the head waiter, over. 'You've got to get a cake on this table before my wife gets back from the powder room.'

'But Mr Broccoli...'

'Joe, I will never come to this joint again unless you have a cake with "Happy Anniversary, Dana" on it, and in minutes!'

Joe delivered. Panic over. Back at the hotel, Arthur Krim's letter had arrived. The deal. James Bond, 007 was about to make his first tentative step onto the world stage. It would change sensationally several lives, not least my own.

[The sequence of events which brought the world of James Bond into Cubby Broccoli's orbit began with its creator, Ian Fleming. Ian Lancaster Fleming (Eton, Sandhurst, Boodles) relished the good life which his grandfather's banking-house fortune had ensured. Tall, sardonic, with hooded eyes that had seen as much green baize as green pastures, Fleming was the favourite of the Mayfair set. He was the archetypal product of the English public school, in which the flaying of bare buttocks was held to be good for the character and the survival of the Empire. Scheduled to be birched at Eton one summer noon, Fleming asked the headmaster whether the punishment could be brought forward to eleven forty-five, to allow him to compete in the marathon. He cantered through the race in bloodstained shorts. It was the kind of stiff-upper-lip bravado which, together with his military background – father killed in World War I, brother in World War II – guaranteed his acceptance into British Naval Intelligence.

He was a gifted writer, a born reporter, an expert skin-diver, a sound bridge player and a marksman – all of which combined to make him irresistible to hostesses and heiresses, and they to him. Fleming's appreciation of sex as an art form, as well as a basic human activity, was evident in his writings, his conversation and, notably, in his chambers off London's Fleet Street. A gold-painted nude, one eye glancing coyly over an eighteen-carat shoulder, looked down from the Regency-striped wall. Other topless beauties were deployed among the rare books, *objets d'art*, or alongside a quill pen on a rare antique desk. The long cigarette-holder, the spotted bow-tie, well-worn dispatch case and the shiny revolver on the inkstand completed the image. Whether Bond was modelled on Fleming, or the other way round, was academic. Clearly the two-tone décor of the esoteric and the erotic was basic to 007, the universally popular hero of postwar fiction.

The story of how James Bond was created places the time: January 1952; and the location: his home GoldenEye, in Oracabessa, Jamaica. Stuck for a name to give the hero of a novel he is working on, Fleming searches around for the 'dullest name I could find'. His eye lights on a coffee-table book, *Birds of the West Indies*, written by an ornithologist, James Bond. Perfect. Short, authoritative and masculine. Fleming steals it, and the novel is completed. It was written, Fleming would say later, 'in a moment of intense boredom'. He was a shade more specific to this writer: 'It was quite extraordinary, really. I invented him to take my mind off that appalling business of getting married at the age of forty-three. (He married Anne Rothermere, divorced from Lord Rothermere, in 1952, in Jamaica. Noël Coward and his secretary were witnesses.) 'It was rather a dramatic step for a confirmed bachelor to take, and I created Bond to sort of insulate myself against the shock.' It was pure Fleming.

Twelve years and eleven books later, the hero of this bachelor boy's antidote to marital shock has become a household name; and two actors who were then scarcely in the Olivier class were close to becoming multimillionaires. The initial attempts to translate Fleming's lightly pitched novels to the screen were abortive. Sir Alexander Korda, the Hungarian producer who helped substantially to create a film industry in Britain, had asked Fleming to send him a copy of *Live and Let Die*. He read it, and returned it with thanks. CBS paid $1,000 for the rights to make a single, one-hour TV production of *Casino Royale*. It starred Barry Nelson, and sank without trace.

The first real movie interest came from actor-director Gregory Ratoff. (Years later, he would make the 'rival' Oscar Wilde film, with disastrous results.) Ratoff bought the film rights of *Casino Royale*. But there is a vast stretch of territory between owning the rights to a film and getting it onto the screen. Ratoff couldn't find a studio interested in developing the subject. Eventually he died, bequeathing the rights to *Casino Royale* to his widow. These were then bought by agent-turned-producer Charles Feldman, who also represented Ratoff. The outcome, unhappily for Feldman, was dismal. Fleming was also courted by Henry Morgenthau III, a wealthy dilettante working at the time as a television producer for

NBC. According to John Pearson, in *The Life of Ian Fleming*, Morgenthau wanted Fleming to write a series of half-hour adventures, provisionally entitled *Commander Jamaica*, named after the location where they would be filmed. The character was clearly based on James Bond. But the idea foundered, drawing the wry comment from Fleming: 'The film and television world in America is a hell of a jungle, and I know how long is the road between specious promises and the actual signing of a contract.'

In 1958 an American, Ivar Bryce, a lifelong friend of Ian Fleming, introduced the writer to a young, rakish Irishman named Kevin McClory. Ambitious and shrewd behind the smile permanently riveted to his Nassau tan, McClory had learned much from working with Mike Todd as associate producer and foreign location director on *Around the World in Eighty Days*, and also as boom operator for Cubby Broccoli on *Cockleshell Heroes*. He had also been a close friend and confidant of John Huston. Todd's hype and Huston's genius were a valuable apprenticeship for McClory's own venture into film production.

McClory and Bryce joined forces to make the film *The Boy and the Bridge*. Bryce liked McClory's style and gave him some of Fleming's novels to read. This led to discussions with Fleming about the possibility of filming Bond. Much of the discussion took place in McClory's home in London's Belgravia, where a black butler supervised the meals and the dubious hygiene of a pet monkey and a green macaw. This alone seemed guaranteed to make McClory Fleming's kind of man. There was a lot more talking between the three, Fleming, Bryce and McClory, which finally produced a decision. They would combine to make the first James Bond feature film, provisionally titled *James Bond, Secret Agent*. Because Fleming had had little experience writing for the screen, a British scriptwriter, Jack Whittingham, was brought in to work on the story. But there were interminable delays, and Fleming became increasingly disenchanted with the idea, if not with McClory himself.

Fleming viewed with some distaste the vibes he was getting from the whole affair. As he wrote to Bryce, 'Showbiz is a ghastly biz and the last thing I want is for you to lose your pin-striped trousers in its grisly maw...' There were now more disagreements over the project. During the hiatus Fleming wrote another book, *Thunderball*, in which he used material, according to McClory, based on ideas in their film script. When the book was published and Kevin saw no acknowledgement to this effect, he petitioned the High Court for an injunction. This, too, dragged on. (It was finally settled in December 1963.) The James Bond books, with the exception of *Casino Royale*, were still on the market. Fleming badly needed to sell them. His precarious health was causing his wife and son increasing concern. Ian was anxious to set up a trust fund for them. He was also determined to upgrade the value of the film rights, which, in the case of *Casino Royale*, had been pitched at the ludicrously low figure of $6000 that Ratoff paid.

Though Harry Saltzman had secured the options, after five months these still remained in limbo. It was at this point that Cubby Broccoli, renewing his early quest for Bond, entered the arena. He talked with United Artists, and this resulted in the deal on which Arthur Krim gave his word, obligingly put in writing to appease Harry Saltzman. The three main characters in the project were unlikely bedfellows. We have the disdainful old Etonian, Ian Fleming, cautiously embracing in public the showbiz he privately despised; Harry Saltzman, the volatile producer, not instantly amenable to dissenting viewpoints; and Cubby Broccoli himself, called upon to orchestrate patiently, not always painlessly, the disparate elements involved. In the event, Cubby's sure footwork would prove to be vital to the creation – and sustaining – of the legend.]

THIRTEEN

A producer starts out on any picture hoping it's going to be great, but with an uneasy gut feeling that maybe he could be wrong. I had the same emotions as I embarked on the first Bond film, *Dr No* – not that I had any doubts that the Fleming stories were great box office. Yet I couldn't ignore the fact that they had been around for a long time, and that none of the leading British and American producers had made a serious pitch for them. A couple of major US TV networks had burned their fingers, and the Rank Organisation came in – and out. Yet here were Harry and I, with a company called Eon Productions, offices in London's fashionable Mayfair and a tight budget of $1 million, rushing in where angels – and Columbia Pictures – had feared to tread.

This is as good a place as any to set one particular record straight. I must state emphatically that although there have been many people claiming to have invested in the first Bond film, this is pure fantasy. United Artists were pleased, in fact eager, to put up all the money for the picture and wanted no other investors or participants involved. There was just no need for it. In spite of that, a fair number of people have gone around claiming they put up money for *Dr No*. But maybe that shouldn't surprise me. Bandwagons tempt a lot of easy riders.

We had originally planned *Thunderball* as the first Bond film. In fact, we had Dick Maibaum write the script. But the day Dick completed it, Kevin McClory brought his injunction against Ian Fleming. United Artists were nervous about getting into a film with a controversy hanging over it, and rejected it. We then set out to make *Dr No*. Harry and I decided that, since Wolf Mankowitz was a fine writer and had acted as the marriage broker in our partnership, he deserved to have a crack at the screenplay.

The story centred on what seemed like science fiction at the time but is highly feasible today: an arch-villain's attempt to topple US space weapons by the use of sophisticated electronics. As Dr No was going to be 007's first, and most fiendish adversary, the situation called for a character of menacing dimensions. This was the brief which Wolf and his co-writer, Dick Maibaum, took away with them. They came back with a treatment which, since I love both these guys, I will simply say was unacceptable. They came over to the office and, as the four of us sat around reading the pages, I had that sinking feeling that my two friends, the geniuses, had blown this one. I searched through the lines for our definitive villain and couldn't find him. Understandably, since they had decided to make Dr No a monkey. I repeat: a monkey.

This threw Harry and me into some dismay. A million dollars was being invested in bringing James Bond to the screen. We didn't think that a monkey, even with a high IQ, could in any circumstances be 007's 'merciless antagonist'. Moreover, I didn't remember a monkey chittering around in Fleming's book, and I'm a great believer in not tampering with an original winner. Also, Harry and I didn't think United Artists would take kindly to the notion of Britain's most feared secret agent pitting himself against a spider monkey, however ingenious the plot. Consequently, the air was blue at the script conference. Dick remembered that meeting:

'When Wolf and I began working on the script, we decided that Fleming's Dr No was the most ludicrous character in the world. He was just Fu Manchu with two steel hooks. It was 1961, and we felt that audiences wouldn't stand for that kind of stuff any more. So, bright boys that we were, we decided that there would be no Dr No. There would be a villain who always had a little marmoset monkey sitting on his shoulder, and the monkey would be Dr No. We wrote the whole thing, about forty pages. Wolf and I thought it was marvellous, and we showed it to Cubby and Harry. Cubby was outraged, in his usual good-natured way. "You've got to throw the whole damn thing out. No monkey, d'you hear? It's got to be the way the book is!" He made a very strong point about it. Wolf withdrew; he just couldn't take it. Now I think about it, it was just a temporary collaborators' aberration. But Cubby wasn't going to forget it. Even now, fifteen films later, if we got into an argument – we argued all the time – he hit me with "DR NO IS A

MONKEY!", which I can't argue with, since he had the treatment on hand to prove it!'

With the monkey off his back, Dick, again with Wolf Mankowitz, rewrote the script (with me looking over their shoulder this time) to bring it more in line with Fleming's original story. Which was just as well, because Ian attended several of our meetings well before the picture started. It was good having him around. His whole persona, the way he held his cigarette, his laid-back style, that certain arrogance, was pure James Bond. He never interfered in any way. There was no agreement giving him approval of the scripts, but we let him see them just the same, partly as a courtesy but mainly because we valued his expertise. He was not concerned about the stories, but occasionally he'd make marginal notes in his minuscule handwriting, mostly on matters of protocol. For instance, Bond should never call M by that title in the Club; he should always address him as 'Admiral'.

Also, Ian took a close interest in the guns Bond used. He had become friendly with the gun expert Geoffrey Boothroyd, who had suggested changing Bond's personal armoury. For instance, he told the author that Bond shouldn't be armed with a .25 Beretta, which he regarded pretty much as a 'lady's gun'. He thought a Smith and Wesson .38 Centennial Airweight would be best for close encounters, and a Walther PPK 7.65mm or .357 Magnum for heavier stuff. (Ian 'rewarded' his expert friend by creating a character in his novels, Major Boothroyd, the armourer who kits out Bond for his dangerous exploits.)

Ian also enlightened us on the derivation of the label '007': the double zero signified that the agent had killed an enemy in personal combat, while the '7' specifically identified James Bond. He and I would talk exhaustively together about Bond over dinner or in our office. His concern with authenticity was evident in his novels. Harry and I wanted to get the same attention to detail in our whole approach to Bond.

After one of our meetings Ian sent me a fascinating memorandum which must be the definitive thesis on the way James Bond should be structured and played. Students of 007 will find Fleming's 'Editorial Notes' instructive. For instance: 'Atmosphere: To my mind, the greatest danger in this series is too much stage Englishness. There should, I think, be no monocles, moustaches, bowler hats or bobbies, or other "Limey" gimmicks. There should be no blatant English slang, a minimum of public school ties and accents, and subsidiary characters should, generally speaking, speak with a Scots or Irish accent. The Secret Service should be presented as a tough, modern organisation in which men may dress more casually than they do in the FBI. Above all they should not slap each other on the back or call each other "old boy". James Bond: James Bond is a blunt instrument wielded by a Government Department. He is quiet, hard, ruthless, sardonic, fatalistic. In his relationships with women he shows the same qualities as he does in his job, but he has a certain gentleness with them and if they get into trouble he is sometimes prepared to sacrifice his life to rescue them. But not always, and certainly not if it interferes with his job. He likes gambling, golf, and fast motor cars.' So, incidentally, did Ian – and guns, espionage and beautiful women, particularly in the uniform of the WRNS. He'd have given anything, I imagine, to have been James Bond.

The notes go on: 'Neither Bond nor his Chief, M, should initially endear themselves to the audience. They are tough, uncompromising men and so are the people who work for and with them.' Fleming continues with a detailed description of the headquarters of the British Secret Service, located, he recommended, on the entire upper floor of a modern block of offices with shops below. 'The list of other occupants of the building is innocuous: Universal Export, Central Radio Communications and so forth. Bond's secretary, formerly of the WRNS, should be attractive, sexy, but extremely efficient and rather severe. She would obviously look much prettier away from the office. She is inclined to mother Bond – brushes his coat and so forth. They have a friendly, businesslike relationship with occasional sparks of flirtation from Bond. The relationship...is rather similar to that between Perry Mason and Della Street. [My late friend borrowed from the best.] Bond's office, looking out over a park, should contain a number of office gadgets, such as a twenty-four-hour clock, Phonodeck, oddments like a shell-base for an ashtray, a shrapnel fragment as a paper-weight, three telephones, two black and one white – the latter direct with M and his Chief of Staff.' Also, M's clothes are described, right down to the bow-tie: dark blue with white spots.

And there was more, all wrapped in upper-class civility, in phrases like 'I am merely suggesting', 'with due humility' and 'I am sure this idea contains no grain of originality but...'. In fact, everything about Ian Fleming made him an 'original'. The success of the films, I have always believed, depended crucially on getting this authentic 'feel' behind the fanciful ideas, the spectacular stunts and the tongue-in-cheek dialogue. This is why we scoured the world for the perfect locations and built vast sets in meticulous detail, whatever the cost. It achieved the sort of visual impact television couldn't possibly compete with.

We had set Dr No's island fortress, Crab Cay, in the Caribbean. Here again, the author's concern with getting the detail right was helpful to us. Years before, Fleming had gone on a scientific expedition to survey the flamingo colony on the island of Inagua. Fleming never went anywhere in the world without noting every detail: the climate, the terrain, the local food, what the people looked like, especially the women. People marvelled at his output. They should have seen his input. He was curious about everything, never missed an opportunity to learn something from somebody.

Once, when we were flying together to a location, I thought I'd leave him alone on the plane to read some of the armful of books he carried with him.

I said, 'Now Ian, I know you like to read, so I'm going to sit in another seat and leave you alone.'

He replied, 'No, no, Cubby, I want you to sit next to me. There are a lot of things I want to ask you.'

And he did: about America, motion pictures, my own life – the genuine interest of a highly intelligent observer. He'd have made a great chat-show host. I felt it was an achievement to have secured the rights to Fleming's books, but it was a big bonus to the production to have this personal back-up from the man himself.

We also discussed casting with Ian. We still hadn't got our Dr No. An idea was floated that we get Noël Coward to play the role. It was an intriguing notion. The character required brains, sophistication and a kind of machiavellian wit. Ian thought it was a brilliant idea. I did, too. Since I didn't know Coward and Ian did, I asked him to cable our offer to Noël in Jamaica. He did so, and received a swift response by telegram: 'Dear Ian, The answer to your suggestion is No...No...No...No! Thank you. Love, Noël.'

The script was getting into shape, and the top priority now was to find the right director. There was no great stampede to take on the job. I asked Guy Green, then Guy Hamilton, both with fine track records, to consider directing the picture. They turned it down. I talked to Ken Hughes, who had directed *The Trials of Oscar Wilde* for me and won universal praise for it, but he declined. Maybe they all thought the idea wasn't good enough, corny perhaps. We finally offered the job to Terence Young, who had done such good work for me before. He was well educated, had done war service and had a rapport with the higher echelons of the British establishment – all useful to bringing out the subtleties of the James Bond character. He also needed the money. I mention this simply in the context of a reported claim of his that he, Terence Young, made Harry and me millionaires.

Terence was a good director; excellent, in fact. I wouldn't have chosen him to direct the picture if I thought otherwise. But, for the record, Harry Saltzman did not want Terence. Nor did United Artists. As I remember it, nobody wanted him except me. Even Ian Fleming, who knew Terence, was said to have had some misgivings. According to Michael Feeney Callan's biography of Sean Connery: 'With Young, whom he knew through mutual acquaintanceship with Noël Coward, Fleming was more cruelly honest – "So they decided on you to fuck up my work..." Young was not shaken: "Let me put it this way, Ian. I don't think anything you've written is immortal yet. Whereas the last picture I made won a Grand Prix at Venice. Now let's start even."' True or not, it didn't concern me. We hadn't hired Terence on the strength of awards gained in the rarefied circles of the Venice Film Festival. We had faith in his ability to put flesh and bones on what was basically a two-dimensional character. He could also write and help out with the dialogue, which is a much tougher challenge than it might seem.

Harry and I offered Terence a smaller (but still sizeable) salary, plus a percentage of the profits. He was adamant: he preferred the cash. That insistence is worth remembering when the Bond bandwagon begins to roll.

Wolf Mankowitz also had doubts. When the script was shown to him and he read it, his response was:

'Look, OK. You guys like the script? You do the script, but I don't want my name on it. And be sure to put that in writing. I want it in writing.'

I said, 'Fine. You're sure you want to do that?'

'Yes...I want to do that.'

'You don't want to wait till you see the picture?'

'No. I want my name off it. I don't want my name on a piece of crap, and that's a piece of crap!'

Dissolve. The picture is made, and Mr Mankowitz sees it. He calls me up and says, 'Listen, I'd like to change my mind on that. I'd like to have my name back on...'

'Wolf, the picture is complete. The titles are done. I can't afford to change all that now. Unless, of course, you're prepared to pay the costs involved...'

'No, no...the hell with it!'

To be fair to Mankowitz, misjudging the potentialities of a script, and the way the public will react to the film, is an occupational hazard in our business. [Wolf Mankowitz died May 21, 1998 in Ireland.] Getting the Bond script right was crucial. The balance between the spectacular action sequences, the focus on exotic locations and the interplay of the leading characters has to be meticulously fine-tuned. With Terence's own ideas thrown in, and useful contributions from Joanna Harwood and Berkely Mather, we finally came up with a finished screenplay.

We now had the toughest problem of all: finding the actor to play James Bond. As written by Fleming, Commander James Bond, CMG, RNVR had a Scottish father, Andrew Bond of Glencoe, and a Swiss mother, Monique Delacroix, from the Canton of Vaud. He went to Eton (like Fleming), where he got into trouble with one of the dormitory maids (which may also have been true of Ian, though I can't recall if he ever said so). Because of his father's work with an armaments firm in Europe, Bond speaks fluent German and French. He is an expert skier, and knows a lot about women, having lost his virginity in Paris at the age of sixteen.

Bond works for the Ministry of Defence in 1941, ending the war with the rank of commander. His flair for languages, his obvious taste for danger, his work at the Ministry and experience with the Royal Naval Volunteer Reserve all make him an ideal candidate for the British Secret Service. His CMG (Companion of the Order of St Michael and St George) was awarded for 'outstanding bravery and distinction', although occasionally he exhibits 'an impetuous strain to his nature, with a streak of the foolhardy that brought him into conflict with higher authority'. All this careful blocking out of the character is there in Fleming's books. The more I read them, the more mystified I was that a major company hadn't snatched them up sooner.

Fleming's physical descriptions of James Bond were also very well drawn. He saw him as 'very good looking. He reminds me rather of Hoagy Carmichael, but there is something cold and ruthless...' (*Casino Royale*, Chapter 5). 'His grey-blue eyes looked calmly back with a hint of ironical inquiry and the short lock of black hair which would never stay in place subsided to form a thick comma above his right eyebrow. With the thin vertical scar down his right cheek the general effect was faintly piratical...' (*Casino Royale*, Chapter 8). Fleming gives Bond's height as a little over six feet, his weight as around one hundred and sixty-seven pounds, and his build slim. Furthermore, the various descriptions confirm that Bond possesses 'dark, rather cruel good looks' and that women find him devastatingly irresistible. Well, we had our blueprint, but where was there an actor to fit it?

Harry and I were absolutely agreed upon one thing: Bond had to be British. There would be none of this business about making him Canadian so that we could use a top American star as a bait to the US market. Not that ideas like this weren't thrown at us. I talked to Cary Grant, who liked the project. He had the style, the sophistication and, in fact, had been born in Britain. He also happened to be a Bond aficionado. But he said no. As a very important actor and world-class star, he didn't feel he could lock himself into the Bond character. Anyway I felt strongly that we had to have an unknown actor, not a star; above all, a man you'd believe could be James Bond.

Rightly or wrongly, we were looking beyond *Dr No*. Maybe we were being wildly optimistic then, but we truly believed it would be a success and that there would be several more Bond pictures ahead. I guess that's the way all producers feel: that they're working on a winner. It's the way they ought to feel anyway.

Our theory was that if we cast a virtually unknown actor, the public would be more likely to accept him as the character. Also, we wanted to build the actor into the role, so that he would grow with it and wouldn't complain if we wanted him to do several more Bonds. (As it turned out, we were wrong. The complaining was loud and persistent.) Patrick McGoohan had been suggested, and might have made a fine Bond. But he was strongly religious, and was uneasy about sex and violence. In fact, in the Bond films these elements are tame compared with the widespread explicitness in movies these days. James Fox was also put forward, but he, likewise, was reluctant because of strong religious scruples. Roger Moore had also been touted as a possible Bond. But at that time I thought him slightly too young, perhaps a shade too pretty. He had what we called the 'Arrow collar' look: too buttoned-down smart. (I could see, though, that he would develop into the character we wanted, which indeed he did, and successfully, too.)

Other names entered the reckoning: Michael Redgrave, David Niven – even Trevor Howard, though I couldn't see Eton behind that wonderful craggy face of his. Harry and I were sure that we had to build on Fleming's 007, giving him coarser shading. Just as menacing, but more overtly masculine, and with a touch of humour. A dozen people claim that they discovered Sean. Fine. Maybe Columbus didn't discover America. The facts are simple, and worth the telling.

While all the discussions about the casting of Bond were going on, one face kept coming back into my mind. It belonged to an actor I had met briefly a year before in London.

He was Sean Connery, who at that time was making a film with Lana Turner, *Another Time, Another Place*. Lana introduced me to him at the house she was using during the filming. He was a handsome, personable guy, projecting a kind of animal virility. He was tall, with a strong physical presence, and there was just the right hint of threat behind that hard smile and faint Scottish burr. The movie he was making with Lana was poor, but it revealed other potential in Connery: a flair for wearing stylish clothes and an easy, confident style in front of the cameras. It was this image that persisted in my mind.

Back in Hollywood I arranged to see the only footage available on him, *Darby O'Gill and the Little People*, at Goldwyn Studios. It was a Disney film about leprechauns and suchlike. But Sean stood out in it. I phoned Dana to come down to see the picture. I wanted to confirm with her that Sean, an uncut diamond at the time, had the necessary sex appeal. Dana's reaction was immediate: 'That's our Bond!' She thought he would be absolutely ideal for the role, but imagined we would never get him, convinced that he must already be under contract. She was astounded when I told her this wasn't so. I knew that her judgement was spot on.

Sean's looks and explicit body language cast him irresistibly as 007. To be candid, all the British actors I had interviewed, while very talented, lacked the degree of masculinity Bond demanded.

To put it in the vernacular of our profession: Sean had the balls for the part. I was convinced he was the closest we could get to Fleming's super-hero. The character was written as a semi-sadistic operator, well manicured but with a streak of mercilessness about him. The more I thought of Connery, the more he seemed to fit the image we had of Commander James Bond, RNVR of the British Secret Service. I phoned Harry and told him to run some film on Sean, call his agent and invite the actor to our office in London to meet us on my return.

[Tommy Connery was born in an Edinburgh slum, a bottom drawer serving as his crib. His Irish father was a truck driver; his mother Effie was a Scottish char who went out to do housework for a large part of her life.

Connery went into the Navy at sixteen, and came out three years later with muscles like tow ropes and the build of a Roman gladiator. His affection for his parents and for the country of his birth was needlepointed with pride on his right forearm: tattooed in blue were 'Scotland Forever' and 'Mum and Dad'. (Only one other passion would get anywhere close, but Connery stopped short of having 'Arnold Palmer' tattooed on the other arm.)

If the best talent is compounded of an infinite variety of experiences, then Connery's tough apprenticeship was invaluable. Oddly, there was an intriguing similarity between his early life and Cubby Broccoli's. Like Cubby, Connery was born and raised in a tenement. For a short period, he was a French-polisher specializing in buffing up the lids of coffins. The only difference was that Connery was on the manufacturing side, whereas Cubby, through the Long Island Casket Company, was concerned with sales. Cubby remembers making a snow sleigh out of beer barrel staves. Connery used the offcuts from the caskets to make his. It was appropriately called 'The Coffin'. He still winces when he thinks about it. On its test run, it careered down a Scottish hillside and crashed into a tree. Fortunately, Connery's granite-hard head required only thirty-two stitches to repair the damage. Fears that the accident might in some way affect his personality were groundless. He emerged from the experience the same cheerful, wary, stubborn, two-fisted charmer as before.

Like Cubby Broccoli, Connery had a variety of jobs, all of which fashioned him – though he couldn't have been aware of it – for the compelling physical impact he would one day make as an actor. He drove a dray-horse hauling potatoes and corn. He did the early-morning rounds with a milkman, manhandling the bottles in metal crates along the Edinburgh streets. And there's an irony here. According to Fleming's stories, James Bond was expelled from the famous Scottish public school Fettes. Connery remembers delivering milk there, at the tradesmen's entrance. In the Navy he had led the boxing team. Later, for a while he was a steel bender, a labourer, then he became a lifeguard on a bleak stretch of beach on Scotland's Firth of Forth.

Connery was now a beautiful specimen of well-honed manhood: six foot two inches tall, with the biceps of a road driller and eyes like chipped anthracite. Here, but for the plebeian tattoos, was a Greek god. He came to London to compete in a Mr Universe contest and won the bronze medal. It seemed only natural after that for him to do part-time work at the Edinburgh Art College, posing in a G-string and pouch, for the students' life classes. For around 6 shillings and 8 pence, or 70 cents an hour – this was more than thirty years ago – Tommy Connery, all one hundred and eighty-five pounds of him, posed standing, or reclining on a plain wooden couch. This was not the body-conscious activity of a beefcake merchant. Connery needed the money. Every penny of his earnings, his mother would say proudly one day, went towards keeping the family afloat – another similarity between him and his mentor, Cubby Broccoli.

Friendships at the college brought him stage contacts. He had been interested in acting from the days when he used to visit the local flea-pit, the Blue Halls, near his home. At twenty-two, and now as Sean Connery, he managed to land a spot in the chorus of the London company of *South Pacific*. To get it demanded a two-day crash course in dancing, and determination. He was also a spear carrier in a touring version of the stage play *The Glorious Years*, starring Anna Neagle.

He was intelligent and learned fast, and did some useful work on stage and on television. He was already becoming aware that his Mr Universe image might well be counter-productive in the future. So he put himself through another crash course, this time in self-education. He took on Shakespeare, Ibsen, Pirandello and Proust, with a side order of James Joyce's *Ulysses* and the plays of Bernard Shaw. There was no immediate pay-off. The big break still eluded him.

As he told this writer at the time: 'I was either too tall, too heavy, too thin, too Scottish, too handsome, too ugly – one geezer even said I looked too Polish!' He was living in London then, at a former convent recently vacated by the twenty-five nuns of the Order of the Adoratrices. His entry into movies was tentative. *Action of the Tiger*, which, incidentally, was directed by Terence Young, did little to advance Sean's ambitions. Young himself admitted that the picture was 'pretty awful'. *Another Time, Another Place*, in which Sean had a leading role opposite Lana Turner, opened to mostly dire notices. It was supposed to have been the film that would give Connery an international showcase, especially in Hollywood. It did not. Three others, *Tarzan's Greatest Adventure*, *Frightened City* and *On the Fiddle*, were equally unmemorable, though Connery himself revealed increasing range and versatility as an actor. Only *Darby O'Gill and the Little People* alerted those shrewd enough to perceive it, that the actor had exciting potential.

The critic Freda Bruce Lockhart wrote at the time: 'It is a mystery to me why no film company has built Sean Connery into a great international star.' By 'film company' she meant Hollywood. They had this star material in their grasp, but had not seen it; just as 007 had been theirs for the taking years earlier. The situation was different now. Sean was about to meet two producers who had staked everything on James Bond and were prepared to do likewise for him – a virtually unknown actor with a somewhat indifferent track record.

As he strode along Park Lane, then into South Audley Street, he had the usual actor's apprehensions. And hopes. But never in his most fanciful imaginings could he have seen their dazzling outcome. History, never mind fortunes, was about to be made.]

Connery walked into our office wearing a brown, open-necked shirt and suede shoes, and had a strength and energy about him which I found riveting. Physically, and in his general persona, he was too much of a rough-cut to be a replica of Fleming's upper-class secret agent. This suited us fine, because we were looking to give our 007 a much broader box-office appeal: a sexual athlete who would look great in Savile Row suits, but with the lean midriff of a character who starts his day with twenty push-ups. Everything about Connery that day was convincingly James Bond. Harry and

I asked him a lot of questions. His answers, in that very appealing Scottish accent of his, were friendly and direct. There was no conceit to him, and no false modesty, either. He didn't come on in the style of a classical actor who thought James Bond was a little too down-market for his talents. Well, not in those days anyway. In fact, he had read Fleming and thought Bond had great box-office potential. There was, though, a slight change of tone in him when we got around to talk about specifics: the image we wanted to create and the money he expected to earn.

The way Bond dressed was intrinsic to the character. We're talking about an ex-Eton type who mixed with the aristocracy, belonged to the most exclusive clubs, gambled at Monte Carlo and wore handmade silk shirts and Sea Island cotton pyjamas. Our search for James Bond was over. Connery had strong notions about the money he was getting. Money and Mr Connery combined to become quite a problem a few years on, but I think there's a point to be made here. Sean has claimed we didn't pay him enough – which is odd, considering the millions that he earned. The fact is, we paid him to the limit within the budget that we were given. When you are making a picture for one million dollars, salaries have to be in line with it. We didn't pay anybody a big salary in that first picture. We were taking a leap into the dark with an untried subject and an actor who still had to make his mark internationally. I never had any doubts about his talents, but we still had to see whether these would capture audiences the world over, particularly in America.

We had tried to persuade Terence Young to take a smaller salary and a piece of the picture, but he didn't want it that way. But everybody else accepted that, on a strictly limited production budget, big salaries were out. When we explained this to Sean the discussion became very lively. He started hammering the desk, his accent becoming even broader: 'I want fooking so much or I won't do the fooking picture! I won't work for fooking nothing!' And so forth. It was quite a performance. Privately, I was quite amused by it. And I gather that Sean himself admitted some time later that it had been a bit of an act. But it all ended in a friendly way. We agreed on his salary, and he walked out happy. He'd have been even happier if he had known that a couple of years later he would be a millionaire.

Terence Young had been promoting the idea of getting that polished British actor Richard Johnson to play Bond. It was a valid idea, but we thought Connery a much more exciting proposition. We had made up our minds, and called Terence in to tell him. He again pressed us to consider Johnson.

I said, 'No, we have already signed somebody.'

'Who?' he asked.

'Sean Connery,' I told him.

'Oh, disaster, disaster, disaster!' was Young's initial reaction. He based this assessment, I imagine, on the film Sean made with him, *Action of the Tiger*. Whether he was querying Sean's acting ability or his suitability as Bond wasn't clear. In any event, he slowly came round to the idea of Sean as Bond, got into the spirit of it and was helpful in the development of the character.

We brought Sean Connery down to Pinewood to shoot some footage of him with various young actresses we were considering for the picture. For some reason Sean wouldn't make a screen test for us. We couldn't understand why he objected, particularly in those days. A screen test doesn't mean you have doubts about the talents of an actor or actress. What it means is that you're bringing a third eye into the proceedings: the camera. It can tell you plenty about what you have and how to shoot it. Still, Sean didn't want to test, but he agreed to our shooting some footage of him with some of the girls we were testing for the film.

We sent some of this material to United Artists in New York, to David and Arnold Picker and the rest of the top brass there. They sent back a telegram: 'NO – KEEP TRYING.' We dug our heels in then. We wired back, insisting that Connery was the man we wanted and we weren't searching any further. Ian Fleming also had initial misgivings about our selection of Sean for Bond. He'd seen *The Saint* series and considered Roger Moore, visually at least, closer to his own concept of the character. Maybe at first he saw Sean as too raw and physical for his high-born ex-public school hero. Later, however, he conceded that Sean was excellent in the role.

Once we had signed Sean Connery – for one Bond film and one non-Bond picture a year – we threw everything into grooming him for the part. We wanted to bring out all those features which are the unmistakable James Bond hallmark. The casual but well-cut suits, the black, soft-leather moccasins – 007 would never tie a shoelace – the silk kimonos – all these were carefully designed to work the Bond style into Sean's macho image.

It is important to understand that we never intended to play Sean Connery exactly as Fleming's Bond: the university graduate, the gentleman and all that. If we had wanted that kind of character, then we might have considered Richard Johnson, or someone in the David Niven mould. The whole point about having Sean in the role, with his strong physical magnetism and the overtones of a truck driver, was that it thrilled the women, but, more important, young men in the audience could feel that there was a guy up there like them. We could then play the role as a kind of subliminal spoof, and it went over beautifully.

But to make it work, Sean still had to look like Bond, and Terence Young deserved credit for the way he helped in this process. He took Sean to his tailor and his shirtmaker, and persuaded him to go out in the evenings wearing the clothes, so that he'd feel more and more at ease in them. There was nothing condescending about it. Sean, sensibly, preferred to go around in jeans and bomber jackets. But we wanted him to get used to his Savile Row gear the way any good actor gets to know his costume. Terence also took him out to lunch and dinner a couple of times in the most exclusive restaurants, with the sole purpose of developing Bond's pretensions as a wine and food expert. We wanted to underscore the character a bit; make him look used to ordering Mouton Rothschild '53 or Taittinger's Blanc de Blanc in restaurants; the sort of chap who'd go to Fortnum's to buy Norwegian Heather Honey on his way to have a last made by the royal shoemaker.

We were lucky in one sense. I believe that Terence Young, like Ian Fleming, subconsciously saw himself as James Bond. He had a fair claim to the fantasy. Harrow, Cambridge, then service with the Guards Armoured Division during the war: he certainly had the background. He'd read the books, too, was a *bon viveur* and knew the odd countess here and there. The upshot of all this was that Sean took all the Bond trappings and used them to play the role the way he saw it.

Dana, too, in her reserved but perceptive way, helped in the creation of the character. Her contribution to Bond was invaluable from the start. She was in on most of the discussions, and being a writer, made some highly practical suggestions. Her input wasn't always visible – Dana is a very low-profile lady – but the writers appreciated the help she gave them. (I would later discover that she also possessed an acute legal sense, quite an asset when lawyers began flying at each other from all sides.)

We now had to get down to the task of putting a crew together. I used most of my Warwick team, people I'd worked with for years. It helps to have people around you who know the way you operate. We hired Ted Moore as cameraman. He had photographed *The Trials of Oscar Wilde*, and was much admired for it. Ken Adam had been the art director, and was rightly acclaimed for his work on the film. He had a fine track record, with films like *Queen of Spades* and *Around the World in Eighty Days* to his credit. Ken turned us down at first. I remember calling him in Italy, where he was working on a big Italian production. I told him we were making a Bond film, and his first reaction was: 'I really don't think I want to do a spy thing. I had to cajole him into doing the picture. There's nothing more cajoling than more money. He worked on the big production interiors, and it is generally recognized that they were brilliant. The other designer was Syd Cain, so we were sure about one thing: the film was going to look great.

But there was still one piece of major casting left: choosing the actress to play Honey Ryder (Honeychile Ryder in the novel). Finding this beauty was not going to be easy. Fleming saw her as 'Botticelli's Venus seen from behind'. We visualized her as a very sexy broad who looked pretty good from the front as well. She is virtually naked in the book, with nothing on except a hunting knife in a leather sheath. She had to be strikingly beautiful, voluptuous, but with a kind of childlike innocence. As Bond's first screen heroine, she had a key role.

The production was due to start in mid-January 1962 and we had only two weeks in which to find the girl. It was when I started sifting through hundreds of photos in our office that I spotted a shot of Ursula Andress. It was a publicity still of her in a pose that became a photographic cliché. She was emerging from the water, her clinging wet T-shirt emphasizing the perfect moulding of her breasts. She was tall and sturdily built, with long, fair hair falling around a lovely, oval face. Without realizing it, she had struck a pose that was exactly the way the script had drawn her.

I said to Harry, 'Who is this beautiful girl?'

'Oh, just a dame that Goulash [the affectionate nickname for the Hungarian-born agent John Shepridge] introduced me to.'

'Well, this is the girl, Harry.' I didn't wait for general approval. We had rejected everyone else, and time was running out.

This girl looked terrific. She had an unusual sex appeal. She had the sturdy shoulders and limbs of a boy, but the rest of her was dazzling. I called Max Arnow, the casting director – a dear friend with whom I had formerly made films at Columbia – and asked him, 'Max, do you know a girl called Ursula Andress?'

'Of course I know her,' he said.

'Is she as beautiful as she photographs?' I asked him.

He replied, 'No photograph can catch the beauty of this girl.'

'But is she an actress?'

Max laughed. 'Well, put it this way: she has a voice like a Dutch comic. But what do you want her to do?'

I told him about the scene and the way she was supposed to look striding out of the water. 'Perfect,' he said, and of course she was. I made a deal, and shipped her out to join the unit in Jamaica. Terence was peeved at this *fait accompli*. But Sean was pleased. The scene where she strode out of the ocean with a hip knife strapped to her bikini became one of the great entrances in movies. Audiences were stunned by it. The chemistry between Sean and Ursula is one of the more potent elements in the film. It was a great plus for *Dr No*.

[It wasn't at all bad for Ursula, either. At the age of twenty-five, the Swiss-born actress had been under contract to Paramount for a year, and had also made a few films in Italy. But none of this had done much for her career. She married the actor John Derek, who was also a fine photographer and an adroit promoter of beautiful women, notably his wives. Bo Derek would become the prime example. Since Miss Andress was married to him, he was privileged to photograph her with the perceptive eye of an appreciative husband. When Cubby phoned her to invite her to play the role, the astute Mr Derek visualized what a shop-window Bond would be for the strapping creature he was married to. He advised her to accept.]

Fleming had written a good story in *Dr No*, and Dick Maibaum's script kept fairly close to the original. There were certain things we couldn't go with. Fleming's Honeychile Ryder, for example, had a broken nose in the book. Nobody knows why he introduced this, but a lot of eager intellectuals have read some deep psychological meaning into it. I never got around to asking Fleming what the point was. Similarly, we couldn't play the villain, Dr No, the way Fleming wrote it. In the book, he has two hooks instead of hands. It was more of a caricature than a character. We substituted two steel hands encased in black leather gloves. The effect was just as ominous, but acceptable.

We were lucky to get the New York stage actor Joseph Wiseman to play the role. He had made some good films, including *Detective Story*, and he was perfect in conveying the cold, sadistic menace of the character. Bernard Lee, who became a very good friend, was selected to play M, one of the best supporting performances in the Bond films. Fleming particularly admired him, having seen his real-life equivalent behind a Whitehall desk.

We flew out to the Jamaica locations on January 16, 1962. Syd Cain, who had worked for me in the Warwick days as a designer on *Zarak* and *A Prize of Gold*, was a former RAF fighter pilot. I had taken him out on an earlier recce, together with Ken Adam, scouting for locations. We had to reproduce Dr No's Devil's Garden, the mangrove swamp where his dragon tank captures Bond and Honey; and the Afro-Chinese section of Kingston, where we staged the now-famous sequence of the three blind beggars marching.

As it turned out, Jamaica, which is a beautiful island, had everything we were looking for. We filmed the beach sequences, including Ursula's she-Tarzan emergence from the sea, at Laughing Water, the secluded estate of a reclusive celebrity on the island, Mrs Minnie Simpson, who, fortunately for us, was a James Bond addict. (Around the same time President Kennedy also pronounced himself a Bond fan, listing *From Russia With Love* ninth in his ten favourite books. 007 was now moving in exalted company!) There is simply no substitute for the exotic values you can get from shooting on location. If entertainment is part escapism, taking the audience into this kind of paradise is the way to achieve it. The waterfalls of Ocho Rios, the Crab Cay shoreline with its tropical backdrop, the blue Caribbean – they're all part of the magic of motion pictures.

Meanwhile Ken Adam had been busy constructing the interiors at Pinewood Studios. We arrived there in late February 1962 to shoot scenes in M's office, where Bond is briefed on the

WHEN THE SNOW MELTS

disappearance of Strangways; the casino, where we first meet
Bond; and the brilliant reactor room, constructed on several levels
with an eerie, phosphorescent atomic pool. Ken excels at this kind
of inventiveness. He was given strong technical back-up by Ronnie
Udell, the construction manager. Having this kind of visual punch
enhances the interplay between the leading characters.

A key sequence in the film was the camera holding on a head-
and-shoulder shot of Sean seated at the gaming table playing
chemin de fer with an attractive woman played by the British
actress Eunice Gayson. We see only the back of his head, his
shoulders and his hands. He wins twice, and we have the woman's
face in close-up as she says, 'I admire your luck, Mr...er...?'

Then we see Bond's face for the first time. He takes a lighter to
his cigarette and flicks the flame, then with precise emphasis
replies, 'Bond, James Bond.' Those words, against the insistent
rhythm of the James Bond theme, was not just good cinema. It
became the signature which has run through all the Bond films.

The music was crucial, as it has been for all the Bond pictures.
Monty Norman composed the original 007 theme for us. This has
become a Bond trademark now. To do the scoring I brought in the
brilliant John Barry, whose soundtracks for this and the other
Bond films – he has worked on twelve of them – are some of the
best in cinema music. He has written the music for most of the
Bond films. Like the rest of the creative bunch, he now has James
Bond in his bloodstream. Barry is a highly respected composer
who won five Academy Awards, for *Born Free* (1966) and *The
Lion in Winter* (1968). He also composed the music for *The L-
Shaped Room*, Harry Saltzman's *Ipcress File*, and also scored
Midnight Cowboy, *The Day of the Locust*, *Out of Africa*, *Dances
with Wolves* and many others.

Linking the powerful beat of the Bond theme and the songs to
Maurice Binder's main titles was a tremendous mood-setter.
Today Binder's work is universally recognized. (Tragically, he died
on April 9, 1991.) He was a modest, round-faced little genius
whose famous gun-barrel logo which opens every Bond picture is
regarded as a classic. This idea, too, has been reworked by
imitators for rival Bond-type movies. In his quiet but persuasive
way Binder managed to attract some of London's most beautiful
models to pose for his titles. His famous sequence of apparently
nude females slowly gyrating in silhouette is beautiful, and was

well within our ground rules of audience acceptability. Our brief
to Maurice was to capture the essence of the Bond – the so-called
'sex and death' – persona in the few brief seconds of the title logo.
I remember we gave him about fifteen minutes to come up with the
idea before calling him in to a production meeting. He produced a
couple of scraps of paper with some squiggles on them, and we had
our Bond titles.

The game plan for matching music to titles in the Bond pictures
hasn't varied. You see the blank screen, the John Barry orchestra
pounds out the Bond theme, then the familiar two white circles
swing onto the screen until they converge, like the focusing of a
camera, into the circle of a gun barrel. Bond walks into the circle
and fires a shot. It works perfectly. By then, the audience's pulse
rate is up a couple of beats. The title sequence usually takes no
more than two and a half minutes, but has the kind of visual clout,
and humour, that Bond movies are all about.

Paying off the frightening situations with a touch of humour is
basic to the whole tongue-in-cheek approach to James Bond. Take
the situation in *Dr No* where Bond is driving along a coast road,
chased by a hearse full of villains who try to edge him over the side
onto the rocks below. He outmanoeuvres them, and it's the hearse
that ends up crashing down to the foot of the cliff. Somebody asks
Bond, 'What happened?'

He replies, 'I think they were on their way to a funeral.'

All the tension is built up in the chase, then it's suddenly
released, like the snapping of a fiddle string. It is menace offset by
humour. It tips the audience into taking Bond, and all the other
elements in the movie, as entertainment and nothing else. The
unexpected shot of the stolen Goya portrait of the Duke of
Wellington – sensational headline news at the time – was an in-
joke which drew a huge laugh from the audience when it was
briefly glimpsed in Dr No's study. (It was a suggestion from
Terence's script associate, Joanna Harwood. The writers on the
Bond films always leave the door open for this kind of outside
inspiration.)

The tarantula sequence, where this hairy monster crawls up
Bond's body in bed, is also teased for maximum effect. It can't be
played straight, like one of those safari films of the thirties. The
only question was how long to keep the tension going before
pulling the relief plug. When we were scoring the music for that

scene, I felt it was too melodic. There was no strong identification with what was happening on the screen. As the tarantula crawled close to Sean's face, the music was too low-key. When he finally dislodges the creature and starts pounding it with the heel of his shoe, I asked for the music to pound – crash...crash...crash! – in unison. At the opening night at the London Pavilion, during that sequence the audience were absolutely silent. You could feel the tension mounting as the spider moves. Then Sean brings his shoe crashing down on it: bang, bang, bang! And there was a loud explosion of laughter inside the cinema. It was relief laughter, when nerves which had been strung too tight are suddenly released. Terence Young was standing alongside me at the back of the theatre. He seemed shattered.

'I told you, Cubby,' he said. 'I told you they would laugh!'

'Of course they're laughing,' I said. 'They're laughing with us, Terence. Dammit, they're enjoying themselves. It's a helluva good scene!'

'No, it's terrible,' he insisted. 'You made me score it that way, and it's awful.'

'Don't worry about it,' I said. 'It's my responsibility, and that scene stays.' And of course it was a great scene. Audiences applaud it to this day.

The film opened in England to almost unanimous praise. The London *Times*, recognizing its intrinsic tongue-in-cheek approach, praised the care and expertise that had gone into the production. Superlatives like 'magnificent' and 'superb' burst out of most of the tabloids. Connery achieved his own personal triumph. The critics liked him and saw an international star in the making. Audiences, specifically the women, reacted strongly to his raw, rugged manliness and his sardonic double entendres. But the ultimate success pivoted on audience reaction in America. An outsider might have imagined that the instant success of the movie in Europe would have encouraged United Artists to give it the big New York showcase it merited. Within a few months, the picture practically recouped its production costs in London alone.

However, the geniuses who made the decisions at the time liked the picture but lacked the courage to go with their hunches. Several of the UA bookers who saw the picture privately in our projection room expressed some doubt that they could sell a picture in the major US cities with 'a Limey truck driver playing the lead'. The fact that the said Limey truck driver was being interviewed around the clock, moving onto practically every magazine cover – as well as attracting audiences that were standing in line right around the block – did not seem to impress them. The result was that, instead of opening the picture in key places like New York or Chicago, they opened at drive-in cinemas in Oklahoma and Texas. Moreover, they sold it on very low terms for a Bond picture. They took 'frightened money', scared it wouldn't do the business. Their reasoning at the time appeared to be: we won't risk spending a chunk of money in promoting the film. Let's see what we can do in the sticks, pick up bucks where we can and get out.

This booking blind spot was nothing new to me. I remember a couple of years before, with *The Red Beret*, Columbia also had cold feet. They changed the US title to *Paratrooper*, on the grounds that *The Red Beret* wouldn't mean anything in the States. And even after it opened to a big success in England, Irving Briskin, who'd seen the print we delivered to Columbia, declared, 'This picture is too goddamn British. We won't recoup the costs of the prints and the advertising on it.' He was wrong, as events would prove United Artists to be on *Dr No*.

When UA told us they were putting the picture on at an Oklahoma drive-in, we were livid. Two things occurred to remove the scales from their eyes. The Oklahoma audiences were ecstatic; American press reaction was enthusiastic. *Variety*, which knows more about movies and trends than any other showbiz journal in the world, declared: 'As a screen hero, James Bond is clearly here to stay. He will win no Oscars but a heck of a lot of enthusiastic followers.' Bosley Crowther liked Sean, and found the film 'lively and amusing'. *Time* led their reviews with the Bond notice, stating: 'Agent Bond, in short, is just a great big hairy marshmallow, but he sure does titillate the popular taste...at last the Scarlet Pimpernel can be seen on screen. He looks pretty good. As portrayed by Scotland's Sean Connery, he moves with a tensile grace that excitingly suggests the violence bottled in Bond.' The magazine asked Ian Fleming what he thought of the picture. He said, 'Those who've read the book are likely to be disappointed, but those who haven't will find it a wonderful movie.' He told Harry and I the same, and he was particularly generous about Sean. All his earlier misgivings faded when he saw Sean's Bond on the screen. He said afterwards to me that our Bond added dimensions to his own character that he wished he'd thought of. Other papers across the country echoed the general approval. Bond was on his way to capturing America.

It was then that United Artists, with exquisite chutzpah, hinted that of course they knew all along that Bond was going to be a hit. But they felt that by opening it cautiously in the sticks, there'd be that slow build-up, etc...It was nonsense, but Harry and I were old hands at this kind of talk. What mattered to me personally was that the big success of the film totally confirmed my belief in Bond when major studio producers were turning it down. The film had cost $1 million. It took back, worldwide (TV residuals were still to come), more than twenty times that. I had to smile. United Artists had seen the test on Sean Connery and had asked if we could do better. Terence Young had protested, 'Oh, disaster, disaster, disaster!' The bookers, dubious about their inability to sell 'this Limey truck driver' to the American people, had expected it to die, and selected an Oklahoma drive-in for the interment. All these forebodings had been royally blown away at the stunning première we had in London. The gasps, the howls of laughter, the ebb and flow of tension, were classic entertainment. Paul Getty Sr was there, and even that lugubrious character smiled happily on his way out of the theatre.

Ian Fleming, who also had been nervous initially, shook hands with Harry and me afterwards. 'It was wonderful!' he said. We had proved something else. Americans, far from not accepting British actors in British pictures, loved everything about Bond. And they were ready for more.

FOURTEEN

The huge impact of *Dr No* was evident not just in its wide box-office appeal around the world, but also in the boost it gave to Fleming's books. Before the film took off, his spy adventures had done well, but his hero was not exactly a household name. Suddenly, after cinema-goers all came out for Bond, the sales of the paperbacks soared. James Bond was away and running. The world had got a new screen hero. The effect of all this success on Sean Connery was fascinating. We invested thousands of dollars in publicity campaigns to hammer home the message: Connery is James Bond.

Sean, at the beginning anyway, played along with it, enjoying all the door-opening, the flattery, the hero-worship that comes with the film-star package. Virtually overnight, *Dr No* had taken him out of the 'promising young actor' category and given him potential – if not actual – international status. The American movie director (quoted in the *Saturday Evening Post*) who said, 'Connery was on the garbage heap of acting until Bond' was strictly out of line. Sean, even in some of his very early films which flopped, was always interesting, often first-class. But in terms of recognition – what else matters to an actor? – 007 was the career boost of a lifetime. Events will show to what extent Connery conceded that fact. Not that he hadn't earned all the kudos he received: he had taken a spoofy character and given it an exciting, appealing and very macho dimension.

In the euphoria that followed he began to flex his muscles not only as a screen performer, but also as a personality. No matter what he might have said in public, Sean could scarcely have objected to his sexy, cult-hero image. He knew that when he walked into a room, or was invited to parties, the women responded to his James Bond aura, not him as Sean Connery. I don't recall him issuing any public rebuttal when a newspaper described him as 'a walking aphrodisiac'. He could see there was a lot to be gained (he would eventually own shares in a bank) by keeping that game plan going. He enjoyed it, too – and why not? When you've been a truck driver and a labourer, it's great to wear Savile Row suits and be chauffeured around. And the fact that he is an excellent celebrity golfer today owes something to the golf lessons we arranged for him on *Goldfinger* for his scenes with the German actor Gert Frobe. We gave him time off to play, and be coached by professionals. Often we juggled with the shooting schedules so that he could slip away to hit a few balls on a nearby course. Nothing special about this. It was a fringe benefit – there were plenty of these – that we were glad to throw in for an actor of his calibre. And, to be fair, he had earned them.

With the next James Bond film still on the drawing-board, Harry and I, through our company Eon Productions, had time to make another picture outside Bond. But what kind of film? Thinking back over that episode and the decision we finally took – with our eyes open – reminds me of the answer Irving Thalberg often gave whenever he was asked the reason for his success: 'Two rules: never take one man's opinion as final. Never take your own opinion as final.' In the event, Harry shouldn't have listened to his own opinion, and I shouldn't have agreed with him! It resulted in both of us missing out on a minor bonanza to the considerable gratitude of certain characters who still can't believe their luck.

My partner, who had been a successful independent producer, never disguised the fact that he liked to spread himself over a variety of interests. He had a low boredom threshold, I guess. Once Bond was launched, he was restless for a diversion and keen to go ahead with an African safari spoof he had in hand. He had already gone a fair distance in persuading Bob Hope to come over to make the picture. (I heard whispers that as an inducement he promised Hope that he could deliver the Pope on one of the comedian's TV specials. Personally, I knew nothing about this and maybe His Holiness didn't, either.)

Anyway, Harry was eager to go ahead on the project when I walked in with an alternative suggestion. Donald Zec had written enthusiastically about a pop group then making quite a few waves up in a city called Liverpool. It was a major layout which was being plugged with the group's photos on billboards outside news-agent shops across the country. I had mentioned to Zec that Harry and I were looking for a non-Bond film to make. Donald thought about this for a while and then said, 'Look, this may not be your line of country, but there's something wild happening in the pop world which suggests a whole untapped goldmine to me. I wrote a spread in the paper today about a group called The Beatles. They're a zany foursome with long hair and Liverpool accents, and I wouldn't be telling you this except that apparently we sold more papers today than we did on the Queen's Coronation. Kids all over the country are crawling out of their beds just to steal The Beatles' pictures off the billboards. I don't see Oscars in this, but it seems to me you have the dream package: four certain stars and a whole new audience out there who might just kill to see them.'

Donald's logic convinced me, but persuading Harry proved to be a bit tougher. I remember looking over at my partner, who lay back in his leather desk chair, shoes off, his feet with the red socks on up on the desk. He is looking fixedly at Donald, who is looking fixedly back at him. Donald, in turn, is giving me that 'what-the-hell-am-I-doing-here-Cubby?' look. And the reason is, Mr Saltzman's round little black eyes are clouding over with disbelief. At which point Donald wrapped up his narrative as fast as he could and left. I turned to Harry and asked, 'Well, what do you think?'

He leaned forward – I recall this vividly – pounded the desk with the palms of his hands, then said, 'Listen, let me ask you something, Cubby. Would you rather make a picture with four long-haired shnooks from Liverpool – what's their name…?'

'The Beatles,' I said.

'The Beatles, who nobody's ever heard of, when we've got Bob Hope – BOB HOPE! – all ready to go.'

Well, of course, when it was put like that, I wasn't sure I could give Harry an argument. By the normal rules of the game, Harry made sense. Bob Hope was a major star with acknowledged box-office appeal all over the world. Could we gamble on these four relatively unknown kids? The euphoria faded. Mr Broccoli and Mr Saltzman joined the ranks of those other geniuses who over the years made the wrong decisions for all the right reasons! One man's poison is another man's meat. We turned our backs on one of the biggest money-spinners in the world of entertainment.

A year later *A Hard Day's Night* is leaping towards a gross of $65 million; Walter Shenson, a publicity chief for United Artists, who made the film, is driving a Rolls or maybe a Cadillac; and the four 'long-haired shnooks' went on to reshape the styles and attitudes of an entire generation. While we went on to make *Call Me Bwana* with Bob Hope and a voluptuous Swede named Anita Ekberg.

In the event, the film did little more than cover its cost. (But it was a big break for Miss Ekberg, dubbed 'The Iceberg' by one newspaper and 'The Bore With the Bust' by another. Having Bob Hope as a co-star raised her professional status enormously. Socially, it brought her into contact with Sean Connery. There was considerable static generated between these two, which kept the gossips going for a while.)

I was glad to see *Bwana* out of the way, so that we could get down to making the second Bond film, *From Russia With Love*. We favoured this film for several reasons. To many people, myself included, this was one of Fleming's best stories. The leading characters were well fleshed out. It was a tough, straightforward spy adventure. The public was familiar with the title, and it gave us an opportunity to shoot in one of the world's most exotic places, Istanbul. The story centres on an attempt to steal a vital decoding machine, the Lektor, and murder 007 in the process. The organization behind it, SPECTRE (Special Executive for Counter-intelligence, Terrorism, Revenge and Extortion), dupes a beautiful Russian agent, Tatiana Romanova, into a plan to seduce, then execute, James Bond.

The popularity of the book, notably among women, was the strong love interest between the female agent and Bond. I liked the fact that it gave Bond an emotional, as well as physical, dimension. But there was an aspect to the story which led me and Harry into making a decision which was to be fundamental to all the Bond films. We decided to steer 007 and the scripts clear of politics. Bond would have no identifiable political affiliation. None of the protagonists would be the stereotyped Iron Curtain or 'inscrutable Oriental' villain. First, it's old-fashioned; second, it's calculated to induce pointless controversy, especially in these days of *glasnost*, with Mikhail Gorbachev (as of March 1988) the Flavour of the Month.

Fleming had made the Soviet Secret Service the 'heavies' in *From*

Russia With Love. He called this murderous organization SMERSH, a name linking two Russian words, '*smyert shpionam*', which translate roughly as 'death to spies'. There was nothing fanciful about Fleming's plot. He'd based it on actual experiences in the 1930s, when he served in the Moscow bureau of Reuters News Agency. One of his assignments was to cover the trial of six British engineers working for the Metropolitan-Vickers Company. They were charged with spying and plotting against the Soviet state by sabotaging equipment at power stations and allegedly bribing Russian officials in exchange for secret information. Also charged with the six Britons was a dark, attractive Russian girl, Anna Kutusova, a secretary who worked for the company. She was supposed to have been the mistress of one of the accused men. It was a classic example of the 'beautiful spy' cliché, and Fleming clearly modelled Tatiana Romanova on her.

It was while he was reporting this case that Fleming built up his extensive knowledge of the way the secret police extracted information or confessions by torture or blackmail. We wanted to keep the motivation, but redefine the villains. Manipulating the seductive Tatiana is Rosa Klebb, a butch, crop-haired villainess, aided by Red Grant, a sadistic psycho drawn into the plan to kill Bond. It was Harry's idea to have the distinguished German actress Lotte Lenya play Rosa Klebb. It clicked with Fleming and me immediately. Ian had given this character – he'd seen the real McCoy in Moscow – evil overtones, with just a hint of lesbianism. (She lightly touches Tatiana on the knee, the girl recoiling in disgust.) The late Lotte Lenya, widow of the composer Kurt Weill, was a fine actress, and she made Rosa Klebb one of Bond's memorable adversaries. Her struggle with him as she attempts to kick-stab him with a switchblade in the toe of her shoe is real edge-of-the-seat action.

The casting of the girl to play Tatiana was not easy. Fleming describes her in the book as 'a young Greta Garbo'. There aren't many of those featured in the casting directories. Harry and I interviewed a couple of hundred girls of several nationalities. Some of these were already well known, including Magda Konopka, who is Polish, and Sylvia Koscina of Yugoslavia. We finally settled on Daniela Bianchi, a runner-up in a 1960 Miss Universe contest. She had fine features plus a touch of class, which brought her closer than anyone else to the Fleming prototype. She had to portray the discipline of a secret agent while also suggesting the vulnerability of a young woman with stirred emotions. (She seduces Bond, as ordered, wearing only a black velvet choker around her neck, but then defies the conventions of espionage by falling in love with him.) Daniela handled this character shift excellently.

Robert Shaw gave us terrific value, too, in his role as Red Grant. This character is a convicted murderer who escapes from a British jail to be recruited by SPECTRE as a top-grade killer. Shaw prepared for the role by putting himself through a ferocious body-building course. He had to look as though he was built to take the vicious test punch to midriff delivered by Rosa Klebb with a knuckleduster on her fist. Both he and Sean had lessons in Turko-Grecian wrestling in a Turkish gymnasium to prepare them for their confrontation on the Orient Express. The result is the most savage, heart-stopping duel you'll ever see in sixty seconds of screen time.

(Robert Shaw's death not long after was a great loss to me, and to the industry. He was not only a fine actor, especially in Shakespearean roles, but also a gifted writer. The film industry on both sides of the Atlantic could ill afford to lose this kind of talent.)

Dana loved Istanbul. She's always had the writer's curiosity about new places, different cultures. But she had other reasons for remembering the place. It was there that she really got to know Ian Fleming. In London he was mostly preoccupied with writing or his business affairs. At production meetings he'd sit there in his detached manner, occasionally, but always diffidently, suggesting an idea or two. He revealed very little of himself. But in Istanbul he was in his element. It was as though he were stepping back into the pages of his book. He loved the sounds, the spicy smells, the bazaars, the street merchants and the belly-dancers. Especially the belly-dancers. I can picture him now in one of Istanbul's exclusive restaurants, a quivering midriff an inch or two off the end of his Turkish cigarette, and his pale-blue eyes locked on the dancer's navel.

Here, away from the world of publishing and the hassle of agents, he could relax. He warmed towards Dana, and even – this was rare for him – discussed aspects of his writing with her. But then Ian always had a weakness for beautiful women! He loved talking about them. The way he describes the women in his books gives no clue as to whether he's seeing them through his own eyes or Bond's. One thing's for sure: Ian appreciated all types, hues and nationalities. His wife Anne, whom he adored, is on record as having written to him, claiming playfully that she seldom visited a capital city where she did not meet some woman with whom Ian had enjoyed carnal relations. But I suspect much of this was myth rather than fact, Fleming coming on with that suave lady-killing manner because he thought it was expected of him.

Dana and Ian went sightseeing together on a boat in the Bosporus. She found him a delightful, charming man and a great guide. He had been to Istanbul a year or so before, on assignment as a journalist covering an Interpol conference. He became very friendly with an Oxford-educated shipowner, Nazim Kalkavan, who knew Istanbul's every treasure, every monument, every secret alleyway. All this information Fleming filed away in his mind, and it reappeared in his book *From Russia With Love*. He told me that the character Kerim, head of the Turkish Secret Service, was modelled on Kalkavan.

Kerim was a pivotal role in our script, and was played magnificently by the actor Pedro Armendariz. Pedro was a big attractive Mexican, a warm personality who'd been a star in his own country before having an even bigger success in Hollywood and Europe. He was not only a great actor but a fantastic human being. I thought he'd be terrific as Kerim, Bond's Secret Service contact in Istanbul. I met up with him in California and offered him the part. I didn't know until we were halfway through the picture that he had cancer. Apparently there were indications of it even before we started, but Pedro was determined to fight it. He had another reason, I was told. If he wasn't going to beat it, he wanted to leave money to his widow.

One of his big scenes involved a chase and a three-car pile-up featuring Bond, a moustached Bulgarian and Pedro. When Bond gets away, the Bulgarian shouts in fury at Armendariz, who reacts by casually flicking the ash off his cigar, saying, 'My friend, that is life.' When Terence shot that scene, we knew then, and so did Pedro, that he was a dying man. It was a delicate situation. We wanted to spare him any pain or discomfort. He was determined to finish the film. He had that kind of discipline, and he had the guts, too. He was desperate to prove that he could see the assignment through. The alternative was to recast the role, but none of us was prepared to do that.

So we figured out a solution which enabled us to shoot all Pedro's remaining sequences at Pinewood in one go. It was a very painful two weeks for the whole crew. To see this fine man, with that 'lovable bandit' smile of his, going rapidly downhill was hard to take. I don't know how, what inner strength he grabbed hold of, but he performed right through to the last shot.

Ironically, when Terence afterwards went to have a drink with Pedro there was an echo of that scene in Istanbul. Terence was sad, and it showed. The Mexican flashed his famous teeth in a smile. He had a cigar in his hand. He remembered the scene. Tapping the ash off, he repeated, 'My friend, that is life.' We had a dinner party before he left to return home to Mexico. It was June 1963.

A couple of years earlier his close friend, Ernest Hemingway, also faced with a crippling illness, had shot himself. While Pedro was at UCLA Medical Center in Los Angeles for special treatment, he asked his wife to bring him his antique pistol so that he could have it repaired in California. Not long after, in his bed, he took the gun from under his pillow and killed himself. It was tragic, of course. But to many of us it was also brave and typical of the man.

The second-unit work on *From Russia With Love* hit quite a few problems. There was sickness among the cast; some of the motor-boat sequences had to be aborted and re-staged in Scotland. An important scene in the film has Bond, Tatiana and Kerim escaping through an underground sewer, chased by an army of brown rats. Under British regulations, we weren't allowed to use wild rats in British films. Syd Cain hit on the idea of coating tame white rats with cocoa, but by the time we got around to shooting the scene they were tired. They wouldn't budge; instead they started licking the chocolate off one another's backs. We now had piebald rats and a lot of spare cocoa. It was a key sequence, so we took a small unit to Madrid, where we'd heard there was a Spanish rat-catcher who could lay his hands on two hundred brown rats. Or two thousand, if we'd needed them. We shot the whole scene in a garage with a sheet of plate glass between us and them. The rat-catcher thought we were being unduly hesitant. But then so did the tarantula handler in *Dr No*.

The final scenes of *From Russia With Love* were shot in the last week of August 1963. There were some brilliant back-up features to the film. It was our first effective use of what became known as the 'Bond gadgets': specifically, the special black attaché case

handed to Bond by the head of Q branch, Boothroyd, played by
Desmond Llewelyn. Based on Fleming's description, it was created
by the special-effects genius John Stears and the art director Syd
Cain. The case contained gold sovereigns, a throwing knife, .25-
calibre ammunition and a folding Armalite Survival Gun with a
telescopic infrared lens. There was also a harmless-looking tin of
talcum powder which, in fact, was a trick canister of tear-gas.

Dick Maibaum wrote some great dialogue for the scene where
the boffin instructs Bond, in the tones of a headmaster, 'Normally,
to open a case like that you move the catches to the side. If you do,
the cartridge will explode in your face. Now, to stop the cartridge
exploding...' It's a great scene, played for humour, but at the same
time it offers an intriguing insight into the hardware of deadly
espionage. Which is what Fleming's popularity was all about.
Another clever idea, superimposing the titles on the sinuous body
of a Turkish belly-dancer, was masterminded by Robert
Brownjohn and Trevor Bond.

The film opened in London to an enthusiastic reception, with
considerable praise for Sean. It became the top money-maker of
the year worldwide. Bosley Crowther in the *New York Times* was
totally enraptured by Daniela Bianchi, and as for the film, he
begged: 'Don't miss it...just go and see it and have yourself a good
time.' The influential *Variety*, predicting 'big box office', declared
unequivocally: 'Ian Fleming's British Secret Service Agent James
Bond cannot miss. *From Russia With Love* is a preposterous,
skillful slab of hard-hitting sexy hokum...directed by Terence
Young at a zingy pace...the cast perform with an amusing combo
of tongue-in-cheek and seriousness and the Istanbul location is a
bonus. Connery...is well served, not only actionwise, but by some
crisp wise-cracking dialogue by Richard Maibaum. Robert Shaw is
an impressive, icy, implacable killer and the late Pedro Armendariz
weighs in with a formidable, yet lightly-played performance.'

Entertainment Today was just as enthusiastic, commenting:
'...the film proved to countless skeptics that the James Bond films
were being made by people who knew what they were doing...'
This was true, although I could not pretend that the successful
partnership between Harry Saltzman and myself looked set to last
for ever. We were different in style, temperament, and in our
attitude to film-making. To me, sustaining Bond as a top
international box-office attraction meant staying with it, living

with it, without hankering after other things. It had achieved a unique success, but there was always the temptation to believe that it had a kind of built-in momentum of its own. It didn't. Each James Bond film is as demanding creatively as the first. The pictures must never have the flavour of tired thinking or recycled scenarios. To me, that meant then – and means now – that Bond is a full-time occupation.

And here I'm exceedingly fortunate, since Dana is just as involved with the Bond pictures as I am. Her name isn't among the credits, but her input has always been valuable, often crucial. There's always been a lot of love in our household, and Dana is at the heart of it. She somehow manages to keep that generating current going wherever any of us might be in the world. Her son Michael, and Tina, Tony and Barbara are all devoted to her. And I'm not exactly at the back of the queue.

While our first two films and the James Bond books swept the world, Ian Fleming, who began it all, was having a tough time. In his early film negotiations with Kevin McClory, which were finally aborted, one controversy remained. It hinged on whether McClory and his associate Jack Whittingham should be acknowledged as having contributed material for his book *Thunderball*.

In November 1963 Kevin brought the case to the High Court in London. It would lead to two years of contentious argument, over which time Fleming became increasingly weary. He was a creative writer, not a showbiz litigant. And even before all that began, his heart condition was worsening – a fact he concealed from most of us. As the case dragged on, our own interest in *Thunderball* had to be shelved again. We turned instead to *Goldfinger*.

This was a strong story with a fascinating villain. Auric Goldfinger's master plan is to detonate a small atomic bomb in Fort Knox, which would hugely increase the value of his own hoard of $60 million worth of gold bullion. Terence Young wasn't sure he wanted to make another Bond picture, and went off to direct *The Amorous Adventures of Moll Flanders*. We approached Guy Hamilton, who had originally turned Bond down but was eager to do this one. I've always liked Guy Hamilton's work. He shoots with a lot of pace and style, and also has a flair for comedy: all the elements intrinsic to Bond. Guy was also a low-handicap golfer, which immediately gave him points with Sean. Before he came to us, Guy had made some impressive films, including *The*

Colditz Story, *An Inspector Calls*, *The Devil's Disciple* and *The Best of Enemies*.

The moment we began casting, we hit a problem. Obviously, choosing the actor to play Goldfinger was crucial. There was initial disagreement over who that actor should be. Harry was all for the American actor Theodore Bikel, who played the adventurous Hungarian in *My Fair Lady*. I was just as insistent that we use the German Gert Frobe. He was a bulky, bullet-headed character who was not only well known in Germany, but had also played a role in *The Longest Day*. What impressed me was that he could be menacing, yet had a great sense of humour. But Harry kept pushing Theodore Bikel until finally I said, 'All right, let's get him over here and make a test.' There was always the chance Harry could be right. We flew this actor from New York to London and made the test. He was no Goldfinger.

Even so, Guy and Harry remained unsure about Frobe. They protested he didn't speak English too well and was not a star, merely a character actor. I said we were not looking for stars. We were looking for the ideal Goldfinger. There was only one way to find out. I flew to Munich to speak to his manager, a German woman. Frobe's hair was sand-coloured, but not as red as the script called for. I told her I'd like to have Gert redden his hair and then come and see us in London. When Guy saw him, his eyes lit up.

'Gee! Who's that?'

'That's Gert Frobe,' I told him.

'We have to test him. He looks the right man to me,' said Guy.

It's true Frobe's English was sketchy. But that was never going to be a problem. We could always dub another voice over his. What mattered was he made a great Goldfinger.

To bring in some fresh thinking to the screenplay, we engaged the late Paul Dehn, a fine writer and distinguished film critic. He and Dick Maibaum sparked ideas off each other in what turned out to be a very productive and highly professional collaboration.

Two important pieces of casting remained: an actor to play Oddjob, and an actress for Fleming's butch but sexually free-wheeling female, Pussy Galore. Casting the Japanese wrestler Harold Sakata as Oddjob was, like Frobe, a spot-on choice. He was not an actor, but I didn't see that as a particular handicap. That square head, the quizzical Oriental eyes, and the sheer tonnage of the man made him the perfect henchman to the master criminal Goldfinger. Instinctively, he managed to convey a hint of icy humour, which made audiences shudder in their seats. If you guessed that offscreen Sakata (known as Tosh Togo in his wrestling days) was probably a bit of a pussycat, you'd be right. He was a friendly, gentle giant who, though he had no dialogue in the film, grunted his way to international recognition. He died some time back, but he'll long be remembered. He created a whole new role model for the screen heavy.

It was Guy Hamilton who suggested Honor Blackman to play Pussy Galore. All her crinkly leather action and shoulder-throws she did so effectively in *The Avengers* virtually clinched it for her to tussle with James Bond. The casting complete, I drove to London Airport with Guy Hamilton and Dana *en route* to the States for the Fort Knox sequences. Also with us just for the ride to Heathrow was Dana's son Michael. He'd been in London only a couple of days.

I began turning over in my mind all the complex problems we were going to have to face on the location. There were intricate flying sequences, ground shots near the Fort, and we'd have to move carefully in a sensitive area guarded by crack units of the US Army.

Michael, before going to law school, had spent two years at a military school, then graduated from Harvey Mudd University in Claremont, California, with an engineering degree. He was on summer vacation and had been accepted at Stanford Law School. I could see that experience being valuable back-up in our contact with the military and also with the technical stuff around Fort Knox. Moreover, we had only a handful of crew on that location and could use a versatile character like Michael. So it was not nepotism or an idle whim which made me say to him as he stood there in just a shirt and pair of trousers: 'Too bad you don't have your passport. You could be of some help on this trip.'

'As a matter of fact, I do have it with me in my pocket,' he said (looking questioningly at his mother – Dana had waited for months for him to come to England to visit us).

I looked at Dana. 'I could use him.'

Michael said, 'Mom?'

Dana smiled. 'Go, if that's what you want.'

'Then consider yourself hired!' I said, and bought an extra ticket to New York. A day later Michael was with us in Kentucky, a hard worker and a very fast learner.

We went through the motions of seeking permission from the US Treasury Department to shoot inside Fort Knox. Firmly but courteously, they refused. Their interest in movies in general, and James Bond in particular, didn't extend to giving us an insider's view of how the greatest concentration of bullion in the world is guarded. But Ken Adam's ingenuity and research produced a spectacular substitute. His concept of what the inside of the depository looked like was close to genius. Built on several levels of chrome and steel, behind which the gold bars were stacked, it was a breathtaking arena in which Oddjob is finally eliminated.

Outside of the Pinewood stages, we constructed the Fort Knox exterior, complete with big electric gates, concrete drive and long stretches of wire barricades. While the engineers were preparing all this, we were within shouting distance of the real thing, under the alert scrutiny of armed elements of the US military.

Permission to use troops was hard to obtain. We were not allowed to pay them, so remuneration had to come in the form of an allowance for cleaning uniforms or whatever. In the event, we received all the permissions we required, and much of that was due to Charles Rushon, a friend of mine and former Army colonel. Ted Moore's photography, together with all the stunt work, created a landmark in spy adventure films. The imitators would soon be climbing on to the bandwagon. (We had to stretch a point with Pussy Galore's flying circus. Flying females were thin in the air over North Kentucky, so I hired some male pilots from a nearby flying school, rigged them out in black jump suits and blonde wigs. They looked pretty good, too, but couldn't wait to get rid of the gear.)

There was now the problem over Pussy Galore. Not the character, but the name. Fleming was no shrinking violet. He'd been around and was familiar with the vernacular of Vegas bachelors and men's locker-room conversation. My mischievous friend knew only too well the double entendre behind the name Pussy Galore. So, apparently, did his American publisher, who read the manuscript of *Goldfinger* and laid it on the line: 'You just can't use this name, Ian.'

Fleming, who'd been to Sandhurst, Britain's equivalent of West

Point, was not used to being told what he couldn't do. 'Oh yes I will,' he said, 'and not only that, we're going to get away with it!' Well, that was fine for Ian Lancaster Fleming. He only had the publisher to contend with.

We were also advised against using the name. But our view was quite simple: we were filming the book; Pussy Galore was a pivotal character in the story; that's what Fleming named her; there seemed no reason to call her anything else. Dick Maibaum was prepared to change it to Kitty Galore, but Fleming, rightly, thought that would be nonsense, since millions who'd read the book would be mystified. In those days we didn't submit scripts beforehand to so-called censors.

Geoffrey Shurlock was the man behind the then influential Production Code of the MPEA (the same sort of character who had come out against *The Trials of Oscar Wilde*). We saw no reason to clear the script with him, and used the dialogue as written. At a Royal Première, Honor Blackman was presented to Prince Philip. The following morning one newspaper gave it front-page treatment under the heading 'Pussy and the Prince'. It was an irresistible heading which amused everybody, including the Palace. Another newspaper had a similar headline.

By then Geoffrey Shurlock had been told that *Goldfinger* had been premièred in London without him having read or approved the script. This upset him. He was even more miffed when he heard there was an actress featured in the picture named Pussy Galore. He began to make waves, and I had to drop everything in London and fly over to the States to talk to him. He said flatly that he was not going to permit me to release the picture.

'How can you do that?' I said. 'We've spent millions of dollars – you can't just censor it because of a name.' (I was never for censorship anyway; the public are the best judges.)

'I know what you're saying, but I can ban this picture,' was his answer.

I then played the ace. I had brought with me all the tear sheets of the British papers which carried pictures of Prince Philip meeting Honor Blackman. Some said, 'The Prince meets Pussy'; others, 'Pussy and the Prince'. I showed them to Shurlock. 'Look at these. If the picture is good enough for Prince Philip and the people of London to see, that ought to be all right over here. Second, look at those headlines. There's obviously nothing wrong with the word 'Pussy'...that's her name! It's been accepted in England, and dammit, if it's OK with them what are you worried about?!'

He looked again at the tear sheets, then at me, paused a while and laughed. 'Ah, OK, Cubby, you win.'

FIFTEEN

Harry and I expected *Goldfinger* to hit big at the box office. It had pace, style, great action, fantastic sets, and the performances, especially from Sean and Gert Frobe, were outstanding. But the overall impact of the film exceeded even the most extravagant forecasts. The picture broke box-office records throughout the world.

These statistics are misleading, however. When you've repaid the distributors, added the cost of prints, advertising, publicity and a barrel load of other charges, including stars' salaries, you've trimmed the grosses drastically. Even so, it was still a considerable achievement at that time. What we had not foreseen was the way Bond would become a cult figure throughout the world. Between 1965 and 1967 Sean was virtually the number-one box-office attraction in the cinemas. No other British actor had come anywhere close. In Germany, Italy, France, Spain and Scandinavia, the fallout from the Bond explosion led to 007 fan clubs, cover stories in the leading magazines, with Sean Connery edging John Wayne sideways as the world's favourite actor. In Japan, Sean Connery overtook the Beatles as the nation's favourite. What had started out as just a film project was now a roller-coasting phenomenon.

Despite this, Sean was now suggesting that Bond was affecting his image. Rarely, if ever, did he acknowledge to me that Bond was at the core of his success. The three James Bond films had lifted him out of the 'talented actor' category and given him the international appeal that not even Larry Olivier, in his best years, could match. *Look*, *Time* and *Life* magazines unanimously hailed him as what we would now call a superstar. He made other films between the Bond pictures, but in those early years, at any rate, they had far less impact, merely confirming what we already knew: that he was a fine actor who slotted perfectly into the character of Bond.

Sean's attitude to all the fêting and fan worship was becoming increasingly ambivalent. Cautious about money, he was thrilled to see his earnings soar, dramatically so, when he asked for and was given a percentage of the picture. But he also had the 'serious actor' syndrome, disliking the 007 label which inevitably he became stuck with. It would be many years later when he would finally – if not grudgingly – acknowledge to an interviewer: 'I'm not ashamed about doing those Bond films. Quality is not only to be found at the National Theatre. Playing Bond is just as serious as playing *Macbeth*.'

The movie business is notoriously over-generous to its stars, but it doesn't permit them to have their cake and eat it. Whatever it is that makes you the idol of millions is the way those millions want you to be. Let's face it, they pay the piper. Humphrey Bogart was also a serious and sensitive actor. But he learned to live happily with the tough screen image that created a cult, made him a legend. Sean's love-hate relationship with Bond was beginning to show. Unwisely, I think, he appeared to denigrate Bond, and those of us who'd given him the chance of a lifetime. It was a familiar scenario, and I saw danger signals for the future of Bond – at any rate with Sean continuing in the role. But I have to say that whatever his reservations – public or private – he went into the next Bond picture, *Thunderball*, with his usual drive.

Sadly, Ian Fleming would not see the production get under way. Five weeks before the big charity opening of *Goldfinger*, he suffered a massive heart attack and died. A year or so before, he had been treated for a similar attack, and warned to take it easy. Imprisoned, as he saw it, in a bed, he 'took it easy' by writing a charming children's story about a magic car, called *Chitty Chitty Bang Bang*. I acquired this with the other Fleming properties and it seemed a great subject for a film. I had a great deal of joy in making it. It brought some old friends together: Gert Frobe, who'd been such an instant hit in *Goldfinger*, and Benny Hill. The film starred Dick Van Dyke and Sally Ann Howes and had some fine songs in it written by the Sherman Brothers. Children loved it. Like *Mary Poppins*, it still appears on the cinema screens and it still has an exciting potential.

The life Fleming had been ordered to lead – no excitement, no dangerous fun, popping nitroglycerine tablets between exertions – was no existence for the man who created James Bond. The family motto he gave 007, 'The World Is Not Enough', suggests perhaps that Fleming wanted a full life or no life at all. Despite the title of one of his best sellers, Fleming was aware you only live once. He made no changes in his exhilarating lifestyle.

In August 1964 he booked into a hotel at Sandwich, Kent. He had been invited to become Captain of the world-famous Royal and St George's Golf Club. He was looking forward to meeting members of the committee. Instead, on August 11, he suffered his second major heart attack. In true-blue Fleming style, he said to the ambulance attendants, 'I'm awfully sorry to trouble you chaps.' He died the next day. Dana and I were tremendously upset.

Not only did we like Fleming immensely, and admire his taste and intellect; we also valued his ideas at the conference table. We were particularly sad he missed the opening of *Goldfinger*, though I'd shown him some of the early rushes. He was pleased with what he saw. All in all, I believed we served him well. Fortunately, Fleming's interest in the films, plus the massive boost they gave his books, achieved his one ambition: to leave a handsome legacy to his family. We were glad of that, but shocked that he should die so young, just fifty-six years old. I don't know how bad his heart was, but maybe if the bypass operation was as common then as it is now, he might be alive. But he was gone, and we had to do the best we could without him.

The court case involving Fleming and Kevin McClory had been resolved, giving Kevin the rights to film *Thunderball*. Although we had bought that story as part of the whole package, the court ruling inhibited us from going ahead with the film. Kevin – and I could understand this – nurtured the idea of filming it. But he could see advantages in talking to us. For our part, we recognized that a 'rogue' Bond might act as a spoiler upon our own productions. We didn't want to see our films confused with other, perhaps inferior, products. I went over and sorted out a deal with McClory which brought *Thunderball* under our banner, with Kevin as the producer.

Terence Young came back to direct the picture, with a slightly amended attitude toward money. Originally, when we had offered him a percentage against a smaller salary, he had turned it down, opting for cash instead. Now, notably after the big grosses of *Goldfinger*, he indicated a preference for a salary and a piece of the picture. We considered the fee he wanted to direct the picture was sizeable enough without the percentage. I said, 'If you want the percentage, then lower the cash.' He didn't want to do that. So he set out to direct *Thunderball* on a salary-only basis, which was a pretty good stipend by any standards. (Like Sean, he'd earned it. And like Sean, he would later question it. As my dear departed father Giovanni observed, 'When the snow melts...!')

Nothing succeeds like excess. After the three Bond blockbusters, spy mania swept through the film-making countries of the world. Producers looked enviously at our grosses and reasoned: if they can do it, so can we. And why not? It looked so easy: get a virile, good-looking actor; surround him with a lot of sexy females; cobble together the semblance of a spy story; put in a lot of bumps and sound-alike dialogue; and you've got 007 Mark Two. Well, the theory may have been sound, but the record reveals the reality was vastly different. Cheap imitations, or for that matter, expensive imitations, never work in movies – least of all with James Bond. The fatal mistake made by most of these upstart productions was to try to send up James Bond. It doesn't work. Audiences don't like to see their heroes lampooned. When Bond pays off a terrifying situation, or kills off an adversary with a quip, it works as a tension-breaker, the audience laughing with relief. But making Bond into a kind of spoof spy doesn't work.

It was amusing to me to sit back and watch the stampede develop. Columbia made an attempt with the Matt Helm novels, Dean Martin playing a sexy secret agent. The fact that his secretary was called Lovey Kravezit indicates the level of humour. As the Matt Helm films were produced by my late friend and former partner Irving Allen, I don't wish to mar the fond memories I have of him. But it's useful for students of the Bond phenomenon to see what some of these imitations were like. Leslie Halliwell, the respected authority on films, said this of *The Silencers*, the first Matt Helm film: 'Adventures of a sexy secret agent – or James Bond sent up rotten. Plenty of fun along the way with in-jokes and characters like Lovey Kravezit, but the plot could have done with more attention and the sequels (*Murderers Row*, *The Ambushers*, *Wrecking Crew*) were uncontrolled disaster areas.' MGM came in with *The Man From UNCLE*, which was a straight steal from Fleming's use of acronyms like SMERSH and SPECTRE. They were not bad on TV, but in the cinema the film was just another spoof on Bond.

Twentieth Century Fox decided anything UA, Columbia or Metro could do, they could do better. In *Our Man Flint* James Coburn plays secret agent Derek Flint. To put it kindly, Coburn was no Sean Connery. The series eventually out-spoofed itself – it even had an organization called ZOWIE (Zonal Organization World Intelligence Espionage). The whole enterprise probably made some money, but it was swiftly and unceremoniously buried on the Fox lot. Columbia, however, still hadn't got the spy craze out of its system. It backed a French/Italian/Spanish effort titled *That Man in Istanbul*, starring Horst Buchholz and Sylvia Koscina. Dino De Laurentiis made his pitch with *Kiss the Girls and Make Them Die*, as the rip-off movies went on and on. *Second Best Secret Agent in the Whole Wide World* was generally written off as a cheap Bond copy.

The long string of bad imitations, some funny, others embarrassing, did Bond no harm whatsoever. They were marginally above the level of drawing a moustache on the *Mona Lisa*. But probably the most unfortunate attempt to make an 'independent' Bond picture was Charlie Feldman's ill-fated *Casino Royale*. At one time I had tried to buy the film rights of this book from Gregory Ratoff's widow. Feldman had been Gregory's agent, and eventually she sold her interest in *Casino Royale* to him. When Charlie saw the enormous success we had had with Bond, he could see rich opportunities for his property – given Sean Connery. I loved Charlie. We had been friends for years. But the deal he proposed was so bizarre, if he had been my agent he would have tossed the offer – and the person making it – out of the window.

He asked us whether we would loan him Sean Connery for the picture. We told him we couldn't do that. Bond is a special kind of animal, and Sean is a special kind of actor. He's our James Bond. We don't loan him out.

'Well,' said Charlie, 'maybe we could be partners.'

I smiled. 'Maybe. Tell me all about it, Charlie. You've got the one Fleming property I was negotiating to buy from you, but you changed your mind. What kind of a deal do you want to make?'

He told us. Seventy-five per cent of the profits for him, twenty-five per cent for Harry and me and United Artists. I told him we hadn't any notion of doing that, which was as deadpan an understatement as I could contrive. 'Also,' I said to him, 'I can't work for you. I already did that and it was great. I like you, too. But on these terms, Charlie, you're going to have to make the picture on your own.' Which was what he did, with near-catastrophic results. It was a mess of a picture, largely because in trying to compensate for not having Sean as 007, he went way over the top. He had David Niven down to play Bond. He had Woody Allen down to play James Bond. He even had Ursula Andress down to play James Bond. I advised him to get a good young actor to play the part, but he had other ideas. He brought in a whole battalion of joke-makers, professional wits and other professional buffoons in a frenzied attempt to make the ultimate spoof.

It was a bad miss. (One reviewer commented: 'This film was shot by five directors – right between the eyes.') I was very sorry for Charlie. And it was no joy to us that it flopped. The reverse. Feldman, who was a marvellous promoter, had secured huge media coverage for the film. Inevitably, many thought we had made it, which did us no good at all. Eventually the film, because of its big names and sexy romps, made its costs and maybe a profit.

But Charlie had learned the hard way that making a Bond film is not a dilettante operation. He was a brilliant agent, a man of great taste and charm, a powerful figure in Hollywood, and as good a friend as anybody could have. But although he was a good film producer – he made *A Streetcar Named Desire* – his judgement on Bond was seriously awry. All of us who were close to him wanted his career to go out on a note of triumph. Unhappily, the *Casino Royale* débâcle did the reverse.

Thunderball opened in the States in December 1964 and soon broke every box-office record in New York and Los Angeles. My mother, Cristina, now a frail but gutsy lady of eighty, was very proud to see the name 'Broccoli' in the producer credits on the marquees. Not that she exactly fell over herself to say so. She retained, to her end, her Calabrian notion of life's priorities. She lived by the basic credo: be good, do good.

Record grosses, rave notices, talking in millions, and lines around the block were fine. OK. You're successful. But my mother's real joy came from seeing Dana and the children coming over to the house, reminiscing about the old days on the farm, fussing around the kitchen, making sure I cooked the spaghetti *al dente* and made the sauce she invented absolutely right. It wasn't easy to persuade her to attend a Bond première – any première. I remember when I took her to the opening of *From Russia With Love* in Los Angeles. It was at the famous Grauman's Chinese Theater. There was a lot of excitement blowing around it. Big crowds were expected. I mentioned all this to Cristina just to tempt her out of her apron and into the car. I wanted to see her face light up in the glow of a typical Hollywood opening.

We drove up to the theatre with my mother and Dana's mother, a wonderful lady, Stella. No lights, no crowds, total darkness. There were groups of people standing around outside the theatre and in the parking lot. The foyer was dark; there were no lights in the ticket booth. I went up to one of the managers. 'What the hell's happened?'

He told me, 'We've just had a riot here. A bunch of wild ones came in demanding tickets. We didn't have any more; we were all sold out. They tried to crash the cashier's cage. They threatened to tear up the theatre. They were going to carve up every seat in the place unless we let them in. We called the police, who advised us to take the heat out of the situation by switching off all the lights. We had no option.' I went back to explain things to Mom. I didn't get far.

'A big opening, huh?' she said. 'What happened? Where is everybody? I don't see anybody here – no lights, no crowds, no nothing!'

When finally we went in to see the picture she was enthralled. Afterwards in the foyer, when celebrities and studio executives came up to congratulate Harry and me, those deep-shadowed eyes of hers shone with pleasure. She was not one to throw compliments around. People were always more important to her than big occasions. But I thought a few words of maternal pride wouldn't be out of place. We'd come a long way since she was on her knees pulling up weeds on Long Island. I waited for the bouquet. Instead she frowned on a thought. 'Tell me, Cubby,' she said. 'What happens to all those clothes on the film?'

I was puzzled. 'What do you mean?'

'Those clothes. They don't belong to the actors. I don't suppose you can use them again, and there are a lot of people who would be glad to have them.'

Echoes of the tough years on the farm; maybe even of Calabria.

She hadn't been awed by the lights or the celebrities. She saw those clothes up on the screen and lined up in her mind just who she could send them to. Which, of course, is why everybody loved her: Dana, the children and the grandchildren. She was a generous, gentle soul. She lived to realize all her dreams. She died on December 27, 1965, after suffering a stroke. We buried her close to Giovanni and John at Sayville, Long Island. The images I have of her, cooking for a dozen farmhands at one sitting; on her knees in the summer heat, thinning out the vegetables; consoling my father when work was scarce, are vivid even today. The influence she had on my life can't be measured. Nor the extent to which I miss her.

Some critics have said there was a change of format in the making of *Thunderball*, with the emphasis on action. This wasn't true, though we certainly made it larger, more lavish, with spectacular visual effects. This was determined by the story, which has Bond tracking down a hijacked Vulcan bomber, loaded with atomic charges, to its sunken hide-out in the Bahamas. With that premise, the underwater action has to dominate. In the event, the hand-to-hand combat; the battle between SPECTRE's underwater army and the aqua-paras; the slow-motion love scene between Bond and Domino (Claudine Auger) – all below the surface of the Caribbean – was, in my view, marvellous to watch. Whatever the odd critic might have said, this was great cinema, and audiences worldwide were thrilled by it.

We also had one of the world's most experienced marine cameramen, Lamar Boren, of La Jolla, California. I had admired his work, particularly after seeing his outstanding underwater camera work in the TV series *Sea Hunt*. He put together a team of sixty professional divers and nearly $100,000 worth of diving equipment. Meanwhile Ken Adam was busy designing SPECTRE's huge underwater hide-out, with its submerged cave into which a two-man submarine sled manoeuvres the stolen atomic charges. The logistics in this area alone were daunting, but UA were now recognizing that all this hardware was vital to the Bond magic.

Just as crucial were the female characters, the key figure being Domino, mistress to Largo, the eye-patched SPECTRE villain, who eventually switches her allegiance, and everything else, to James Bond. Fleming's description of this beauty places her as someone of peasant stock, wilful, hot-tempered and sensual, and accordingly no pushover for 007. Harry and I were convinced that Raquel Welch, though still a comparative newcomer, would be ideal for the role. She had been featured in *Life*, made one film, and was stunning to look at. We went to Hollywood and signed her for the role. Not long after I had returned to London, I had a panic phone call from Dick Zanuck, then production chief at Twentieth Century Fox.

'I'm awfully sorry, Cubby,' he pleaded. 'I'm in trouble. I really need this girl. Would you release her?'

'I'll have to talk to my partner Harry,' I said. 'We like her, we'd still like to use her, but it's no big deal. She is still virtually unknown.' We finally agreed to release her – which may or may not have done her a favour – and renewed our search for the ideal Domino.

So again it was a question of bringing in girls from all over Europe; looking through hundreds of photographs; interviewing scores of girls. Favourites were Yvonne Monlaur, a striking Parisienne who had made a few interesting films; Maria Bucella, a former Miss Italy and Miss Europe; and Claudine Auger, a one-time Miss France who was causing rising excitement in France's cinema world. The latter became our Domino, and was highly effective in the role.

The love sequence between Claudine and Sean was, I guess, the first time such a scene was shot underwater. The sequence ended with Domino's bikini floating to the surface in a burst of air bubbles from the lovers down below. The more I looked at it, the more I was convinced that it was too suggestive. We cut it from the scene. There is a great temptation to go over the line with Bond, but Harry and I always resisted it. We were not prudes, just realists. Bond's high level of acceptability to all ages and different cultures hadn't happened by accident. We knew how far we could go, should go, with Bond in this area, and would never exceed it. For the most part, sex in the Bond films is lightweight, mostly played for humour. The rest is a matter of style, and taste. Proof that we've got it right is in the way the public have come back again and again to Bond in spite of the competition from other big action thrillers.

Sean coped well with the underwater work. Physically strong, enjoying the Caribbean sun, he contributed his usual mix of humour and threat with easy self-assurance. The film out-grossed all the previous Bonds. Four films, all of them major successes. And in the process we had smashed box-office records everywhere and put Sean Connery in the international reckoning as a solid, bankable actor. We had swept away the barrier – which I had breached with *The Red Beret* – against British films and the notion that no British actor could make it big in America.

Moreover, we had achieved all this as independent producers under the noses of the Hollywood majors, who had claimed for years that Bond couldn't be filmed. Put simply, we worked hard, prospered well and, according to the experts, were creating a legend. It was unique, even by Hollywood's standards. Maybe the leading characters weren't exactly expected to fall on their knees. But who couldn't be content, associated with a series of films which even then looked set to make motion-picture history? Well, Sean Connery for one.

Even before I flew out to Japan to commence location shooting of *You Only Live Twice*, the Indian signs were unmistakable. Sean never came to me directly. Actors never do. The agents come in. They unspool a whole tale: Bond is harming Sean; Sean wants to be free to do this or some other thing; he doesn't want to be known as 'Mr Bond' but as 'Mr Connery'. Meanwhile Sean himself was spreading it around that he'd had enough, that *You Only Live Twice* was going to be his last Bond. 'After this,' he told reporters, 'I will only do the things that passionately interest me for the remaining thirty-five years of my life.' Not the most encouraging noises an actor should make as he starts a film that will cost close to $10 million and in which he has a handsome stake.

Sean was reportedly sounding off in London and New York, saying, 'One should be paid what one is worth!' (I wouldn't argue with that.) He continued, 'Money gives you freedom and power... I want to use that power I now have, as a producer.' He further commented apparently, with a little less style, 'What I'm really tired of is a lot of fat-slob producers living off the backs of lean actors.' That outburst, from an actor I admired and respected, was a little light on good nature and short on truth. For a 'lean actor', he was doing pretty well, as his bank manager or agent would have confirmed. But I wasn't going to spend my time rebutting these gripes, unfair though they were. I had a picture to make. The Japanese location was going to be tough enough without souring it by confrontations with the star of the picture. But I feared that it was inevitable.

I also knew that Harry Saltzman and I wouldn't be able to conceal our own disagreements much longer. It wasn't just a conflict of personalities, which other partnerships have survived. It was, at least the way I saw it, two totally contrasting attitudes to Bond. Harry could make his own case. But to me there was a growing imbalance between us in the commitment to the Bond films and the effort put into making them. I say this without any animosity towards Harry, whose talents I have always respected. And when we first started out on the Bond films, he put all those skills behind the pictures. But Harry was a maverick. Once Bond was away and running, he began looking for other projects, new territories to conquer. And some of these were successful, too. He made Michael Caine a star with *The Ipcress File* and *Funeral in Berlin*.

Harry Saltzman's generous but overpowering hospitality occasionally misfired. On the Istanbul location for *From Russia With Love*, a dinner party was organized at a fashionable restaurant at which Ian Fleming was present. Any acquaintance of Fleming's, or student of his books, would have recognized the author as a gourmet of class. A prudent host might have sought the famous *bon viveur*'s views as to the menu and the choice of wines. But the expansive Mr Saltzman was a commander, not a consultant. This was his territory. Good food was his subject. He decided he'd order for everyone. The food arrived, and a dozen or so forks were poised for the first mouthful. There was a sudden commotion and we froze, forks in mid-air. Harry had seen the dish and in a reprise of many similar incidents, he had all the food returned to the kitchen.

Fleming, seated stiffly in his chair, raised his eyebrows in disbelief. To be served food he had not ordered was not on, old chap. Then, to have it swept away from under his aristocratic nose, compounded the offence. He immediately distanced himself from the captive eaters around the table, and beckoned to the waiter. In a voice loud enough to be heard at the top of the table, he said, 'I would like to order something for myself.' Ears and eyes swivelled in the direction of the famous connoisseur – the man who had written in *Casino Royale*: '"You must forgive me," he said, "I take a ridiculous pleasure in what I eat...it comes mostly from a habit of taking a lot of trouble over details..."'

Harry's exotic offering had been delivered and then removed. What esoteric masterpiece, we wondered, would Fleming order in its place? The waiter licked the tip of his pencil. 'Bring me,' the author said, 'a Spanish omelette, not overcooked, with two slices of toast.'

'An omelette!' echoed the waiter.

'Exactly!' smiled Fleming. My partner seemed relieved to see the belly-dancer appear.

Despite the fact that Sean blew cool on Bond, once he started working on *You Only Live Twice* he was as cooperative and as professional as ever. This time we had Lewis Gilbert directing, following our pattern of bringing fresh thinking into each production. Lewis observed that Harry and I were having problems, but is on record as saying afterwards, 'Once the picture got going, the producers were terrific. With their vast experience, I had people to turn to when I was in doubt and, good God! at times you needed support.'

We had engaged Roald Dahl, the renowned short-story writer, to script the film, with some later additions by the writer Hal Bloom. Roald had a sharp, sardonic style. His storyline was close to science fiction: Blofeld is hired by international master criminals to hijack American and Soviet space capsules, leading each to accuse the other and thus trigger World War III. Just how this would be staged depended crucially on the kind of spectacular terrain we could scout in Japan. Meanwhile, since Roald was a newcomer to Bond, we briefed him on the basic formula.

I remember that meeting well. So did Roald Dahl, who wrote an account of it for *Playboy*. (I wouldn't say it was exactly the way I remember it, but then I wasn't the best fairy-tale writer in the world.) Dahl recalled:

'You can come up with anything you like so far as the story goes,' they told me, 'but there are two things you mustn't mess about with.

The first is the character of Bond. That's fixed. The second is the girl formula. That is also fixed.' 'What's the girl formula?' I asked. 'There's nothing to it. You use three different girls and Bond has them all.' 'Separately or *en masse*?' One of them took a deep breath and let it out slowly. 'How many Bond films have you seen?' he asked. 'Just one. The one with the crazy motor-car.' 'You'd better see the others right away. We'll send them out to your house with a projector and someone to work it.' This was the first small hint I was to get of the swift, efficient, expansive way in which the Bond producers operated. Nobody else does things quite like them. 'So you put in three girls. No more and no less. Girl number one is pro-Bond. She stays around roughly through the first reel of the picture. Then she is bumped off by the enemy, preferably in Bond's arms.' 'In bed or not in bed?' I asked. 'Wherever you like, so long as it's in good taste. Girl number two is anti-Bond. She works for the enemy and stays around throughout the middle third of the picture. She must capture Bond, and Bond must save himself by bowling her over with sheer sexual magnetism. This girl should also be bumped off, preferably in an original fashion.' 'There aren't many of those left,' I said. 'We'll find one,' they answered. 'Girl number three is violently pro-Bond. She occupies the final third of the picture, and she must on no account be killed. Nor must she permit Bond to take any lecherous liberties with her until the very end of the story. We keep that for the fade-out.'

Though we had a basis of a story with Fleming's book and Dahl's outline, we still had to find a visually stunning centrepiece, which is the essence of a Bond picture. We decided to recce the Japanese islands to see if the terrain would produce an idea. I took a plane; Harry went off with his wife, Hal Bloom and Maurice Binder in search of salt mines. As far as I know, there aren't any salt mines in Japan. Harry was just as convinced there were. So while the salt-mine contingent drove away, I took to the air. What we needed was a vast enclave with a spread of water that would serve as the artificial lake featured in the story. We did a lot of island-hopping in helicopters. I went to the famous castle of Himeji (where the fighting Ninja agents were filmed doing their training). I wanted to find another castle somewhere on the coast which we could use as Blofeld's fortress. It wasn't to be found, and I realized the reason: the Japanese never built castles on the coast, because these would take the full force of the typhoons which rip through that area.

We had been flying around for days and still hadn't found the ideal location. We made one last sweep over the island of Kyushu, which is at the southern tip of Japan. It is a great landscape of mountains and extinct volcanoes. Weaving through the steep ranges, we looked down and spotted exactly what we were looking for. It was the volcano Aso-san, which has the largest crater in the world. At the centre of it was a lake, the whole arena circled by volcanoes. It was perfect.

I decided we could place everything in this crater area: Blofeld's fortress and all the space hardware, including the launching pad for Blofeld's capsule-grabbing operation. Now and again the Bond scriptwriters are accused of being too outlandish in their ideas. In fact our storylines, intentionally or by coincidence, frequently reflect today's, or even tomorrow's, headlines. While the script was being written, US astronauts were walking in space. Off the coast of Spain, a US Air Force B52 bomber was lost with two atomic bombs on board, leading the newspapers to speculate whether an unfriendly country might try to grab them. Both stories gave our scripts a strong flavour of authenticity.

It was a tough location and, shooting at the height of the Japanese summer, brutally hot and uncomfortable. Officials in Tokyo – Bond fanatics many of them – gave us all the help and facilities we needed. But it was still rough going for the crew, with temperatures hitting a hundred degrees.

Sean Connery, who, like any other major star, can make waves occasionally, is also capable of an act of instant kindness and concern. Dana and I had brought Barbara with us to Japan. As she was then only five years old, Dana didn't want to leave her alone in England. We were sleeping Japanese fashion on thin mattresses laid out on the floor. There were no sheets or proper pillows. Barbara became ill with a fever and her temperature hit one hundred and four degrees. Dana said, 'I don't know how we do it but I've got to get this child a bed with a proper mattress and some sheets.' It was essential for Sean, who worked all day in the heat, to have a bed. But the moment he heard about Barbara, he gave his bed, mattress, sheets and all. This was one of his many likeable qualities, which owe a lot, I believe, to his solid upbringing in the backstreets of Edinburgh.

When the film started I wondered how Sean and Roald Dahl, who is a pretty good needler himself, would get on. Dahl had brought his wife, the actress Patricia Neal, to the location. She had suffered a stroke, but was recovering remarkably well. One afternoon, in the stifling island heat, we took a dip in a pool, then slipped into kimonos. It was the sort of garment to wear with the temperatures in the nineties. Dahl arrived with Patricia Neal. He was rigged out in gear of the typical English colonial: shirt, long khaki shorts, black socks and white tennis shoes. He stared at us in our kimonos and sniffed, 'You all look a strange, ridiculous, motley group in those Japanese costumes.'

Connery stared back at Dahl. 'Well, you, Roald, look like an English asshole in your long khaki shorts, or to be more precise, a Norwegian asshole!' Laughter and Dissolve.

Roald's deceptively brusque manner intrigued Dana, particularly in his handling of his wife's recovery. Sometimes he appeared to come down very hard on Patricia. In fact, it was extremely subtle and effective therapy. Dana, involved in one particular incident, was convinced it was this treatment that really helped Patricia fight back. They had both stepped out of a helicopter onto the burning sand along the island beach. Even Dana found it hard to walk, let alone Patricia, who stumbled once or twice. She fell into a nest of bees, and was crying when Dana helped her to her feet. 'I'll never be all right,' she said, in tears.

Roald Dahl, who had observed the whole scene from the top of a stairway leading from the beach to the hotel, made a show of scolding his wife. 'Well, you are making a great spectacle of yourself! Falling all over the place!' To any outsider, it might have seemed inhuman. To those who understood, Roald was simply playing the tough coach to get every ounce of effort from Patricia. But I know Dana was quite upset for her before she caught on to the 'treatment'.

The final casting of the picture involved the actor to play Blofeld and the two Japanese heroines in the script, Kissy Suzuki and Aki. We needed more than just attractive girls. They had to be able to perform and have good enough English for the roles. There were a few candidates in Europe and Hawaii, but they were too American or generally Westernized. Moreover, the Japanese were keen for us to use their home talent, so we finally chose two lovely kids: Akiko Wakabayashi to play Aki and Mie Hama as Kissy Suzuki. We brought them to London and put them on a crash course to improve what little English they had. Akiko had the edge on Mie, who was finding it hard to get the words out. Lewis Gilbert said he didn't think she could handle it, and we decided to drop her. Lewis, who achieved a great rapport with the Japanese contingent, worked out a way of letting Mie down gently, maintaining all the essential courtesies. He spoke to Tetsuro Tamba, who plays the Japanese Secret Service chief in the film, told him of our decision and asked him to explain the whole thing nicely to Mie.

Tamba took her out to dinner and broke the news. The following day he came to our production meeting and we asked him if Mie understood the situation.

'Yes, I told her,' Tamba said.

'And how did she take it?'

'She said OK, if she was out she'd commit suicide. She couldn't go home to Japan and face the loss of honour after all the pre-publicity, with James Bond being the king in Japan and she having this big role opposite him.'

True or not, I decided prudence was called for. I said quickly to Lewis, 'She's not that bad, is she?'

Lewis nodded. 'Not when you come to think about it.'

'Well, that's settled,' I said to Tamba. 'Tell Miss Hama she's back in the picture. We'll fit her in somehow.'

Tamba bowed. Mie dried her tears. Working on a Bond picture calls for great dedication, but not hara-kiri.

Casting the arch-villain Blofeld was a tougher proposition. Gert Frobe's masterly Goldfinger had been the benchmark of sophisticated evil. Every subsequent Bond protagonist would be, whether we liked it or not, measured against him. Time was short and, odd as it may seem, there weren't many actors around who could effectively play this part. Eventually we chose Donald Pleasence, who was a very successful British actor specializing in a kind of pale-eyed menace. We were criticized for this, some people saying he was miscast. I don't accept this. His icy, deadpan style, and a formidable track record of screen villains, made him as good a candidate as anybody else.

But none of these casting problems – or any other headache on the picture – added up to a row of beans compared with the tragic helicopter accident which overshadowed the entire production. It was the afternoon of September 22, 1966. Johnny Jordan, a cameraman with extensive experience in aerial photography, was filming from a French Alouette helicopter. He was racing above a couple of other helicopters featured in the dive attack on Bond. One of them got caught in an updraught which threw it straight into the path of Jordan's helicopter. One of its rotor blades hit a skid of the Alouette, slicing through Jordan's extended foot. All of us watching from below were horrified. A group of surgeons were holding a symposium not far from where the accident occurred. It was a great stroke of luck. An operating room was being used for demonstrations, and doctors swiftly pushed everything out of the way and operated to stitch the foot back on using micro-surgery, a comparatively new procedure at the time.

Later, when he was able to speak, I asked Johnny what he wanted to do. He said he wanted to get back to London. We flew him back with a Japanese nurse detailed to take care of him. Dana and I went to see him in the London Clinic. This guy had guts. It had been a gruesome, traumatic experience, but he made no big scene over it.

'Well, Johnny,' I asked him, 'is there anything you'd like?'

'Yes, Cubby,' he said, 'I'd like to have this foot taken off. It's still not quite right to me. A friend of mine who went through a similar experience tells me the pain, especially in bad weather, can be quite rough. I'd rather have the thing off.'

I wasn't going to buy this and I told him so. 'You'd better think this over, Johnny,' I said.

'I've done that, Cubby. I really don't want this foot any more.'

We shook hands, and a couple of days later the surgeons carried out the amputation. He had an artificial foot fitted, and months later he was back filming again.

Good luck, bad luck, I've learned to take both with caution. On our recce in Japan for *You Only Live Twice*, Ken Adam and I stayed for a while at the Tokyo Hilton. We had got to know several guests at the hotel who were flying to Hong Kong. The day they left we said our goodbyes and watched them all drive off in limousines. Not long after, their plane crashed into Mount Fuji. There was one survivor. The next day Ken Adam and I had a booking to fly out of Tokyo. I had a phone call telling me that an Army film I particularly wanted to see, of the Ninja Fighters, could only be seen on that day. I told Ken we'd have to cancel our flight. He said, 'No...I've got to get to Hong Kong.'

'I'm sorry, Ken,' I replied, 'I have to see these Ninjas, and so do you. I'm cancelling our flight.'

That plane crashed, too. All the passengers were killed. The sole survivor of the first disaster died in the second crash.

SIXTEEN

Exit Sean Connery. Tired of the Bond image, he threw off what he saw as a strait-jacket and strode out in search of a new identity. Sean's parting shot to a columnist was: 'It's finished. I don't want to know. Bond has been good to me, but I've done my bit. I'm out!'

If that was the way he felt, so be it. An actor is a free agent. Sean had no contractual obligation to us, and in any event, I never fight to retain a reluctant performer. There was some brief media hysteria predicting that Connery's abdication would force the 007 empire into oblivion. It didn't happen, because of one fundamental truth: James Bond 007 is the real star. It is always one notch bigger than the actor who plays him. It is like a space station – it stays in orbit whichever hero is up there at any given time. And in that respect, it can take on board any kind of character, except a dissident. So if Sean had decided he'd had enough, there would be no feelings of bereavement in our office. Connery was right about one thing: Bond certainly had been good to him; in fact, to all of us. I wished him good luck.

I had always been happy about my relationship with Sean despite his occasional churlishness about the way we were supposed to have treated him. If he had a less pleasant relationship with Harry Saltzman, I wouldn't necessarily blame my ex-partner. Sean is supposed to have threatened now and again to walk off the set if Harry was there. True or not, I would never have supported him. No actor can ever be allowed to pull that number on a film.

Sean was great in the pictures he did for us, and he'd probably concede they were great for his career, too. Certainly if we did nothing else, we gave him a tremendous financial boost. Looking at it objectively, Sean was hardly well known when we signed him. Not that he didn't have the looks or the talent. He obviously had both or we wouldn't have signed him in the first place. But it was undeveloped material: raw merchandise that needed to be recognized, processed, restyled into something attractive and exciting. He was – and I was convinced of this from the outset – a star in embryo. There was a lot of animal virility and banked-down energy which nobody else had seemed aware of. He came to us with a track record that had shown all the promise but nothing significant had happened

Maybe Fox, who had him under contract, never found the right subjects. Perhaps the characters he'd associated with originally were unable to discern his immense screen potential. They saw a ruggedly handsome Scottish giant, but nothing of the humour or the fire inside the man. They put him with Lana Turner, and the two of them cancelled each other out. In almost everything else he did before Bond, he was marking time, going no place. And not getting paid much into the bargain.

From the day he started with us he had money in his pocket. More important, he was groomed, polished and given maximum exposure before a world audience. It's what an actor dreams about. He deserved his success. He was the tenement kid who'd made it. And nobody was more delighted than me. Having been up that mountain myself, I understood what it meant to him and his family. But it wouldn't have happened if we hadn't fought off the top brass at UA, who, when we picked him for Bond, urgently cabled back asking us to keep on looking. But we ignored them, and in less than five years we had made Sean Connery an international star.

Now he has claimed we underpaid him. My answer to that is: if becoming a millionaire with us meant we short-changed him, then simple arithmetic means different things to different people. Also, Sean should reflect whether he would have become a millionaire without us, or more specifically, without James Bond. A fair acknowledgement might not be amiss. It all happened years ago, and situations like this have long ceased to bother me. Bond's future is assured, and in any event it isn't going to be affected by what anybody said, or didn't say, in the late 1960s. But some professional observations can be made. First, the notion that Bond somehow stifles an actor. Wrong on two counts. One:

surprisingly, 007 offers great scope to any actor smart enough to see the several dimensions of the character. Two: if Bond was that limiting, it's curious how so many famous actors have wanted to play the part. They are not merely attracted by the huge box-office returns of the Bond films. They recognize that Bond helps them grow as an actor.

Far from restricting Sean, we went out of our way to help him. He had the right in his contract with us to make one non-Bond film a year. In fact he could have made these films with us too, but he didn't favour that idea. Maybe he thought we didn't know how to make pictures. Still he had this urge to step out of 007's shadow now and again, and we did what we could do to help. We asked him who he wanted to work with. 'Fooking Hitchcock!' he replied, the vernacular, in this instance, being Sean's way of expressing admiration. I went through the correct rituals and spoke to the agent Lew Wasserman, who was connected with the studio where Hitchcock was working at the time. He was surprised. 'What's the matter, isn't Sean doing well enough with you guys?'

I said, 'Sure, but he has this desire to make a picture with Hitchcock. And I can understand that.' So I spoke to Hitchcock and Sean made a picture for him. It was called *Marnie*. 'Hitch' was disappointed in it. I don't think Sean will list it among his best efforts, either.

He followed that episode with a film for Sidney Lumet called *The Hill*. It got good notices, though it was not a commercial success. Ken Hyman, who produced it, had approached me saying he would dearly like to have Sean for the film. I told Sean that Ken and Sidney Lumet were eager to talk to him. 'Sure, I'll talk to them,' he said. And that's how he got to make *The Hill*. As for the first batch of films he made after leaving Bond, the records speak for themselves. When Sean left, we shook hands and I wished him well. And I meant it. I get a kick out of success and rejoice at nobody's failure. The plain fact is that, apart from *The Anderson Tapes*, in which he was first-class, Sean's first films after Bond were no great shakes. Much later on he had some brilliant successes and deservedly won an Oscar for *The Untouchables*. I'm delighted for him.

So now we had to find another Bond. The ground rules hadn't changed. Everybody knew the kind of hero we were looking for:

he had to be British, personable and built to fit the Fleming blueprint. Above all, he had to have all the elements of strong box-office potential. It involved us in another massive search and, as before, we threw the net across the world. Harry and I interviewed several possibilities. We brought in Peter Hunt as director to honour a pledge. He is an excellent film editor whose work on the early Bond films was outstanding. He had always wanted to direct, and we promised to give him his chance with the sixth Bond film, *On Her Majesty's Secret Service*. Dick Maibaum, the writing mainstay of the Bond films, came back to do the script.

The man we eventually chose to play Bond was a former Australian model named George Lazenby. I had, in fact, spotted him three years earlier at Kurt's barber shop in Mayfair. I looked across to the next chair and saw this handsome character with a strong jaw, great physique and a lot of self-assurance. I remembered thinking what a good Bond he would make, but I figured if he was having his hair cut at Kurt's – which doesn't come cheap – he was probably a businessman, and a wealthy one at that.

What I didn't know at the time was that, according to insiders, Lazenby had done a bit of shrewd sleuthing and discovered that I went to Kurt's shop. He made it his business to find out about my next appointment so that he could be there at the same time. This was acknowledged by Kurt, who became a kind of a co-conspirator. Afterwards, when I got back to the office, I had someone ring Kurt's to find out who the customer was. I discovered he was earning £20,000 a year (1968) doing TV ads. So I always had him at the back of my mind, and when Sean left we brought him in for tests.

Everyone, particularly Peter Hunt, was impressed by Lazenby. The infallible litmus test was to parade him in front of the office secretaries. Their eyes lit up as he swung past their desks and through to our office. Six foot two inches tall – the same height as Connery – he was a hundred-and-eighty-six-pounder who knew how to walk tall and put himself over. We tested him along with three other short-listed actors. What clinched it for Lazenby were the fight sequences we filmed to test what kind of an action man he was. The key scene was the tussle Bond has with a would-be assassin in a Portuguese hotel. Lazenby, whose modelling experience hardly prepared him for it, gave an excellent performance. United Artists in New York saw the tests and backed our judgement that he was the best actor available to succeed Sean Connery.

[Born in Goulburn, Australia, in 1939, Lazenby was the son of the greenkeeper at the local bowls club. His first job was as a used-car salesman. He came to England in 1964, and it was a photographer who persuaded him he could make more money as a model. He styled fabrics for the rag trade, sudded his thick, dark hair in shampoo preparations, and extolled High Speed Gas for British Petroleum. But his commercial with the most sex appeal was the one for Fry's Chocolate, in which our smiling hero strides like a gladiator bearing a giant-sized crate of chocolate on his massive shoulders. As a result, his personal rating soared with the advertising companies. When the search for the new Bond made headlines, his agent contacted Eon Productions, enclosing Lazenby's photo. Cubby Broccoli looked at it, matching his face with that handsome customer in Kurt's barber shop. Lazenby was signed…and would never have to hoist chocolate on his shoulders again.]

We put together some fine talent in *On Her Majesty's Secret Service*. We brought in Telly Savalas to play Blofeld, developing a talent that would later be acclaimed worldwide in his portrayal of Kojak. Diana Rigg, a British actress I have always admired, ideally suited the role of Tracy, the rich but disillusioned playgirl who falls in love with Bond.

The story is pure Fleming: Blofeld plans to unleash biological warfare on the world using a string of beautiful dupes unknowingly equipped with deadly atomizers. Blofeld's fortress is embedded high on a peak in the Swiss Alps, giving us scope for the breathtaking Alpine action shots in which Johnny Jordan filmed some of the best aerial sequences of his career. Dangling from a helicopter in a sort of parachute harness, he swung through the peaks and the tall pine forests, producing cinematography that made the heart leap. In the controversial logistics of film-making, one thing is for sure: not a dime is overspent in creating visual masterpieces like these.

(The saddest sequel to it all occurred a year or so later. Filming action material for *Catch-22* in Mexico, Johnny fell out of a plane and was killed. There are a lot of unsung heroes in the motion-picture business. Johnny Jordan was among the best of them.)

John Barry's score for the film was one of his finest. It featured the song 'We Have All the Time In the World', a beautiful number and a great favourite of Barry's. The title was taken from the last page of Fleming's novel. It needed to be sung with a mature, reflective kind of voice. Barry immediately thought of Louis Armstrong, one of the few performers who could justly be described as a legend. But Armstrong had been in hospital for nearly a year and had still barely recovered. I suggested they raise the idea with him gently. He was frail but, born trouper that he was, he somehow managed to sing our song. At the end of the recording session in New York, he took Barry's hands and grinned, 'Thanks for the gig, man!' He died soon after.

Considering he was a beginner walking in Sean Connery's shadow, Lazenby, in my judgement, made a good James Bond. He could easily have fallen into the trap of doing a smart but fatal imitation of Sean. Instead, he fought his corner as a fledgeling actor, avoided tricks and gave a surprisingly effective performance. The *Variety* critic, while conceding George suffered inevitable comparison with Connery, declared him to be 'pleasant, capable and attractive in the role'. Generally, though, critics passed on Lazenby, giving him points for trying, but reserving judgement until his next Bond picture.

Unfortunately, that wasn't going to happen. In my opinion, George ruled himself out of the reckoning by behaving like the superstar he wasn't.

The fact is, film production, especially on arduous locations, can't tolerate an over-assertive ego, not on a film costing millions. Lazenby didn't get on too well with the director, Peter Hunt, nor, apparently, with his co-star, Diana Rigg. We put limousines at his disposal and he ended up quarrelling with the chauffeurs. I was astounded. Here was a guy taken out of the modelling business; a man who had seen Sean Connery parlay James Bond to millionaire status; yet here he was, in professional terms, sawing off the branch he was sitting on.

Dana remembers one particular incident: 'There was already

much uneasiness about George when we arrived on location in Switzerland. He seemed to be at odds with almost everyone. In fact, it became so apparent Telly Savalas took him on one side and read him a lecture: "Listen, George, why are you being so difficult? Most actors would give their back teeth to get this kind of a break. You should be paying Cubby, not the other way round, so why don't you cool it?"

'Normally the atmosphere on a Bond picture is wonderfully friendly. But at one point feelings were so charged, people not talking to each other, I said to Cubby, "It'll be Thanksgiving in a day or so. Why don't we give a party for the crew?"

'Cubby thought it was a great idea. "Invite the lot, every single person doing any kind of job on the picture," he said. We only had a day to put the plan together. It was such a big undertaking, one hotel on its own couldn't handle it. But in hours I'd persuaded other hotels to help out with the food, which was brought in heated containers from all over town. There was no time to send out individual invitations. Instead, we pinned notices up in the hotel elevators, putting it on the call sheet which everyone would read, announcing the James Bond party. Some of the crew wondered whether George Lazenby, who was having this arm's-length relationship with everyone, would actually appear. About a half-hour into the evening, everybody having a good time, Lazenby arrived, standing alone at the door. Nobody went to talk to him, since he looked too gloomy. So I went over to him.

'"Hello George...Come over here and sit down."

'He did, but continued to pout.

'I said, "George, what seems to be the trouble? Why are you so unhappy?"

'"Well, I didn't receive a special invitation to this party."

'"But George," I explained, "this whole thing was just pulled together in twenty-four hours. The announcement was posted everywhere. Everyone was notified the same way."

'He frowned and said, "But I'm a *star*!"

'I laughed. I thought at first he was joking. In my whole experience I have never heard a star describe himself or herself that way. But George wasn't joking. Cubby, who was sitting close by, didn't think it was funny, either. He was clearly fed up with George's behaviour. He leaned across and said, "Listen, George, you're not a star – yet. You are not a star just because you call yourself a star, or the publicity people call you a star, or the director calls you a star. You're only a star when the public says so. And this we still have to see!"'

Years later, Lazenby conceded he'd blown it on Bond. He told Peter Haining, 'The trouble was I lived Bond out of the studios as well as in. I had to have a Rolls-Royce to go around in, and women just threw themselves at me if I stepped into a nightclub. I couldn't count the parade that passed through my bedroom. I became hot-headed, greedy and big-headed.' Unfortunately, the remorse came just a little too late.

There were good things happening that year, too. I went back to Astoria, Long Island, where I was born. The Board of Directors of the Boys' Club of Queens honoured me with their Man of the Year Award. [This cited Cubby's 'dedicated efforts' on behalf of several youth organizations.] They produced a fine dinner at the Waldorf Astoria. I was delighted and touched when Bob Hope turned up unannounced as a tribute to me. He cracked a couple of jokes, then Tony Bennett looked in and sang. It was generous of the Board, but in fact I felt I owed something to Astoria, to a new generation of kids having their shot at the American Dream.

It was an odd feeling standing on the familiar sidewalks again, walking past my first school, PS No. 7; along Hoyt Avenue, where I worked behind the counter of Iorio's Drugstore and where Marietta, my grandmother, helped out as the neighbourhood midwife. It was a semi-rural area then. Now the town has spilled over into the fields; Giovanni and old man de Cicco would today see concrete and tarmac where once they planted vegetables. For all the struggles my family endured, I had some happy years in Astoria. If I've done anything at all for the kids here it was, in a sense, the repayment of a debt. There was a lot of humanity here among the hardship. I looked at their faces – a microcosm of the big-city racial mix – and hoped that one day they would have the same pride I was feeling nearly sixty years on. My inspiration had been Charles Lindbergh, routed – or was it fated? – to overfly the farm where I was working, on his landmark flight across the Atlantic. But this was the 1960s generation I was now looking at, and I wondered who their inspiration would be. It was an enjoyable day for me, Dana and the family. We all had the same thought: a pity Marietta, Giovanni, Cristina and John weren't around to see it.

The nostalgia of New York dissolved swiftly into the realities facing us in London. We urgently had to find another James Bond for *Diamonds Are Forever*. With Connery gone, Lazenby a non-starter, the field was again wide open. It was the mixture as before: another worldwide search, names being thrown at us from all sides. Burt Reynolds was a name which surfaced several times. He was not the major star he is now, but he had a big following, particularly among women. If he'd been British, he'd have been a strong contender.

After weeks of interviews, looking at hundreds of photos, talking to agents, we found we were reshuffling the pack. We couldn't find a British actor, known or unknown, exciting enough to handle a character who had now become a cult hero. Harry and I decided that reluctantly we might have to bend our rule about Bond having to be British. If we were forced to use an American, however, he would still have to have the stamp and style of a British Secret Agent. We needed a good actor, but without the star label, which would have worked against the creating of a new Bond.

We found the one person who matched up to that requirement: John Gavin. He had worked for Kubrick on *Spartacus*, playing the young Julius Caesar. He starred in *The Cardinal* and had been in a couple of television series. He was tall, a good athlete and a fine actor. He performed well in some action tests we made. We finally signed him for the role, and the pre-production process began. The script was already well advanced, and Guy Hamilton returned as the director.

In New York, however, David Picker of United Artists was simultaneously pursuing an alternative plan. Wisely or unwisely, he was manoeuvring to bring Sean Connery back as James Bond. He wanted him so desperately he flew over to London and offered Sean a monumental deal in which the actor virtually wrote his own ticket. It was a basic salary of $1.2 million, plus a percentage, plus a hefty sum if the film overran its schedule, plus an agreement in which UA backed two further films of Sean's choosing, which he could star in or direct.

Sean had turned his back on Bond. He was clearly a restless actor, anxious to discover whether he could repeat his triumph as

Bond in other roles. And to be fair to Sean, he did. He had declared himself to be 'sick of the Bond image'. But then along comes David Picker dealing him a handful of aces, sweetening the pot with more money than he had ever dreamed of. It was then that the shrewd Scot decided it was an offer he couldn't refuse. Harry and I had misgivings about taking him back. But we couldn't ignore UA's insistence, nor overlook Sean's strong hold on the world box office. So we honoured our 'pay or play' contract to Gavin and he left. He later became US Ambassador to Mexico. Only he can say whether, in the long run, he got the better of the deal. He is certainly a good ambassador. He might also have made a first-class Bond.

Audience reaction to the previous Bond showed humour to be a big factor. We hired Tom Mankiewicz, a witty writer, son of the distinguished director Joseph Mankiewicz, to work on the script. We intended to keep fairly close to the Fleming story of Bond infiltrating a diamond-smuggling organization run by American gangsters linked to England, South Africa and Las Vegas. But we all felt the story a little tame, too much like any other spy thriller. We were sitting around discussing ideas, when I mentioned a frightening dream I'd had the previous night.

I dreamed I was on the terrace of Howard Hughes's apartment in Las Vegas. It was mid-afternoon, and I walked up to a picture window of Hughes's suite, looked in and saw a man seated there with his back to me. I rapped on the window and called out, 'Sam...' The man turned round, but it wasn't Hughes; it was some kind of impostor. It was a weird, unnerving dream. The writers were groping around for ideas. I told them the story of the dream. It seemed to me to be as good as anything they had in mind. The script took on a whole sea change, with a threat to the world powers using a diamond-powered laser satellite and Blofeld kidnapping this Hughes-like character (building satellites for the US) and impersonating him: a plausible scheme, since the public had never seen him. The idea worked well. But I couldn't guarantee to have a dream for every script.

My friendship with Howard Hughes was sustained in those days largely through third parties. He had now become a total recluse, locked behind sealed doors, with Mormon retainers standing guard outside. Getting more frail each day, terrified of virtually any kind of human contact, he was a pitiful contrast to the vital, attractive character I'd had so much fun with years before. Hughes had his flaws, his crazy obsessions and his infuriating demands on your time. But he was for America as passionately as anyone I've ever known. The most uncanny feature of our friendship was the way he kept tabs on my activities even when he'd sealed himself off from the world. There were two intriguing examples of this when we moved into Las Vegas to start filming there.

We needed a ranch to shoot certain sequences. I knew Howard had bought one some time before from a German industrialist, but, as we might have expected, no one could get in to see it. I wanted to see if it was suitable for our purposes. I talked to Howard's friend and associate Walter Kane and told him what I wanted. He came back to me saying he had 'word from the penthouse' that it was OK for me to go into the ranch. We went there with art directors and the crew, identified ourselves to the guards on the gate and were waved in. 'Word from the penthouse' had filtered through to them, too. The ranch was lovely, though too small for the scenes we had in mind.

So we passed on the ranch, but we needed some shots in the hotel where we were staying: Ted Moore wanted to shoot a scene from the top of the lift shaft to the bottom. But the hotel manager refused. Hughes owned the hotel, so I had another conversation with Walter Kane, who talked to 'the penthouse'. The word came back, 'Tell Cubby he can shoot anywhere anytime, in any of the hotels I own.'

The Hughes connection was also significant in an incident at our hotel. We came in late one evening and went to bed. In the middle of the night, one or more intruders crept in and stole Dana's purse off the night-table, a piece of antique English jewellery that she especially liked, and some money we'd forgotten to put into the hotel safe. We had slept right through it. The security people were convinced the robbers had squirted a chloroform spray in the room to put us out so that we wouldn't hear them. It was a frightening experience, especially for Dana.

In the evening we came back from the location to find two men posted outside our door. They had apparently been there all night and all day. I asked the front desk if this was standard hotel procedure. They were surprised. The two men were nothing to do with them. So I asked the men who'd sent them.

'Compliments of Mr Howard Hughes, Mr Broccoli. Our orders are to stay here round the clock until you leave.'

Reviewers of Connery's performance in *Diamonds* say he gave one of his most relaxed and confident performances. He seemed, they said, to be enjoying himself; and when that happens with an actor, he's at his best. The main location, Las Vegas, was certainly a conducive factor. If Sean couldn't relax in Vegas, then he had a problem. In addition to providing a luxury suite at the best hotel in town, we fixed it for him to play golf at one or two of the great desert golf courses nearby. Once he had decided to come in from the cold, so to speak, Harry and I did what we could to keep him happy. If this was to be his last Bond film for us, then we wanted to part as friends. The odd critic complained that Sean 'walked' through the picture, didn't give the production all he had. I refute this. He may have his faults, but Sean is too much the professional to short-change himself, let alone us, as an actor.

There were some good ideas in the movie. The two assassins in the original story, Mr Wint and Mr Kidd, came as the conventional thugs. Hamilton and Mankiewicz pushed for them to be camp and funny. It was a risk, but it worked. Audiences loved these villainous gays. By then, 1970, it was an acceptable theme in the cinemas. A few years earlier and I might have objected. In this connection, the criteria we apply in the making of the Bond pictures have been worked out with a lot of care and a lot of listening. I read what the critics say; I read reports from sneak previews; but most important of all, I go night after night to theatres where our pictures are playing to sense the way audiences react to particular, perhaps controversial scenes. Also, I talk to the house managers to find out if there have been any complaints and, if so, what their substance is.

It is essential, however, to give writers a free hand. Fleming's stories were tailored for the light read. They were never constructed with films in mind. Which is why we have to build on them, restyle them for the age of lasers, computers, space travel and genetic engineering. The balance has to be carefully drawn between fantasy and credibility. You can go just so far with Bond. The only time I blow the whistle on the writers is if they get too smart and try to upstage the audiences. I like to keep the dialogue simple. If it is likely to go over the heads of the audience, then it

goes out of the window. Of course, writers will fight their corner
if they think they're right and I'm wrong. They've got to do that.
I wouldn't respect them if they didn't.

[One such writer, Tom Mankiewicz, recalls a confrontation he
had with the late Harry Saltzman on *Diamonds Are Forever*:
  'Everybody had told me to look out for Harry. He had this
reputation as a talent picker but not for the finer sensitivities. He
stormed into one of the bungalows at Universal one day – we'd
rented bungalows at the studio – and he said to me, "I understand
you're doing a good job. I understand it's OK, but tell me, what
is the threat? That's what it's got to get down to: what is the
threat?"
  'I said, "The threat is, Harry, Blofeld's gonna destroy the
world."
  'He shook his head, said, "It's not big enough," and walked
out.']

We had always been tempted by the notion of making a Bond film
in the Soviet Union. *From Russia With Love* had been one of our
biggest hits. Fleming himself, with his Foreign Office contacts and
as a former Reuters correspondent in Moscow, knew his way
around the dark corners there better than most. By the mid-1970s,
perhaps because the Soviet regime was beginning to see the
writing on the wall, it set out to woo the West. Getting film-
makers in from Hollywood was high on its list of priorities. By
then the enormous success of James Bond had penetrated the Iron
Curtain, and the Soviet film authorities officially invited us to
Moscow in April 1975 in the hope that we might make a picture
there.
  Not a Bond film, though. As Dr Edward A. Aikazian, Chief of
the US Section of the State Committee of the USSR, Council of
Ministers for Science and Technology, Moscow, explained
straight-faced, the Soviet Union was not quite ready for James
Bond. 007's Turnbull and Asser Sea Island cotton shirts, silk
pyjamas, Pinaud Elixir shampoo and Guerlain's 'Fleurs des Alpes'
were frowned on as capitalist decadence in those far-off, pre-
Gorbachev days.
  So when we flew from London on the Aeroflot flight to
Moscow on April 13, we expected to hit a cultural stone wall;

certainly no empathy with the world of 007. Instead, I was surprised to discover that the film chiefs knew all about me and the Bond pictures and couldn't wait to see the film we'd brought with us for a special embassy screening, *The Man with the Golden Gun*. The wife of the American Ambassador, who was hosting the evening, told Dana she had no idea how many guests would be arriving. Apparently it's an old Soviet custom not to reply to invitations. The diplomats either turn up or they don't. In the event, a huge gathering of ambassadors and other diplomats arrived with their wives and it was a highly successful evening.

The Soviet officials looked with some envy at the high artistic and technological quality of the production. The President of Sovinfilm, Otar V. Teneishvili, discussed a couple of possible ideas for co-productions in the Soviet Union. One was a story which had been around for a while called *The Cowboy and the Cossack*. It turned out that Warners apparently held a prior interest in the subject, which ruled it out for us. Another idea was the story of the American journalist John Reed, the Communist who, after being indicted for sedition in the States, fled to Russia, where he died and was buried in the Kremlin. It was not my kind of subject and in any event the picture was later made by Warren Beatty. I was pleased, though, to learn that *Goldfinger* so impressed the Soviet film-makers it is used in film schools there to train future directors.

In the Leningrad studios, where, incidentally, Elizabeth Taylor was filming, Soviet technicians were well clued in to the Bond pictures and, like film-makers the world over, were spellbound by the stunts. Michael Wilson had the opportunity to talk with a group of bright young student intellectuals. A book buff himself, Michael sympathized with them when they told him that half the books they wanted to read were on the officially banned list. They got round that problem by taking their vacations in Helsinki, where they could get all the books they wanted to read without someone leaning over their shoulder.

In those days, co-production deals with the Russians bristled with problems: political, cultural and so forth. But since then barriers have been crashing down almost daily. Suddenly Soviet citizens no longer feel guilty about wanting democracy and all the good things in life. They may even be ready now for James Bond.

SEVENTEEN

Sean Connery's swansong as our James Bond (he would do a controversial one-off for someone else later) hit a high note at the box office. *Diamonds Are Forever* opened simultaneously in Britain and America at Christmas 1971, and broke all existing records. It was the runaway box-office champion of the year.

But now casting the right actor as his replacement was crucial, though that challenge never bothered me. I was sure that whoever played Bond, it was the film millions went to see. This time the search was much shorter. Ten years earlier we probably would have cast Roger Moore for *On Her Majesty's Secret Service* but for his commitment to the television series *The Persuaders*. Now he was free, and unreservedly my choice for the new James Bond. I made out a strong case for him. He had been Fleming's first choice as the Secret Service agent. He looked more the public-school drop-out, the socially well-connected gent, than did the more coarse-grained Sean Connery.

Harry and I split on the idea, however. He felt, not unreasonably, that Roger was too closely identified as Simon Templar, of the networked TV series *The Saint*. This cut across our belief that an unknown actor should be cast to create a new James Bond. But balancing that was Roger's talent as an assured actor. With a Niven-like touch in his humour, six-feet two and handsome, Roger had a claim on 007 that was stronger than all the other possible candidates'.

United Artists made dissenting noises, fearing that Roger couldn't step competently into Sean's shoes. Again they suggested we get an American actor with a big name. Burt Reynolds was floated again. Even Steve McQueen. All fine actors, but not James Bond. I could never see Burt or Steve as Bond; and Fleming would have spun in his grave. Also, without my knowledge, UA approached Clint Eastwood. He laughed at them. 'I couldn't play that part. For one thing I'm not British, and for another, I couldn't follow Sean Connery. No matter how much money you offer me, I can't play Bond.'

I wouldn't compromise on my choice of Roger for Bond, and eventually Harry and UA went along with it. But I wanted no repeat of the problems we'd had with Sean. Before we signed Roger, I laid it out for him. Sean had complained that Bond had shackled him as an actor, that people saw him as nobody else but James Bond, and so forth.

Roger widened his pale-blue eyes in astonishment. Complain about an opportunity like this? 'Me?! Never!' he said. 'Frankly, there's no way it's going to ruin my image. Personally,' he added, quoting an old showbiz saying, 'I'll kiss your backside in Macy's window if we make the picture a winner!'

I said, 'It's a generous offer, Roger, but I'll pass on that one. You don't have to do anything more than give us your best shot.' And we signed him.

[Roger Moore was no street-smart tearaway born on the wrong side of the tracks. Streatham, London, where he was raised, was solid, comfortable, lower-middle-class. Sean Connery had to battle his way out of the poverty trap. Roger had no such problems. Born on October 14, 1927, he had the contented and disciplined childhood you'd expect from a father who was a police officer and a mother who was the daughter of an Army sergeant-major. (Roger's fastidiousness with clothes, the immaculately combed hair and flawless look must owe something to this spit-and-polish background.)

Out of grammar school, he got a job in 1943 working on animated propaganda films to help the war effort. It was this that sparked his enthusiasm for motion pictures. His début was as an extra brandishing a spear in Gabriel Pascal's *Caesar and Cleopatra*. His spear-carrying was no different from anybody else's, but led to no alert-eyed scout picking him from the crowd. So he took himself off to the Royal Academy of Dramatic Art, where a useful career was predicted by his tutors. Then he did National Service, where his RADA training and very personable manner convinced the military he'd be a cinch with the Combined

Entertainment Section. He was, too. His mates there, admiring his elegance, nicknamed him 'The Duchess'. Out of uniform, he looked for stage and film work. With only small parts initially on offer, Roger did what most actors do when 'resting': washed dishes, became a waiter, a salesman and then a male model. This last was smart casting for the six-foot two-inch charmer with his twinkling blue eyes, boyish smile and a smooth self-assurance in a variety of outfits. Front covers of knitting magazines where he sports Fair Isle sweaters and thick-knit jerseys are now much sought after by his fans.

His first marriage, to a professional ice-skater, Lucy Woodward, foundered. He then married the volatile British songstress Dorothy Squires. They went to America together, she to sing, he to try his hand in Hollywood. He landed several film parts, among them *The Last Time I Saw Paris* with Elizabeth Taylor and Van Johnson, *Interrupted Melody* with Eleanor Powell, and *The King's Thief* with his friend David Niven (also a future Bond, in Charles Feldman's ill-fated *Casino Royale*). It brought him the TV series *Ivanhoe*, followed by *The Alaskans*, 1959, and *Maverick*, 1961. He continued to make films between the TV assignments, one of them, *The Rape of the Sabines*, taking him to Rome. There he met and fell in love with a beautiful Italian girl, Luisa Mattioli. His eventual marriage to her followed acrimonious divorce proceedings between him and Dorothy Squires.

Moore's role as Leslie Charteris's Simon Templar in *The Saint* series was a hit from the beginning. Roger was perfect as the debonair hero fighting crime. Six years in the role brought him a huge fan following, wealth and a weakness for hand-rolled Havana cigars. The fateful phone call from Cubby Broccoli would one day ensure a never-ending supply, plus a villa in the south of France, a chalet in Switzerland and a home life of some splendour in Beverly Hills, and – perhaps the ultimate accolade – an invitation to be a nude centrefold for *Cosmopolitan*.]

So it was decided that Roger Moore would star as James Bond in *Live and Let Die*. But we would have to make changes. His TV image was too glossy and soft-centred compared with the virile dynamite we had in Sean's James Bond. Essentially, we had to bury the Saint and all that lightweight giggling of *The Persuaders*.

Apart from cosmetic stuff like cutting his hair, getting rid of that naughty-boy smile and the one raised eyebrow, and making him look altogether leaner and tougher, we had to make Roger believe he was 007. He had to take on whole new dimensions, recognizing that Bond could be a mean bastard at times, a bit sadistic if the situation called for it, and that even his love scenes might need a touch of menace now and again.

I told Roger to walk like Bond, think like Bond, act like Bond, be Bond. Not that this meant he had to be another Sean Connery. That would be wrong and it wouldn't work. Anyway, any actor worth his salt would want to put his own imprint on the character, and by any objective judgement, Roger's Bond was immediately successful. He had a lighter touch, bringing the humour of the eighties into the role. There was less threat, less a feeling that things were about to explode around him. But his performance, though on a different level from Sean's, was pleasing and effective. And as I've said, it came closer to the Fleming original.

Again we departed from the novel in areas where we thought it wouldn't work in the film. I didn't care too much for the condescending way the book treated racial minorities. Also, the crooks were local villains whom we turned into international criminals. Tom Mankiewicz's screenplay was tailored to exploit Roger's sophisticated style of humour. It also produced some of the most daring boat-chase sequences on film.

All those who publicly or privately predicted Roger would hit the deck as Bond now said how good he was in the part. He prepared for his second 007 film, *The Man with the Golden Gun* (ninth in the series), with all the confidence you might expect of a Bond actor who'd proved he could hold his own against Sean. It had not been easy, as he himself admitted. He was well aware that when people, especially women, sized him up, they were subconsciously measuring him against Connery. But he handled that problem well. Whatever private fears he might have had, he was his own man in public. All credit to him, then, for succeeding in a role most actors regarded as one of the toughest in movies. He was enjoying himself. Box-office takings were still breaking records, in spite of our switching to a new James Bond. It was the kind of situation producers dream about.

But it was all overshadowed by the gathering storm involving

Harry Saltzman and myself which had been rumbling on for some time. This was no longer the normal disagreements between co-producers fighting it out over such things as casting, scripts or production costs. Nor was it merely a clash of personalities, though that had happened, for sure. The conflict between us went far deeper than that. Ultimately, it would involve heavy flak between tough attorneys, with Swiss banks and other interested parties watching intently from the sidelines. This is my version of the trouble between us as I remember it all. Years have passed since then, during which Harry lost his dear wife, Jacqui, and suffered a serious illness himself. But in reviewing my life and career, I can't ignore an episode which threatened to bring down everything I had worked for, and put in jeopardy not only the fortunes of Dana and myself, but also of our whole family. It was one of the blackest periods I ever had to face. But for Dana's fantastic resources and devotion, I might have thrown in the towel. As it was, we took on the battle of a lifetime – and won.

My initial disenchantment with my volatile former partner arose from what I saw as his hot-and-cold relationship with Bond. This is a personal opinion, but in essence Harry saw the 007 properties as the first step to conquering the world. Given a dozen pair of hands, Saltzman would be happiest having all the fingers in different pies. By contrast, James Bond, cruising along to becoming perhaps the greatest success in motion pictures, was a sufficient challenge as far as I was concerned. So even as far back as our second or third picture together, Harry had one eye over the other side of the mountain. He'd make an appearance on the set or on location, do a lot of shouting, then he'd be off to France, Italy or someplace else, making a film, taking over a company, doing what he loves most of all: playing the celebrated entrepreneur.

This hit-and-run technique was a pain to me because it would frequently upset the equilibrium of the production. Maibaum and Mankiewicz can speak for themselves, but both would concede, I believe, that life was made no easier for them, or the picture, by Harry's noisy entrances and exits. I'm not just talking about some of his wild ideas. We all have those. And I give him points for having some of the funniest.

When we were shooting in Thailand for *The Man with the Golden Gun*, Harry had this idea that we should have a big elephant chase in the picture. I said it didn't seem to fit into our script. An elephant chase would be very slow, and at that particular point we didn't need to stop the action. Harry disagreed. He'd been talking to the local villagers, who told him they could make shoes for the elephants which would speed up the chase. So he went out and ordered sixty pairs of shoes for these elephants. I don't remember how much it cost, but he didn't tell me he was having them done. One day I got a bill for the shoes. 'Who the hell are we buying these shoes for?' I said.

'For the elephants,' he replied.

'Where did you get them made, Harry – Gucci's?'

I refused to pay the bill, told the shoemakers to get the money from Harry – or from the elephants. I wasn't about to add that cost to the budget. Harry was furious, and of course we didn't shoot the scene.

[Tom Mankiewicz recalls a couple of even more hilarious anecdotes:

'Harry could be enormously bright. At a story meeting, he could shotgun six ideas at you. One or two might be absolutely wonderful. Four would be no good. But Harry would push each one with equal vigour and not be able to discriminate between one and the other. *In Live and Let Die* he had this scene which he kept wanting me to put in and I kept fighting him on it. It is a scene where Bond is lying in bed thinking that Solitaire (Jane Seymour) is lying next to him – this is not a scene in the movie! He reaches over for her and there is this huge crocodile in bed with him.

'I said, "Harry, Bond is asleep, right?"

'"Right," he said.

'I said, "Then why doesn't the crocodile eat him?"

'"Well, the crocodile just got on the bed."

'"But crocodiles have tiny little legs. How did this one get on the bed?"

'"He's in the bed, he's in the bed!" Harry insisted.

'"Well, how did the crocodile get in...? Who put him in the bed ...and why?"

'"I don't know who put him there!" Harry shouted.

'"So all Bond has to do to get away from the crocodile is roll out of bed?" I asked.

'"No, no – it's too dangerous."

Cubby and Dana Broccoli with Sean Connery, and Harry and Jacqueline Saltzman on location in Jamaica for *Dr No*.

Ian and Ann Fleming with Cubby at a private screening of *Dr No*.

Barbara's birthday party at Cubby and Dana's home in Green Street, Mayfair, on 18 June 1963. *Left to right, bottom*: Tina, Barbara and Tony; *left to right, top*: Cubby, Michael and Dana.

Left: Ursula Andress makes waves as Honey Ryder in *Dr No*.

Left: Pedro Armendariz in *From Russia With Love* (with Nadja Regin) shortly before his tragic death.

Below: Police hold back the crowds at the première of *Goldfinger*, 7 September 1964.

Chitty Chitty Bang Bang film poster, 1968.

Cubby and Dana being presented to HM The Queen at the première of *Chitty Chitty Bang Bang* on 16 December 1968.

George Lazenby faces the press as James Bond.

Boys Club of Queens, Inc.; Spyros Skouros presents Man of the Year Award to Cubby Broccoli, accompanied by Dana, in 1968.

Cubby, Harry Saltzman and Roger Moore take a break from filming *Live and Let Die* in Florida.

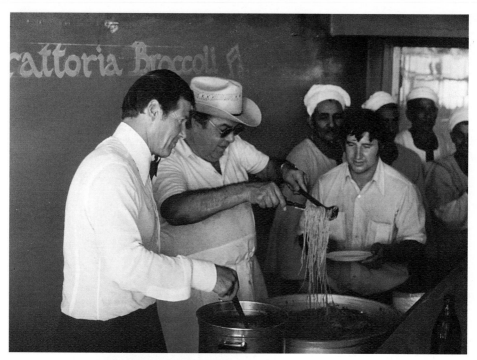

Cubby caters for the film crew at 'Trattoria Broccoli' with the help of Roger Moore during filming of *The Spy Who Loved Me*.

Cubby on location in Cortina, Italy on *For Your Eyes Only*.

Broccoli, Bond and backgammon: on the set of *For Your Eyes Only*.

Lady Diana Spencer, Roger Moore, HRH The Princess Margaret, Cubby Broccoli, and HRH The Prince of Wales at the première for *For Your Eyes Only*.

Speaker of the House (now Lord Weatherall), Mr and Mrs A. R. Broccoli and the then Prime Minister, Margaret Thatcher.

An informal Prince Philip and a smiling Broccoli at a Variety Club celebration.

President Reagan
shakes hands with
Cubby Broccoli: a
signed souvenir of
their meeting at the
White House, 10
April 1984.

Cubby, Dana and
George Bush. 'The
Broccoli the
President Really
Likes'.

Dear Cubby ~ Very Best Wishes +
Regards Ronald Reagan

Dana and Albert Broccoli
Now we're talking about the Broccoli I really like ~
Warm Regards. Gg Bush

Cubby and his Associate Producer, daughter Barbara Broccoli, on location in Austria for *The Living Daylights*.

France honours Cubby with the award of *Commandeur de L'Ordre des Art et des Lettres,* 1987.

The Broccoli star: Cubby backed by his family at the Hollywood sidewalk ceremony, 16 January 1990.

Cubby and Dana arrive at the première of *For Your Eyes Only*.

Timothy Dalton, Roger Moore and Pierce Brosnan at the tribute 'Celebrating the Life and Work of Cubby Broccoli', London 1996.

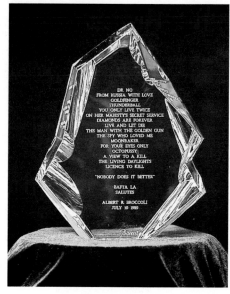

An honour rarely given,
the Irving G. Thalberg
Memorial Award, 1982.

BAFTA Award, 1989:
'Nobody Does it Better'.

Star of the Hollywood Walk of Fame, 1990.

'"And how does the crocodile get out?" I said. "I mean, he can't jump..."

'Four days later I met Harry and he said, "What happened to the crocodile scene?"

'I replied, "Harry, I just don't know how to write that scene," and he got mad. But finally he would give up and forget all about it.

'He floated another idea. For some reason he saw Bond in a giant spin-drier. Now, he didn't know why or where, but somebody was going to lock him in a spin-drier and he was going around and around in this giant machine.

'I said, "Harry – where is this spin-drier? Does the villain have a big spin-drier in his home...? Is there a spin-drier that can hold a six-foot three-inch human being?"

'"The villains throw him in," he insisted.

'"But what for, Harry? Are they going to spin him to death?"

'It never got into the movie, but he loved that idea.']

All this was the harmless, fun side of Harry Saltzman. And in any event, great ideas often emerge from characters throwing crazy notions to each other. The trouble starts when actors start complaining, writers get cheesed off and the atmosphere on the set becomes highly charged. And that is what was happening, first on *Live and Let Die* and later on *The Man with the Golden Gun*. If the problems had been restricted just to two partners falling out over the way the films should be made, there could have been a civilized separation, as happened between me and Irving Allen.

But Harry, against my advice, had taken on enormous outside ventures and was finding his knees giving way under the weight of it all. Flushed with the success of 007, believing in his own omnipotence, he went out and took over Technicolor, bought a couple of doomed camera companies, made a Beatles-type pop film which died at birth; he was in up to his neck and floundering. I was his partner and tried to dissuade him, but he wouldn't listen. He wanted to go out and buy films, some of dubious potential, borrow money from the company for this and other ventures, and with all these things there was a constant fight, a struggle to keep him from doing the things which could eventually ruin him. I don't think he ever consciously set out to bring me down. The plain fact is, he was in a spot, he was in a corner with his back against the wall, and he wanted to get out of it by using me and Dana – our money – to pay the banks. Well, there was no way I was ever going to let this happen.

The effect of this battle I was having with Harry, and all the financial questions involved, was a miserable period for Dana and me. Michael, my stepson, who had now spent two years with a prestigious law firm in Washington, came to London to help untangle the web being drawn around Danjaq, our Swiss company. He was going to be an enormous help in the oncoming confrontation.

The problems were aggravated by Tom Mankiewicz falling out with Guy Hamilton on *The Man with the Golden Gun*. This was Fleming's last novel, and became a best seller. Mankiewicz had written a good first draft, but for some reason he and Guy Hamilton weren't getting along. The situation came to a head in the summer of 1973, when Tom asked me if I'd take him off the picture.

[Tom recalls:
'We had come back from Iran – Cubby, Guy and myself. I'd finished this first draft. Guy and I were disagreeing, and it was getting worse and worse. I didn't know why. Guy was the person I was working with every day, more than with anybody else. Maybe I was a little nervous of the picture. It was the first picture where I was getting a piece of the profits. But all through the trip it had been getting very difficult, and Cubby had witnessed it. I made the decision I was going to leave, and told my father [Joseph Mankiewicz] I was coming back to New York.

'He said, "You've got to call Cubby."

'I did, and went over to see him. I remember he was in that little study of their house in Green Street, Mayfair, playing backgammon.

'I said, "Cubby, I want to leave."

'We sat and talked, and Cubby was sad about it. I told him I didn't want to hurt the picture, but I felt it was best if I left.

'Cubby, in his typical way, said, "That's OK, Tom. I understand."

'We shook hands, and I left."]

I asked Dick Maibaum to come in and work on Tom

Mankiewicz's script. He did this with some reluctance. His own relationship with my partner was a knife-edge situation. But once he started hitting the typewriter, Dick was as professional as ever. Roger Moore was now in his stride as Bond, and building his own battalion of aficionados. But as we started on *The Spy Who Loved Me*, the bomb which had been ticking away for a couple of years finally exploded. Danjaq was in peril, with Swiss bankers claiming Harry had pledged a hundred per cent of the company to cover liabilities said to be close to $20 million. Neither of us could do this under the rules of our partnership. In fact, the Swiss banks were holding the lettered stock which expressly prevented either party from pledging its stock for any personal reasons. The Swiss banks may have been convinced their loan to Saltzman was secured by Danjaq. But this was erroneous under the agreement and we strenuously contested it.

The immediate outcome was a dramatic freeze on the production. Our bitter row was now in the open. At that point Guy Hamilton decided to leave the picture. He claimed he couldn't continue to work with this terrible commotion going on between myself and Harry. His success with Bond meant that he now had 'play or pay' guarantees. In other words, if we didn't use him we'd have to pay him. About this time he had received offers to direct *Superman*. The legal wrangling was certainly the major reason for his leaving; *Superman* just sweetened the prospect. Dana and I were now in a siege situation. With the financing in jeopardy and the director gone, the production of *The Spy Who Loved Me* was in limbo.

The battle lines were drawn between lawyers representing Saltzman, the Union Bank of Switzerland (UBS) and other interested parties; and my attorneys, Norman R. Tyre and our son Michael Wilson. At stake: our survival. On the face of it, their team had the edge, if only in numbers. Halfway through the wrangling they produced what they thought was an ace: they wheeled in the famous and fashionable attorney of the Kennedy clan, Sargent Shriver. If this was meant to make us go weak at the knees, it failed. The hostilities, fought in a five-star Swiss hotel, and with cordon bleu meals between arguments, were complex, bizarre, close to black comedy. If their side thought we'd be a pushover, they soon learned how wrong they were. With all their legal overkill, they found Norman, Michael and myself could match them for stamina as well as for argument. And there was Dana: shrewd, devoted and formidable. Whatever their rules of engagement were, Mrs Broccoli would give no quarter!

[Norman R. Tyre, of Gang, Tyre, Ramer and Brown Inc., Attorneys at Law, Los Angeles, is tall, courteous and disarmingly soft-spoken. A much-respected lawyer, he fights cases the way he cultivates his roses in Beverly Hills, with meticulous preparation and a sharp eye for the best vantage point. An expert on the fine print of Hollywood, he had been on first-name terms with almost every mogul or movie star in the business. A seasoned campaigner in the jungle of film litigation, he is wise to the territory, knows the nature of the beast. He has been friend as well as legal adviser to Cubby and Dana for many years. His concern, therefore, to protect their interests, fight off marauders, was as much personal as professional. In two years he would chalk up a sheikh's ransom in fees, all of which he admits (though not in writing) he'd have willingly paid Cubby for the intense satisfaction the outcome of the case brought him. He would say at the end of it all, 'It was an experience of a lifetime, and without doubt one of the toughest.'

Michael Wilson is a taciturn six-footer you would not immediately place as an expert in the martial arts. His varied interests include collecting rare books, photography and writing. Scriptwriters and other walking wounded find his half-smiling inscrutability unnerving. Even the way he listens, some say, puts you on your mettle. But it is precisely this low-profile adroitness which brought him, after graduating from Stanford Law School, several top jobs and partnerships in leading law firms in Washington and New York. He specialized first in international law, working on government engineering and defence contracts. Later he moved into the tax area, handling, as a managing partner, tax situations in the international field.

In 1973 he took two years of absence from his law firm and came to London to help Cubby with tax matters and the burgeoning problems with Harry Saltzman. But his creative talents soon extended into the Bond world, where, as we'll see, he became first executive producer, then, additionally, co-writer on several of the Bond films, and finally co-producer with Cubby. He was to prove himself to be an incisive protagonist in the battle with Saltzman. But then he had an added incentive. Somebody was threatening the family silver.

Norman R. Tyre sets the scene:

'When Cubby Broccoli first asked me to become his personal attorney, the primary objective then was to create a contract that would protect him against any possible invasion of the corporate asset, Danjaq. I had to build a wall around it against any possible attempt by Harry Saltzman and his attorney, Irving Moskowitz, to encroach on this total asset shared equally by the two partners. We created an agreement between them based on the principle "it takes two to tango".

'In essence it ensured that neither party could do anything, in Company terms, without the approval of the other. Events proved what a prudent safeguard it was. Harry Saltzman, as a result of several abortive enterprises, had incurred a total indebtedness said to be in the region of $20 million. He went to the Union Bank of Switzerland and left them with the strong impression that he, on his own, would pledge the hundred per cent shares of Danjaq to secure the loan which the Bank was making to him – in other words trying to pledge the whole Company. If the pledge succeeded and was registered in the Company's books, it would give them a proxy to vote the shares. More basic than that, it would give Saltzman the millions to keep him afloat. Harry claimed this was not his intention, and I am not going to say it was what he was attempting to do. But what I do know is that UBS, at the very highest level, believed that is what they expected to receive. Accordingly , we were forced to do all we could to prevent that happening. It was not quite clear in my mind what he presented to them. But he certainly presented his own Danjaq shares, which must have reinforced their belief that he had the right to offer Danjaq as security.

'There were many meetings between the Bank and Michael and I, in Zurich, initially, with the top echelon of UBS. We had to persuade them that they did not have a valid lien on the Danjaq shares to become, in effect, a partner with Cubby in the Company. This, we asserted, violated the shareholders' agreement between Cubby and Harry. Neither partner independently could hock the shares of the other, or, in fact, his own shares. These had to be offered first to the other shareholders. (In fact, the shares were all lettered, confirming that they could not be individually pledged by either partner. This was another significant restraint.) The scenario widened to take on additional characters aligned with Saltzman. The key figure was a financier, a Monsieur Dolivet. Dolivet sought to underpin Saltzman's parlous financial situation by giving him literally "eating money". In return, Harry could provide the right, by transferring his shares to him, to assert his position with them, which of itself probably violated the Company agreement. Dolivet took up a very aggressive position, because we had at that time frustrated the Bank from doing anything with the lien they perceived they had. Until then, the picture *The Spy Who Loved Me* was proceeding, albeit with a lot of harassment and much ill feeling between the partners.

'But when Dolivet came in, he asserted certain rights which effectively blocked any operational decisions being made on the production. This resulted from the appointment of a sequestrator, set up under Swiss law which, in theory at least, meant Danjaq was operated by a trusteeship. This sequestrator was a charming lady whose sole aim was somehow to make peace between the parties. But the series of meetings which subsequently took place in Lausanne were very vitriolic, very belligerent, with a lot of raised voices disturbing the Alpine peace. The main contenders at that time were Dolivet, the attorneys for Saltzman, Cubby, Michael and myself. As tempers flared and the tension rose, one elderly gentleman, a dignified veteran with the Fiduciaire Générale, decided he couldn't take any more. Somehow the fierce arguments got to him, and he resigned. His assistant, M. Gerald Schleppi, took over.

'Throughout all this, Cubby sat and listened impassively, despite the very serious threat the situation posed. Dolivet had arranged with another financier, Serge Semenenko, for a Boston bank to loan Harry Saltzman $1 million to tide him over. This, Dolivet assumed, gave him authority to speak for Harry's interests, which in effect would make him Cubby's partner; or more fancifully, Cubby would sell his shares to Dolivet, giving him control of the Bonds. I doubt, though, if Dolivet ever seriously thought he could bring that off. More likely, he was hoping to work out some kind of compromise.

'Everything was now poised for the "summit meeting", which took place at one of Europe's finest hotels, the Beau Rivage at Ouchy, Lausanne. A large public room was closed off for the meeting. It had this immensely long table running almost the length of the room. Arrayed along one side were Harry Saltzman, his man Irving Moskowitz, Peter Schiller and his assistant. In addition, they had three Swiss lawyers, one from Zurich, the second from Lausanne, a third from Geneva. Reinforcing them was Sargent Shriver, representing the Charlie Allen group. He also had his assistant with him. Shriver was a senior partner with a substantial New York law firm, and as I recall he was getting $400 an hour. This was more than twenty years ago, but it is still high by today's standards. In addition, he was drawing $2,000 a day for travelling expenses.

'This battery of attorneys was aligned along one side of the table, spilling around two sides. In the middle, sat the lady sequestrator. On our side of the table – and this never ceased to amuse me – sat Cubby, Michael, Escherman, an excellent Swiss lawyer chosen by us, and myself. But for the Alps, visible through the tall windows, and the acrimony in the room, a comparison with the Last Supper was irresistible.

'Their side wanted to have the entire proceedings recorded, and hired engineers with expensive sound equipment, boom mikes and everything placed strategically close by. Our side couldn't trust their recording, so we did the same. Heaven knows what the technicians involved must have made of the scene.

'The meeting became more and more heated. There was a lot of yelling and shouting and bickering. But came lunchtime and the civilities were observed. There was a temporary armistice in order to savour the Alsace wines and the *haute cuisine*. Then it was battle stations again. I marvelled at Cubby's composure through it all.

'The meeting continued all day. Their side were asserting – or more correctly, they were putting on soundtrack – some kind of excuse for dissolving the Company. They were hoping to show, with tapes, that there was an irrevocable dispute between the two partners. This would mean that if it couldn't be settled any other way, the court could order an official dissolution. But that manoeuvre failed. There was now a hiatus, with their side falling back to regroup.

'Monsieur Dolivet, however, had not finally given up his position. He invited Michael and me to lunch at his home, somewhere in the Bois de Boulogne, just outside Paris. It was so obvious to us why he'd invited us. The way he treated us eliminated all doubt. He picked us up by a chauffeured car. We were told later it probably was not his chauffeur, but one he had hired for the purpose. We believe, though we're not sure, that even the apartment might have been rented for the occasion. In any event, it was one hell of an apartment. I remember the dining room was reached by walking downstairs, the waiters wore white gloves and there was a butler who saw us in. There was nobody else there except Dolivet, Michael and myself. There was champagne, caviare, beautiful *hors-d'oeuvres*: it was a most elegant and beautifully set-up meal from beginning to end. During the luncheon, it emerged that his primary purpose was to get our respect and acquiescence to what he wanted to do, which was this: he thought it was the perfect time to buy gold, and he wanted us to agree that the Danjaq cash that was available should be put into buying gold. He was convinced that gold was going to go up and the price of oil was going up, and therefore we should take all of our assets and put them into gold. Neither of us reacted favourably to that suggestion. Dolivet's attempt having failed, the meal ended rather abruptly...and as I recall, I'm not even sure he saw us to the door. Nor was there any car to take us back to Paris. So there we were, Michael and I, in the middle of the Bois de Boulogne...the roads going every which way, and no taxis to be found. We had to walk about half a mile before we could get a cab back to Paris.

'The impasse between the two sides continued for a considerable period. This was holding up the making of the picture. Arthur Krim of UA was very anxious to get the picture started. So was Cubby. We prevailed on Arthur to let us go ahead without Danjaq and then, at the appropriate time, Cubby's Company would come back in. In the meantime, contracts would be entered into in Cubby's name which would later be assigned over to Danjaq, UA financing those contracts.

'Perhaps one of the most acrimonious meetings of all was with one of the top executives of the Union Bank of Switzerland. It was really a terrible meeting, because we were telling him that his Bank didn't have the rights they thought they had; they couldn't deal with the shares in the way they thought they could. It came out of the blue to this guy. A lawyer for the Bank later told me that this executive was convinced I was some kind of highbinder trying to hornswoggle the Bank out of their security, and they could see $21, 22, 23 million going down the drain. Plus interest. Which was enormous. Meanwhile other parties, tempted by the huge potential of Bond, entered the scene. Sargent Shriver – who, incidentally, was well disposed towards Cubby and respected him – left, as the Charlie Allen group backed out. Then we had a parade of other characters in whom Dolivet was trying to stimulate some interest. The idea was to find someone who could convince Cubby to take him on as a partner. Dolivet having failed to impress Cubby himself – and that went for the rest of his initial coterie – he directly, or indirectly, introduced more appealing candidates. We had a meeting with John Daly, of the Hemdale Group. Then I had a meeting with David Frost. Nothing materialized, but David was keen to make a cordial exit. He paused at the door, and in front of all the secretaries, blew me a kiss and said, "Goodnight, sweet prince!" I appreciated the gesture. It had more style than the words from the man at UBS.

'Lord Hanson, then Sir James, a close friend of Cubby's, examined the possibilities of taking over Harry's position. Hanson himself came to London with a whole group of accountants and managers, and we had days of discussions, but I believe they considered the price of salvaging Harry's situation was too high. With Harry Saltzman implacably opposed to selling his shares to Cubby, eventually Arthur Krim of UA, ostensibly acting for Cubby Broccoli, bought out the position of Dolivet and Saltzman, which meant his fifty per cent of everything, including the copyright. Later on events would show that Mr Krim was not so disinterested as he appeared and that, in fact, he was markedly reluctant to hand over his Company's interests. The Bank was paid something in the region of $15 million, Harry Saltzman $5 million. The Bank was more than happy. They settled, I guess, for about half of what was due to them, having waived all the interest, which would have been at least fifty per cent more against the loan. UA were the new partners, but Cubby was the sole producer. He had the artistic control. He chose the cast and whoever would play James Bond. He was effectively, as he had been for some time, solely in charge. The battle was won.'

EIGHTEEN

I found the whole confrontation with my business partner strange, embarrassing. Here was a man whom I had tried to save from falling into the pit dug by his own ambition, looking at me across a table with a lot of characters who, whichever way you looked at it, were trying to wipe me and Dana out. I knew Harry Saltzman was in deep trouble, and I was genuinely sorry for him. But I couldn't allow the roof to crash down on us, too. I was fighting to preserve everything that Dana and I had built up over the years for ourselves and our family.

Now, maybe without realizing it, Harry was getting close to ruining me. I can't begin to measure the support Dana gave me during this crisis. She wondered how I could, years later, shake hands with my partner and end up feeling sorry for him. My answer was, 'You have to be sorry for those who eventually fall on their own swords.'

I was relieved when it was all over. Glad to see this big exodus of lawyers, special pleaders and other characters who'd hustled in, hoping to pull off a big coup. I didn't see Harry Saltzman afterwards to shake hands. But there was no animosity, no enmity. His life was not without its tragedies. The whole painful episode underscored my belief that partnerships in the film business are rarely successful. It worked for Zanuck and Brown, Spielberg and Lucas; but they're exceptions.

[Dana Broccoli remembers the legal battle with more pride than bitterness. Her son Michael Wilson had been tested on the anvil and had proved himself to be as tough and as smart as his highly paid adversaries. Of Cubby, she says: 'He was a remarkable man in so many ways. He was fearless. When he's making the films and the people around him are frightened, wondering, God! Should we do this, dare we do that? – Cubby, if he believed in it, would say, "Sure, go ahead, let's do it...What can happen?" That was his style. That was the way he was in this big battle. There was never a moment when we weakened, never a second when we wavered or might have capitulated. But Cubby was also a good man, who cared for people, understood people. Which means he forgave them. I don't have that gift, unfortunately. But in the end, Cubby just shrugged it off. It takes a big man to do that.'

For Michael Wilson, it had been a special triumph. Working with Norman R. Tyre – now a close friend – had been instructive and enjoyable. Tyre came into the fracas as a seasoned campaigner who actually relished the fight. 'But here I was,' recalls Wilson, 'a young man who, in a sense, had the fortunes of the family on my shoulders as well. It was a big responsibility.' He was fortunate. Both he and Tyre had a pretty gutsy client. 'Cubby was always a great pillar of strength,' says Michael. 'He exuded tremendous confidence and nothing defeats him. It was emotionally trying for everyone, especially Dana, but she's very good, too, when it comes to the strategy in a fight. The predominant thrust of all their decisions was to keep fighting, whatever it took. That was their position, and ours, too.']

The legal tangle resolved, the most important thing for me was that I had the green light to go ahead and shoot *The Spy Who Loved Me*. No more discord, and a clean sheet. I felt good about it. Stand or fall, I was on my own, in full control of operations. The question that some raised amused me: can Broccoli go it alone, without Saltzman? I'd been 'going it alone' for much longer than I cared; doing what was required while my entrepreneurial partner was taking on the world.

But now, with this new Bond picture, I was up against tougher problems. First, I had to get everybody back into the enthusiasm we always had on Bond. Spirits had understandably plummeted with all the rows going on, Guy Hamilton leaving the picture and the brakes being put on the production. Michael Wilson was becoming more and more involved in the creative side of filming, and was a great help to me as associate producer. Lewis Gilbert had come back to direct, and we were ready to go. There's no special magic to making a picture when you know what you want and have a good crew to back you. I've been very fortunate here. We've built a great team over the years. But this new Bond was one of the toughest of the whole series. It presented major logistical problems, with locations in the Bahamas, Switzerland, Sardinia, Egypt, Scotland and Baffin Island.

The biggest problem I had, however, was getting the script right. The basic story was simple enough: an attempt to hijack nuclear submarines and use them as blackmail against the major powers. But somehow, developing a story for the kind of action I wanted defeated one writer after another. Christopher Wood did a first draft, but though I respect his talents as a writer, I don't think they're best used on a screenplay. I brought in another scriptwriter, Anthony Barwick, who produced a story with some useful ideas; then other very accomplished characters like Sterling Silliphant, John Landis and Anthony Burgess, who had written *A Clockwork Orange*. In total, we had fourteen writers, all very clever men with established reputations. But, in my view, they couldn't write Bond. Michael and I felt they had locked themselves into creating great set-piece sequences which didn't slot into a strong storyline.

Dick Maibaum got us back to basics with his usual skill, but we still didn't have a clear, coherent structure for an exciting Bond movie. The more I talked to our writers, the more futile it seemed to be. We were now under pressure. One day Dana and I were at our home in California and we had all these scripts, close to a dozen of them, spread out all over the room. We sat and talked for hours, with Dana scribbling ideas down on paper. We rewrote the whole story, collected all the pages together and took the polar flight from Los Angeles direct to London. There was no time to sleep. We went straight from the plane into a meeting with Lewis Gilbert and Michael. Lewis looked through the pages, nodded and said it was the first time a producer had come to him with a storyline that worked.

A couple of problems remained. One of these involved the character Jaws – a great spoof villain built like a giant, with cobalt-steel teeth that could munch on iron girders. He is caught in a deadly battle with a shark close to the end of the picture. I liked the character (played by Richard Kiel) so much, I wanted him to survive the shark so that we could use him in another Bond. I remember Michael bantering, 'Oh, what happens then...Jaws bites the shark?'

'Michael, you said it! That's it! The duck came out the ceiling!' (An old Groucho Marx expression meaning 'You hit the nail on the head.')

Lewis Gilbert frowned. 'Oh no! We can't...'

'What do you mean, we can't? Man bites dog, Jaws bites shark! It's perfect!' I said. It worked hilariously.

All these changes or additions we made to the words of the original writers is not meant in any way to disparage their work. All of them have impressive track records. I merely want to underscore the uniqueness of Bond. There are scriptwriters, and there are Bond scriptwriters. They are not necessarily the same animal.

Richard Kiel had reason to be glad he beat the shark. Up to then, he was virtually an unknown player in television dramas. Jaws made him an immediate cult figure. He went on chat shows around the world, and he has been much in demand ever since. One other problem – a legal one – caused us to do some swift adjustment to the story. When we negotiated to buy the Fleming properties, we obtained the right to create new Bond stories, in addition to filming those written by the author. But Ian had stipulated that we could not use the title or the story of *The Spy Who Loved Me* because it was so different from his other Bond books. It took much negotiating by Michael with the Fleming estate before we obtained final clearance to go ahead and use the title and write a new screenplay.

We began production in 1976. This film had some marvellous action in it: the fight in the train compartment between Bond and Jaws; the combined attack by the enemy in high-powered automobiles, helicopters and rocket-propelled sidecars; Roger racing his Lotus Esprit into the Mediterranean, where it doubles as a submarine. They're all great scenes and a tribute to the special-effects crew and the stunt men.

But for me, and a million others, perhaps the greatest stunt ever was the incredible ski-jump in the pre-credits of the film. Those who've seen the film will remember that Bond is being chased on skis by the Russian assassins. At full speed, he turns and shoots their leader with his ski-stick gun. But when he faces ahead again, we see he's zooming straight for the edge of a precipice. He hits space, and we see him falling and somersaulting into the abyss, his skis flying off into the distance. The fall seems endless, leaving the audience gasping and wondering what on earth can save Bond. Suddenly a parachute snaps out of his backpack, with the Union Jack painted on it. It has to be one of the most daring stunts ever risked. I wince even now when I see it.

Michael and I got the idea for this sequence from a TV ad. In the commercial, this genius of a ski-jumper is supposedly doing this spectacular leap off the ridge of the three-thousand-foot Asgard peak in the Auquittug National Park, Baffin Island, Canada. In reality, he took his leap off the El Capitan peak in the Yosemite Valley, California; but it didn't matter to me where he did it. It was outrageous, took staggering courage and would obviously be a sensational curtain-raiser to the film. Michael located the jumper and called him up.

He was a guy named Rick Sylvester. This daredevil kid turns out to be a nice Jewish boy from Beverly Hills. Born with an irresistible urge to cheat death, preferably on skis, he is naturally a worry to his mother. After she saw the clip of his leap off El Capitan, she complained, 'He wants to climb, he wants to jump off mountains, my boy's crazy! A lawyer he couldn't be. An accountant isn't dangerous enough. A doctor's too safe. Find him a mountain to fall off and he's happy!'

Well, I was with her all the way. But Rick Sylvester became more enthusiastic the more we talked about it. What he wanted, he said, as though we were planning a barbecue, was a really good vertical cliff with a good ski-run top. There was only one place, he insisted, and that was Mount Asgard (which was where he'd intended that commercial to be shot, but was thwarted by bad weather). The fact that it was three thousand feet high was in its favour, because the longer the fall, the more time he'd have to open his parachute, get rid of his skis and watch out for obstructions on his way down.

'Anything else?' we asked.

Well, yes: the wind conditions would have to be right, otherwise he could get blown into the ice wall. Then a safe landing area would have to be clearly staked out: he didn't want to drift into anything unpleasant. We said we didn't want him to drift into anything unpleasant, either.

Mount Asgard lies about four hundred miles from Frobisher Bay. We could only get to its summit by helicopter, which immediately gave us problems. We couldn't fly helicopters all the way. We had to dismantle them, put the parts into crates, fly the crates to the take-off point in the area, then reassemble them. John Glen, who was second-unit director and editor, was in charge of the team arranging and photographing the stunt. They arrived in July 1976, and made their base in an old hunting lodge in the village of Pangnirtung.

All this planning and movement were beginning to cost money. When United Artists had their specialists figure out how much the stunt should cost and what the snags were likely to be, they became dubious about the whole thing. I said we had to do it for two reasons: I wanted it, and it was in the script. They had an accountant up there and every time we added ten cents, it was reported back. Their reaction was, hell! – this is gonna cost a fortune! It did. In fact, the whole operation cost a quarter of a million dollars. The circumstances dictated that. We had to wait for weather conditions that were not merely ideal for shooting, but safe enough for Sylvester to do the jump.

Also, the sequence was dangerous and required special personnel to provide the expert back-up. Sylvester wanted his friend Bob Richardson, an experienced climber, to be on hand, close to the peak, in case there had to be an emergency mountain rescue. We needed a parachute expert, Jim Buckley, to repack the chute if something went wrong with the first jump. Add a doctor, several cameramen, two helicopter pilots and mechanics, and that quarter of a million doesn't seem that steep. Not for what we were about to get on film.

Sylvester flew with John Glen to the summit. When they looked over the edge, according to what I was told, John Glen went a fine shade of green. They obviously hadn't expected anything quite as awesome as this. A three-thousand-foot cliff looks a lot higher when you're staring down from the top of it. Sylvester's experience told him also that the strong crosswinds could blow him back against the cliff face. He would need to go like a rocket to get maximum lift-off, to give him time and space to kick off his skis and release the parachute. The agreement Michael and Norman R. Tyre had worked out with him gave us the right to ask for three jumps. We needed this guarantee because if one jump failed, we would have to repeat it quickly in case bad weather intervened, when the whole sequence might be lost.

John Glen reported to me that Sylvester was prepared to go

ahead, though I'd heard he didn't care too much for the view from the summit. But I had qualms. I decided, great as the shot was likely to be, it was still only a motion picture. (I also thought of his momma back home in Beverly Hills.) So I sent a message to him:

'Look, Rick, I know you've been up there. You've agreed to do it and you're committed. But if you have any second thoughts about it, if you think it's too risky, I'll release you from your contract. All you have to do is tell John Glen you want out and we'll wrap up and come home.'

I didn't pause to wonder how the top man at United Artists might react to this. But then, he wasn't skiing off the top of a mountain. Sylvester was grateful for the offer, but said he'd always wanted to do this jump and he was damned well going through with it. And one afternoon, after nearly ten days of waiting, the sun broke through the clouds. We had about fifteen minutes. Sylvester got the signal and skied like a bullet towards the cliff edge. He zoomed off it, fell like a black speck in space, and then suddenly, with the whole crew holding their breath, that parachute opened. It was brave, and it was beautiful. It was the pure essence of James Bond.

This boy had given a lot of thought to the jump. He had rigged up special release hooks on his legs so that when he was flying out into space he could jettison his skis at a certain point, allowing them to fall before he dropped. He didn't want to risk them falling on top of him or the parachute. Nevertheless, if you look at the jump you can see that one of the skis did hit the top of the chute. Fortunately, it didn't tear the canopy, otherwise it would have been a disaster.

For all its problems – the drawn-out lawsuit with Harry Saltzman, Guy Hamilton backing out, the hassle with the script-writers – *The Spy Who Loved Me* was a smash at the box office, the biggest hit since *Thunderball*. Roger Moore had finally laid to rest the ghost of Sean Connery. And if anybody mentioned the Saint, he'd ask, 'Who's he?'

The film had some inspired gadgetry: Bond's wristwatch, which fed out ticker-tape messages from M; a cigarette box and lighter which combined to form a microfilm reader; a ski-stick that doubled as a rifle; and a motorbike which skimmed over the surface of water. This last item, called a 'wet-bike', was marketed commercially after the film's release. Bond's famous Aston Martin (last seen in *On Her Majesty's Secret Service*) is replaced by a remarkably versatile Lotus Esprit, which, apart from the usual complement of evasive devices and dazzling fire-power, can travel underwater to a depth of forty feet. Ken Adam's set designs, which received an Academy nomination, were masterly. The gem was the *Liparus*, Stromberg's supertanker, constructed to open its huge bows and swallow submarines at one gulp. Inside, there are monorails, walkways, elevators and an operations room.

To house all this at Pinewood Studios, we had to construct the biggest stage in the world. The '007 Stage' was 336 feet long, 160 feet wide and 53 feet high. At one end was a giant tank, 38 feet square. The stage, which cost UA and Eon Productions more than £600,000 to build, eventually paid for itself with rentals from other productions.

The critical response to the picture was predictable. Nobody would love it quite as much as the public. There was plenty of praise from some critics, reservations by others. Meanwhile the public were standing in line around the world. Everybody agreed, though, that the film was great entertainment. Can there be any other criterion? The picture gave me a lot of personal satisfaction. Michael Wilson's many talents, fully tested as a lawyer, associate producer and creative input to the script, made an immensely important contribution to the film. He'd earned his spurs and the role of executive producer on the next Bond picture, *Moonraker*.

It was around this time that my cousin Pat de Cicco died. I loved this man. We'd had a great deal of fun together and much of any success I might have had began with him inviting me out to Hollywood when I was out of a job. I was away in Europe when it happened. Pat had originally been taken ill in New York with lung cancer. He had surgery there which, though it didn't remove the tumour, apparently arrested it sufficiently for him to be discharged. It looked as though he might make a good recovery.

About seven months later he came to stay with us in California, which he did every six months or so, staying a week or two. He liked being with us, and we enjoyed having him. I had to leave for England after his first week with us. He was very excited about a deal he was involved in with John Wayne. In fact, he was looking forward to going down to Wayne's home to discuss the details. My colourful cousin, who had been involved in many different enterprises, was now about to corner the market in – let's not be coy – bat shit. I am no expert in this field, but apparently this commodity was valued very highly indeed by the cognoscenti as a very high-grade fertilizer. Well, they had this disused mine where he and Duke Wayne had the biggest accumulation of bat shit in the county. (Personally, I told Pat, I could take or leave the stuff, but he behaved as though he'd really struck gold.) So I left him in California and flew to London.

What happened afterwards is one of Dana's sadder memories:

'We had dinner together, then Pat went to bed. Around midnight I heard this loud noise blaring away from his TV. It struck me as odd. It was so loud I decided to try and get some sleep in another room. I wanted to get up early because I knew Pat was leaving to join Wayne at his home. I got up about seven o'clock and there was still this wild music coming from Pat's room. I was puzzled, then worried. It wasn't like Pat to have that noise going on around him. I buzzed his room and there was no answer. I went down and knocked on the door. There was no response. The TV was on full blast. I opened the door, but couldn't see him in the bed. I thought at first he might be taking a shower. I walked to the other side of the bed and saw him collapsed on the floor. He seemed unconscious. I called the paramedics and then his doctor in New York. He was away on holiday but had left instructions that if Pat suddenly became ill arrangements had been made to take him into UCLA. The paramedics rushed him there, and meanwhile I phoned Cubby in London, where he was having dinner at the White Elephant with Frank Sinatra. I told him that Pat had had a stroke, was unconscious, and the doctors weren't sure whether they'd be able to revive him. Cubby said he'd grab the first plane out of London, but the doctors told me, "There's no point. He's in a coma there's nothing anyone can do."

'At that point an intern came over to me and said, "This fellow will never regain consciousness and he can't stay here."

'I looked at him. "What are you saying? He must stay here."

'But this doctor was adamant. Fortunately, at that point Pat's doctor, Dr Beattie, had returned and phoned me from New York. He said, "If you can make arrangements to have a plane bring him here I will fly over and then accompany him on the flight. I think we might be able to help him. But you must realize he could die on the way in the plane; going up in the hospital elevator, anywhere and at any time." I told him I understood that "but there's no hope here". The problem then was to find a plane. By then Frank Sinatra had returned from London to Palm Springs. I rang his home. His wife Barbara answered the phone. I said, "Where can I get a plane at once?" Frank thought quickly and suggested we get a special ambulance plane. This seemed the best idea, so I called Dr Beattie. "It will take too long," he said. "Eleven hours or even more. It could be too late. You need a plane that will do the flight in six or seven hours at the most. And there's got to be oxygen and everything else for emergencies on board." It was a lawyer friend, Sydney Korshak, who came up with the solution. He called Sinatra, who had a house guest at the time, George Barrie of Fabergé. George said, "Tell Dana she can have my plane for as long as she needs it." Pat was flown to New York with Dr Beattie and Pat's niece, Frances Savino, his closest relative. Pat was operated on and he regained consciousness.'

As it turned out, that rescue operation was a great bonus to Pat. He was able to put his affairs in order. He could say a personal goodbye to his close buddies. Greg Bautzer, his friend and lawyer flew out from California to help Pat make out his will. Greg, who loved Pat as we all did, was wonderful. Even towards the very end, my cousin retained some of the old de Cicco humour. When they got down to figures, he said to Greg, an executor, 'Listen, take a little but leave a little – you know what I mean? Otherwise you'll be hearing from me up there...!' and he pointed ominously to the ceiling.

As he lay dying, my cousin Pat was unaware of one visitor who had entered the hospital room. Gloria Vanderbilt, his former wife, had arrived to pay her last respects. The gesture was curious, to say the least. Their marriage had been a disaster which had ended acrimoniously. I wasn't surprised when it struck a reef. My cousin Pat was certainly no shrinking violet; nor, for that matter, was Miss Vanderbilt. But the fact that their marriage had been a catastrophe made that scene in the hospital room hard to take. I was there at the bedside with my cousin Frances Savino when Gloria swept in. Pat lay there unconscious, his head shaved. His eyes were closed. He barely moved. Gloria Vanderbilt rushed in, flung herself on the bed and hugged this unconscious figure. 'Oh Pat, Pat...' she sobbed, 'you're the only man I ever loved...!' Maybe she meant what she said, but I found it hard to square that demonstration with the blasting she gave my late cousin in her memoirs. Still, a late conversion, I suppose, is better than no conversion at all!

Pat was buried in New York in the marble mausoleum built for the de Cicco family. Greg Bautzer, Henry Ford Jr, Bill Hearst, Frank Sinatra and myself were pallbearers. Other friends came in from all over. Then we went to the 21 Club, Pat's favourite place in New York. It was absolutely the right setting and atmosphere in which to say our final farewells. Bautzer was so impressed, he said: 'Just look at this. When I die I want you guys to do the same for me.' His wife Niki did not forget.

Dana and I had plenty to be happy about as preparation for the new Bond picked up momentum. The siege on Danjaq had been lifted, the pressure taken off our lives. Tina, Barbara and Tony were growing up, following their own paths in life but remaining devoted to each other and to Dana and me. Dana's strong concern for family – which I was raised on – is reflected in her charitable work. It's significant that most of the royal premières we've had were targeted mainly towards children's charities. It was a great honour for us when the Queen, Prince Philip, the Prince and Princess of Wales, the Princess Royal, and the Duke and Duchess of Kent, attended our charity premières. It's also a great night out for Londoners, who pack the West End's famous Leicester Square to see the 'royals' and celebrities arrive.

The big bonus is the money these events raise for organizations like the Prince's Trust (created by the Prince of Wales), the British Deaf Association, the Princess of Wales Charities Trust, the Stars' Organisation for Spastics, the Variety Club of Great Britain, King George's Fund for Sailors, the National Playing Fields Association and the Police Dependents' Trust. Ian Fleming could never have envisioned that his tales, written in 'a moment of boredom' would one day benefit thousands of needy and unfortunates.

Dana's involvement in this fund-raising work, both in England and in the United States, was taking more of her time. But after the script crisis on *The Spy Who Loved Me*, I needed her input on the new productions.

While writing began on *Moonraker*, we returned to our home in California. To sad news. Gloria Blondell, to whom I was briefly married way back in the 1940s, had become critically ill. She'd seen all the doctors and finally she accepted that there was no hope. Knowing that she was terminally ill, she had made up her mind that if she was to die it should be in a hospice. She had heard so much about them and the gentle way in which they help terminal patients to face their death. On one of our visits to her she begged Dana to organize it.

As Dana remembers it:

'Our dear friend and devoted doctor, Dr Rex Kennemar, helped us get Gloria into Cedars Sinai Hospital in Beverly Hills. The tests there proved, tragically, that Gloria was nearing the end and at her request she was transferred to a hospice. The nursing there relied as much on gentleness and love as upon drugs. Gloria knew that her life was coming to an end, but she smiled when we went to see her. The only problem she had – and it clearly distressed her – was the future of her cat, Angelina Ballerina. This cat meant everything to her. It had been left alone in her house for a neighbour to care for. But she was worried. She was leaving $1,000, she said, for anyone who'd take the time to care for the cat. But she had to know that it was a good person.

'I didn't know anything about cats, but I knew our daughter Tina liked them. I called her and explained the situation. She said, "Oh, I'll call Uncle Bill – he has twelve cats."

'When he heard about Angelina Ballerina, Bill was over the moon, because she was half bobcat, and he had a cat which was also a bobcat. He would now have thirteen, and $1,000. He was ecstatic. We told Gloria, and she sank back against the pillows, relieved and happy.'

I went to see Gloria at the hospice again towards the end. As I left, I heard a woman in an adjoining room call out. The door was open and she beckoned to me.

She said, 'Would you hold my hand?'

I said, 'Sure' and took her hand in mine. I asked her, 'Are you comfortable?'

'Oh yes,' she said, 'I'm fine. They're all so wonderful here. It's just that I felt so happy and peaceful, I wanted to hold someone's hand.'

I left her sleeping, and at peace. Dana and I felt pretty miserable that day. But everybody else, it seemed, was happy, including Angelina Ballerina.

The initial success of the US Space Shuttle was the key to the scripting of *Moonraker*. We had originally planned *For Your Eyes*

Only as the next Bond film, announcing it on the tail end of the last one. But with space technology, and films like *Close Encounters of the Third Kind* strong in the public's mind, we went with *Moonraker* instead. Putting James Bond in orbit brought Ian Fleming into the space age.

Tom Mankiewicz worked on the original story with Lewis Gilbert, the director. Once we had agreed on the treatment, Christopher Wood would write the shooting script. To make sure our science fiction was based on science fact, Mankiewicz went to NASA's testing complex in northern California, focusing on the centrifugal-force test chamber. We had an interesting villain, Hugo Drax, in this picture, played with low-key menace by that excellent actor Michael Lonsdale. The plot: billionaire industrialist hijacks an American space shuttle and plans lethal extinction of whole populations using poisoned orchids. Some critics have argued that this, in part, updates ideas already used on earlier Bonds. This overlooks the fact that if you wanted to put Bond in space, the shuttle was, at that time, the only realistic vehicle he could take. Also, though threatening Bond is basic to the whole series, technology had by then moved into entirely new and fascinating areas. In updating plot ideas, we were also updating our hero.

It may be that by then we had overworked the sophisticated hardware in our pictures. Dana, Michael and I discussed this at great length. We began to wonder whether we should get back to the more human values that worked so successfully in *From Russia With Love*. In the event, *Moonraker* broke all the existing records of Bond films. Nevertheless, Maibaum and Michael, preparing the script of *For Your Eyes Only*, decided to focus more upon character and story than the familiar set-piece fireworks.

With this change of format came a new director, John Glen. Apart from being a very likeable individual, Glen had all that it takes to make a fine film director. He had produced some excellent second-unit work on *On Her Majesty's Secret Service*. He had also masterminded Rick Sylvester's ski-jump in *The Spy Who Loved Me*, a task which required toughness and the ability to handle people. He was also a skilled film editor. And he'd been with us long enough to have Bond in his bloodstream.

Everything was set to begin principal photography in September 1980. The locations were in the Bahamas (for the underwater sequences), Corfu and Cortina d'Ampezza in Italy.

Early in 1981 Bernard Lee, the much-loved actor and popular M of every Bond film, died. He was a great personal friend, liked by all of us, and unquestionably one of Britain's most gifted actors. His quiet authority and totally convincing manner were absolutely flawless. His death was a great loss to the series, but especially to Dana and me. In fact, it was demoralizing for the entire production. He had been in every Bond film, and was as close to their heartbeat as any of us who'd been with the pictures from the beginning. Dick Maibaum and Michael had to rework the script, changing those scenes in which Bernard would have appeared as M.

Julian Glover, playing Bond's chief adversary, the Greek agent Kristatos, is very convincing. I agree with the general opinion that he was one of the best-written villains in the Bonds. He is a sinisterly flawed human being instead of a conventional monster – and all the more menacing because of it.

The writers achieved the same effect with Carole Bouquet as the Melina Havelock character, on a revenge-killing mission. Her motivations go deeper than just ending up between the covers with 007. She came to us as a noted French actress with problems. She had a boyfriend who, unknown to us, was addicted to drugs. It became a problem largely because of its effect upon her. She was trying to keep him under control, but was losing out. He was in the hotel with her, and would do all kinds of crazy things: he had a fight with the doctor who was treating him; he would run naked down the hall, and had to be chased back and locked in his room. And here's this fine young actress worried sick and having sleepless nights. Inevitably, she was late on the set, which was a nuisance to John Glen and to Roger. It had been the first time we'd encountered this sort of situation on a Bond film. (The poor chap died not long ago.) Though Carole was deeply affected at the time, she came through with a strong performance.

The notices for *For Your Eyes Only* strongly justified our decision to get back to basics, to bring Bond back to earth. *Variety* was unusually warm in its praises: 'It emerges as one of the most thoroughly enjoyable of the twelve Bond pics despite the fact that many of the usual ingredients in the successful 007 formula are missing.' And the writer added this accolade: 'The entire film is probably the best directed on all levels since *On Her Majesty's Secret Service*. John Glen, moving into the director's chair after a long service as second unit director and editor, displays a fine eye and as often as not keeps more than one thing happening in his shots...'

Public reaction was extremely strong, and the picture did exceedingly well. In certain key places it overtook Spielberg's blockbuster *Raiders of the Lost Ark*. This was very rewarding, especially to Michael Wilson and Dick Maibaum, who had worked hard on the story. Here was the twelfth James Bond film, up there among the most successful films of the year. At the beginning they called Bond a 'phenomenon'. Now they were calling it a legend.

I'd been in the business too long to be deluded by those superlatives. But then, on the night of March 29, 1982, something happened that made me feel that those thirty years and thirty-eight films from *The Red Beret* to *For Your Eyes Only* were perhaps more than just a string of movies. The Academy of Motion Picture Arts and Sciences, at the Oscar ceremonies at the Dorothy Chandler Pavilion, honoured me with the Irving G. Thalberg Award.

[The award, which is not given every year, is presented to the producer whose body of work reflects a consistently high quality of motion-picture production. Alfred Hitchcock, Walt Disney and Cecil B. De Mille were previously among the chosen few.]

Many stars and producers over the years have heard their names called in the auditorium, and taken that long walk from their seat up onto the stage in a haze of spotlights, flashing cameras and applause. It's a euphoric moment. Each recipient has had his or her thoughts as they approach the podium: a flashback to the early struggles, a stab of nostalgia as they think of those they dearly wished were there. I had all those thoughts. It had been quite a journey from the Long Island Casket Company to Oscar night, March 1982.

My dominant thought as I held the sculpted head in my hands was of the day when, as a young jewellery salesman, I brought samples to show Mr Thalberg. Fifty years on I held the rare tribute given in his name. Some Oscar winners, out of true modesty or professional chic, have dismissed the award as 'a useful doorstop'. I have to say I'm proud of mine, and have it up there on the mantelshelf where we can look at each other now and again. The rest of the Broccolis were just as pleased as I was. Dana especially.

She had soldiered alongside me through the débâcle of *The Trials of Oscar Wilde* and the battles of the Saltzman era. The simple truth is there would have been no victories, no glittering prizes without her.

The titanic problems in making the Bond films have to be seen in the context of the life and chequered times of United Artists. Financially and creatively, we were locked in together. A tap on them induced a knee-jerk on us. Their own problems inevitably had their effect on our productions. They were bound to affect all of us, embroiled as we were in a tough, unpredictable and brutally competitive business. The corporate convulsions which I was caught up in will emerge. But when we look back over the years, the title United Artists could not have been more incorrectly named. Their history is a movie in itself.

When, on February 5, 1919, Mary Pickford, Charlie Chaplin, D.W. Griffith and Douglas Fairbanks created United Artists, their objective was plainly set out: to give independent film-makers greater artistic freedom and flexibility. It was a noble idea, but the venture appeared doomed from the start. After five years Griffith pulled out. He was nearly broke and he drank too much. The other three hung on for a while, bringing in 'Honest Joe Schenck', as he was called, as Chairman of the Board. But Honest Joe, Chaplin, Fairbanks and Mary Pickford woke up one day to find themselves almost put out of business by Asa Yoelson, the rabbi's son. More famously known as Al Jolson, he sang his way into the talkies era and demolished those giants of the silent films virtually in the first reel. Mary Pickford, who could put the Bourbon away as efficiently as her ex-partner Griffith, dismissed the talkies with a memorable phrase: 'Putting sound to movies would be like putting lipstick on the Venus de Milo.'

By 1930 the partners were fighting one another. Profits drooped from $1.3 million to $300,000. Five years later they might just as well have had a revolving boardroom door, the way presidents swept in and out. Schenck had gone. Vice-president Al Lichtman took over, but for an embarrassingly short period. In came Dr Attilio Henry Giannini, from the Bank of America. Whether he fell, or was pushed, was academic. What matters is his rueful comment afterwards:

'All my life I've been an adventurer and have been in a lot of tough situations. But let me tell you I never saw fights like the ones at UA board meetings. Criminations, recriminations, cuss words, even physical violence became standard boardroom procedure.' After he departed, Murray Silverstone and Sam Goldwyn entered the arena, Sam not endearing himself to Douglas Fairbanks by calling him 'a crook'. According to UA's counsel at the time, Charles Schwartz: 'Fairbanks, the retired swashbuckler, vaulted across the table and grabbed Goldwyn by the throat. Giannini had to separate them.'

The rot continued to set in. In 1950 Chaplin floundered in murky political waters. Fairbanks had long since died. With the company facing bankruptcy, Mary Pickford turned for help to the prestigious New York law firm of Phillips, Nizer, Benjamin and Krim – Louis Nizer having established a reputation as one of America's most famous trial lawyers. The invitation to Arthur Krim and Robert Benjamin to take over the company made good sense. Both were experts in film financing and had handled a considerable amount of business in Hollywood. They took over in 1951. Writing about this move years later in his highly revealing book, *Indecent Exposure*, David McClintick declares:

'Since taking control of United Artists in February 1951, Arthur Krim, Robert Benjamin and later Eric Pleskow consistently displayed an unusual combination of ingenuity, taste and business acumen and had come closer than most in the modern era to mastering the still mysterious process of making movies. There were many reasons for UA's success. But perhaps the most important was the company's sense of how to strike the right balance between the film-maker's creative independence – essential for artistic integrity – and the studio's financial control – essential for corporate health and stability.'

Which, of course, was why I was eager to bring James Bond to Arthur Krim at the outset. These men certainly had taste, ingenuity, and the skill to back winners. *Around the World in Eighty Days*, *Twelve Angry Men*, *Some Like it Hot*, *The Moon is Blue*, *The Man with the Golden Arm*; and in later years, *In the Heat of the Night*, *Midnight Cowboy*, *West Side Story*, *Elmer Gantry*, *Judgment at Nuremberg*, *Tom Jones*, *Sunday Bloody Sunday*, *One Flew Over the Cuckoo's Nest* – and, of course, all our Bond films. The list speaks for itself. In one year, 1976, three of the films nominated for the Oscar as 'Best Picture' were distributed by United Artists: *Rocky*, *Network* and *Bound for Glory*. (*Rocky* won.)

Once UA had given their approval, they let me get on with it. No producer can engage in the fragile exercise of making motion pictures – one eye on the budget, the other on turbulent talents involved – with the front office breathing down his neck. In 1976, when the problems with my partner Harry Saltzman were coming to a head, Krim was having troubles of his own. With several other majors being taken over by industrial combines eager to diversify into movies, it was only a matter of time before United Artists would go the same route. They had been taken over in 1967, becoming a subsidiary of the $3-billion-dollar Transamerica Corporation, which had holdings in insurance, charter airline turbines and a rent-a-car business. It worked reasonably well for a while. But in later years the relationship drifted towards a reef. None of this came as any particular surprise to me. When this giant conglomerate took over I had my private doubts whether the marriage would last. Krim and Benjamin were not the types to dance to someone else's tune, especially if they didn't like the music.

Transamerica's vow to allow them total freedom to run their own show began to wear thin. 'Artistic integrity' and 'creative freedom' are great concepts until the accountants get their thumbs in the soup. Characters who knew slightly less than nothing about the complex problems of making motion pictures began looking over shoulders. Krim and his partners who had acquired distinguished reputations as film backers found themselves boxed in, hampered by financial busybodies. We felt some of the backlash. Bonuses awarded for exceptional work were blocked; pay structures that had operated for years were suddenly changed. It was irritating enough at the time, but much worse was to come.

By the start of 1978 Krim, Benjamin, Eric Pleskow and two senior associates, Bill Bernstein and Mike Medavoy, decided they had had enough. In the parlance of our trade, they 'walked' to film interests elsewhere. It made waves in Hollywood. On January 24, 1978 leading figures in the industry wrote an open letter to Transamerica's boss, John Beckett, reproduced across two pages of the *Hollywood Reporter*:

Dear Mr Beckett,
    We, the undersigned, have made films in association with Arthur Krim, Eric Pleskow, Bob Benjamin, Bill Bernstein and Mike Medavoy.

The success of United Artists throughout the years has been based upon the personal relationships of these executive officers of United Artists with us, the film-makers.

We seriously question the wisdom of the Transamerica Corporation in losing the talents of these men who have proven their creative and financial leadership in the film industry for many years. The loss of this leadership will not only be felt by United Artists but by all of us.

The letter was signed by, among others, Robert Altman, Lindsay Anderson, Bernardo Bertolucci, Richard Brooks, Bob Fosse, Mike Frankovich, Norman Jewison, Stanley Kubrick, Claude Lelouch, Sidney Lumet, Ralph Nelson, Sidney Pollack, John Schlesinger, Martin Scorsese, Sam Spiegel, François Truffaut, Sir John Woolf and Fred Zinnemann. I was in England at the time. But I shared the general apprehension about the effect of corporate interference in the creative process. The maxim about not hiring a dog then barking yourself applies particularly when a film company is a subsidiary of a large conglomerate where profit is the only spur.

So now two new chieftains moved into the UA hierarchy: James R. Harvey, Chairman, and Andy Albeck, President and Chief Executive. A case of *plus ça change*...and another drama. *The Spy Who Loved Me* had been made on a budget of about $17.5 million. That figure represented the accepted cost of a Bond film around that time. But *Moonraker*, because of its locations and special hardware, involved far greater financial commitment: we're talking about $30–33 million.

It was a big jolt and Andy Albeck flew to Paris, where we were preparing to shoot, to discuss the situation. We showed him the budget, which he studied and then told us to go ahead with the picture. The film grossed over $100 million. (This was the film that brought our daughter Barbara into Bond, working as second assistant director.)

On May 21, 1981 Transamerica sold United Artists to Metro-Goldwyn-Mayer for $380 million, bringing that soft-spoken entrepreneur Kirk Kerkorian into the picture. 'Here we go again,' I mused to Dana as fairly swiftly Messrs Harvey and Albeck left. They begat Norman Auerbach, who begat Frank Rosenfelt, who begat David Begeleman, who begat Frank Rothman, who begat Freddie Fields, who...There was so much begatting, buck rabbits could have learned a trick or two. And while they were doing the begatting it was Eon Productions suffering the labour pains. But while all these changes at the top were taking place, the new executive intake brought in their own departmental subordinates. This meant that by the time you had worked out a publicity and marketing schedule on a picture the guy you were talking to was already clearing his desk.

Michael Wilson confronted this situation with his usual calm expertise. The problems involved every aspect of film production: finance, casting, production schedules and the script. Michael handled all these elements with immense skill and patience. His firmness in standing up to the incompetents who ran interference on our productions was widely acknowledged. It is not easy to make movies in that kind of wind-tunnel atmosphere. Bankers, accountants, lawyers moved into creative territory, most of them unable to comprehend the basics, to the considerable detriment, in my view, of our business.

Now another, unrelated problem loomed over the horizon. It involved Kevin McClory, Sean Connery and a rival Bond picture they planned to make, *Never Say Never Again*. That title is ironic, since it seemed a tacit admission by Sean that his ritual declaration, 'I'll never make another Bond!' was a shade unconvincing. When McClory joined forces with us to make *Thunderball*, to which he had certain rights, the deal was that he wouldn't shoot another version of it for ten years. After that time had elapsed, Kevin touted the idea of a remake round all the Hollywood majors. At that time he still called his story *Warhead* (written in conjunction with Connery and Len Deighton). Most companies backed off because of what they saw as legitimate objections from our company. Eventually McClory joined forces with Jack Schwartzman, an ex-tax lawyer and former executive vice-president at Lorimar. He left them to become an independent producer, presumably because he was convinced that McClory's right to film an update on *Thunderball* was valid.

We sought an injunction against them, claiming, among other things, that they would be trading on our success, that they had milked ideas from previous Bonds, and by remaking *Thunderball*, would be using more of our material than their own. We lost, not because of the weakness of our claim, but because it was held that they were so far advanced on the production it would be unfair to pull the switch. But it was obviously going to be an irritant: two

Bonds virtually being released at the same time. (It had happened before, with Feldman's *Casino Royale* and our *You Only Live Twice*.) I had no doubt at all that our product could hold its own against anybody else's Bond. What soured the issue was the feedback of rumours from the 'rival' camp. According to Michael Feeney Callan's book on Sean Connery:

'Rumours started to circulate, wry rumours that confused the general interpretation of Connery's motives in returning. Most popular on the grapevine was the hint of a grotesque spoof, some elaborate put-down of Broccoli's Bond. The casting of English comedian Rowan Atkinson as a "bumbling British agent" was seen by some as an accurate pointer to the likelihood of spoof...'

Well, I don't go by rumours; but if Sean felt that with this film he was going to knock everybody out of the box, the results proved otherwise. Their film took thirty per cent less than ours at the box office. In saying this, I'm not trying to score a point. The movie business is a game where anybody can throw their hat into the ring. But not with Bond. There's more to it than saying, 'Great, I've got the story, I've got Sean Connery, I'm going to make another Bond film.' The question is: how are you going to make it? Who is the right person to direct it? How do we cast it? Is this authentic Bond or a scissors-and-paste job? The picture, which I'm sure they thought would wipe us off the map, didn't even come close. The reason: we'd learned a lot from making the previous Bonds. They went out on a caper and, in my view, got it wrong.

[*Variety*, comparing estimated grosses, put *Octopussy* at $81.424 million worldwide against *Never Say Never Again*'s $51 million. A modest return, based on the accountancy which requires a film to take at least three times its negative costs – in their case $36 million – just to break even.]

Their film had not been the spoiler they may have intended, nor the bonanza they certainly hoped for. The public demonstrated, as they had with *Casino Royale*, a dislike of spoof Bonds, of seeing their heroes sent up.

The whole episode was buried and forgotten as Michael Wilson, actively writing as well as being executive producer, prepared the fourteenth Bond, *A View to a Kill*.

In April 1983 I received a letter which brought back vivid memories and renewed controversy about Howard Hughes. When

Howard died, in 1976, what angered me most about the media coverage was the ghoulish emphasis on his wretched physical condition at the time. Not much was said about his remarkable achievements in aviation and engineering, nor about his contribution to his country. I believe history will do him greater justice than did the commentators of his time. Now suddenly, seven years after his death, came this letter which again projected my old friend into public scrutiny. It was from a firm of San Francisco attorneys involved in litigation which turned precisely on where Howard Hughes had been officially domiciled at the time of his death.

'Our desire to speak with you arises from the fact that you knew Mr Hughes during his years in California,' they wrote.

'Mr Hughes's activities in Nevada are relevant to the issue in this case. Information as to where and how Mr Hughes lived in California and what he thought about the states of Texas, Nevada, and California is thus highly relevant...'

What my old friend thought about the states in question might have been more than instructive to the hearing. And in any event, the legal squabbling over the Hughes Estate was a ritual I would have preferred to stay out of. I had rich and vivid memories of great times with a much happier man. Now, lawyers were fluttering down from the branches establishing claims or counter-claims. They wanted to know where we met; how we met; what places we visited together; which planes we flew in; who was at the controls – everything bar the flight plan. Sometime during the questioning they got out of me the dark secret that when we had dinner together in Las Vegas, Hughes favoured charcoal-grilled lamb chops, slightly burned, with a baked potato, followed by apple pie. Not much help to the Supreme Court, where I was questioned as follows:

Q. Did you have occasion to meet Mr Hughes on a movie set?
A. Yes.
Q. What was your first job?
A. My first job was to take a very lovely young lady on a train up to Flagstaff, Arizona.
Q. Was that Jane Russell?
A. Yes.

There was a bit of a stir among the listeners which may have been envy. I continued. It was very cold in Flagstaff. In the morning I had to rouse all the Indians sleeping in the sagebrush and they'd appear with their hair full of frost, but none of this was in the picture because Hughes scrubbed it all, sacked the director and took over the film himself.

I told them how I was finishing a four-ball golf match in Palm Springs with Bruce Cabot, Charlie Farrell and Pat de Cicco, when Hughes swept us all off by plane – we're still in our golf shoes – to Reno.

Q. Right then and there?

A. Right then and there.

Q. What golf handicap were you playing to at the time Mr Hughes flew you all to Reno?

A. I refuse to answer that on the grounds it might humiliate me!

Q. Did he ever come to your house, pick you up at your house?

A. Yes.

Q. Did you ever see him at 211 Muirfield Road, in Los Angeles?

A. On several occasions, yes.

Q. Did you have occasion to go to other places in the southern California area with Mr Hughes besides these various nightclubs that you mentioned?

A. In California?

Q. In the southern California area.

A. He would fly Pat de Cicco and I to various places.

Q. Did Mr Hughes fly the plane himself?

A. Yes.

The hearing went on and on. Vultures arguing over succulent game. Finally...

Q. When was the last time you spoke to Mr Hughes?

A. During the shooting of *Thunderball* in 1963 he called me at my home in London. My wife, Dana, answered the phone. He said, 'This is Howard Hughes calling. I'd like to get in touch with Cubby Broccoli.' She thought it was a joke. She said, 'Who is this?' He convinced her and she told him to phone me at Pinewood Studios. I was on the set at the time. I went back to my office and spoke to him. He wasn't calling me for any special reason. He was just getting in touch, apologizing for not having spoken to me for all these years. Someday, he said, he would explain. I never spoke to him again.

Q. Did he sound lucid?

A. Oh yes.

Thank you, Mr Broccoli.

You're welcome.

And that was that. I was glad to get out into the sunshine. Personally, I didn't give a damn where Howard Hughes had been domiciled. It was his life that mattered to me.

NINETEEN

On June 27, 1984, just as we were preparing to shoot *A View to a Kill*, a devastating fire destroyed the 007 set at Pinewood Studios. It took barely minutes to reduce the largest studio stage in the world to a heap of blackened, twisted metal.

When I got there, this marvellous complex, where we had shot *The Spy Who Loved Me* and later Bond films, was just a shell. At the time, it was being used for the filming of *Legends*, and fortunately no one was hurt, everyone having broken for lunch. The immediate dilemma we faced was whether to write the whole thing off and film interiors on another set, or rebuild the stage at an estimated cost of £1 million. The studio held its breath. Pinewood had been home to the Bond films for more than twenty years. There were rumours that I might switch the studio work to Hollywood. I met amid the ruins with Cyril Howard, managing director of the studios, and Michael Brown, the talented young architect with the original builders, Delta Doric. There wasn't much left to see except the charred remains of the sign saying '007 STAGE'. Brown, who had helped create the stage, seemed as though he'd suffered a personal bereavement. To Howard, the idea of Bond being filmed anywhere but at Pinewood just wasn't on. In a sense it had been my home, too. 'OK,' I said, 'let's build it again.' Less than five months later, ahead of schedule, we were in there shooting.

It was not just a case of commercial considerations, either. For all its immediate shock and massive logistical problems, a fire is a containable situation. It affects you as a producer because of the delays, which can cost a lot of money. But these are the hazards you have to face in motion pictures. Far worse are the personality hazards, when stars begin playing up or production executives, eager to pull rank, start making waves.

Frank Yablans, then the top production chief at MGM/UA, may or may not be a man of great talent. It is possible that before he started breathing down our necks during the making of *A View to a Kill*, he had a fair track record as a production executive. I have to be less than sanguine, however, about his actions as far as the Bond film was concerned. Because he had been appointed by Metro's top people, Kirk Kerkorian and Frank Rothman, Michael Wilson and I duly offered him all the courtesies and full cooperation. Unfortunately, when you have sweated making Bond films for nearly twenty-five years you're a little wary of new characters coming in and telling you how to do it.

Mr Yablans, regrettably, showed little finesse, criticizing subordinates in front of others. Difficulties arose even before we started shooting *A View to a Kill*. Michael had agreed the budget for the picture with David Wardlow, the head of production at UA. Then Yablans came in claiming to have no knowledge of this arrangement in spite of the fact that Michael had sent him a detailed breakdown. Yablans went further. 'The budget's too big,' he said. 'No one told me anything about it. I'm cancelling the project.' If he thought he had intimidated Michael, he soon learned otherwise. Michael called him up.

'Listen, Frank, I'm on a private line here,' he told him. 'This is just between the two of us. Let me lay this out.' He then went on to spell out meticulously the whole budget which had been agreed. Yablans listened, then said, 'OK, I'll tell that to the board of directors.' But when Michael referred to this last sentence, Yablans interrupted, saying, 'No, no, I did not say that. I said, "I tried to *sell* that to the board of directors."'

It was the wrong tactic to pull on a lawyer.

That skirmish out of the way, we went ahead with the shooting. But then Yablans raged over a location sequence we had planned. We were shipping equipment over to Paris and Chantilly, north of the city. Everything was set, but then Yablans walked into my office insisting that the whole location be dropped. Tom Pevsner, one of our production chiefs, told him with more patience than Yablans deserved, that he could not agree to a cancellation. Yablans started shouting, 'No, you're not going to Chantilly, we don't need that scene. It's too expensive. And you don't need to go to Paris either to shoot the Eiffel Tower...!' Tom Pevsner stood his ground. 'I'm sorry, but I can't agree to that.' Yablans shouted back, 'You work for me. You don't work for anybody else.' It was the wrong tack. Pevsner said, 'I don't know about you. I've just met you. As it happens, I work for Mr Broccoli.'

In spite of this Yablans continued his offensive, this time from behind the ramparts of a letter written by an MGM executive, addressed to Pevsner:

Dear Tom,
   A VIEW TO A KILL.
   As requested, this is to confirm that I have been specifically instructed by my Company not to authorise any advances or commitments, nor to countersign any cheques relating to:
   1. The fire and elevator sequences and fire engine chase set in San Francisco (whether studio interior or location.)
   2. The Chantilly location.
   Also, I have been asked to confirm that we will not authorise or accept any expenditure or commitments in respect of any other cuts that were discussed at the meetings on July 25th and 26th between Frank Yablans, Dan Rissner, Cubby Broccoli and Michael Wilson.
   Yours sincerely,
   R.E. Atkinson.

If all this had concerned any film other than Bond, I might have tolerated Yablans's argument, if not his style. But the whole showy display was simply a trial of strength, to show who was the boss. Unfortunately for him, his power base was shifting perilously towards the rocks. We went ahead and shot the scenes we had planned in France.

Two incidents illustrate this fascinating aspect of the colourful Mr Yablans. The first concerns an important UIP Convention at which the whole advertising, marketing and publicity strategy for the film was discussed by the executives involved. Departmental heads were brought in from all over the world. The discussions climaxed with a presentation of the film, for which about a hundred and fifty people were present. We sat down and waited for about half an hour for Yablans.

He finally arrived and sat down in the front row about five seats away from me. Jerry Juroe, then our marketing and publicity director, made a few introductory remarks from the stage while Yablans yawned and stretched. Jerry continued speaking and in the middle of it Yablans called out to me, his voice drowning the commentary, 'Hey, Cub, I'm thinking about buying a Rolls-Royce. Do you think I should go to Jack Barclay or is there another place in town?'

And then there was the incident at the royal première of the film. Yablans and production chief Freddie Fields insisted they sit in the front row across from Prince Charles and Princess Diana. They took their seats close to the royal party. But as soon as the lights were down and the credits and opening sequences were over, they stood up and walked out of the auditorium. They may have been unaware, but this was a rare and unacceptable discourtesy at a charity première in the presence of royalty.

Dissolve. Fade in: Exterior Thalberg Building, MGM, some time later. Yablans is standing on the steps, a shade paler than usual. He has reversed the umbrella in his hands and is practising golf swings.

As I walk up, he looks at me and says, 'Cubby, you can't imagine what happened to me today.'

I didn't know what he was talking about, but I knew it was nothing pleasant. I said, 'What is it, Frank?'

'I have been told that I have to get out of this studio today. Not tomorrow, not the following day, but today!'

'I'm sorry to hear that, Frank. Who would do that?'

'Laddie.'

He was referring to Alan Ladd Jr, then Chairman and Chief Executive Officer of MGM Pictures, Inc. It was out of character. Alan Ladd Jr was not the kind of man who would summarily dismiss a senior executive, ordering him out that day. But it was obvious to me that buttons were being pushed higher up the totem pole. I guess I had to pity him in the end. As I said before, such people eventually fall on their swords.

The Yablans affair was not unique. Boardroom assassinations are as commonplace in movies as they are in any other industry. I was more concerned with its effect on the production and morale than its irritant effect on me. What was beginning to peeve me was an unwelcome change in Roger Moore's attitude and behaviour. Ego can be very contagious. One star sees what another star appears to get away with, and soon you have a very stubborn actor on your hands.

When I hired Roger – albeit with some resistance in high places

– his reaction had been, 'Wow! This is the biggest break in the world! I ought to be paying you for letting me do it!' And that's the way he behaved for the first three or four pictures. What happened after that was almost a cliché.

He was suddenly asking for things like private planes to locations. He didn't want to appear here, do this charity thing or that personal appearance. He was expected to go to a special film event in Deauville but kept us all dangling, saying he wasn't sure whether he'd attend. Then he declared he wouldn't go if Grace Jones, his co-star, was there at the same time. This was very awkward for all of us. How do you tell someone as volatile as this actress that she can't go to Deauville because the male lead in the picture apparently doesn't want her there?

Suddenly all these bizarre, neurotic little tricks were being pulled. They were all the more bewildering coming from Roger, who at first had been so cooperative. Like Sean, we had made him a millionaire, taken him into a world he'd never have got close to, doing those lightweight series like *The Saint* or *The Persuaders*.

I said to him, 'Quite frankly, Roger, you're being a bigger pain than Sean Connery used to be. This surprises me, because you know you have a percentage interest in this picture. You're not doing me a favour by attending these events. You participate. The success of the picture depends on your being there in person. It's as beneficial to you as it is to everyone else.'

He heard me out. Finally, he said, 'OK, Cubby, I'll sleep on it.'

This attitude was not like the Roger I knew – and liked. He went to Deauville. And so did Grace Jones.

This rock singer with the West Point hairdo is a formidable lady, even off the screen. She comes on like a kick-boxer, all flashing eyes and bared teeth. With all this going for her, she was perfect as the villainess Mayday in the film, particularly since after once being mugged in New York, she'd become an expert in unarmed combat. She was already notorious for punching a well-known English TV presenter (the late Russell Harty) before an audience of twelve million viewers. It should have warned us that, unlike her ash-blonde co-star, Tanya Roberts, Grace might be just a shade unpredictable. There was only one person on the production with the staying power and the delicate counter-punch who could handle her: Barbara, our daughter. Barbara, who inherited Dana's striking good looks and the touch of steel when it matters, remembers twenty-four hours with Grace Jones that, on reflection, she'd sooner forget.

She recalls: 'Cubby had been very interested in Grace Jones before she had become a major star. He'd seen her on a video programme playing the accordion and singing 'La Vie en Rose', which, to my knowledge, was her first hit in Paris. Cubby saw this woman on television and he called me and said, "Who is this girl? She's absolutely amazing. She's a very androgynous, lethal-looking woman!" We did some investigating and found out that she had originally been a model and was now starting out on a recording career. She had just played a role in *Conan the Destroyer*. I called up Raffaella De Laurentiis, whose company made the film, and asked her what she was like to work with.

'She said, "Look, she's a rock 'n' roller, she's not used to film schedules, she's not used to getting up at five in the morning. But if you have someone around to try and help her, it's really worth it, because on the screen she's dynamite!" So as I was an assistant director at the time I was nominated to make sure Grace kept to her schedule. Grace is a unique human being. She has many, many personalities. She can be extraordinarily generous, extraordinarily funny – and very kind. She can also be totally crazy. I got to know her fairly well and we became friends, but it took some adjusting to her personality.

'Grace was dating a guy whom we knew as Hans Lundgren, a Swedish kick-boxing champion. (He has since changed his name to Dolph Lundgren and is now a big star after his appearances in *Rocky* and *Masters of the Universe*.)

'We were in Paris doing a scene on top of the Eiffel Tower, where Mayday dives off the top and parachutes down to escape from Bond. We had to find a stunt man who could double for her. Now, although Grace is very tall and muscular, she's very slender, and the only stunt man we could find in England is a guy we've used a lot, called Clive Curtis, who is six foot four, and about two hundred and sixty pounds – he's a big man! And we needed him to do a jump off the top stage of the Eiffel Tower into some box mattresses about ten, fifteen feet. Clive came out, all ready, and Grace just pushed him aside and said, "Hell, I'll do it." She just took off and dived into the mattresses – with such style!

'We finished that sequence and had to go to Chantilly from Paris, where we were doing a big château sequence – a three-, four-hour drive. We had planned to leave Paris around four in the afternoon, needing to arrive in Chantilly before ten-thirty at night, because the little country hotel we'd be staying at locks the doors at ten-thirty. I had arranged with Grace and Dolph to pack up and be ready to leave the Hilton in Paris at four, drive comfortably to Chantilly, getting there in good time to have dinner. Grace also had her little son, Paolo, with her, who was about four years old, and the son's nanny, who was about sixty. She'd had two hip replacements – a very sweet lady, but she waddled and couldn't walk up stairs with or without the many, many trunks, bags and suitcases she had. We finally got everything together by about seven in the evening.

'We had ordered a van to take the luggage and a Mercedes to take the people. We put all the luggage into the van and started to put Dolph and Grace, the nanny and the kid into the car. I'd decided I would go with the luggage van. Then Paolo said, "No. I wanna go with Barbara, in the van!" I said I wasn't going to take the child alone with the driver, and said if he came in the van, then the nanny had to come, too. Fine. So he leapt into the van, and the driver had to come round and lift the nanny up.

'As we're about to pull off, Grace said, "By the way, we've got to stop off at Antonio's" – a well-known French dress designer who had been doing some of the wardrobe for us. She said she had to go there to pick up a jacket to wear in the scene. We drive to Antonio's workshop, get out of the van and out of the Mercedes onto the street, and it's a real strange mixture of people. There's Dolph – six foot four inches tall, big body-builder type – the nanny, Grace, the kid, myself and the two French drivers, and we're standing on the street. Antonio lived on the top floor of this apartment building. It didn't have any doorbells, so we had to scream up to try and get him to come to the door. It's eight o'clock on a Sunday night in Paris, and it's the kind of area where ambassadors and diplomats live, so there are lots of guards around. We're making a lot of noise, and then the dogs start barking everywhere. Finally, a little figure appears at one of the top windows. "Oh, come up, come up."

'We went to the elevator; that didn't work, so we had to trudge up six flights of stairs. I had to get one of the drivers to carry the nanny. We huffed and puffed to the top, and there was this wonderful character, very tiny little man, with this little poodle called Pattapouf, who was a vicious little creature, and immediately he and the little boy started having a fight, chasing each other around.

'We walked into the workshop and I said, "Antonio, look, we're in a terrible hurry, we have to drive to Chantilly and be there very soon – we've just come to pick up the jacket."

'He said, "Oh, come over here, come to my work table." I looked and there wasn't a jacket there. There was a sleeve and a pocket and a zip, and this and that – all in pieces. So I panicked.

'I said, "Antonio, we need this – *now*. We have to leave and Grace has got to wear this tomorrow."

'"No problem, no problem," he said. "I'll put this on the machine and you'll have it in twenty minutes."

'So, fine. Then Dolph said he was hungry and had to get some food. He and the driver went off to get some Chinese, and the boy and the dog were fighting and screaming at each other, and the nanny at this point was lying in a heap on the floor, exhausted. And Grace was going through Antonio's collection. Eventually we all piled back as before into the van: the nanny, the kid and I. I sat in front, and Paolo wanted to sit in front with me, but the driver said, "No, I'm sorry. In France, if you're under twelve years old you have to sit in the back." The child refused to get in the back. The nanny tried to grab him and bring him to the back. So the kid socked the nanny right in the mouth! A tooth fell out, and she starts screaming. She wouldn't spank him – just tried to get him in the back with her, and he just slugged her, twice, in the teeth. It's now eleven o'clock, eleven-thirty, and we're nowhere near Chantilly. I had these instructions about what to do when we arrived. We'd find Grace's keys planted in the dirt of the geranium pot. Everyone went to sleep, except me and the two drivers, who were taking turns to drive.

'Finally we pull up, having arrived in Chantilly, in this really lovely, quaint country hotel that's normally frequented by elderly people who go to Chantilly for the summer, for a rest. It's the dead of night, absolutely dead still, quiet and beautiful. We started unloading the baggage, and one of the drivers suddenly hit the side of the car with his arm or something – and suddenly the alarm system to the car went off – Wah-wah-wah-wah – and all the lights in the hotel went on, all the windows were thrown open, and there was screaming and yelling. I thought, we've made our entrance!

This is a Grace Jones entrance into Chantilly. We've woken up the entire village at one-thirty in the morning.

'Then the drivers had to hump all the baggage up this narrow stairway in total darkness. Not one outside light. Grace and Dolph went up and one of the drivers carried the child, the other one carried the nanny up the stairs, and we finally packed them all in.

'But the Grace Jones saga did not end in Chantilly. There is a royal première and she is being presented with others to Prince Charles and Princess Diana. A crisis blows up about her dress. The designer in Paris has a problem and is trying to reach her urgently in London. It was now my mother Dana's turn to get caught up in Grace's slipstream.

'It's the day of the royal première, and they are all at the Dorchester. Grace has an army of odd characters in her suite. Dana is with her friend Eleanor, an Italian countess, in an adjoining room and there's an hysterical man on the phone screaming in French, 'We cannot reach Grace Jones and unless we get to talk to her she will have no dress for the opening!'

'Dana said to Eleanor, who spoke good French, "Look, talk to this man and whatever you do, calm him down."

'Eleanor phones him. Her eyes widen, she puts her hand over the mouthpiece and tells Dana, "He just said, '*Merde* on Madame Broccoli!'"

'"Agree with him...agree with him..." Dana urges her. "That dress has got to be here!"

'So Eleanor talks to the man, then turns to Dana again. "He just said shit on me too!"

'"Don't argue with him, Eleanor," Dana pleaded. "What are friends for?!"

'Finally they find Grace, who calls the man herself. And the dress arrives in time.'

TWENTY

It was inevitable that we would have to make changes. Nothing lasts for ever. Actors are no different from producers, or Secret Service agents: we all grow older. But we're not in the superannuated Bond business. Our 007 had to look young and virile enough to match Fleming's heroes and the new ideas we had for the future. When *A View to a Kill* was released, the results pointed to a couple of uncomfortable truths. First, it just didn't do the kind of business we had been used to. Second – and not unconnected with the first – we urgently had to find a new James Bond.

Michael and I had sensed even before we shot the picture that Roger had a shade too much mileage behind him for 007. And there had been rumblings from Roger himself. Not only was he saying he didn't want to play the role any more, but his wife, Luisa, was saying the same, even more forcibly. Whether Roger genuinely wanted to back out, or was merely squaring up to the inevitable, was now irrelevant. Critics had been giving him the rough treatment, not just saying he was too old for Bond, but almost counting the lines on his face. Basically, they were right in their judgement, but unfair in their observations. What they tended to overlook was what a success he'd been as Bond: probably better than most other available actors twenty years younger might have been. Moreover, the public paid a lot of money over many films to prove it. If, at the end, Roger started playing up, demanding this and that, I suspect it was most likely others provoking him into it. Outside of that, we always got along fine making the pictures.

Roger had done everything possible to keep in good shape and sustain his vitality. He did regular exercises, daily workouts; Luisa saw to that. In fact, he looked great for his age, but obviously he couldn't move the way he used to. And the camera kept reminding us of it. We were shooting hundreds of stills and he was discarding eighty per cent of them. His secretary took over, viewing all the contacts under the magnifying glass, and she, too, began discarding stills. But the crucial fact was the box office. The figures alone signalled an urgent message: find a new Bond – and quickly. How do I go about this? I thought. Roger had not only been a terrific Bond, but was a friend. He had taken over the role in Sean's shadow and had to fight that off as well as his soft-centred TV image. The challenge would have daunted the best actors. Roger worked at the problem and beat it. He had made seven Bond films and created strong audience support throughout the world. But as I said, nothing lasts for ever. We both happened to be in California at the time. I rang and invited him over to the house.

I said, 'You realize, Roger, we're going to have to make a change. I think you probably understand that. You've had a great run, but I think we now have to call it a day. I want this to be a businesslike arrangement. It would be better if it looked like your decision rather than ours. If you want to say, officially now, that you're not going to make any more Bonds, I'll happily go along with that. Either way, I'd like it to happen quickly, before we start on the next picture.'

The news obviously came as a shock. I believe Roger thought for a moment that perhaps this was some ploy on my part to keep his salary down, or to head off requests for a lot more money. But then it sank in, and I felt sorry. I had to be grateful to him, but I was ending a very important and lucrative era in his life. I had made it as easy as I could for him, but whichever way I cut it, it was going to hurt. The actor who makes a success of James Bond achieves a professional power base most other superstars would envy. It means fame, status, and security in the millionaire class. Roger had achieved all that, with luxury homes in the sun and a lifestyle that went well with his hand-rolled Havanas. And now I was calling it all in. Well, he was a capable actor, he could direct, he could produce. Let's face it, he wouldn't, like some retiring stars, have to end his days in the Actors' Home. I'll say this for Roger: he accepted the decision well. He looked at me, smiled and put out his hand. 'I agree, Cubby,' he said. 'I think it's time…'

He bowed out in public with the same style.

On May 17, 1986, the New York Friars Club gave a testimonial dinner in Roger's honour at the Waldorf Astoria. It was a lavish occasion, with stars and other celebrities from both the US and Britain paying their tributes. Roger deserved it, and I was pleased for him. Any movie actor in the world would be happy to settle for that career peak in his life.

But now we had to get on with the show. Michael and I decided we not only needed a new 007, but an entirely fresh concept for the fifteenth James Bond film. It was a new challenge. Actors who can be first-class Bonds are a rare breed – but we'd been this route before. The new concept on the film was going to be worked out initially by Michael and Dick Maibaum, writing together. Given a fair degree of production equilibrium, we could get on with finding a Bond for the next picture, *The Living Daylights*.

Unfortunately, the upheavals at Metro, the firing of Frank Yablans, the new regime taking over, all made me think, here we go again! It had happened during our tenure with United Artists. Now the ritual dance was taking place at Culver City. These changes always have a disruptive effect on production.

We were told a new genius was coming in to run the studio. He was Jerry Weintraub, a pleasant sort of guy, full of energy and very successful in his own field, which was music, musicians and singers: top artists, too, whom he sent touring around the world. He had also made a film, *The Karate Kid*, which had taken money.

I liked him. He was a rambunctious character. Having dealt with Yablans, I hoped for an improvement with Weintraub. But it meant we had to pick up the pieces again, reintroduce ourselves and our production personnel to the new regime. Alan Ladd, Jr had been the third production chief at MGM/UA in four years, and one of the most competent. Frank Rothman and Frank Rosenfelt, Vice Chairman Emeritus to the then Chairman, Yablans, had hung around a little longer, Rothman longer than most. A former lawyer, and a long-standing associate of Kirk Kerkorian, Rothman knew a lot about the nuts and bolts of making movies. Meanwhile we had to carry on trying to cast and make a picture through all this hassle.

We dispatched Barbara to Australia, where there'd been an explosion of exciting young talent, to look for possible Bonds. Her brief was to come back with three or four that we could test. She brought back videos of twelve actors. None was the ideal Bond, but two had great looks and personality. We decided to test them, along with a couple of others, in the studio theatre at Culver City. Jerry Weintraub wandered into the screening room with a posse of sidekicks and said, 'Hey, mind if I come in? I'll just sit at the back.'

'Sure, come on down,' I said. We had no obligation to do this, but I was happy to show him what we had. A couple of these actors were established performers, drawing big audiences in Australia.

When the tests had been run, he got up and turned to me and asked, 'Do you want me to tell you what I think of these people? Do you want my opinion?'

'Of course.'

'Well, let me sugar-coat it for you: they stink!'

And that was the beginning of the 'new relationship', suggesting that conceit can be just as contagious as ego. It was irritating, but in this business you have to take the rough with the crude. By now the permutations on the company name, let alone the rapid turnaround in corporate executives, were forcing the trade papers into a round-the-clock updating of their stories. It is not easy to make motion pictures when the company which holds your destiny in its hands is up for grabs. Despite United Artists being a fully owned subsidiary of Transamerica since May 1981, we'd had three or four years of comparative peace. I didn't feel any corporate breath on the back of my neck at the time. But on August 7, 1985 MGM/UA was sold to Ted Turner of TBS for $1.45 billion, with Kirk Kerkorian buying back UA for $480 million.

That was just the opening gambit. In October the terms were revised and the air was thick with talk of share options, new issues, cash payments, preferred stock, junk bonds and all the other features of motion-picture finance. Inevitably, when a huge company and upwards of $1 billion of financing is being discussed by accountants, lawyers, brokers and other romantics, the making of motion pictures is pushed onto the back burner. We were involved in the crucial search for a new James Bond as well as the preparation of another picture. But back at the ranch the Kerkorian–Turner two-step continued into January 1986, when the selling price to TBS was revised downwards for the third time, with further permutations on the share price, the cash payment and other sweeteners.

I watched all this happening first with misgivings and then with some sadness. The great studio complexes, which had made history and created legends, were being bartered and carved up in an orgy of financial manipulations. Producers, directors, writers and other creative personnel stood around while young attorneys and accountants in designer denims and jogging trainers punched calculators and talked percentages. And as the film side of their operation shrank, so those who had in their different ways helped to create the wealth, found themselves tossed out into the wilderness.

Asset-stripping, the inevitable consequence of a shrewd takeover, is bound to result in casualties. But to see United Artists in recent years lose much of its highly talented personnel around the world so that auditors will have something to sing about, is depressing. Whole departments of this once great film company have gone to the wall. Of the 3500 personnel it once had, at that time only a few hundred now remained. We could not foresee how much worse that situation would become. Under Kerkorian's stewardship the huge Tracinda Corporation, with its vast hotel and entertainment holdings, has been a considerable success. But in essence he is a buyer and seller. He is not a picture-maker. He admits that. He is forced to put that side of his business into the hands of these other characters. They make mistakes. Kerkorian admits that, too. They make life tough for us just by being there. That was true of Jerry Weintraub, though he, too, went the way of all flesh.

We started interviewing potential Bonds in our London offices, hoping to find a British actor who could measure up to what we wanted. Weintraub was keen for us to consider an Australian actor, Mel Gibson. When we discussed his price, Weintraub said, 'Well, I can get him for you, but you have to give him $10 million for a two-picture deal: five for the first, five for the second.' The point was academic. I had no wish to cast Mel Gibson in the part. Then suddenly Weintraub was gone. His had been a short but lively reign. However, nothing that happened altered my liking for him. Whether he walked, stumbled or was pushed is not clear. I doubt if he went into shock. Nobody in that hot seat expected to see in their pension as production chief at UA.

After Weintraub had gone, Frank Rothman called Michael and me into his office for a most stimulating conversation. He spoke like a born-again film-maker. 'Boys,' he declared, 'we're going to have a great time. We're going back to talented projects. I've had the green light from Kerkorian. Everything's going to be great. You've had a rough ride, I know. But with me, everything's going to be all right.' About six weeks later Michael and I met him on the steps of the Thalberg Building. He was waiting for his car. 'I'm resigning,' he said. I couldn't help thinking how much blood had been spilt on those famous steps.

By this time Ladbroke's, Britain's leading bookmakers, were taking bets on who would play James Bond. We tested an actor named Lambert Wilson. I favoured him, but Michael didn't. Michael was impressed by the Australian actor Sam Neill, whereas I had my reservations. Michael, Barbara and John Glen were all keen on Neill. Ladbroke's had him as a clear favourite.

Meanwhile a new contender entered the scene: Pierce Brosnan, a young actor, star of the hit TV series *Remington Steele*. UA were strongly behind him, largely because of his successful TV image. In terms of looks and style, he'd have probably taken us along the Roger Moore route. But we were looking for a harder-edged actor who could take Bond into a new dimension. Still, of all these we'd seen, Brosnan appeared to be the best compromise. The case against him, from our point of view, was that the TV company would be getting mileage out of the 007 magic internationally, while to audiences, rather than something special, he would be just another TV star. There was a moment when I thought we might just use him. We made this stipulation to his agent: if he could be cleared completely out of the TV series, cutting all ties with the network, we would consider him. He was wildly keen to play the part. But when talks began with the network, there was a lot of stalling. In the end, his TV contract was renewed, and our search continued.

Throughout all this flurry in Hollywood and London, there was a patient but persistent voice in the background. It was Dana's. 'Why don't you have another look at Timothy Dalton?' she suggested. Seven years earlier I had twice talked to him about playing Bond. Those were the occasions when we were having some differences with Roger, and we had to be prepared with a replacement. But Timothy considered he was too young. He also said the part intimidated him, which I found interesting, coming from an experienced Shakespearean actor. Also, Michael detected in his reluctance some uncertainty about our genuineness in looking for a new 007. Dana was absolutely convinced from the start that he would make a first-class Bond. Now, seven years later, she was just as certain. I told her that Timothy had gone on record saying he didn't want the part. Dana, with that enervatingly sweet insistence, replied, 'Why don't we have him over for a drink at the Dorchester?'

When we met with Timothy we saw that those seven years had added poise, experience and self-assurance. Dana was right. He stood out from the bunch. He was obviously excited at the idea. He said he'd read the Bond books, and would want to play the character closer to the way Fleming wrote it. I said that was fine with me. He saw Bond as being more serious, just as ballsy as Connery's 007, but carrying his own personal imprint. Well, this, too, was in line with the sort of Bond we had in mind.

Timothy was playing in *The Taming of the Shrew* opposite Vanessa Redgrave in London at the time. He also had a commitment to film *Brenda Starr* in Puerto Rico, with Brooke Shields. But we were prepared to wait the six weeks until he became available. At first he didn't want to test for the part. He felt his track record as an actor was sufficient. But Michael explained to him, 'Look, nobody doubts your talents. But we have to see you as Bond just to get an idea of what we're dealing with, what we have on camera.' He was reluctant, but finally agreed. We tested him in a couple of scenes from *On Her Majesty's Secret Service*, as a lover and as a killer. All his years of training and experience showed. We had our new James Bond.

[Timothy Dalton has been described as the 'thinking woman's James Bond'. What the women are supposed to be thinking isn't examined. But assumptions can be made. The most persuasive of these is that this tall, lithe actor with the jungle-cat eyes suggests thrilling relationships rather than whistle-stop sex. Six foot two, with the intense, darkly handsome looks of a young Olivier, Dalton brought 007 back full circle: to that sharply intelligent secret agent Fleming created. He was no Superman, nor was he cast in the mould of the Connery stallion or Roger's raised-eyebrow charm. Timothy's exciting macho appeal, already revealed in his earlier work, had the crucial ingredient of believability. This is precisely the element Cubby Broccoli and Michael Wilson sought to create in the new-style Bond of *The*

Living Daylights. If the 007 eras of rough and tumble sexuality and raised-eyebrow capers were dead, Timothy Dalton was the right actor to bury them. Not that he didn't acknowledge Connery's excellent début in the role, or Roger's effectiveness as Sean's successor.

Nevertheless, he came to Bond determined to re-create the character, and delved through Fleming's books for his source material. This was the actor's approach, appropriate for someone of Timothy's training and experience. Born in Wales, raised in Manchester, he learned his craft, like so many other famous players, at the Royal Academy of Dramatic Art. He was much praised for his first film, playing the King of France in *The Lion in Winter*. He was only twenty-one, but the word went round that here was an actor to watch. He followed this with some excellent portrayals on TV, notably Heathcliff in *Wuthering Heights*, and Rochester in *Jane Eyre*. A critic, raving over his Heathcliff, declared: 'Dalton is one of the greatest acting finds of the decade.' Another confidently predicted that he would bring back the era of the matinée idol.

Timothy's reaction to all the hosannas was revealing. 'This absolutely isn't me,' he complained. 'I think the Americans must have gone completely mad!' They hadn't, of course. It was merely the diffidence of an actor concerned with his craft and not celebrity. Inevitably, there were a couple of flops, but even here, Timothy managed to go down in style. Playing Mae West's sixth husband in her disastrous movie swansong, *Sextette*, he rose ruefully from the ashes, grateful, he said, for the experience.

Back on TV with roles in *Mistral's Daughter* and *Sins*, Timothy proved that a good actor can sometimes rise above dud material. He starred in them with Vanessa Redgrave, the controversial actress with whom he has had a lively, close relationship for more than fifteen years. Inevitably, as 007 projected him into the limelight, he was questioned about that friendship, but declined to discuss it. As the media persisted, he became aware of the price an actor might have to pay for one of the biggest breaks in motion pictures. It is not enough to be Bond. You have to help sell him, too. Roger, more a media creation, was a pussycat at first, but then he, too, began to show his claws. Michael Wilson, intent upon heading off this problem early, invited the new prospective Bond to his home in London's Hampstead.

'I said to him, "Look, Timothy, if you want to play Bond for us, you've got to be prepared to help sell the picture. That is absolutely vital." I explained to him that these pictures are now mass media events. We have to stimulate the publicity in order to get the public out to see them. He gave me his word that he would do what was required.'

In the event, Timothy regretted giving this assurance. He said it had been a 'terrible mistake'. Not the complaint of a temperamental star; nor a symptom of what Cubby Broccoli calls the 'contagion of ego'. Just the lament of a very private person discovering he's a major public possession. He had to learn to live with it, if not love it. After all, as an enthusiastic angler, he could now afford to fish in exotic and distant waters, travelling in style, cosseted all the way. True, everybody's eyes were fixed on him wherever he went. But actors can suffer worse afflictions. And it's a small price to pay for the kudos that comes with the James Bond package.]

I was impressed by the way Timothy took on the new James Bond. He was also a rare sample of a vanishing breed: a gentleman actor with a highly tolerable ego. I think he was smart in having no preconceptions based upon what Sean and Roger had done before him. He was his own man, and played Bond that way. In the event, he received general critical approval. Most observers agreed that he gave the role an exciting new dimension, which is what we had set out to achieve.

Michael Wilson and Dick Maibaum, who collaborated on the script, cut down on the tricks and the gadgets. But we brought back Bond's famous Aston Martin, upgraded to the Volante model, fitted out with an array of devices which included laser-beam cutters, automatic missiles, rockets, a head-up display (as seen in the cockpit), studded tyres and protruding skis for driving on ice. Bond also has a lethal key ring which responds to a selected whistle. (Whistle 'Rule Britannia' and it emits a stun gas with a range of five feet.) We demonstrated these and other devices to Prince Charles and Princess Diana when they visited our set at Pinewood Studios. The Princess stole the show by smashing a prop bottle (made of sugar-glass) over Charles's head. Few wives could resist that!

[A slightly more friendly royal gesture occurred on February 19,

1987, when Cubby received an honorary OBE. The British Embassy in Washington announced:

'At an investiture ceremony at the British Embassy Residence today, the British Ambassador, Sir Anthony Acland, will present the insignia of the Order of the British Empire (OBE) to the distinguished film producer, Albert R. Broccoli. Mr Broccoli is receiving his award in recognition of his outstanding contribution to the British Film Industry. Based in London for 27 years, he has produced many films there including all fifteen of the highly successful James Bond series... During his time in Britain Mr Broccoli constructed the world's biggest sound stage, the "007" stage at Pinewood Studios.'

This award, together with France's Commandeur de l'Ordre des Arts et des Lettres and other honours and testimonials, is kept in Cubby's private office at his home in Beverly Hills. Framed, leather-bound, on pedestals or behind glass, these show the distance he has travelled since those days on the farm on Long Island.]

The Living Daylights introduced another fascinating actress to the Bond scene, Maryam d'Abo, who plays a Russian cellist. She is a very attractive and accomplished performer. Her love scenes with Timothy achieved the maturer level we were aiming at in Bond's amorous relationships. The film did well, the *Newsweek* critic declaring: 'The plot, thank goodness, is as outlandish and fast-paced as ever, with plenty of topical turns. This Bond inhabits a more ambiguous universe than his predecessors – a world where he acts on instincts more than orders. When an officious British agent whom Bond has grown to respect is suddenly killed, 007 actually looks grieved before he turns coldly furious and dashes off to avenge his colleague's death.' This endorsed our thinking about the way Bond should go in the future. It also proved that Timothy Dalton, physically and intellectually, was the man to play him.

The success of a movie, however, depends as much on the selling as upon the performance of its stars. Timothy did his job, but once the cameras had ceased to roll the tub-thumping began, for producers have to go out and court an increasingly diffident public.

There was an intriguing example of this one night in Westwood, Los Angeles, where *The Living Daylights* was being shown. Dana and I strolled into the Hamburger Hamlet opposite the theatre for a cup of coffee before the ten-thirty screening. We sat at the counter, and were kept waiting for an inordinately long time. A young man close by noticed this, and complained to the manager, saying, 'These people came in some time ago and nobody has bothered to take their order.'

I appreciated this gesture very much, and a conversation ensued in which I asked the young man if he had seen the film showing across the road.

'No,' he replied, 'and I have no intention of seeing it, either.' He'd decided this, he explained, on the basis of unfavourable verdicts by a couple of critics.

'Why be influenced by these characters?' I asked him. 'Surely you should rely upon your own judgement?'

'Why, have you seen it?'

'I made it,' I said. 'Furthermore, I would like you to see the film as my guest.'

The young man protested. I insisted. The three of us then trooped across to the theatre, where I bought a ticket. The manager, recognizing me, leapt forward.

'Did I see you buy a ticket, Mr Broccoli?'

'Yes,' I said. 'I bought it for this gentleman here.'

The manager's embarrassment dissolved in laughter. 'I know you believe in backing your pictures all the way, Mr Broccoli – but you really don't have to drag the customers in off the streets!'

Further confirmation of Timothy Dalton's talents came from an unexpected quarter: Sean Connery also thought he was right for Bond. It was generous of him, revealing his curiously ambivalent personality. At one moment he recognized what he owed to Bond; at the next he was quoted making accusations about my integrity.

[There were other problems with Sean, as Cubby's lawyer Norman R. Tyre explains:

'When Sean Connery first made an employment agreement with Danjaq, it provided for a series of pictures to be made and further modifications, each of which gave him bigger benefits than before. He ended up, finally, in a position whereby he had a percentage of the profits which Danjaq would make from merchandising: selling various items bearing the Bond image: toiletries, clothing, jewellery and so on. These referred to Sean's pictures or his name.

For this syndication right to use his name in connection with his Bond image, he was given a percentage of the net receipts from merchandising. (This was in addition to a percentage of the profits from the distribution of the films themselves; that is, the films in which he appeared.)

'However, even after he ceased to appear in the pictures, whenever merchandising with his name or likeness was used he was still contractually entitled to his percentage from the merchandising. But he claimed that under the agreements, even if his name or likeness was not used, as long as the name of James Bond was used in merchandising, he was entitled to his percentage, in perpetuity. This seemed to be an erroneous interpretation of the agreements to me, and it involved protracted legalities involving Danjaq, Eon Productions, UA, Glidrose (now in the Fleming estate) and lawsuits filed in the Federal Court of Los Angeles and later in the State Court. Armies of lawyers were being deployed on all sides, largely because, in addition to the merchandising dispute, Connery was claiming he was not properly treated by UA in connection with the distribution of the pictures. UA were aware they were liable to a portion of the claim. They had gone through four or five changes of management, and Frank Rothman, who himself was a litigator, wanted to get the matter out of the way. Perhaps Connery's well-known tendency towards thrift finally persuaded him to settle. This was achieved not unfavourably to Cubby.']

I was open-minded about Connery fighting his corner about what he considered his legitimate rights. What I resented was his making me a target for disputes which had nothing to do with me or my company. His beef about money was with UA. We never handled his money. This was handled by UA, as the distributors. So if he had a complaint at all it was with them, not with me. Yet this didn't prevent him from making unjust slurs. A London newspaper quoted him as saying he'd been 'screwed' by the Bond producers. It was clearly libellous, implying that, to put it in plain language, I was a crook. In fact, he had reportedly said a lot of things about me that were unfair and I overlooked it until the newspapers picked them up and quoted him. Apparently Sean later claimed that the statements in the newspaper to which I objected had been made two years earlier. I didn't see that this mitigated the insult and instructed our lawyers to seek a full retraction. On August 16, 1991 the London *Sun* published this statement:

CUBBY BROCCOLI:

On November 13, 1989 we published remarks by Sean Connery about Cubby Broccoli, the world-famous producer of the James Bond films which suggested that he had defrauded Connery of £170,000 and was obsessively greedy. We accept that these allegations are untrue. Also we wish to make it clear that Mr Broccoli had no involvement whatever in the making of the film *Never Say Never Again*, which was criticised in the article. We apologise to Mr Broccoli and will be paying him substantial damages and costs.

I demanded a similar retraction from the *Sunday Times* of London, which repeated the same kind of allegations. On August 3, 1992, this apology appeared in that paper:

CUBBY BROCCOLI AND THE SUNDAY TIMES

Last week, Times Newspapers apologised to the world-famous producer of the James Bond films, Cubby Broccoli, over an article in the *Sunday Times Magazine* (November 5, 1989) about Sean Connery headlined 'No one says no to Sean'. In the article, Mr Connery criticised the production arrangements for the Bond film *Never Say Never Again*. The article failed to state that Mr Broccoli had not produced *Never Say Never Again*. In the same article, reference was made to Mr Connery's claim in the American courts that Mr Broccoli had defrauded him of a substantial part of the profits from the Bond films. In fact, Mr Connery had abandoned the American litigation some time before the article was published. The *Sunday Times* therefore accepted that Mr Connery's claim and allegations against Mr Broccoli were untrue and unfounded and apologised to Mr Broccoli for any embarrassment caused by the article.

The apology was not exactly commensurate with the insult, which cut too deep to be shrugged off in a couple of paragraphs. Fortunately, the substantial damages paid by the paper, like all ill winds, blew somebody some good. I sent the cheque, to which I added a much larger amount, through Roger Moore to UNICEF, the children's charity to which the late Audrey Hepburn, bless her heart, had devoted so much of her energy right until the end.

It's hard for me to understand this side of Sean's nature. By any standards, Bond was the best thing that ever happened to him. But that is for him to judge. To have him complain that I was dishonest with him was hurtful, and, as he well knew, untrue.

Finally Sean quit. He might have made things difficult for us making a rival Bond. This didn't happen. Frankly, it couldn't happen. Sean was a good Bond, but he was never going to be the only one. Really successful film series outlive their stars. The package scores over the personality. Just the same I never underrated Sean's gifts as an actor. I was pleased to see how he confirmed this by winning the Golden Globe and then, in 1987, the Oscar for Best Supporting Actor for his performance in *The Untouchables*. I myself voted for him in the Academy Awards that year. To my mind he was the best actor of them all. But he seized the opportunity in his acceptance speech to take another oblique swing at Bond. He grinned at the audience, saying: 'My name is Connery – Sean Connery!' The implication was clear: don't confuse me with James Bond. That's over! Which amused me. No matter how many different roles he plays, the subconscious image in the public's memory will always be of him as 007. More than thirty years on, Connery would receive an Academy Fellowship – a considerable achievement for an actor and the highest honour in the industry.

We began work on the new Bond film, *Licence to Kill*, caught in the slipstream of more top-level company manipulations. At last we had two characters in charge of production at MGM/UA who had paid their creative dues: Lee Rich and Tony Thomopoulos. When Lee Rich, who had been president of Lorimar, arrived on the scene, MGM/UA were going through a lean period. The London *Times* spoke of 'an impressive comeback by MGM/UA under Mr Lee Rich. It has pared costs, reduced losses which amounted to $14.3 million on sales of $237 million in 1987, and produced several big hits including *Moonstruck*, which won three Academy Awards, and *The Living Daylights*.' For a moment at least there appeared to be some respite from the battle. We were back in the motion picture business.

Toward the end of 1987, my old friend Greg Bautzer died. He was one of the great, colourful characters of Hollywood. Tall, with a powerful physique, he could roar like a bull, but had a lot of heart and was a fiercely loyal friend. He was one of the town's most fashionable lawyers, and had been Howard Hughes's attorney for years. He was part of the small group who remained Howard's friends to the end. He had also been famously known as Joan Crawford's boyfriend. I watched this affair develop with as much alarm as amusement. Joan's real-life persona wasn't all that different from her screen image of a fierce, tough, demanding lady.

Greg had been a fighter almost from his childhood. He worked his way through law school, flew with the Navy during the war. Raised on San Pedro's rough waterfront, he was generous and attentive but short on the hand-kissing finesse demanded by Miss Crawford. I knew her well. I knew Greg even better. I stood back and waited for the fireworks. Joan was the complete movie star – on and off the screen. She made a fine production of having her escort light her cigarette. He was also required to unfold her dinner napkin and spread it on her lap, walk a couple of respectful paces behind her in public and generally behave like a well-heeled slave. As her friend Bill Haines once observed: 'To be Joan Crawford's boyfriend a man must be a combination of bull and butler.' Greg was neither. And once I saw him glowering behind her carrying her poodle I knew that rigor mortis was fast setting into the romance. Mr Bautzer was as volatile as all hell, and playing gin or backgammon with him could end in arguments that would have neighbours dialling the Beverly Hills police. Touch a raw nerve, and his pale eyes behind thick lenses could freeze you at ten paces.

I recall a formal dinner party at the Bistro to which I had brought a lawyer friend from Washington. This innocent dared to take issue with Greg on some small point, which angered him so much he was close to exploding. Everyone looked nervous as Bautzer turned a murderous glare on this upstart who'd flown in from the East Coast.

'Who the hell are you!?' he roared.

'Greg, he's a friend of mine,' I said.

Greg simmered down and said to the young lawyer, 'In that case you have diplomatic immunity!'

Dana, who had been expecting a catastrophe, sank back with relief.

I remembered that dinner party when we were in the church, listening to all the graceful tributes being paid to Greg. Of course, my friend was all that they said of him: kind, respected, charitable, and all that. But I kept wondering what my late cousin, Pat de Cicco, and Henry Ford Jr would have made of all these rose petals being heaped on Bautzer. Here in the church they were making him out to be some kind of saint, which in some ways he may have been – but somehow it didn't match the rampaging s.o.b. we'd all known and loved. I looked across at Sidney Korshak and he looked across at me, and we both knew what the other was thinking. Mike Frankovich looked across at both of us and he was thinking the same, and we were all close to falling apart. The high-profile image of Mr Bautzer we had in mind didn't exactly go with the reverential atmosphere and the stained-glass windows.

Still, Greg was entitled to his day in church. And he had the last laugh. One thing was for sure: the pallbearers were going to suffer. As I sweated and heaved under the weight of the casket, Beldon Katleman and Korshak didn't look like they were enjoying it either. It occurred to me that I could use a little urgent diplomatic immunity myself!

As happened with Pat de Cicco, Greg's wife, Niki, and his friends gave him the sort of send-off he would have liked: caviare and champagne at the Bistro Gardens in Beverly Hills, a great favourite of his. We saw him out as royally and affectionately as we had said goodbye to Pat. I miss them both.

Not long after we buried Greg Bautzer, Irving Allen died. He had been ill, unable to walk for some time. I saw him occasionally, and it was sad. He had lost none of his old sassy spirit, but his legs could no longer carry him. We talked a lot about the old days, and also about the state of the game today. There wasn't the slightest echo of the disagreements we'd once had. We had walked away from our partnership with a handshake. Anyway, neither of us put movies above our families in importance. Irving doted on his wife, Nita, who was devoted to him; not easy with a man as volatile and as forthright as Irving. But he was extremely kind, and behind the boisterous act, a very human individual. I still chuckle over an episode concerning Irving and a horse he bought. This is a story he often told against himself, so I don't consider I'm being disloyal to my old friend. It concerned a racehorse he paid a lot of money for. When it was delivered, he rounded on the dealer. 'This ain't the horse I ordered,' he bellowed. 'The one I chose wasn't so sway-backed as this. This is a jackass – I don't want it!'

The owner vehemently disputed this allegation, so Irving sued him. He won his case in court, and the guy had to take the horse back. Put back into training and carefully groomed for the track, it became one of the biggest money-spinners in the business: Halo. It later went to stud and earned millions. Whenever anybody talked about having blown it on something big, Irving topped it with, 'I'm the smart-ass who won a lawsuit over a horse and lost a fortune!'

We had planned originally to make the next James Bond film in China, where the regime was trying to encourage commercial interest from the West. There was plenty to tempt us in this big, strange country with its contrasts between primitive rural areas and ultra-modern cities with luxurious Western-style hotels.

But first, Michael, Barbara, Dana and I flew to the film festival in Tokyo, where we screened *The Living Daylights*. The Japanese love everything about James Bond, particularly the stunt work. Having seen all the Bond films now, Japanese audiences are tuned in to the nuances and tongue-in-cheek humour that goes with 007. They liked Timothy Dalton's style, recognizing the experienced actor beneath the James Bond persona.

Ian Fleming had often talked to me about his experiences in Japan. Although many of his friends had suffered as prisoners of war, he loved the country and the Japanese people. He knew the philosophical basis to judo. He could give an expert commentary on sumo wrestling. He knew all the different kinds of sake and which brands to drink with different dishes. He understood all the subtleties of the Tea Ceremony and, according to the geisha who years ago ceremoniously entertained him in Tokyo, he was the essence of gentlemanly British decorum. To me, it was just another indication of Ian's professionalism. He had to get to the essence of any country he visited. It showed in his conversation, and above all in his books.

From Tokyo, Michael, Barbara, Dana and I, with an entire film crew, flew to Hong Kong and then, in early October 1987, on to Beijing. We planned an extensive recce of China, including seeing what must be another Wonder of the World. The incredible Terracotta Army is a masterpiece comprising sculpted soldiers in full uniform and marching gear, each face individually modelled. What a set-up for a Bond picture! The most curious feature of this subterranean army was how close they were to the ground surface.

The soil above was loose and trampled on by thousands of visitors, yet strangely the figures remained intact and awesome to look at. So too was the Great Wall, another art director's dream.

I'm certain the Chinese film authorities would have liked to become involved with a James Bond film. In fact, when we showed *The Living Daylights* to them in Shanghai they were excited by the idea. This proves how successfully Fleming's hero adapts to totally different cultures and why internationally 007 has remained a top box-office attraction for so long. Like the Russians, the Chinese officials were excited by the action sequences and bowled over by the stunts.

Our hosts gave us a splendid banquet, preceded by formal tea drinking. Dana was quick to notice that the evening was a strictly men-only affair, with the officials' wives noticeably excluded, though as a courtesy Western wives were allowed to attend. In spite of the determination of the Chinese to break out of the Communist mould, the cultural differences struck us immediately. For instance, at the studios we visited everybody who worked there lived on the complex: the actors, the technicians and their families. Protocol was strictly observed, and introductions conducted with solemn regard for the pecking order. The Chinese revere the older generation, equating age with wisdom. At eighty-three I wasn't disposed to quarrel with that. All our hosts stood in line, and the introductions began: 'This is the elderly Mr So-and-So, and here is the elderly producer...' and so on. Michael responded with his usual charm but stopped short of introducing 'the elderly Mr B'.

The Chinese film co-production people were attentive and good-natured hosts. But eventually we decided the conditions and the logistics ruled out our making a picture there. The bureaucracy was stifling and the political intrusions, with scripts having to go back and forth between officials, would not have given us the essential elbow room to operate freely. I suspect it will be a long haul before China is ready to open all its doors to 007.

With that option closed, I would have liked to have gone back to England's Pinewood Studios, where Bond was born and raised, and where I had so many friends among the crews. But with a Bond picture costing more than ever, I couldn't ignore the arithmetic. Filming in Mexico offered immediate advantages: there was a favourable exchange rate, there were film studios – of a kind

– in Mexico City, and the terrain offered plenty of scope for good action locations.

Michael and Dick Maibaum had produced a treatment based on our recce in China. Michael and I talked around the subject for a long time and decided that we would go for an altogether more realistic, gutsier James Bond. We had no doubts about Timothy Dalton in the role. It was just that our story, based on a theme of personal revenge, required this additional, more muscular dimension. The central character, a plausible monster with political muscle running a massive drugs operation, was criticized by some as being too fanciful. This was ironic, considering the script was based on a real-life character named Noriega.

I liked the new treatment and so did United Artists, and after Barbara Broccoli and Tom Pevsner made a long, on-the-spot survey of the studio facilities and locations, we shifted the entire operation down to Mexico. I didn't expect making a film down there to be a picnic. And I wasn't wrong. I am not criticizing the Mexicans: they did the best they could for a country strapped for cash. The facilities were primitive. Some of the stages had holes in the roofs, and when it rained, water poured down onto the sets. Two other films were being shot there at the time; one of them was *Old Gringo*, starring Jane Fonda. There wasn't much of a prop department, so we had to buy most of the furniture and other things we needed. The Mexican craftsmen were good, but we brought nineteen technicians from the UK who had worked with us and knew what Bond was all about. (One of Barbara's big discoveries there was Ramón Bravo, a Mexican underwater director and cinematographer, who produced some first-class underwater footage for us.)

I don't deny I was apprehensive. This was a big leap for me. Quite apart from the emotional ties I had with Pinewood, we were shooting in uncharted territory and in a Catch-22 environment. The higher you climbed to escape pollution the less oxygen there was to breathe. Moreover, any notion that the new regime at UA would make for a more peaceful operation was soon knocked out of the ballpark.

Stephen Silbert, the new head of production, sent his lieutenant, Dean Stolber, down to kibbitz around the activities. It was the mixture as before: another expert, keen as a Boy Scout to earn a company medal. Again it was an attempt at a cost-cutting operation as though we ourselves weren't aware of the need to keep within a budget.

I had no objection to UA keeping an eye on their investment. What annoyed me was some of their money-saving ideas. Dean Stolber is a competent executive who had been with the company since the departure of Arthur Krim. He should have recognized that every dollar spent on Bond is aimed at getting a first-class production. Any unnecessary extravagance hits us as much as anybody else. But all of us, working for months in the heat under primitive conditions, found these nit-picking intrusions trying, to say the least.

Michael had his own personal cross to bear in all this. A woman from UA who accompanied Dean Stolber wandered into a Mexican bar that had been set up for a scene. She looked around, turned to Michael and said, 'Gee, this seems to be an awfully big set for just a five-minute scene.'

By this time a veteran in this sort of caper, Michael replied patiently, 'It isn't all that expensive, considering much of the stuff has been given to us by the beer companies.'

'Yes, but look at those bottles. Look at those cases of booze...!'

Michael stared at the woman in disbelief, then said, 'You don't think those bottles contain real booze, surely? They're filled with water. And those cases you're looking at. They're just empty boxes.'

This upset her. She thought she had nailed a clear case of extravagance. She frowned, looked around and muttered, 'Well, what do you need a pool table for?'

At this point we made it clear that we were marginally better off without their kind assistance.

Eventually *Licence to Kill* was released to impressive box-office figures throughout the world. But the American public didn't respond the way they always had to previous Bond pictures. The film just didn't seem to go right in the US. This was a rare experience for us and we spent a lot of time thinking about it. The timing of the release was certainly a factor. We came up against two blockbusters, one of which, *Batman*, was hyped like no other movie in my experience. What I also found hard to take was the harsh reaction of the British censor in restricting the age group for our picture while giving *Batman* a clean bill of health. Dog doesn't eat dog in our trade, but in a volatile market few motion pictures could compete with the multimillion-dollar hype behind that film. The other competition, *Lethal Weapon II*, was something else. It was a good movie, though it was stacked with foul language which, regrettably, appeared to have been a factor in its popularity. There is no way we can do that with James Bond.

The press were less than fair. They criticized our plot and totally misunderstood our intention to expose top-level corruption in the drug scene. If Noriega had been nailed a year before, the same critics might have accused us of milking the situation. That aside, it was obvious that Michael and I had to do some serious rethinking. We agreed that in making Bond an altogether tougher character, we had lost some of the original sophistication and wry humour. Bond is not a Superman, or a Rambo. He is the kind of guy who has a tremendous will. He capitalizes on his luck and tries to limit the downside. Sometimes it works, sometimes it doesn't. But he's not superhuman. He is, as Fleming insisted, a skilled professional: ruthless and sardonic in his work; gentle, witty and stylish off duty. That is the way the public want him and it's clear we had to get back on to that track. Back to a lighter touch, with more fun and capers like we had with the earlier Bonds.

For all its problems of style and logistics, filming James Bond has always been a great experience, and sometimes a lot of fun. But that fun was noticeably diminished as MGM/UA went into further financial convulsions – inevitable when a great company is being kicked around in the market-place. Kirk Kerkorian had always been a considerable figure on the entertainment scene, and was always courteous when we met. But we had different motivations; differences that would later force us to challenge him in court. His preoccupation with billion-dollar deals and huge financial juggling distanced him from the day-to-day problems of making motion pictures.

As the pack of top executives of MGM/UA was constantly reshuffled, the casualty rate among subordinates in the marketing, publicity and similar areas was mind-boggling. Several independent producers were ditched as the financial whiz-kids scythed their way through the organization. In October 1988 a couple of investment bankers were brought in to run the company. What they both knew about the making of motion pictures did not seem to be relevant to Kerkorian's game plan. Those on the inside track had no doubts that these characters – on $1 million-plus salaries – had been brought in to fatten the goose; to make the company an appetizing buy for another hungry conglomerate.

There was a flirtation with the Sony Corporation which fell through. Then, on March 31, 1989, MGM/UA announced the sale of UA and certain MGM/UA assets (including the valuable library and distribution organization to the Quintex Group of Australia for $1 billion plus $400 million in assumed debt, Kerkorian buying back MGM/UA television, the name, the logo and the headquarters.

Suddenly another face with baby-blue eyes was sauntering around, allegedly boss of the company. His name was Christopher Skase, a flamboyant multimillionaire whose office in Brisbane has an indoor waterfall complete with marble cherubs. Hardly the appropriate backdrop for a character the Australian magazine *Bulletin* described as 'among the hundred most appalling people in the country'. It continued: 'young and very *nouveau riche*, he loves to party in his two-piece suits with his glamorous wife Pixie of the blonde bangs and gold bangles. He zooms about the world in King Hussein's hand-me-down jet with faded maps of the Mediterranean on the cabin walls.'

Which was fine for Mr Skase, and I am never one to knock the good life. But as it turned out, the announcement of the Quintex-MGM/UA deal was premature. There appeared to have been some delay in coming up with the hard cash: around $50 million as a deposit. I was forewarned of this possibility by an Australian who was familiar with the Quintex style of operation. In the event, the deal fell through.

When one predator falls, another pounces. In came Rupert Murdoch, via his News Corporation and Fox Inc., with an eleventh-hour bid of $1.8 billion for the whole of MGM/UA. The offer was stalled while further negotiations continued with Quintex. The absence of actual cash on the table prompted Kirk Kerkorian to return to Murdoch. But this suitor wasn't interested in a marriage on the rebound, and backed away. The company created by Chaplin, Mary Pickford, Douglas Fairbanks and D.W. Griffith, and built up over the years by some of the most famous figures in motion pictures, was now just a negotiable asset.

Hollywood's dominance as the entertainment capital of the world was not achieved by 'creative accountancy' nor corporate raiding. It was achieved by people who, good or bad, tyrants or benevolent megalomaniacs, loved motion pictures. Not that I should have been surprised to see key Wall Street figures moving into the boardrooms of the film industry. As Neal Gabler wrote in *An Empire of their Own*: 'Wall Street had few compunctions about loaning money and placing its officers on the boards of movie companies. By the early 1920s Wall Street was well represented on the boardrooms of almost every film company. Some saw this as a tragedy. "When we operated on picture money," Cecil B. De Mille once said, "there was joy in the industry. When we operated on Wall Street money, there was grief in the industry."'

The line between 'picture money' and 'Wall Street money' was clear-cut in those far-off days. Today, the distinction is largely academic. Technological advances in the film business have been enormous. The computer is now part of the creative process. And the Japanese, ahead of almost everyone in these technological miracles, now dominate the majors in Hollywood with mixed success. I ought not to have been surprised at the way events turned out towards the close of 1990. But I wasn't exactly thrilled, either.

For two years now Kirk Kerkorian, in his attempt to sell off MGM/UA, had flirted with a whole array of assorted individuals, but the projected deals had been aborted for one reason or another. Throughout that time we rarely met. He had bigger fish to fry, seeking a buyer with the $1 billion-plus which was the price tag pinned on the movie empire Louis B. Mayer had built.

I was equally preoccupied sustaining Bond, which was built up with just as much sweat and dedication. I have no prejudices against money or against those with a rare skill at manipulating it. But the feverish activity which went into the selling of MGM/UA inevitably induced shock waves upon those caught in the fallout. In these massive financial operations involving billions of dollars certain elements were kicked into the sidelines. I was determined that this was not going to happen to James Bond. Other producers caught in the same slipstream were equally apprehensive.

That apprehension increased when a new player took to the field. At that time Giancarlo Parretti was just a name to me. His holdings in the entertainment world were apparently huge, dominated by the giant US subsidiary Pathé Communications. On the face of it, Parretti had the credentials to bid $1.3 billion for the great and prestigious Metro-Goldwyn-Mayer. His chances of raising this sum appeared rosy when he all but clinched a deal with Time Warner, who agreed to put up a large share of the money in exchange for long-term video rights to both Pathé and MGM/UA movies. Eventually, after some energetic fiscal cliff-hanging, Parretti appeared to come up with the cash.

While all this was going on, my attorneys, with Michael alongside, were closely observing the state of play. Then we discovered that James Bond appeared to be a sizeable sweetener in the pot. We learned that our sixteen Bond pictures were being sold off as part of Parretti's cash-raising in order to clinch the purchase of MGM/UA. Moreover, it was clear – to us at least – that these pictures were to be sold off at bargain-basement prices in a number of foreign TV and video licensing deals. The longer we looked at the fine print, the more our attorneys, Michael and me were convinced that not only an alleged breach of contract was involved. This was becoming a question of the virtual survival of James Bond.

Accordingly, our company, Danjaq, filed suit against MGM/UA Communications and Pathé Communications in a move to block international TV licensing agreements which, allegedly, would cause 007 films to be sold to foreign TV (France, Spain, Italy, South Korea and Japan) at well below market rates for the remainder of the century. Our action was a matter of simple prudence to guard against the consequences of a possible failure by the company which, if it were to occur, would make Bond just another creditor, the properties part of the prime assets. I was determined that this was not going to happen. The stakes were just too high. Friends and associates warned me that I was in for a tough and costly battle. But there was no way I was going to permit these people to knock me out of the box.

In any event, there was more to this battle than the preservation of a cinema legend. What we were also seeing was the death by a thousand cuts of a great studio. On November 20, 1990 an old friend, Charles Champlin, the distinguished critic and Arts Editor of the *Los Angeles Times*, wrote: 'The purchase of the MGM/UA Communications Co. by Pathé Communications Corporation completed at the start of November is the last cutting of the cord to the MGM that was. The new logo will be MGM/Pathé. And at the same time the UA logo will disappear into history after 71 memorable years. From somewhere up in the clouds, Louis B.

Mayer and his arch-rival Columbia's Harry Cohn must both be gazing down with extremely mixed emotions at what Mammon hath wrought. From adjoining clouds Charlie Chaplin, Mary Pickford, Douglas Fairbanks and D.W. Griffith could look down with equally mixed emotions...The decline and demise of a studio or a production company...is very much like the death of a magazine or a newspaper. It is the silencing of a voice...'

Champlin couldn't have put it better. At their peak, MGM and UA carved the benchmarks of highly popular and prestigious film-making. They created some of Hollywood's greatest stars, enhanced its prestige, kept faith with the talented pioneers who had staked their lives and their fortunes on the industry. James Bond is a cinema legend because the studio that backed it was not obsessed by greed. The men who ran it respected the many independent producers whose primary objective was the making of good, profitable motion pictures. Optimism, confidence and creative freedom are the essence of successful independent production. In the period of MGM/UA's – and Giancarlo Parretti's – long travail there wasn't much of these qualities around. Just fear, and gloom at the top.

During the protracted lawsuits that arose from this situation we were forced to put James Bond on hold and carry on with our lives.

TWENTY-ONE

Christmas 1990, as always, centred on family and friends, with Dana the focal point of the festivities. She shared my anger at the way we were having to fight to protect everything we'd built together. But she kept it in perspective. The lawyers could be kept at bay for a while. We were going to have our family Christmas: the tree-dressing party, fun with the grandchildren.

New Year took us to Las Vegas to see one of my oldest friends, Frank Sinatra, give another one of his unique performances. It was his kind of crowd, and despite what he says about Chicago, his kind of town. At tables close by were his kind of people, too: friends from way back, hosted by his attractive wife, Barbara. Frank sang with all his old, inimitable magic: casual, intimate, witty, but always in total control of his music. It was close to perfection. And memorable. I have known him a long, long time, and can tell when the man is taking over from the performer. He has had his bouts of ill health. Perhaps that is why I detected a special sincerity in the way he wished the audience a happy, healthy and peaceful New Year. I suppose there comes a time in life when each new year arrives as a bonus. He must feel that now. And so do I.

Towards the end of his performance he addressed a personal tribute and then a song to his wife. There was a special tenderness to it. Barbara rose in the full glare of the spotlight and smiled at him. It was a rare moment of intimacy, caught instantly by the audience. Those of us who've known Frank and Barbara over the years sensed something special about that moment. Frank has never given less than his best. I hope the oncoming years for both of them will be just as generous. [Frank Sinatra died on 15 May 1998.]

But Fate knows how to call in its markers. We flew back from

Nevada still caught in the afterglow of the New Year celebrations. We had barely unpacked when a phone call told me that Dick Maibaum had died. It was a tremendous blow to me: sudden and without warning. Dick may have been eighty-one, but in his quizzical, smiling way he'd always seemed to me to be indestructible. I was immensely saddened. Everybody knew he was an extremely talented writer, highly respected by his peers. But behind that skill was a man of great sensitivity. He was, as was said in the eulogy at his funeral, a *'mensch'*. The best translation of this Yiddish accolade – as any good Catholic would tell you – is 'a good, decent, honourable and charitable man'.

Well, Dick Maibaum was all those things. But he also had a fine sense of humour and, a valuable quality in a writer, good taste. In the forty years or so that I knew him, he never compromised his integrity as a writer nor his principles as a human being. His contribution to Bond, from *Dr No* right up to *Licence to Kill*, was invaluable. Maibaum understood Fleming. But more important, he had a special insight into the nuances integral to the character and Englishness of James Bond. Two of the most respected newspapers in Britain, *The Times* and the *Guardian*, wrote admiringly of his life and work. Our tribute placed in the trade papers after the funeral expressed precisely how we felt:

> 'Remembering Richard Maibaum...
> A gentle friend and gifted colleague,
> with respect, admiration, and love.'

One blow was followed by another. Mike Beck, one of my oldest friends and the watchdog of our company, died in New York. I was prepared for it because he had been dreadfully ill for some time. But there was something unique about this man which made the loss hit much harder. He had been blind for many years, but he could steer his way around the desks in the New York office as confidently as anyone else. I'll never know how he managed it, but he dealt with company business, signed letters, ran the store as though he had twenty-twenty vision. Now and again I'd take his elbow when we went out to lunch. It wasn't really necessary: more a gesture of friendship. 'I know where I am, Cubby,' he'd say. Flying from the West Coast to the funeral in New York, I saw him in my mind the way I will always remember him: patient, wise and ever smiling. He was in many ways like a brother. And one of the bravest men I've ever known. When we sit around, I often think of him, of Dick and of all the others who've played such a large part in my life. Pat de Cicco, Henry Ford Jr, Howard Hughes, Bruce Cabot, Errol Flynn, Charlie Feldman, Joe Schenck, Greg Bautzer, Irving Allen...and especially the late Abba Schwartz, a loyal and much-respected associate of the late President Kennedy and one of the most devoted friends we ever had. I miss them all. Each name triggers memories. All of them added something special to the total of my life.

I did not expect to have to add to that list so quickly and so unexpectedly. On April 9, Maurice Binder died. He was just seventy-two. It was another blow, the loss of a close friend and valued associate. Maurice's famous screen titles made an enormous contribution to the success of James Bond. His death shocked us all, particularly Dana and Barbara, who loved this gentle, dapper little genius whom we treated as part of the family.

Maurice and I had similar beginnings. Like me, he moved into the entertainment world out of the services. He'd been in the navy section of the US Army during the war. Born in New York, the city he loved as much as he loved London, he displayed an early talent for design. He began his career creating catalogues for Macy's department store. This took him into advertising, creating posters for stage and screen productions. Many of those posters, particularly the one he designed for *The Jolson Story*, are collector's items today.

When Harry Saltzman and I discussed the titles for our first Bond film I happened to see Maurice's opening credits for the Stanley Donen picture *The Grass is Greener*. They were totally innovative and brought enthusiastic responses from the experts and the general public. Maurice had hit on the brilliant idea of parading a line of babies toddling around on a lawn, each rigged up as one of the stars or leading figures on the production. The sequence was hilarious, and the audience fell about even before the movie had got under way. We needed to look no further. Binder's definitive opening logo, with Bond striding into the circle of the gun barrel and firing a shot, is now a renowned trademark. With that one sketch, which took him all of fifteen minutes to create, Maurice had pencilled himself into instant celebrity, and the titles for a total of fourteen James Bond films.

Occasionally I had to curb his frisky enthusiasm for filming seductive silhouettes of models making daring manoeuvres across the screen. Sometimes that enthusiasm took him close to the edge of acceptability and I had to blow the whistle. This my late and much-loved friend took more in sorrow than in anger. Grudgingly, he'd get to work with stick-ons and so forth on the more provocative outlines, somehow managing to satisfy us, the censor and himself. His credits included *Indiscreet*, *Damn Yankees*, *Charade*, *Arabesque*, *Two for the Road* and the memorable titles for *The Last Emperor*. But he always regarded Bond as his greatest challenge and, I believe, his greatest joy.

The motion-picture industry demonstrated its affection and admiration for Maurice Binder at the memorial tribute paid to him at London's National Film Theatre on June 16, 1991. Some of the best-known figures in films and in the media assembled to pay their respects and share amusing anecdotes. There was rich material to draw on. Harry Saltzman's son Steven, who, like us, had been very close to Maurice, made a witty speech containing vintage tales of the volatile little guy at his best.

Unfortunately, Harry, who had been ill for some time, couldn't make the trip from Paris, where he lived. I was sorry about that. As with the Broccolis, there was much affection between Binder and the Saltzman family. Inevitably, seeing young Saltzman there brought back memories of my ultimately ill-fated partnership with his father. It was more than twenty years since we went our separate ways. It was a bad scene at the time, but I prefer to forget it. No point in reliving old battles.

'How is he?' I asked Steven.

'Rather poorly.'

'Give him my love,' I said, 'and wish him well for me.' I'm sure Harry got the message.

Frustration was the dominant theme in the early months of 1991. We should have been filming, but legal wrangling had put the film in limbo. A variety of legal roadblocks prevented an early hearing of our action against MGM/UA Communications. We had terminated our contract with them; our claim was that they had broken agreements with us concerning the sale of Bond films to TV and video outlets around the world. With the hearing not scheduled until 1993 or later, our production as far as the next

Bond film was concerned, was stymied.

In any event, our legal action was vastly overshadowed by what the media were now describing as the Parretti Affair. I could only sit back, not without some alarm, and observe what the melting snow uncovered. I had nothing personal against Parretti. But I had the strongest objections to his using the Bond pictures as cut-price sweeteners in his scramble to raise the $1.3 billion to buy MGM/UA. The more I read and heard, the more I wondered what kind of man we were dealing with. I wouldn't have to wonder for long.

TWENTY-TWO

It was frustrating not being able to get on with the next Bond picture. Meanwhile nobody kicked their heels. Michael Wilson and Barbara were determined to keep the momentum going, developing projects like the animated film *James Bond Jr* for theatre and video outlets. Barbara commuted between Los Angeles and London, talking to writers, commissioning outlines for future film production. Michael, in his quietly effective way, kept an expert eye on our various legal activities.

Michael is no mere spectator when he sits in on the complex legal discussions concerning our affairs. He is a clear thinker and has a very wise head on young shoulders. He earned his stripes the hard way. To practise law means passing exceedingly difficult exams. These are different from state to state, but are equally tough. This meant that all through his years as a lawyer Michael virtually had to relearn the law every time he moved from one area to another. He qualified in the California Bar, in Washington DC and at the New York Bar. These were tough but prestigious hurdles to overcome. The challenge made him the fine lawyer that he is.

He is also recognized as an important collector of rare books, and, more recently, of fine-art photographs. He has assembled what is probably the largest private collection in England of rare photographic stills, remarkable original art creations centred mostly on nineteenth-century America. This shows the serious, enquiring mind Michael brings to his role as a producer and writer on the Bond films. While he waited for Bond to get back on track, he wrote two excellent non-Bond scripts.

I see the same single-mindedness in his son, David. Deciding he wanted to learn Japanese, David rolled up his kit and moved to

Tokyo, installing himself in a remote Japanese inn where only Japanese was spoken. Within a year not only was he able to speak fluent Japanese, but he taught English at a Japanese college, edited a newspaper and also acted as the *Hollywood Reporter's* man in Tokyo.

In Timothy Dalton's situation, other actors might have been intimidated by Bond and maybe haunted by the shadow of Sean Connery. Timothy was neither intimidated nor overshadowed. Drawing on his considerable experience, he decided that his strongest weapon was his talent. He didn't come to us as raw material which needed to be worked on and developed. He already had an impressive track record on the stage and screen. Nevertheless, I've never known any actor put so much into getting into the skin of a role. He read everything Fleming wrote, studying meticulously all the shadings of 007, and came up with an intelligent characterization much closer to the Fleming blueprint. He wanted to be judged on that alone and I respected him for it.

Ultimately, of course, the commercial success of a movie rests on the number of backsides it puts onto seats. Every star has a vested interest in getting his or her work seen by the widest possible audience. This means beating the big drum when the film is ready to go into the market-place. At first, Timothy was unsure about that. We were asking him to undertake certain publicity chores connected with the promotion of the picture which he was reluctant to do. He did not consider this to be part of his job, and we had some early difficulties. But later we gained his trust, and he could see that nobody could speak for James Bond more forcefully than the actor who plays him. He became less nervous about the media and a crucial player in the team.

In our estimation Timothy did a fine job as 007. Interestingly, in a recent college poll, students were asked to vote on the best Bond performances ever out of all the actors who have played the role. They put Connery as number one in *From Russia With Love*; second was Dalton in *The Living Daylights*; third, Connery in *Goldfinger*. No small achievement, considering it was Timothy's first shot at the role. Sensibly, he has kept his machine on a full rev count during the production hiatus. He has made other films, earning excellent public response. Recently he appeared on the stage in Los Angeles, in *Love Letters*, with Whoopi Goldberg. The play was a sell-out, with both performers receiving standing ovations. As I heard it, there was some initial resistance to the casting of Whoopi Goldberg, a fine actress, as his co-star. Timothy, with his smiling, courteous style, politely declared that it was Whoopi Goldberg – or nobody. His instincts and his judgement were totally vindicated on the night. Those same instincts would persuade him to look beyond Bond in the advancement of his career.

All things change, but not always for the better. The motion-picture business has never been more hazardous as the costs for a major movie shoot up into the stratosphere. The budget on Schwarzenegger's *Terminator II* was close to $110 million. That means, in simple terms, that it needed to earn $300–350 million just to break even. Good luck to Mr Schwarzenegger, who walked away with $20 million or so. [The most recent table showing the price tag of leading Hollywood players puts Tom Cruise, Harrison Ford and John Travolta at $20 million per picture; Eddie Murphy at $16 million; Demi Moore at $14 million; and Julia Roberts and Sigourney Weaver at $13 million.]

We're seeing overkill in that market today. The public may well tire of these macho, hardware-heavy movies, as they frequently do when too many people repeat the same tricks. Gimmicks do not make legends. As Goldwyn said, 'It's the story that makes the movie.' But good scripts with the talent to sustain them will be harder to put together as the Schwarzenegger Factor raises the ante beyond the budgets of most motion pictures. Personally, I have no apprehension about it. I believe James Bond, who was never going to stomp into *Terminator* territory, will always have an audience out there.

Giancarlo Parretti aside, other factors were stacked against us. Producers, determined to price a picture to show a fair return, are up against a fairly new kind of sabotage. TV piracy – the hijacking of our products for video reproduction – is crippling the business. The situation is worsening. There was a time when you could depend on the conventional theatre distribution, followed by a sale of your films to a TV network. Now, anybody can see the picture just once on television, record it, then show it to their friends. The result is, networks no longer want to pay a fair price for a film, arguing that TV piracy has flooded the market with cassettes, which effectively rules out TV repeats.

The success of James Bond has always depended upon the values we put up there on the screen. People may argue about the relative merits of the Bond films, but few would deny that they reveal the highest production values and technical skill.

No series of films based upon one central character has ever generated such a sustained love affair with cinema audiences. True, other quality film-makers will have their blockbusters, achieving grosses exceeding our own. Good luck to them. Success is the adrenalin that works for us all. But it's good to hear Spielberg acknowledge, as he did not long ago on TV, the trend-setting influence of James Bond. It was a generous compliment from a very accomplished film-maker.

I've been lucky with the crews I've worked with over the years. James Bond could never have succeeded if these skilled craftsmen regarded 007 as just another movie. They didn't. They gave us and Bond a special kind of allegiance which is reflected in what you see up there on the screen.

Even so, there were moments when, professionally at least, my survival was in the balance. The fact that I did survive I attribute to the single motivating influence in my life: my family. What I owe to Dana for her love and resilience under fire is hard to put into in words. There were three severe challenges over the last thirty years when we were truly hammered on the anvil. The first was the collapse of the distributing company Irving Allen and I had formed. That failure left us shattered and virtually broke. Coupled with the disastrous opening of *The Trials of Oscar Wilde*, in which a great movie was lost to distributor incompetence, this left my career hanging on the edge. The second challenge was the protracted battle with my then partner Harry Saltzman, which again threatened everything we'd built up over the years. That conflict, fought with no holds barred by squads of lawyers, was a depressing period for Dana and me. The third and most bizarre conflict was our case against MGM/UA and additionally Kirk Kerkorian. By the fall of 1992 we had loaded our cannons for the imminent hearing of our case.

[While Cubby Broccoli and others were preparing their depositions, the *Los Angeles Times* reported in mid-October 1992 that the FBI were examining 'alleged criminal transactions' by Giancarlo Parretti. In addition, the Securities and Exchange Commission were reported to be conducting separate investigations. So much for the man who dreamed of becoming another Louis B. Mayer.]

But now Giancarlo Parretti was now out of the picture. Frankly, his problems did not affect me personally. Nevertheless they do indicate the extent to which a producer's hard work can be dangerously sidetracked when he gets caught up in conglomerate bargaining. With Parretti gone, our case was directed at far more substantial targets.

Our claim against MGM/UA brought me – in legal terms at any rate – into direct conflict with Alan Ladd Jr, who, as head of the studio, was there to take the flak. We had become very close friends. He had a considerable success at Fox. Then he moved on to other major companies before being selected to pull the fat out of the fire at MGM. He was driven to defend a position which I suspect he privately must have regarded as indefensible. In a sense we were both victims, caught in the crossfire between the big corporate battalions. With the studio losing about $1 million a day, he must have felt as frustrated as I was, and wondered why he and I were now on opposite sides, cast in the role of adversaries. I never regarded him as an enemy. I could never do that: he was part of my family.

But it was the lawyers who were being kept busy instead of all the gifted people I'd been forced to keep on hold for more than a year. Our case added up to a sizeable laundry list of claims. We alleged a wide range of financial manipulations which operated to our considerable detriment. I don't want to go into the details, but briefly, we saw ourselves as the victims of a straightforward piece of fiscal hijacking. In any event, we claimed they had undervalued our films by several million dollars, using a fascinating system of corporate accountancy. We knew we had deployed a powerful case. But when it drew close to the court hearing the lawyers, quite properly, were concerned to point out the risks.

'You do realize, Cubby,' they cautioned me, 'that once we go in we're talking about millions.'

'Sure,' I said, 'but let me worry about that.'

It was a test of nerves which was nothing new to me, or Dana. Principles don't come cheap.

In my depositions I was asked about my feelings as far as Kirk Kerkorian's role was concerned. I gave the honest answer: 'He was my friend. I felt betrayed.' This was not said with any animosity. On the contrary: I felt no personal antagonism then towards Mr Kerkorian. I was just defending Danjaq against predators; it was as simple as that. But, as the jurors were being selected, I had to weigh up several factors. The reasons that finally persuaded me to consider an out-of-court settlement centred wholly on Dana and the children. Plain horse sense said I could not be as active as I had been. Michael and Barbara – with Dana's strong back-up – were the ones who were eventually going to have to carry the torch. So when I learned that the other side were interested in settling, I viewed the option entirely from their perspective. Finally we agreed on terms that not only involved our receiving money. We also secured a variety of new and more favourable arrangements in the production of the next Bond picture. We had not just vindicated our position. We had cleared the decks for action. Our case against Kirk Kerkorian was settled soon after, to my satisfaction.

It was a long battle. And, reflecting on it now, I realize how much confidence I drew from Dana's calm but determined input. Having her beside me through all those traumas was worth a thousand reinforcements. Sure, she was angry and upset. Anything that hurt me, or threatened to sabotage the prosperity of Bond and those who had helped create it, affected her deeply. But Dana believes in fighting fire with fire. Off the battlefield, she is devoted to the children. Their concerns are hers. I'm proud when people remark on Dana's graciousness, taste and compassion and of the work she does for children's charities, hospitals and the church. These qualities can't be contrived. They're second nature to her, and just as discernible in our children.

Tina, like many others, has had her difficulties. But if character is measured by the way one confronts problems, then Tina comes through with flying colours. Married to a talented young stunt director, Charles Brewer, she is stronger now, and happy. She has turned her love of flowers to advantage, running a florist shop in Santa Monica. It was never going to be easy for her or Tony to come to terms with the loss of their mother so early in their lives. Fate was the villain here, as I'm sure Tina and Tony recognize now. Taking life as it is and making the most, and the best of it, is the only option we have. Add the ingredient of love, given and returned, and there's very little that can't be squarely faced.

The relationship between the different generations in our family is strong and caring. At birthdays, Christmas parties and other celebrations, it is a joy for us to see how close the family is. Ultimately, what people are in life is more important than what they do. Success has to be kept in perspective. It's great when it happens, but no terminal disaster when it doesn't. Of course, there's a good feeling when the work you do is appreciated. The trophies, the statuettes, the film awards and international recognition are rewarding, and it would be coy to pretend I don't get pleasure from them.

But alongside them stands the picture of my grandfather with his black moustache and the medals he won soldiering for Garibaldi. He had a part in that success too. I glance occasionally at the Irving Thalberg Award, which generously acknowledges a body of work notched up over several years. And then I think of the conflicts and the creative hassle on which much of that work was poised. Well, my grandmother Marietta in the tenements, my father on the building sites around New York, had it worse than I did. They worked hard or they starved. But beside that they had to overcome the humiliations and prejudices which were the downside of the immigrant experience. Survive all that with dignity and charity, and you hand on something more valuable than worldly goods. Those Broccolis won no awards or citations. But they were good citizens who spat on their hands and did what was necessary to raise the family. This puts them high on my list of great achievers. All experiences in life, even the most painful, teach us something. I hope the roots we've planted will be strong enough to keep the family tree flourishing. They should be, if the Broccoli bloodstream is as resilient as the vegetable that bears its name.

Of course, I recognize that broccoli is very much an acquired taste and I neither promote it nor defend it. It's only an upper-class cabbage, after all. All the same I was highly amused a couple of years back when former US President George Bush no less, announced a distinct distaste for the inoffensive little plant. This did not please a lot of broccoli lovers, not to mention the growers across the country. Speaking with all the authority of his office, George Bush warned his aides that he never, ever wants to see another sprig of broccoli on his plate whether he is on Air Force One or at the White House or anywhere else in the land. 'I do not like broccoli!' he complained, 'and I haven't liked it since I was a little kid and my mother made me eat it, AND I'M PRESIDENT

OF THE UNITED STATES AND I'M NOT GOING TO EAT
ANY MORE BROCCOLI!'

Well, if the President didn't want to eat broccoli, that's perfectly
in order with me (though smoke may be coming out of old man de
Cicco's ears, wherever he happens to be). Fortunately, George
Bush drew a distinction between the plant and the character who
just happens to have the same name. Around this time, Dana and
I were invited to a private lunch at Jimmy's in Beverly Hills to meet
the President and senior members of his staff. It was a privilege as
well as a pleasure and I have to admit that when we shook hands
my mind flashed back to that dawn when Lindbergh flew over
Long Island. My ambitions were fired, but they hardly envisaged a
future that would include lunch with the President of the United
States. Some time after that meeting he sent us a signed photo. It
was inscribed: 'Dana and Cubby Broccoli: Now we're talking
about the Broccoli I really like. George Bush.'

It was a delightful gesture, typical of the man and of a President
I greatly admired. I think of that day and of the friendly encounters
I had with his predecessor, Ronald Reagan at the White House;
and also of those premières meeting members of the royal family
in England. Not a matter of ego or self-congratulation: I'm too old
a campaigner for that. Anything I may have achieved stems from
the pride I have in my birthplace, reinforces my gratitude to the
country that took my family in, offering them safety and a good
life. For me, that handshake with George Bush no less than that
dawn wave from Charles Lindbergh, proves that almost anything
is within your grasp if you're prepared to go for it. A little luck
doesn't do any harm, either!

As one gets older it is sad to see old friends depart. Not long ago
Hal Roach, one of the true legends in our business, died, having
lived for more than a hundred years. He was already a major figure
in motion pictures, and one of the first people I met, when I came
to Hollywood. He was a marvellous man, with a sharp mind and
quick wit even in his nineties. We became friends and in later years
shared a passion for horses. He, Dana and I had many happy hours
together. We would sit around chewing the fat at the racetrack, at
lunches or at premières, mostly talking about the old days.

Hal started out in a disused shack with a crank-operated camera
and, like those other pioneers Sam Goldwyn and Louis B. Mayer,

created a great industry on the desert wastes of California. It is a legacy none of us in motion pictures should forget. He was a great human being. Hollywood cannot honour him enough. Ironically, however, though the church was full, Dana and I spotted none of Hollywood's leading film-makers in the congregation.

And then, in January 1993, another friend, another legend, faded from the scene. Sammy Cahn, one of this country's best-loved songwriters, died. I remember the many occasions he came over to the house and played some of his greatest songs. For all his fame, he was a modest little guy. He won four Academy Awards for 'All the Way' 'Three Coins in the Fountain', 'High Hopes' and 'Call Me Irresponsible' – songs the whole world sang. But to look at him, you could easily mistake him for the chap who shortens the cuffs on your trousers. (I suspect he could have done that too.)

Sammy resembled everybody's favourite uncle, which, in many ways, he was. Everything he composed, everything he did, was from the heart. He was a pushover for needy causes. As long as Dana and I knew him he was always ready to pick up a telephone or hit the piano keys for underprivileged kids, needy friends or strangers down on their luck. I went to see him at the Cedars Sinai Hospital and mercifully he didn't understand the full measure of his illness. Dana and I were at his funeral. It was sad. But there were laughs, too. All his old friends there remembered him with a smile. The eulogies demonstrated what we – and America – had lost.

But life is fairly even-handed with the pleasures and the pain. There's a lot of human suffering in this world. Every request Dana and I receive to help one cause or another reveals yet more areas of pain. We slit the envelopes and steel ourselves for what the contents might reveal. It is then that we apply the age-old bromide, and count our blessings. In the summer of 1992 two new grandchildren arrived: a daughter, Angelica, for Barbara; and Colton, a son, for Tina. Both children are a total delight to us. These two lively and handsome infants make the family tree look pretty strong to us.

Both Barbara and Tina have moved to new homes. Tina's husband, Charles, is doing very well as a stunt coordinator. Barbara's husband, Fred Zollo, is, at the time of writing, producing a play in New York and preparing a film. Fred won several awards for Broadway plays and was nominated for an Oscar for *Mississippi Burning* and *Quiz Show*.

Another grandchild, Michael Wilson's elder son David, graduated from Brown University, having become expert in the Japanese language, and is planning to go to law school. The future looks bright for him, as it does for his younger brother Gregg, who looks like becoming a mathematician and scientist. Heather, Tina's daughter by her first marriage, is a beautiful and intelligent young lady. She rides well and competes in show-jumping events. Tony is happily working up the ladder, learning as he goes. All this gives Dana and me a sense of fulfilment; of a mission accomplished.

And now, with Michael and Barbara confident producers of the new Bond film, I can lean on the shovel awhile. I can now enjoy one of the pleasures of my later life: my racehorses. I've always loved horses and breeding, and training and racing them has always fascinated me. You get a quickening of the pulse, looking out across the turf at Santa Anita, the sun rose-tinting the distant mountains, the crowd rising as these fine animals turn at full gallop into the finishing straight. I enjoy talking to the jockeys, the trainers and the handlers, who are a world apart from the pressures of producing motion pictures. But it's more than just a hobby to me. The breeding and training of racehorses, the improvement of the stud and the racing lifestock, is a serious business with important potential. I like to feel that in my modest way I'm contributing something to the development of the sport.

With Timothy Dalton moving on to other things, we have a new Bond. Pierce Brosnan has now brilliantly confirmed our original short-listing of him for Bond, which at that time he couldn't accept because of TV commitments. He is a fine actor who instantly gave his own individual imprint to 007 with the record-breaking *GoldenEye*. We have a new director, Martin Campbell, and a highly original script which takes on board the dangerous elements at work in post-Communist Eastern Europe. The writers have taken chances, like making M, a key Fleming character, a woman. True, the present Director of Public Prosecutions in Britain is a woman, Barbara Mills. Nevertheless, it's a gamble that only a really fine actress could get away with. Casting Britain's distinguished actress Dame Judi Dench in the role was an inspired idea. I'm a little more enthusiastic about this than I was when a couple of writers suggested we make Dr No a monkey!

That was more than thirty years ago. At the time many of the top studios said the stories couldn't be filmed. We are now into the seventeenth Bond. It's all systems go...

[Unfortunately for Cubby, those systems came to a sudden, unexpected halt. It is the afternoon of Thursday, February 23, 1995. Cubby is seated in a wheelchair outside his home in Beverly Hills, wrapped well against the cold Pacific winds. Two male nurses, immaculate in white tunics, hover close by, occasionally bending down to share some secret jest with their celebrated patient. With the seventeenth James Bond film in production in England and around the world, Cubby Broccoli should, of course, be continuing this narrative. But an event of some magnitude abruptly interrupted proceedings. More specifically, it temporarily reduced Cubby's voice to a whisper; though whatever my old friend may have lost in resonance was offset by the cheerfulness he still managed to transmit. One of the reasons for his good humour that afternoon was the activity going on all around him. A posse of young creative talent had breezed in from all corners for a production meeting with Dana Broccoli. The project, *Florinda*, was a period musical set in Spain which Dana adapted from her own novel. It opened in Los Angeles in July 1995 to excellent audience and critical response. Cubby signalled me to move closer the better to hear him. 'I'm so proud of Dana,' he murmured. 'She's a very talented lady. And I tell you this, I wouldn't be here but for her – and a little help from the Man Upstairs!'

In May 1994 Cubby Broccoli went to the Johns Hopkins Hospital in Baltimore for a routine eye examination and possible surgery. Dr Walter Stark, Professor of Ophthalmology of the hospital's Wilmer Institute, had come highly recommended by Cubby's friend the influential producer Ray Stark (no relation). Ray, whose own eyesight had been dramatically improved by his distinguished namesake, insisted his friend be treated by nobody else. The surgeon examined Cubby's eyes and proposed surgery for cataracts and glaucoma. Cubby agreed. No point in delay.

But hold on: the Broccolis had a horse, Brocco, running at Belmont in the last of the so-called Crown Jewel Races (the other classics being the Kentucky Derby and the Preakness). Now Mr Broccoli takes his owner's duties seriously, and Brocco having already beaten several of the other horses in the opposition, Belmont seemed a more enticing engagement than Baltimore. It was therefore mutually agreed by surgeon and patient that the operation would take place on June 15, the day after the big race.

But one hour before starter's orders a phone call from the trainer, Randy Winick, caused dismay in the Broccoli household. Brocco had injured a foot in training. 'I'm scratching him from the race,' Winick said. A brief announcement, but a major setback to any racehorse owner. No less so to Cubby, Dana and the Winick camp, who had every reason to expect their horse to triumph. A tragedy of sorts (though Brocco went on to perform splendidly at stud, where an injured foot is no impediment). But the eye surgery could now go ahead. The day after, June 16, Dr Stark visited his patient in the recovery room. Cubby was scarcely prepared for what he was about to hear. The surgeon knew he could be candid. 'Cubby,' he said, 'the routine chest X-ray we took before the operation has shown up an aneurism on the aorta and it is very large. I think you should see the heart surgeon while you are here.'

Dr Stephen C. Achuff, Director of Clinical Services at the hospital's cardiac department, confirmed the diagnosis. And then spelled it out more graphically: 'Your aneurism is ready to rupture. There may only be three to four months before this could happen.'

Cubby did not need to ask what that could signify. 'Go on,' he said.

Then Dr Achuff offered a lifeline. 'There is a surgeon at this hospital,' he told Cubby, 'who feels sure he can remove the aneurism and do the necessary triple bypass in the same operation. If you would like to talk with him I can arrange it.' Cubby agreed, and he was unlikely to forget the options laid out by Dr John C. Laschinger, Associate Professor of Surgery at Johns Hopkins Hospital. Dana Broccoli, who was beside Cubby throughout the whole critical episode, recalls the surgeon's words.

'He said to Cubby, "I can do this operation, but you must realize that whenever one is operating around the aorta there are risks because of the vital nerve centres close by. You could become paralysed, perhaps extensively. You could, considering your age and other factors, possibly die during the operation." He continued quite openly to list some of horrors that might result during the surgical procedures. "On the other hand," he said, "you're eighty-four years old. We could let nature take its course. That has to be a decision which only you can make."'

Cubby Broccoli was accustomed to making decisions. But a life-

and-death one required a little extra thought. 'All right, let me talk to my family, let me think about it,' he said. 'We'll see what we're going to do.'

Bringing the family into the equation was entirely in character. They were, and always had been, at the core of Cubby's existence. The decision was as much theirs as the patient's.

Moreover, professional as well as personal imperatives added to the dilemma. Pre-production was well advanced on *GoldenEye*. Michael Wilson and Barbara Broccoli, the co-producers, had supervised the completion of the script. Locations had been set in France, Switzerland, Puerto Rico and Russia. Pierce Brosnan had received his baptismal benedictions from a huge media turnout as the new 007. A gigantic set would be built on a former Rolls-Royce factory which the producers found and turned into 1.25 million square feet of interior stage space and a back lot of Culver City proportions. Ordinarily, Cubby Broccoli, who started the Bond bandwagon rolling with *Dr No* in 1962, would have been on this, as on every previous location. A routine X-ray had changed the schedule.

Dana Broccoli brought the family in for the bedside conference at the Johns Hopkins Hospital. They flew or drove in from all over: Barbara and her husband Fred, Michael Wilson and his wife Jane, Tina, Tony. If Cubby Broccoli had a fight on his hands, everyone wanted to be in his corner. The pre-surgery tests, X-rays and other procedures gave Cubby and the family a week to decide. The children had their say. Finally Cubby turned to Dana. She well remembers the moment. 'He asked me, "What do you think I should do?"

'I said, "Please don't ask me, Cubby. That is a decision I couldn't make in a million years. Only you can do that." The decision was starkly poised. Do nothing, and his life hung by a thread. Four months or less. Have the operation, and maybe there was an even chance of a few more years with the family, especially the grandchildren.

The decision was predictable. 'I've always been a gambling man,' Cubby smiled. 'I'm going to go for the operation.'

Dr Laschinger felt obliged to observe one final ritual. The night before the operation he spoke to his patient.

'Cubby,' he said, 'I know you have had to make a terribly difficult decision. I just want you to know that if you should change your mind, now, later tonight, tomorrow morning, even while you're being wheeled into the theatre, you just tell me and I'll cancel everything.'

The gambler in Cubby Broccoli instinctively rejected hesitation on a bet. Anyway, the day of the operation was July 7, and seven was his lucky number. 'Thank you, doctor,' he said, 'but no, I'm going for it.'

Miraculously – the word is not used lightly – he survived the eight hours of intricate cardiac surgery. He suffered the almost inevitable minor stroke, but recovered from it. His vocal cords were taking longer to get back to full throttle. But each day saw an improvement in communication. That process was enhanced by his family and his friends. Frank Sinatra came by, and left, the tears showing. Their mutual affection goes back many years. Sinatra's last double CD soothed Cubby through his convalescence.

Robert Wagner called frequently. There was much reminiscing over the forty years or so of their friendship. It was Wagner, at that time an unknown young actor, whom Cubby brought to MGM studios, only to be told that he was barred from the lot. Nothing personal: merely that, as Cubby tells it earlier, his then associate, the famed agent Charlie Feldman, was having an affair with the mistress of Louis B. Mayer. Hell hath no greater fury than a cuckolded mogul. But Cubby dug his heels in and the doors opened – and so did the future for his client.

Roger Moore drove by to embrace the man who had propelled him to international rating. If there were ever hard feelings about being replaced by Timothy Dalton, that was ancient history now. Lush homes in California and Europe, and skiing in Gstaad, work wonders on a bruised ego. Cubby was touched by these visits. Timothy Dalton, now living in some splendour in the area, was a constant caller. Unquestionably, his casting as Rhett Butler in the TV mini-series *Scarlet* owed much to the added dimension Bond gave him as an actor. He had now handed over his Beretta .25 to Pierce Brosnan. But he remained close friends with Cubby. When the casting of Brosnan was announced, Dalton sent his replacement and the company this message: 'Very best wishes and great good luck with the new James Bond. Yours, with love, Timothy.'

Sean Connery was told about Cubby's illness and phoned immediately. The bitterness and controversies that had clouded a good friendship was water under the bridge now. There was genuine concern in the questions he asked about his one-time sponsor. Genuine appreciation in Cubby's response.

If Sean's gesture implied belated acknowledgement of the career blast-off that Bond had given him, the death of Terence Young at eighty must have been an equally salutary reminder. Young's contribution to Bond – *Dr No*, *From Russia With Love* and *Thunderball* – established the cult and the legend. Young's handling of Connery, as we know, went beyond the required duties of a film director. He refashioned the actor's raw and rough persona into Fleming's sophisticated blueprint of Bond. Of course, Sean Connery was bound to have acquired the same finesse over the years. But the producers urgently needed an overnight conversion. It was Young's cultural crash course that did the trick.

Cubby Broccoli was immensely saddened by Terence's passing. And in spite of past antagonisms, by Harry Saltzman's death, too. Time softens attitudes. The reverberations of that legal battle between battalions of lawyers in Switzerland have long faded. At the memorial service to Terence Young in London in the fall of 1994, Michael Wilson read out this message from Cubby:

'Sadly in the past few months, the world has lost several of the Bond originators. First Arthur Krim of United Artists, who believed so fervently in Bond from the beginning. Then my partner Harry Saltzman – a film visionary who helped fight the good fight on no less than nine 007 adventures. Now Terence, who set the style for the entire series...Terence and I met some forty years ago. What I always cherished about him – apart from his obvious film-making talents – was the enthusiasm, compassion and razor-sharp wit he brought to everything he did. Dana and I would dearly have loved to be with you all today, but the doctors tell me I am not quite ready to make the journey. The cinema industry is greatly in his debt as are we all. I find it almost impossible to sum him up in a few words. So simply: farewell to a very fine English gentleman who will be sorely missed.'

Felicitations to a departed friend. The file had also closed on the turbulent saga with Harry Saltzman. Cubby now felt only sorrow. 'He was OK,' he murmured. 'He just had some bad problems.'

Other phone calls brought happier echoes of the early years. Bryan Forbes, the British film director, now a best-selling author, called from his home in Arizona. The line between Scottsdale and Beverly Hills buzzed with memories of jubilant lunacies on the set. Notably, *The Black Knight*, on which Forbes was hauled in over a weekend to write scenes for the not overly verbose Alan Ladd.

'What kind of dialogue do you want?' Forbes asked Cubby's then partner, Irving Allen.

'Make the bum monosyllabic!' was the Muse's instruction to the writer.

Forbes acknowledges the pivotal opportunity he received from his recuperating friend at the other end of the line. 'Quite simply, I was flat broke; he hired me and it was upwards and onwards from then on. He had read, much to my surprise, a book of mine. He commissioned me to write a treatment for a film called *Vacant Lot*. He paid me $70 a week, which was the difference between starvation and the stipend of your average Hollywood road-sweeper. He liked the draft I delivered, but nothing came of it. I sat all winter in a flat loaned by a friend staring at the fireplace praying for the phone to ring. One day it did ring. It was Cubby with *The Black Knight*, which launched me as a scriptwriter.' (The princely establishment in Arizona and a spate of blockbusting novels just naturally fell into place from then on.)

These notes were inserted, appropriately enough, on April 5, 1995, Cubby Broccoli's eighty-sixth birthday. Another happy day with the family. Another bonus according to Mr Broccoli, with much thanks to the Man Upstairs. We can now let him complete his story.]

As I was saying before I was rudely interrupted, it's great to be alive! The surgeons and the nursing back-up know how grateful I am. Faith was a big factor here. But it was Dana's strength and determination, the way the family pulled for me, that tipped the scales. I'm sorry not to be out there on the seventeenth Bond picture. But the movie is in safe hands. Success can be measured in countless ways. For me, as for Dana, it exists in the bright intelligence and the mutual devotion of our children. It's there in the joyful welcome the latest grandchildren, Angelica and Colton, lay on for us as they see us approach up the driveway. The movie credits and the awards are the icing on the cake.

As Dana and I sit together on the patio in the morning sunlight, we feel a rare sense of contentment. It thrills me that Dana, with all her commitment to me and the family, is now masterminding the musical *Florinda*, helped by a fine array of young talent. I saw the rushes on *GoldenEye* every day and I liked what I saw. We have both worked hard for anything we might have achieved. I hope I can claim we have done so by the book. Success has enabled us to spread some modest comfort and joy for those less fortunate. We know our children, and their children, will do no less. So, offered the chance to rewrite the scenario of my life – heart surgery aside – the answer would be: 'Thank you, but no.' I'm happy with the way the chips have fallen. And anyway, God willing, there's still a lot of living ahead of us! Cut and Print.

Beverly Hills, September 1995

EPILOGUE

Cubby Broccoli died at his home in the early evening of June 27, 1996. He was eighty-seven. As she had been throughout the protracted torment of his illness, Dana Broccoli was at her husband's bedside. The end was mercifully, and deservedly, peaceful. It was a tranquil ending to a triumphant life. And in the event, Dana and the family felt intuitively that, in his generous-hearted way, Cubby had somehow contrived to ease the burden of their grief. Their instinct persuaded them that he had clung on beyond the clinical forecasts in order to prepare them gently for his passing. The ultimate kindliness from the man who lived for others; his unspoken message: 'Don't worry. All will be well.' And that is how it was: Cubby still there in spirit, consoling, encouraging, pointing the way.

In the obituaries published throughout the world old hands in the trade noticed a refreshingly different aspect of celebrity. Genuine affection for the man. The complete antithesis of the familiar stereotype.

Earlier in that sad week yet another accolade came Cubby's way: the Life Career Award. Fred Zollo, one of Hollywood's most successful young producers, received the award on his father-in-law's behalf. The applause in a hotel auditorium on Century City's Avenue of the Stars was particularly warm. There was a simple explanation. The film-makers present, many of them famous names, clearly liked the man they were honouring. Quentin Tarantino, Hollywood's Oscar-winning wunderkind, approached Zollo. 'I have to tell you,' he said, 'Cubby Broccoli was enormously helpful to me. His films are as fresh and innovative as ever.'

That view was shared by others among the gathering. They recognized that Bond had become the benchmark of a whole spate of spy-adventure films that followed. They marvelled at its prodigious staying power against an array of assorted blockbusters. Grosses are the yardstick of success or failure at the box office. The first-run figures for *GoldenEye* was upwards of $350 million. A formidable and significant statistic; and powerful confirmation that the future for James Bond, and its latest exponent in the role, Pierce Brosnan, was brighter than ever. Cubby Broccoli could rest content. Rarely has a veteran Hollywood producer taken his final curtain in the glow of such acclamation.

Yet he did not concede the battle too readily. Perhaps he wanted to see his stepson Michael Wilson and daughter Barbara Broccoli safely launched on the eighteenth Bond. Maybe he wanted no cloud to hang over Barbara's birthday on June 18 or his and Dana's wedding anniversary three days later. Both occasions, he may have felt, required his presence and a shared smile in celebration. Thus he dutifully submitted to the unrelenting regime of round-the-clock nursing.

He was a shade less enthusiastic, however, about his sessions with the speech therapist, Professor Elaine P. Hannah, PhD. A kindly but no-nonsense practitioner, the lady was concerned to bring Cubby's stricken voice back to normal resonance. It would be fair to say that initial exchanges between the professor and the producer were not all sweetness and light. Mightily laid low by intensive surgery and its painful aftermath, Cubby was unlikely to list playing Eliza Doolittle to the professor's Henry Higgins among his favourite pastimes. But, being Broccoli, he tolerated her with good grace. And not without the occasional flash of his well-marinated humour.

In one session, the speech therapist instructed her patient: 'Now we're going to proceed with a group of sentences. I will give you half a sentence and I want you to complete it.' Some sentences are more judicious than others. Hers began innocently enough: 'I have a bucket full of...'

'SHIT!' retorted Cubby cheerfully and in unexpectedly loud tones.

'Now *that's* the voice I want to hear!' beamed the good lady, delightfully unfazed. 'Let's try it again.'

'The relationship thereafter between the patient and the 'good egg' professor became increasingly cordial.

But ultimately and sadly, to no avail. At around five-thirty p.m. on June 27, 1996 it was all over. An avalanche of messages, flowers, telegrams and phone calls deluged the Broccolis' home in Beverly Hills. Sean Connery phoned from Europe. He had been Dana's personal choice for the first James Bond. That spontaneous piece of casting in a darkened screening room made him and movie history. Now the man who had made it all a multimillion-dollar reality had died. Sean said with evident sincerity how sorry he was to hear of Cubby's death.

Roger Moore phoned from Copenhagen, where he was filming. He was deeply upset. His affection for Cubby and the Broccolis persisted long after he was discreetly pensioned off from Bond. Any residual hard feelings had long faded in the afterglow of his personal success.

Timothy Dalton, whose friendship with the Broccolis was also strengthened despite his mutually agreed exit as 007, was one of the first callers at the house. He was in constant attendance on the whole family. He has worked for many producers the world over. 'But none like Cubby,' he says simply. 'He was a friend and a noble gentleman.' A few days later he joined members of the Broccoli family as a pallbearer.

Many other famous names came to the house on Hillcrest to offer their condolences. Only illness prevented Frank Sinatra from paying his respects in person to one of his oldest and closest friends. His wife Barbara spoke with feeling for them both.

The funeral was at the Church of the Good Shepherd, Beverly Hills, on July 1. Warm Californian sunshine spread across the boulevards as the crowds of mourners arrived. The family was unanimous in deciding the tone of the occasion: it would be more the celebration of a life rather than the solemn rituals of a funeral. Because of the suddenness of Cubby's passing, the official obituary notice had not yet surfaced in the Los Angeles papers. It was a fortunate omission, for instead of the familiar Hollywood-scale funeral – which neither the family nor Cubby would have relished – the ceremony was attended mostly by a congregation of intimates. Family and close friends. But several passers-by gathered at the back, adding their prayers for the man they knew only by reputation. The producer in Cubby Broccoli must have noted with serene satisfaction that every seat was taken and there were crowds outside.

Composer John Barry, who had scored a dozen Bond films, helped choose the softly poignant music which ushered the casket into the church. A labour of love from the man whose variations on the 007 theme are almost as familiar as the opening notes of Beethoven's Fifth Symphony.

There was no shortage of famous people eager to take to the rostrum in honour of their departed friend. But many others, more humble characters on both sides of the Atlantic, would have jumped at the chance to say their piece. Grips, stunt men, secretaries, drivers, parking valets, waiters and the even smaller fry would have all happily testified to the generous civilities of this gentle film-maker. If you can judge a man by the way he treated those who built the stages, served his food or parked his car, then Broccoli emerges as a man apart.

The flowers that filled the house or wreathed the simple resting place at Forest Lawn affectionately remembered a fine human being who happened to be a famous film producer. This was the theme of the eulogies in the church where Albert Romolo 'Cubby' Broccoli, at peace under a mountain of dark-red roses, was duly and appropriately honoured by the great and the good.

The State Governor of California, Pete Wilson, addressed the packed congregation less as a politician, more as an admirer and friend. He acclaimed the producer and his triumphs; the proud American and devoted husband and family man. And he referred to Charles Lindbergh and that inspirational encounter with Cubby on Long Island nearly seventy years before.

Gregory Peck, a greying but still striking figure as he stood at the rostrum, spoke of the innate goodness and spiritual certainty of the man who had long been his friend.

But actor Robert Wagner – R.J. to his intimates – eschewed the stained-glass overtones. As a Broccoli intimate he correctly assumed that his old friend had had enough of the glowing eulogies (or whatever choice sobriquet Cubby might have used to describe them).

'When I was eighteen years old,' Wagner began with a faint smile of nostalgia, 'Cubby was my agent. All I ever wanted was to be in the movies. I was at home looking into my mirror doing my Clark Gable and Cary Grant impersonations. The telephone rang; it was Cubby. "Meet me in the parking lot in front of the Thalberg building at MGM. L.B. Mayer has some new producers and I want them to see you." I was waiting for Cubby. He drove up looking absolutely super, as always. There were two policemen behind the reception desk...' Wagner recounted how the producer who had done so much for his career had been barred from the lot.

He went on with evident affection for Cubby, 'who knew the names of every man and woman on his crew and involved himself personally in their lives. He was a proud man, proud of his work, his personal integrity, and most of all of his wonderful wife and family. I loved him.' As he stepped down Wagner paused to touch the casket with his fingertips. 'Goodbye, old friend,' the gesture said.

The former actor turned diplomat John Gavin, and the Reverend Terrance Sweeney, who delivered the Eulogy, maintained the celebratory theme. The Reverend Sweeney had been more than Cubby's spiritual confidant. He was an old friend who had been deeply moved by the way Cubby had confronted the imminence of his passing. What he witnessed in the end was not a man fighting a personal battle of survival, but a devoted husband and father determined to lighten the burden on his wife and family. The unspoken message that day in the Church of the Good Shepherd suggested that, in one way or another, Cubby Broccoli would somehow remain on call: still the focus of the family and the unceasing inspiration for Michael Wilson and Barbara Broccoli's new stewardship of Bond.

It fell to Cubby's friend and lawyer Norman R. Tyre to observe that Bond had been a battlefield as well as a bonanza. He reminded us of one of the threats to the glittering 007 package.

'About four years ago Cubby was confronted with a choice between accepting a reduced position for future Bonds or facing a drawn-out lawsuit. He was informed crystally clear that the chances of success were less than fifty per cent and that the cost of litigation would be between $3 and $4 million. Without a moment's hesitation he announced loudly and clearly, "Let's go." So typical of our Cubby.'

Tyre also told of the many other career-threatening obstacles that had to be, and were, overcome. And he concluded by quoting from Clarence Darrow's eulogy over the body of William Jennings Bryan, from the play *Inherit the Wind*: 'In that body a giant lived.'

The final words were spoken by Michael Wilson.

'I first met Cubby thirty-seven years ago when he took me to the

Luau on Rodeo Drive to tell me that he had asked Dana, my mother, to marry him. From that moment on he invited me into his family, unequivocally and without reservation. He treated me as his son. He and Dana were married in Las Vegas, in June 1959. It was a small wedding. I gave away the bride, Cary Grant was the best man and Mike Romanoff (the famed restaurateur) and his wife were the witnesses.'

Michael went on to sketch out Cubby's career from the early Warwick Films, and the triumphant *The Trials of Oscar Wilde*, to the ongoing legend of James Bond. But then he talked about the man, the husband, the father and grandfather. 'Cubby was a man without enemies. A man of integrity. Meticulously fair and scrupulously honest in his business and personal dealings. He was my mentor and friend; and I loved him.'

The source of Cubby Broccoli's resilience under fire came from the family, and principally from his wife Dana. Among the few whispered words Cubby was able to utter to me in the last months of his illness was, 'I'm so proud of her...'

Nurturing and consoling the family, Dana has yet to articulate her own grief. But she has much to smile at, too. Cubby's life brimmed over with priceless, anecdotal humour – not surprising, considering the acerbic Calabrian input of his father Giovanni Broccoli. He had warned Cubby long ago that people are not always what they seem. That some, stripped of their pretences, are revealed as charlatans and deceivers. 'When the snow melts,' the elder Broccoli cautioned, 'you see the dogs' mess.'

Maybe so. But it is also true that the snow gives way to the green shoots of renewal. And the sturdier the roots, the more resilient the plant. 'This is particularly so,' say the experts 'with broccoli, which has the strongest roots and flourishes under the most adverse conditions.'

On that score, its famous namesake Cubby Broccoli can truly, and proudly, rest content.

FILMOGRAPHY

THE EARLIER FILMS

1953 The Red Beret (USA: **Paratrooper**)
Screenplay by Richard Maibaum and Frank Nugent
Story by Hilary St George Saunders
Adapted from his book *The Red Beret*
Produced by Irving Allen and Albert R. Broccoli
Directed by Terence Young
A Warwick Production for Columbia Pictures

1954 Hell Below Zero
Screenplay by Alec Coppel and Max Trell
Adaptation by Richard Maibaum
Based on the novel *The White South* by Hammond Innes
Associate Producer George W. Willoughby
Produced by Irving Allen and Albert R. Broccoli
Directed by Mark Robson
A Warwick Production for Columbia Pictures

1954 The Black Knight
Story and Screenplay by Alec Coppel
Associate Producer Phil C. Samuel
Executive Producers Irving Allen and Albert R. Broccoli
Directed by Tay Garnett
A Warwick Production for Columbia Pictures

1955 A Prize of Gold
Screenplay by Robert Buckner and John Paxton
From the novel by Max Catto
Produced by Irving Allen and Albert R. Broccoli
Directed by Mark Robson
A Warwick Production for Columbia Pictures

1955 Cockleshell Heroes
Screenplay by Bryan Forbes and Richard Maibaum
Executive Producers Irving Allen and Albert R. Broccoli
Produced by Phil C. Samuel
Directed by José Ferrer
A Warwick Production for Columbia Pictures

1956 Safari
Screenplay by Anthony Veiller
Produced by Adrian Worker
Executive Producers Irving Allen and Albert R. Broccoli
Directed by Terence Young
A Warwick Production for Columbia Pictures

1956 Zarak
Screenplay by Richard Maibaum
Based on the novel by A.J. Bevan
Produced by Irving Allen and Albert R. Broccoli
Directed by Terence Young
A Warwick Production for Columbia Pictures

1956 Odongo
Screenplay by John Gilling
Based on an original story by Islin Auster
Produced by Islin Auster
Executive Producers Irving Allen and Albert R. Broccoli
Directed by John Gilling
A Warwick Production for Columbia Pictures

1957 Fire Down Below
Screenplay by Irwin Shaw
Based on the novel by Max Catto
Produced by Irving Allen and Albert R. Broccoli
Directed by Robert Parrish and Irving Allen
A Warwick Production for Columbia Pictures

1957 Interpol (USA: **Pickup Alley**)
Screenplay by John Paxton
From a story by A.J. Forrest
Produced by Irving Allen and Albert R. Broccoli
Directed by John Gilling
A Warwick Production for Columbia Pictures

1957 How to Murder a Rich Uncle
Screenplay by John Paxton
Produced by John Paxton
Executive Producers Irving Allen and Albert R. Broccoli
Directed by Nigel Patrick
A Warwick Production for Columbia Pictures

1957 High Flight
Screenplay by Joseph Landon and Kenneth Hughes
Original story by Jack Davis
Producer Phil C. Samuel
Executive Producers Irving Allen and Albert R. Broccoli
Directed by John Gilling
A Warwick Production for Columbia Pictures

1958 Tank Force (USA: No Time to Die)
Written by Richard Maibaum and Terence Young
Associate Producer Phil C. Samuel
Produced by Irving Allen and Albert R. Broccoli
Directed by Terence Young
A Warwick Production for Columbia Pictures

1958 The Man Inside
Screenplay by David Shaw
Novel by M.E. Chaber
Associate Producer Harold Huth
Produced by Irving Allen and Albert R. Broccoli
Directed by John Gilling
A Warwick Production for Columbia Pictures

1959 Killers of Kilimanjaro (USA: Adamson of Africa)
Screenplay by John Gilling and Earl Fenton
Screen story by Richard Maibaum and Cyril Hume
From the book *African Bush Adventure* by J.A. Hunter
and Dan P. Mannix
Produced by Irving Allen and Albert R. Broccoli
Directed by Richard Thorpe
A Warwick Production for Columbia Pictures

1959 The Bandit of Zhobe
Screenplay by John Gilling
From a story by Richard Maibaum
Associate Producer Harold Huth

Produced by Irving Allen and Albert R. Broccoli
Directed by John Gilling
A Warwick Production for Columbia Pictures

1960 Jazz Boat
Screenplay by Ken Hughes and John Antrobus
From a story by Rex Reinits
Produced by Irving Allen and Albert R. Broccoli
Directed by Ken Hughes
A Warwick Production for Columbia Pictures

1960 The Trials of Oscar Wilde (USA: The Man with the Green Carnation)
Warwick Film Productions Ltd in association with Viceroy Films Ltd
Produced by Harold Huth
Directed by and screenplay by Ken Hughes
Executive Producers Irving Allen and Albert R. Broccoli

1960 Johnny Nobody
Screenplay by Patrick Kirnan
Based on a story by Albert Z. Carr
Produced by John R. Sloane
Directed by Nigel Patrick
Executive Producers Irving Allen and Albert R. Broccoli
Columbia/Viceroy

THE BOND FILMS

1962 Dr No
Screenplay by Richard Maibaum, Joanna Harwood and Berkely Mather
Produced by Albert R. Broccoli and Harry Saltzman
Directed by Terence Young
Eon Productions Ltd

1963 From Russia With Love
Screenplay by Richard Maibaum and Joanna Harwood
Produced by Albert R. Broccoli and Harry Saltzman
Directed by Terence Young
Eon Productions Ltd

1964 Goldfinger
Screenplay by Richard Maibaum and Paul Dehn
Produced by Albert R. Broccoli and Harry Saltzman
Directed by Guy Hamilton
Eon Productions Ltd

1965 Thunderball
Screenplay by Richard Maibaum and John Hopkins
Produced by Kevin McClory
Executive Producers Albert R. Broccoli and Harry Saltzman
Directed by Terence Young
Eon Productions Ltd

1967 You Only Live Twice
Screenplay by Roald Dahl
Produced by Albert R. Broccoli and Harry Saltzman
Directed by Lewis Gilbert
Eon Productions Ltd

1969 On Her Majesty's Secret Service
Screenplay by Richard Maibaum
Produced by Albert R. Broccoli and Harry Saltzman
Directed by Peter Hunt
Eon Productions Ltd

1971 Diamonds Are Forever
Screenplay by Richard Maibaum and Tom Mankiewicz
Produced by Albert R. Broccoli and Harry Saltzman
Directed by Guy Hamilton
Eon Productions Ltd

1973 Live and Let Die
Screenplay by Tom Mankiewicz
Produced by Albert R. Broccoli and Harry Saltzman
Directed by Guy Hamilton
Eon Productions Ltd

1974 The Man with the Golden Gun
Screenplay by Richard Maibaum and Tom Mankiewicz
Produced by Albert R. Broccoli and Harry Saltzman
Directed by Guy Hamilton
Eon Productions Ltd

1977 The Spy Who Loved Me
Screenplay by Christopher Wood and Richard Maibaum
Produced by Albert R. Broccoli
Directed by Lewis Gilbert
Eon Productions Ltd

1979 Moonraker
Screenplay by Christopher Wood
Produced by Albert R. Broccoli
Executive Producer Michael G. Wilson
Directed by Lewis Gilbert
Eon Productions Ltd

1981 For Your Eyes Only
Screenplay by Richard Maibaum
Produced by Albert R. Broccoli
Executive Producer Michael G. Wilson
Directed by John Glen
Eon Productions Ltd

1983 Octopussy
Screenplay by Richard Maibaum and Michael G. Wilson
Produced by Albert R. Broccoli
Executive Producer Michael G. Wilson
Directed by John Glen
Eon Productions Ltd

1985 A View to a Kill
Screenplay by Richard Maibaum and Michael G. Wilson
Produced by Albert R. Broccoli and Michael G. Wilson
Directed by John Glen
Eon Productions Ltd

1987 The Living Daylights
Screenplay by Richard Maibaum and Michael G. Wilson
Produced by Albert R. Broccoli and Michael G. Wilson
Directed by John Glen
Eon Productions Ltd

1989 Licence to Kill
Screenplay by Richard Maibaum and Michael G. Wilson
Produced by Albert R. Broccoli and Michael G. Wilson
Directed by John Glen
Danjaq S.A.

1995 GoldenEye
Screenplay by Jeffrey Caine and Bruce Feirstein
Story by Michael France
Presented by Albert R. Broccoli
Produced by Michael G. Wilson and Barbara Broccoli
Directed by Martin Campbell
Eon Productions Ltd

1997 Tomorrow Never Dies
Screenplay by Bruce Feirstein
Produced by Michael G. Wilson and Barbara Broccoli
Directed by Roger Spottiswoode
Eon Productions Ltd

OTHER FILMS

1962 Call Me Bwana
Screenplay by Nate Monaster and Johanna Harwood
Produced by Albert R. Broccoli
Executive Producer Harry Saltzman
Directed by Gordon Douglas
Eon Productions Ltd

1968 Chitty Chitty Bang Bang
Screenplay by Roald Dahl and Ken Hughes
Produced by Albert R. Broccoli
Directed by Ken Hughes
UA/Warfield/DFI

AWARDS

1968 Man of the Year Award: Variety Boys Club of Queens, Inc.
1982 Irving G. Thalberg Memorial Award, March 29 (54th Ann. Acad. Awards)
1986 Order of the British Empire (OBE): from HRH Queen Elizabeth II, via Ambassador, British Embassy, Washington DC, September 29
1987 Commandeur de l'Ordre des Arts et des Lettres (France)
1989 BAFTA Baccarat Award, July 10
1989 American Red Cross: Recognition of Gratitude for victims of the 1989 Disasters
1989 World Fellowship: Cubby and Dana Broccoli: First husband and wife team to become members and receive letter of thanks from the Founder, July 18
1990 Dwight D. Eisenhower Award of Honor upon an Admirable American of Achievement and Wisdom
1990 City of Los Angeles, State of California: Star of the Hollywood Walk of Fame; Proclamation of 'Cubby Broccoli Day', both January 16
1990 Producers' Guild of America Inc.: Congratulations on being first member to receive a 'Star' on the Hollywood Walk of Fame, January 23
1990 Commanders Club of San Francisco: Letter of Thanks
(Date unknown) Variety Boys and Girls Clubs of Queens (NYC): Annex Dedication

ACKNOWLEDGEMENTS

The following sources were most useful in the completion of this autobiography and their help is much appreciated:

Playboy magazine, Chicago; Charles Champlin and the *Los Angeles Times*; David McClintick, *Indecent Exposure* (William Morrow and Co. Inc., New York); A. Scott Berg, *Goldwyn* (Alfred A. Knopf, New York); Neal Gabler, *An Empire of their Own* (Crown Publishers, New York); Otto Friedrich, *City of Nets* (Harper and Row, New York); Michael Feeney Callan, *Sean Connery* (Stein and Day, New York); Peter Haining, *James Bond: A Celebration* (Planet, London); Bob Thomas, *Joan Crawford* (Futura Publications, London); Anthony Summers, *Goddess* (Gollancz/Sphere Books, London); Byron S. Miller, *Sail, Steam and Splendour* (Times Books, New York); Raymond Benson, *James Bond Bedside Companion* (Dodd, Mead, and Co., New York); Nathan Glazer and Daniel P. Moynihan, *Beyond the Melting Pot* (MIT Press, Cambridge, Mass., and London); John Pierson, *The Life of Ian Fleming*; Donald L. Barlett and James Steele, *Empire* (Penguin Books, Ontario).

Particular appreciation is due to Norman R. Tyre, Cubby's close friend and legal adviser, for his skilled and detailed review of the weighty sub-plot to Cubby's narrative. Gratitude also to the Reverend Terrance Sweeney PhD, who provided touching testimony as Cubby's old friend and spiritual aide. Thanks also to Meg Simmonds for her painstaking searches among the vast collection of stills held in the Eon archives.

On a more personal level, one other acknowledgement may be taken for granted: gratitude to Dana Broccoli and the family for their own special recollections of Cubby.

INDEX

PICTURE
ACKNOWLEDGEMENTS

First section
Courtesy of Mrs Dana Broccoli: p.1, p.2 bottom, p.3, p.4 top, p.5 top
and bottom, p.6 top, p.7 bottom, p.8 top and bottom, p.9, p.10, p.12,
p.13 top and bottom, p.15 top
© 1953 Columbia Pictures: p.11
Washington Library of Congress: p.2 top
©Mansell/Time Inc., Katz: p.4 bottom
J.R. Eyerman & Allan Grant, Life Magazine © 1972 Time Inc., Katz:
p.6 bottom
Associated Press Photo: p.7 top
© 1957 Columbia Pictures: p.14
© 1965 Warwick Film Productions, Ltd. All rights reserved. Courtesy
of MGM Clip and Still: p.15 bottom
© 1962 Danjaq, LLC and United Artists Corporation. All rights
reserved: p.16 all pictures

Second Section:
Courtesy of Mrs Dana Broccoli: p.7 top, p.13 top and bottom, p.16 all
pictures
Published by courtesy of Mrs Dana Broccoli and with permission from
The Ronald Reagan Library: p.11
© Danjaq, LLC and United Artists Corporation. All rights reserved: p.1
top (1962), p.2 (1962), p.4 top (1963), p.5 (1968), p.7 bottom (1973),
p.8 top (1976), p.8 bottom (1981), p.9 top (1981), p.12 (1987), p.14
(1981)
© PIC Photos Ltd: p.1 bottom, p.3, p.4 bottom, p.6 top and bottom,
p.9 bottom
Published with permission from Central Office of Information: p.10 top
Published with permission from the Variety Club and H.R.H. The Duke
of Edinburgh: p.10 bottom
Photo by Merrett T. Smith, published by courtesy of Mrs Dana Broccoli
and with permission from The Bush Library: p.11 bottom